International Order and the Future of World Politics

In this volume distinguished scholars from different social science disciplines assess the emerging international order. The volume is divided into three main sections. In the first, theories and strategies of order – realism, liberalism, institutionalism, and post-positivism – are presented. In the second, the prospects of the major likely contenders for world leadership are analysed. The strategic possibilities for the US, Russia, China, the European Union, Japan, and India are examined in detail. Part III discusses some key challenges to world order, with contributors examining the problems posed by globalization, nationalism, ethnic and religious conflicts, environmental degradation, and the diffusion of weapons of mass destruction. This book offers a comprehensive and interdisciplinary account of the prospect for a peaceful international order into the next century.

T. V. Paul is an Associate Professor of Political Science at McGill University. He is the author of *Asymmetric Conflicts: War Initiation by Weaker Powers* (1994), and co-editor of *The Absolute Weapon Revisited: Nuclear Arms and the Emerging International Order* (1998).

John A. Hall is Professor of Sociology at McGill University. His books include *Powers and Liberties* (1985), *Liberalism* (1989), *Coercion and Consent* (1994), *International Orders* (1996), and *The State of the Nation: Ernest Gellner and the Theory of Nationalism* (edited, 1998).

International Order and the Future of World Politics

Edited by

T. V. Paul and John A. Hall

 CAMBRIDGE
UNIVERSITY PRESS

PUBLISHED BY THE PRESS SYNDICATE OF THE UNIVERSITY OF CAMBRIDGE
The Pitt Building, Trumpington Street, Cambridge CB2 1RP, United Kingdom

CAMBRIDGE UNIVERSITY PRESS
The Edinburgh Building, Cambridge, CB2 2RU, UK http://www.cup.cam.ac.uk
40 West 20th Street, New York, NY 10011-4211, USA http://www.cup.org
10 Stamford Road, Oakleigh, Melbourne 3166, Australia

First published 1999

Printed in the United Kingdom at the University Press, Cambridge

Typeset in Plantin 10/12pt [VN]

A catalogue record for this book is available from the British Library

ISBN 0521 65138 7 hardback
ISBN 0521 65832 2 paperback

Contents

List of figures and tables

Contributors

STEVE CHAN is Professor of Political Science at the University of Colorado

MICHAEL W. DOYLE is Professor of Political Science at Princeton University

JACK A. GOLDSTONE is Professor of Sociology at the University of California, Davis

JOHN A. HALL is Professor of Sociology at McGill University

K. J. HOLSTI is Professor of Political Science at the University of British Columbia

G. JOHN IKENBERRY is Professor of Political Science at the University of Pennsylvania

KAREN T. LITFIN is Assistant Professor of Political Science at the University of Washington

MICHAEL MANN is Professor of Sociology at the University of California, Los Angeles

LISA L. MARTIN is Professor of Government at Harvard University

MICHAEL MASTANDUNO is Professor of Government at Dartmouth College

HUDSON MEADWELL is Associate Professor of Political Science at McGill University

JUAN DIEZ MEDRANO is Associate Professor of Sociology at the University of California, San Diego

BALDEV RAJ NAYAR is Professor Emeritus of Political Science at McGill University

T. V. PAUL is Associate Professor of Political Science at McGill University

T. J. PEMPEL is Professor of Political Science at the University of Washington

STEVE SMITH is Professor of International Relations at the University of Aberystwyth

JACK SNYDER is Professor of Political Science at Columbia University

PETER VAN DER VEER is Professor of Religious Studies at the University of Amsterdam

Acknowledgments

This volume originated from exchanges between a political scientist and a sociologist on the question of international order. During 1994–5 John Hall was writing his book *International Orders*, while T. V. Paul was beginning to develop a new project on peaceful change in the international system. Our common interest led to endless discussions about differing conceptions of international order, particularly in light of our perceptions as to what the future may hold.

In order to gain real purchase on the subject, we invited a group of internationally distinguished scholars from political science, sociology, religious studies, history, and anthropology to attend a conference at McGill University in May 1997, in the belief that an interdisciplinary discourse would provide the greatest illumination about both the nature of new challenges to the traditional currencies of power and the ways in which major powers and dominant strategies of order might respond to them. The response of our colleagues was overwhelmingly positive, and you hold in your hands the fruit of our collaboration. We are deeply indebted to our team of authors, but quite as much to critical comments offered by Michael Smith, Steven Toope, Desmond Morton, and Ferry de Kerkhove which did much to deepen the sustained process of revision that followed the conference. We specially thank Mark Brawley, Robert Brenner, Bradley Thayer, Michel Fortmann, and Andy Knight for their presentations.

Financial assistance came from Canada's Center for Foreign Policy Development and Security and Defence Forum, the Université de Montréal–McGill Joint Research Group in International Security, and McGill University's Faculty of Arts as well as the University's Conference Grant program. We wish accordingly to express our gratitude to officials of these agencies, and in particular to Steven Lee, Patrick Wittmann, Marc Wittingham, Michel Fortmann, Pierre Martin, and Carman Miller. Doctoral students who provided able research assistance included Saira Khan, Marc Lanteigne, Liliana Riga, and Tamara Sorger. We are particularly grateful to Kirsten Rafferty for her able assistance in formatting the chapters. John Haslam, Social Science editor at Cambridge University Press, offered enthusiastic support from the beginning. T. V. Paul also thanks the support extended by the Center for International Affairs and the Olin Institute for Strategic Studies at Harvard University, where he was a visiting scholar during 1997–8. Last, but not least, we express our profound gratitude to the members of our families, to Rachel, Kavya and Leah, and to Linda, Molly, Jackson and Matthew.

T. V. Paul and John A. Hall

Introduction

John A. Hall and T. V. Paul

If sustained thought should always be given to questions of war and peace, two developments have turned prescription into urgent necessity. Most immediately and obviously, the contours of international politics have been thoroughly changed by the end of the Cold War. History is again, to use Arnold Toynbee's phrase, on the move. Thought is especially mandated given the ever-so-sudden change from initial optimism to eventual pessimism, that is, from "transitions from authoritarian rule" (O'Donnell, Schmitter and Whitehead 1986), "new world order" (Bush 1990), and "the end of history" (Fukuyama 1992), to "the breakdown of democratic regimes" (Linz and Stepan 1978), "new world disorder," and "the return of the repressed" (Ignatieff 1993) – even, indeed, to "the clash of civilizations" (Huntington 1996). Equally important, however, is the claim that the currencies of world politics are changing: military power is held to have lost its efficacy in an era of globalized geo-economic competition, concern with human rights seems set to undermine the norm of non-intervention, whilst "the state" is sometimes considered to have lost salience, as it is supposedly hollowed out both from above and from below (Spruyt 1994; Ohmae 1995). Added to all this is the fact that we are approaching not just the end of a century but the closing of a millennium, something which may well occasion the gloomiest of prognostications.

The purpose of this volume, the result of sustained collaboration by experts from different disciplines, is to increase understanding of the changing contours of world politics. We are concerned with a myriad of analytical and prescriptive issues. What does international order mean in the changed context of world politics? Can elements of the existing approaches to order be utilized – on their own or in various syncretic mixtures – to find concrete solutions to pressing problems in world politics? What role do major powers play as makers and challengers of a given international order? Can rising major powers and regional powers be integrated into the international order without conflict? Can order and change be achieved simultaneously without violence? Can international governance become more democratic and humane?

No inquiry is without presupposition, and so this short introduction lays bare the minimal set of concepts upon which our collaboration depended. Attention is given first to our guiding concept of international order, and to the careful and essentially open way in which it is treated here. This is followed by a brief reminder of some of the mechanisms of the Westphalian system of international order. As it happens, the editors do possess theoretical hunches of their own; their synthetic model, derived from a sociological interpretation, is laid out as clearly as possible in chapter three. Let it be stressed that nothing in the volume hangs on this model. The varied discussions querying the relevance of the lessons of the past in changed circumstances challenge us quite as much as they do the other theories presented in the first part of this volume.

Defining international order

Attempts to define international order produce immediate controversy. "Order" is a term that carries normative and ideological connotations, as it bears particular conceptions about how social, political, and economic systems are and ought to be structured. Order and peace to one group of nations may be perceived differently by another. For instance, the long periods of peace of the nineteenth century and the post-1945 era were viewed differently in the East and the West, and in the South as compared to the North. Differences also arise due to the normative concern as to whether order implies a minimum condition of co-existence in which nation-states are able to avoid destructive warfare or a larger conception in which all can "live together relatively well" and "prosper simultaneously" (Hoffmann 1970: 2). Avoidance of armed conflicts must be the primary function of any international order, as without the control of violence many of the other values states and individuals seek can be disrupted, especially in an age when nuclear and other lethal weapons have spread to several nations and sub-national groups. Still, the success of an international order is predicated on the extent to which it can accommodate change without violence.

The conceptualization of international order at the back of the minds of the authors in this volume is that provided by Hedley Bull's masterly *Anarchical Society* (1977).[1] The considerations made by Bull that are vital here can usefully be rapidly summarized in a series of points.

1. The initial focus of interest must be that of whether the international system is or is not orderly. The historical record sees lulls, less of peace than of the regulation of conflict, between vicious escalations to the extremes. Bull himself tended to conceptualize the difference between

these two types of period in terms of a contrast between a "society of states" and mere anarchy: we make use of this distinction in chapter three.

2. Orderliness needs to be explained. A distinction can usefully be drawn here between general principles of order and the mechanisms which operate within them. General principles have varied across the historical record, but it is easy to see that feudalism and empire stand as alternate systems to the system of states to which most attention has been given by occidental scholars. It can clearly be said that the focus here is firmly on the mechanisms at work within a multipolar system of states. There is an obvious justification for this: Europe had the power to extend to the whole world the system whose essence was more or less codified at the Treaty of Westphalia in 1648 (Krasner 1993). Some of the mechanisms at work within this general principle endorse, others seek to amend, the logic of Westphalia.

3. Bull proved to be a fertile source of ideas in large part because he wobbled, in interesting ways, on a number of key issues. This is particularly so in regard to the morally loaded notion of order. On the one hand, Bull's famous distinction between world order and international order, that is, between a world of full justice in which every state would recognize a stranger as a citizen and one in which there is simply a system of settled expectations, points firmly to a realization that order is *not* being admired uncritically.

This deserves underscoring, and extension. For one thing, none of the authors in this volume belong to any party of order; all recognize that every system of order benefits some at the expense of others. The general purpose of much of this volume can usefully be seen as that of calculating costs and benefits, and of emphasizing the ways order appears from different vantage points. This sort of felicific calculus may assure us that the long peace of the nineteenth and twentieth centuries were, despite differential costs and benefits to varying national actors, considerable positive achievements – in contrast, very probably, to the international order that might have been established had Hitler won the Second World War.

4. Kalevi Holsti's magnificent *Peace and War* (1991) has made it absolutely apparent that the designs of statesmen and other active agents, themselves often believers in the mechanisms to be identified, have played a major role in the creation of particular international orders. Still, designs only have force when backed by structures of power, just as structures of power have their greatest impact when they benefit from clearly articulated ideas. Differently put, an appreciation of agency should never be allowed to introduce, as it so often does, any form of

licentious voluntarism. Key historical figures are themselves "macro" actors embodying social structural powers (Mouzelis 1995); if this gives them the capacity to affect events, it remains the case that their actions are never unconstrained.

The mechanisms of the Westphalian order

Seven familiar mechanisms of the state system, moving roughly from realist to liberal camps, can usefully be distinguished. These are grand affairs: each offers plans for limiting war (and sometimes for establishing peace) as well as theoretical reasons explaining why wars take place in the first place. Most of these mechanisms aim to sustain the primary goals of the society of states, i.e., war avoidance and the maintenance of states as sovereign entities. Every order attempts to deal with the negative effects of anarchy, although some claim to transcend this condition while others simply attempt to manage its consequences. Each order emphasizes either the individualistic, sovereignty-oriented elements of state behavior or the collectivist-multilateralist vision of order designed to curtail unbridled pursuit of self-interest. While some give prominence to military means, others assign importance to economic and institutional mechanisms. Each one of these approaches has descriptive and normative components, making it necessary to judge them in practical as well as theoretical terms. They involve in varying degrees the juridico-political conceptions defined by the principles, pragmatism, and self-interest of the leading actors of an era. They also attempt to give legitimacy to a given politico-military and economic distribution of power of a winning state or coalition of states after a major conflict by enshrining what is permissible and what is considered threatening to the state system. In addition, they revolve around certain norms, rules, and values of behavior among national actors and their success depends upon how these rules, norms, and values are imbibed and observed by all major and a large number of minor (especially regional) powers. A given order fails when one or more key actors within it violates its norms through forceful actions.

It should be noted right at the start that these seven mechanisms are often in mutual contact with each other, making hybrid forms – as will later be demonstrated in the form of our own synthetic model – a distinct possibility. Secondly, not every conceivable approach is considered here, the claim being that no other approach has a fundamental claim on our attention.[2]

The main tenet of *realism* (whether classical or neo-realist) is that states live in an anarchical system, one which lacks the central governing authority familiar to us in the domestic sphere. In this competitive system, self-help is taken for granted with every state being responsible for its own security and economic welfare (Waltz 1979). States, seen as rational entities, seek to maximize their national interests, but worry about the losses and gains they make relative to other actors, friends, or foes. Wars and conflict are natural outcomes of this state of affairs as states seek power, territory, and resources, sometimes at the cost of other states. The temptation to dominate other states increases with the growth of power capabilities. Cooperation is rare and it is anyway likely to be evanescent given the inevitability of changes in national interest. While classical realists and neo-realists agree on these basics, the latter give importance to system structure, defined in terms of the distribution of power among major power actors, in determining war and peace. A bipolar structure with nuclear-armed superpowers is favored by the latter, while multipolar power structures are viewed as likely to occasion war (Waltz 1979; for classical views, see Morgenthau 1967). The major prescription of both types of realism for creating and sustaining order is through the attainment of a balance of power, both internationally and regionally. The mechanisms for obtaining balance vary, but states are held to ally together in the face of a rising power with hegemonic pretensions. Balance of power is predicated on the assumption that peace is preserved only when an equilibrium of power exists among great powers as well as among regional powers, otherwise the strong will be tempted to attack the weak. Countervailing power is essential in curtailing the power aspirations of a threatening state. Parity in power capabilities preserves peace, as the aspiring state cannot achieve its objectives militarily and would therefore desist from using force even if the opportunity arose.

In the classical accounts, it was necessary for powers to shift from one side to another in order for a balance to be achieved; no permanent set of allegiances could be allowed, for to admit them would be to rigidify the system, and so to cause disaster. In the modern versions, balance of power is buttressed by strategies such as deterrence and containment of challenging states. Status quo states align and deploy military forces to prevent a revisionist state being able to upset the balance, while political and military efforts are made to contain the aspirations of such states. When key actors imbibe the norm of non-aggression and smaller states align against a rising power, a balance of power system emerges. There are, however, disagreements as to whether states align in order to balance in the face of rising power capabilities or only in response to increasing threats from such an entity (Walt 1987). In many historical situations, states failed to balance – with balance of power anyway being only one among several strategies of war avoidance that were utilized. A more general difficulty with this approach is, of course, that much violence can be involved in order to discover exactly where the balance lies – with nuclear weapons accordingly putting the whole strategy somewhat into question.

A *concert* of great powers represents a second mechanism for international order. It too is broadly realist in spirit. Thus Metternich sought to convince his colleagues that revolution could be arrested were they to deal with international crises and territorial change by means of concerted action (Kissinger 1964). This system was meant to persuade rather than confront, that is, to make the then great powers – France, Britain, Russia, Austria, and Prussia – realize their collective responsibility for peace. The concert system has been credited with preventing major power wars in Europe in the nineteenth century. The rules and norms of the concert made conference diplomacy the chief instrument to deal with international crises, with all territorial changes subject to the sanction of the great powers. Further, all the major powers of the system had to be protected, whilst no great power could be humiliated, nor their vital interests and honor be challenged (Elrod 1976). In the post-Cold War era, a new concert system has been effectively resurrected by having five permanent members of the UN Security Council play the leading role in maintaining international order. Elements of a concert in specific issue areas are equally evident in the efforts by the nuclear weapon states to prevent the rise of new nuclear states. A clear example of this was evident in their attempts to cap the nuclear activities of India and Pakistan following their open nuclear tests in May 1998. Great power concert was similarly manifested during the 1991 Persian Gulf War and in the Dayton Peace Accords of December 1995 that ended the Bosnian conflict. Yet, at the turn of the new century, the apparent solidarity of the great powers is marred by lingering suspicions, particularly by Russia's opposition to the expansion of NATO.

Concert systems are often criticized for their lack of goals broader than that of simple management of great power relations. The European concert system failed to deal with issues embarrassing to any of the great powers, and it violated the basic principles of democratic governance by lending the great powers the right to determine the fate of small states without their consent (Elrod 1976). Further, a concert could tolerate high levels of repression within the system and treat "violence outside the framework of great power relations as acceptable" (Falk 1975). More generally, in the past great power cooperation often lasted only for short periods, and it was often followed by violent rivalries.

Hegemonic stability theory offers a final broadly realist approach to international order. The starting point of this school is the insistence that uneven development within capitalism causes terrible adjustment difficulties for international politics. Capitalism works effectively if and when a hegemonic power provides leadership – above all, in supplying the public goods of free trade, a top currency, and capital for development. Nineteenth-century Britain and the United States after 1945 are seen as having acted as such benign hegemons (Kindleberger 1973). Modern realists have applied this theory to the arenas of peace and security. Accordingly, a hegemonic power such as the United States provides collective security (e.g., Gilpin 1982) by imposing positive and negative sanctions towards challengers. The decline of the hegemonic state or its withdrawal from global affairs is seen as likely to lead to disorder and chaos. Efforts by American scholars and statesmen to maintain American primacy in the post-Cold War era are often driven by such convictions.

Criticism of hegemonic stability theory has concentrated on two points. First, the air of Anglo-Saxon self-congratulation has been punctured by scholarly awareness that hegemons often end up exercising their undoubted powers in a predatory manner. Second, it is by no means the case that peace within advanced capitalism has always depended upon hegemonic leadership. Nineteenth-century order rested most of all upon a balance of power, making it at least possible to hope that any future decline of the United States would be peaceful. The center of capitalist society has never remained in the same place for long, and the ability to develop and use the most up-to-date equipment and methods tends to diffuse throughout capitalist society, inevitably creating relative decline of the hegemonic power. Hegemonic decline can also be the result of geopolitical exhaustion and self-inflicted overextension (Kennedy 1988). However, the growth path of the most advanced state can remain strong and its economy healthy even as its share of total world product diminishes – as the United States attests at the dawn of the new century.

Before specifying three full-scale liberal mechanisms of international order, it makes sense to say something about *Marxism* for the simple reason that it stands between the two broad currents of thought to which attention is being drawn. On the one hand, Marxism at times resembles realism, particularly in the form of hegemonic stability theory, in suggesting that war is inevitable within capitalist society. On the other hand, Marxism envisages the possibility of an entirely new world, based on a non-antagonistic mode of production able to abolish states and war. Obviously, the belief that the solidarity of an international class was of more importance than allegiances within states has taken a severe beating due to the collapse of socialism in Eastern Europe. However, Marxist thinking still dominates some alternate conceptions of order, and its influence is strongly felt in the developing world – and still more so in the Western academy. But Chan demonstrates in this volume that China, the remaining communist great power, behaves more according to the dictates of *Realpolitik* than to those of Marxism: power and interest seem to matter more here than does international working-class solidarity.

Whereas realists take anarchy and war for granted, enlightenment thinkers hope to transcend or change them. Their contempt for politics as normal is beautifully expressed in Kant's insistence that the idea that peace will be achieved by the balance of power is pure illusion, "like Swift's story of the house which the builder had constructed in such perfect harmony with all the laws of equilibrium that it collapsed as soon as a sparrow alighted on it" (1970: 92). Although there are several strands to liberal thinking, in general liberals believe that human nature is malleable and that, despite obstacles, order, justice, and freedom can be achieved gradually through the creation of proper economic conditions and institutional mechanisms (Latham 1997: 34). Cooperation among nations is necessary "to maximize the possible benefits and minimize the possible damages of interactions and interdependencies and to capture opportunities for realizing greater peace, welfare and justice" (Zacher and Matthew 1995: 109–10).

Kant gave us the most striking of all liberal theories of international order. His 1795 proposal for *Perpetual Peace* enshrines the notion of a *republican order* spreading globally. His proposal rests on three "definitive articles." First, governments must be republican, offering legal equality to citizens on the basis of representative government and separation of powers. Second, liberal states will form a pacific union or a federation among themselves that respects the rights of each member state. Third, liberal states will establish a cosmopolitan law of hospitality which respects the rights of the foreigner while allowing free exchange of goods and ideas among themselves. After several trials and tribulations this liberal order will spread, adding new adherents to it until it reaches the far corners of the world so as to create perpetual peace.

To proponents of this order, Kant's philosophical arguments have been validated by the rise of a separate democratic peace. As Doyle (1986) pointed out, empirical evidence shows the prevalence of a distinct peace among democracies as democratic states have rarely fought each other.[3] Although the Anglo-Dutch wars of the seventeenth century, the American-British War of 1812, and the Spanish-American War of 1898 are counter-examples, in the twentieth century democracies have desisted from engaging in war against each other. Continued analysis (e.g., Russett 1993) draws a useful distinction between institutional and normative explanations for this remarkable achievement. Yet questions remain whether it is the political system or other factors such as the structural and ideological competition in the international system that cause peace among democracies. The test for the theory lies ahead as the number of democratic polities increases worldwide and in whether democracies in troubled spots avoid warlike behavior between one another.

Another approach to order enshrined in classical liberalism but very much in vogue among contemporary liberal theorists is one based on economic *interdependence* between states, arising out of the expansion of capitalism and international trade (Rosecrance 1986). Deepened interdependence increases the mutual costs of war, as fear of vulnerability to each other's actions generates cautious behavior among states. Case studies show states in interdependent relationships as less apt to give priority to military security or high politics in their dealings vis-à-vis one another (Keohane and Nye 1989). However, the interdependent relationship between Britain and Germany before 1914 did not of course generate peace, but it may be that a genuine international division of labor is now creating domestic constituencies for peace in such a way as to lend credence to the theory (Milner 1987).

A final mechanism of order is best termed *liberal institutionalism*. International institutions can both provide a much-needed avenue for cooperation and act as constraints on predatory national policies. The United Nations provides collective security whilst the World Trade Organization (formerly GATT) facilitates free trade. Woodrow Wilson's ideas (Knock 1992) typified an extreme version of this order while modern regime analysts have provided a more realistic, functional basis to this conception of order. To the latter, even if institutions and regimes are the creation of a particular dominant power, they acquire a life of their own, often creating rules and regulatory mechanisms for the behavior of all adherents – including the powerful – long after the decline of the hegemonic state (Keohane 1984). Institutions help to develop new norms of conduct, enforce these norms, create confidence among a multitude of actors, and help deepen inter-state collaboration. Multilateralism flourishes under such an order since it allows states to conduct their relations and pursue their interests jointly, based on certain shared rules of conduct (Ruggie 1994: 554).

In the security realm, liberal institutionalists focus on mechanisms designed to prevent wars. Although the origins of collective security can be traced to idealists who founded the League of Nations, it is valued and maintained under the United Nations Charter. The rationale behind collective security is that it can function as a deterrent against aggression, and if aggression ever takes place, rescue the target state before much damage is done. The problem though is that institutions work slowly, especially in the absence of powerful actors leading the way – for all that such leadership is often self-interested. And it is worth noting that if many liberals believe in the collective security system, so too do supporters of new versions of a concert of great powers.

Trying not to prepare for the last war: the contents of this volume

We have no desire to be the equivalent of French generals who, the standard quip has it, always prepare for the last war.[4] Differently put, understanding the past may not be the same thing as being able to master the future. For it may be argued that the world has changed, that we are now faced with a new context. The Westphalian system was dominated by a small group of European states possessed of fairly strong state structures whose intense conflictual interactions demanded that war and peace be accorded the primary place on the international agenda. New actors and issues now bestride the stage of world politics. What will the future be like? That is the question that this volume addresses, and it has led us to a particular organizational structure that deserves to be highlighted.

The first part of the volume naturally begins with realism and liberalism, the two overarching mechanisms at work within the Westphalian system. Michael Mastanduno's central argument is that realist calculation is as present now as it was in the past, for all that the stakes at issue are different – as is the exceptional strength of the United States. The liberal strategy of peace through democratization is endorsed by Michael Doyle, in contrast, on the grounds of its increasing global relevance. Our own chapter offers a sociology which first explains the circumstances which allow realism to work effectively before then suggesting, in consequence, that realism and liberalism, especially in modern circumstances, should be considered allies rather than enemies. These positions by no means exhaust all possibilities. Hence Lisa Martin offers an account of liberal institutionalism, both because of its significance in resolving collective action problems and its scholarly interest. In addition, we include a chapter by Steve Smith that springs from critical theory, and which questions the very idea of international order. We dissent from this post-positivist approach in our concluding chapter.

The second section of the book turns to an examination of leading states. There is an obvious justification for this. Even if the globalization thesis proves in time to be correct, the behavior of great powers in the short run still matters enormously.[5] Differently put, we need some assessment of the contenders for power, even admitting that their struggles may occupy only a transitional period. Furthermore, some of the challenges identified in this volume may well be such as to undermine the structure of world power. Is it not the case that the Soviet Union, whose demise has caused so much re-thinking of strategy, lost the Cold War because it could not compete in a globalized world economy? Can the United States maintain its supremacy in the face of economic rivals, differently advantaged both on the periphery and in the core, and in the face of the potential spread of nuclear weapons? Do the conceptions of order held by these major power states vary and, if so, how will they clash in the ideational and strategic realms? What conceptions of order do they hold and how can they be compromised to allow for peaceful systemic and sub-systemic changes?

The third section of the book analyzes seven key challenges to the Westphalian system. World politics in the twenty-first century is likely to be more complex than in previous eras. Both centrifugal and centripetal forces are at work simultaneously in the international system. In classical international politics, the main goals of the society of states, as Bull stated, included: preservation of the system; maintenance of internal and external sovereignty of states; peace between states – as well as the limitation of violence habitually caused by inter-state warfare (1977: 16–19). While these main goals of the society of states remain, they are by no means exhaustive as we enter the new century. This is because challenges or threats to the new international order may be coming from non-traditional sources, some as a result of increased economic interactions and global ecological changes among nation-states and the acceptance of new conceptions about equality, especially in terms of gender and race.

We do not by any means assume that the seven topics we identify are the only challenges that the future will bring. Issues relating to poverty, uneven development, human rights violations, and ethnic genocide of various forms may generate considerable pressure on nation-states and, in turn, international order in the coming century. However, we believe that the challenges we identify have the highest immediate salience for international order. The contributors do not necessarily agree on the precise way in which these challenges will affect international order, but all concur that the following challenges have the potential to upset order in varying degrees. First, is it indeed the case, as so many take for granted, that the world is now so globalized that the sovereign state – that is, the central pillar of the Westphalian system – has lost its importance? The second issue addressed is closely related in that the specific claim most often made about globalization is that the power of the state has been hollowed out from above quite as much as from below. This is meant to refer to nationalism, unexpectedly so much in the news in the last decade. And are these two forces related? Is it the case that the appeal for identity rises in the face of international forces? This in turn leads to a third issue. The Westphalian order rested upon the activities and designs of the great powers. One change in the international system has been the emergence of new states, through the process of decolonization: where just two decades ago it seemed that an orderly challenge from cartels of such states might change world politics, our current fear is of chaos, brought on by anarchy resulting from the weaknesses of what now often seem to be mere pseudo-states. All three of these challenges suggest a fourth, namely the rise of religious fundamentalism so central to Samuel Huntington's best selling *The Clash of Civilizations* (1996). The fifth challenge comes from that of environmental degradation. There is a great deal to be said in favor of the view that the advanced core of capitalist society eventually found social peace through industrial progress, that is, by replacing the politics of redistribution with a system of universal bribery. The cost of that to the environment has been huge. If the politics of growth are needed for most of humanity, then the environment may throw up challenges that states cannot deal with. In any case, by what right should rich countries presume to tell the poor not to aspire to what they already possess? The sixth challenge is related to this, and indeed to most of the challenges identified. Scientific breakthroughs in the North have provided medical technology which has sometimes resulted in demographic explosions of force sufficient to undermine state structures. What price does Westphalia exert in societies where three-quarters of the population is below the age of twenty? Finally, we feel it necessary to consider again nuclear weapons and other weapons of mass destruction. The exemplar of modern science did not initially undermine the Westphalian system because such weapons were hard to acquire. That is no longer the case. The nuclear tests by India and Pakistan in May 1998 and the continuing search for such weapons by several other countries show that these capabilities are likely to spread. Will great power status, with all that means for international order, be altered when additional smaller powers possess the ultimate weapon?

In the final section of the volume, we provide a concluding chapter. In this chapter we begin by highlighting general findings and then return to our synthetic model so as to present our own view of the forces at work within world politics together with prudential prescriptions. This chapter, we believe, summarizes the main arguments and prescriptions for achieving order and change simultaneously, the central purpose of this volume.

NOTES

1 Bull's position has been interestingly criticized by proponents of "world order," notably Falk (1977).

2 There is an extensive literature on international and world order, as well as criticisms of both concepts. A partial list includes: Mueller (1989), Miller (1990), Rosenau and Czempiel (1992), Singer and Wildavsky (1993), Dewitt, Haglund and Kirton (1993), Falk (1995), Hall (1996), and Cox and Sinclair (1996).

3 It must be remembered, as Doyle recognizes, that despite their pacific record with each other, liberal states have fought both often and with extreme cruelty against non-liberal states. If one can see touches of this mentality in the history of British foreign affairs, it has equally affected the conduct of American foreign policy – most obviously, in the crusade against communism.

4 This quip stands at the heart of Holsti's magnificent treatise on war and peace (1991), since it argues that the makers of international order failed to prepare for the future because they were so obsessed with the recent past.

5 The rationale for selecting only these states needs to be specified. Of the five permanent members of the UN Security Council, we include the US, Russia, and China, as states whose military behavior has the largest consequence for international order. The other two members, the UK and France, along with Germany are included in the European Union umbrella as their unilateral security behavior is partially constrained by their participation in European institutions. We include Japan as its economic and military behavior have significant consequences for international order and it is a likely candidate for nuclear acquisition in the future, especially since the East Asian region does not contain institutional mechanisms to manage regional conflicts. The inclusion of India is based on the fact that, among the developing countries, it is likely to be the leading candidate for major power status. Its economy is already the world's fifth largest, measured in terms of purchasing power parity. The test explosions of nuclear and hydrogen bombs in May 1998 and acquisition of missile capability attest to India's growing power position in the military realm as well.

REFERENCES

Bull, Hedley 1977, *The Anarchical Society: A Study of Order in World Politics*, New York: Columbia University Press.

Bush, George 1990, *Address to the United Nations*, September 11.

Cox, Robert W. and Sinclair, Timothy 1996, *Approaches to World Order*, Cambridge: Cambridge University Press.

Dewitt, David, Haglund, David and Kirton, John (eds.) 1993, *Building a New Global Order*, Toronto: Oxford University Press.

Doyle, Michael 1986, "Liberalism and World Politics," *American Political Science Review* 80: 1151–69.

Elrod, Richard B. 1976, "The Concert of Europe: A Fresh Look at an International System," *World Politics* 28: 159–74.

Falk, Richard 1975, "Toward a New World Order: Modest Methods and Drastic Visions," in *On the Creation of a Just World Order*, Saul H. Mendlovitz (ed.), New York: Free Press, 211–58.

1977, "Contending Approaches to World Order," *Journal of International Affairs* 31: 171–98.

1995, *On Humane Governance: Toward a New Global Politics*, University Park, PA: Pennsylvania State University Press.

Fukuyama, Francis 1992, *The End of History and the Last Man*, New York: The Free Press.

Gilpin, Robert 1982, *War and Change in World Politics*, Cambridge: Cambridge University Press.

Hall, John A. 1996, *International Orders*, Oxford: Polity Press.

Hoffmann, Stanley (ed.) 1970, *Conditions of World Order*, New York: Simon and Schuster.

Holsti, Kalevi J. 1991, *Peace and War: Armed Conflict and International Order 1648–1989*, Cambridge: Cambridge University Press.

Huntington, Samuel P. 1996, *The Clash of Civilizations and the Remaking of World Order*, New York: Simon and Schuster.

Ignatieff, Michael 1993, *Blood and Belonging: Journeys into the New Nationalism*, Toronto: Viking.

Kant, Immanuel 1970, *Kant's Political Writings*, H. Reiss (ed.), Cambridge: Cambridge University Press.

Kennedy, Paul 1988, *The Rise and Fall of the Great Powers*, New York: Random House.

1993, *Preparing for the 21st Century*, New York: Random House.

Keohane, Robert O. 1984, *After Hegemony*, Princeton: Princeton University Press.

Keohane, Robert O. and Nye, Joseph S. 1989, *Power and Interdependence*, 2nd edition, New York: Harper Collins.

Kindleberger, Charles P. 1973, *The World in Depression, 1929–1939*, Berkeley: University of California Press.

Kissinger, Henry A. 1964, *A World Restored: Metternich, Castlereagh and the Problems of Peace 1812–22*, Boston: Houghton Mifflin.

Knock, Thomas J. 1992, *To End All Wars: Woodrow Wilson and the Quest for a New World Order*, New York: Oxford University Press.

Krasner, Stephen D. 1993, "Westphalia and All That," in *Ideas and Foreign Policy*, Judith Goldstein and Robert O. Keohane (eds.), Ithaca: Cornell University Press, pp. 235–64.

Latham, Robert 1997, *The Liberal Moment: Modernity, Security and the Making of Post-War International Order*, New York: Columbia University Press.

Linz, Juan J. and Stepan, Alfred (eds.) 1978, *The Breakdown of Democratic Regimes*, Baltimore: The Johns Hopkins University Press.

Miller, Lynn H. 1990, *Global Order: Values and Power in International Politics*, Boulder, CO: Westview Press.

Milner, Helen 1987, "Resisting the Protectionist Temptation," *International Organization* 41: 639–65.

Morgenthau, Hans J. 1967, *Politics Among Nations*, 4th edition, New York: Alfred A. Knopf.

Mouzelis, Nicos 1995, *Sociological Theory: What Went Wrong?* London: Routledge.

Mueller, John 1989, *Retreat from Doomsday: The Obsolescence of Major War*, New
York: Basic Books.

O'Donnell, G., Schmitter, P. and Whitehead, L. (eds.) 1986, *Transitions from
Authoritarian Rule*, Baltimore: The Johns Hopkins University Press.

Ohmae, Kenichi 1995, *The End of the Nation State*, New York: Free Press.

Rosecrance, Richard 1986, *The Rise of the Trading State*, New York: Basic Books.

Rosenau, James N. and Czempiel, Ernst-Otto (eds.) 1992, *Governance without
Government: Order and Change in World Politics*, Cambridge: Cambridge
University Press.

Ruggie, John G. 1993, "Multilateralism: The Anatomy of an Institution," in
Multilateralism Matters, Ruggie (ed.), New York: Columbia University Press,
pp. 3–50.

Russett, Bruce 1993, *Grasping the Democratic Peace*, Princeton: Princeton University Press.

Singer, Max 1993, *The Real World Order: Zones of Peace, Zones of Turmoil*,
Chatham, NJ: Chatham House.

Spruyt, Hendrik 1994, *The Sovereign State and its Competitors*, Princeton: Princeton University Press.

Walt, Stephen 1987, *The Origins of Alliances*, Ithaca: Cornell University Press.
 1996, *Revolution and War*, Ithaca: Cornell University Press.

Waltz, Kenneth N. 1979, *Theory of International Politics*, New York: Random
House.

Zacher, Mark W. and Matthew, Richard A. 1995, "Liberal International Theory:
Common Threads, Divergent Strands," in *Controversies in International Relations Theory*, Charles W. Kegley (ed.), New York: St. Martin's Press, pp.
107–50.

Part I

Theories and strategies

1 A realist view: three images of the coming international order

Michael Mastanduno

There is no single or unified theory of realism, even though critics and proponents are sometimes tempted to treat it that way. Realism is both a way of thinking about the world and a research program containing a set of assumptions from which various realist theories and arguments can be derived, developed, and analyzed. It is not surprising that a recent scholarly attempt to test realism *per se*, as opposed to particular realist theories, found that "the scientific study of realism is difficult because it is not often specific enough to be falsifiable" (Wayman and Diehl 1994: 26). Other scholars, in recognition of this problem, have begun to disentangle the various strands of realist theory and subject each to logical and empirical scrutiny (e.g., Deudney 1993; Brooks 1997; Mastanduno 1997; Johnston 1999).

This chapter proceeds in that spirit. I contrast three realist images of the international order that are emerging in the wake of the Cold War. The first highlights economic competition among major industrial powers as the central feature of the post-Cold War environment. The second foresees a return to a traditional multipolar balance of power system. The third depicts an American-centered order, in which the United States continues to play the dominant role in a unipolar international system.

Each of these competing models contains a baseline degree of plausibility. The same is true of several non-realist images, including the clash of civilizations thesis put forth by Samuel Huntington, the vision of a liberal international community stressed by Michael Doyle, the predicted withering of the nation-state in the face of environmental and demographic stress popularized by Robert Kaplan, or the depiction of a world divided into "zones of peace and zones of turmoil," in the words of Max Singer and Aaron Wildavsky (Huntington 1993a; Doyle this volume; Kaplan 1997; Kaplan 1994; and Singer and Wildavsky 1993). My purpose is not to survey all plausible models, but to distinguish among the leading realist contenders analytically and identify which has the most promise empirically. After a brief examination of the common features of realist thought, I discuss each realist image of the emerging order in terms of its underlying logic and assumptions, its expectations for the behavior of major actors in the system, and its fit with the preliminary empirical evidence available since the end of the Cold War.

My overall argument is that neither geoeconomic competition nor the multipolar balance of power adequately captures the current dynamics of relations among major powers. The third image – that of an American-centered international order – best characterizes the contemporary system. I analyze the features of that system – the roles and behavior of the United States and other major powers, and the manner in which order is maintained. I also assess the durability of this international order in light of a series of challenges. I conclude that although unipolarity will not last indefinitely, US officials have the opportunity to prolong the "unipolar moment" by managing simultaneously external relations and internal constraints. Put differently, the durability of the current order will depend significantly on US statecraft, or in the words of the editors of this volume, on the "capacity to calculate" of US officials.

Realism: world view and assumptions

As a way of thinking about the world, realism is distinguished by its "pessimism regarding moral progress and human possibilities" (Gilpin 1986: 304). Realists view history as cyclical rather than progressive. They are skeptical that human beings can overcome recurrent conflict and establish cooperation or peace on a durable basis. This pessimism is rooted in both human nature and the international system. Classical realists emphasized the former. Thucydides, in accounting for the catastrophic Greek war, assured his readers that "human nature being what it is," these tragic events would be repeated in the future (Thucydides 1954: 48). Hans Morgenthau began his classic text by observing that the conflict-ridden international arena was the consequence of "forces inherent in human nature," and that the best humanity could hope for was the "realization of the lesser evil rather than of the absolute good" (Morgenthau 1978: 3–4).

For contemporary realists, pessimism is more apt to be rooted in the nature of the international system. The absence of a higher governing authority leads to insecurity, conflict, and the routine resort to organized violence. States can mitigate the consequences of anarchy by relying on time-honored instruments such as diplomacy and the balance of power. But they cannot escape it altogether. Statecraft is more a matter of damage limitation than of fundamental problem-solving.

Both classical and contemporary realists would accept the following set of assumptions as central to their intellectual and scholarly endeavor.[1] First, the most important actors in international politics are "territorially organized entities" – city-states in antiquity, and nation-states in the contemporary era (Keohane 1986; Gilpin 1986: 304–5). Nation-states are not the only actors on the current world scene, but realists assume that more can be understood about world politics by focusing on the behavior of and interaction among nation-states than by analyzing the behavior of individuals, classes, transnational firms, or international organizations. Realists assume further that the state – the central decision-making apparatus of the nation-state – continues to be a viable political actor and meaningful analytic construct. Stephen Krasner articulated this realist assumption clearly in 1976: "In recent years, students of international relations have multinationalized, transnationalized, bureaucratized and transgovernmentalized the state until it has virtually ceased to exist as an analytic construct. This perspective is at best profoundly misleading" (Krasner 1976: 317).

Second, realists believe that relations among nation-states are inherently competitive. Nation-states compete most intensely in the realm of military security, but compete in other realms as well, in particular in economic relations. To say that nation-states "compete" means that states care deeply about their status or power position relative to other states, and that this concern guides state behavior. Competition is a consequence of anarchy, which forces states ultimately to rely on themselves to ensure their survival and autonomy. This does not imply cooperation is impossible, only that states will approach cooperative ventures with a concern for their impact on relative power positions (Grieco 1990).

Third, realists emphasize the close connection between state power and interests. States seek power in order to achieve their interests, and they calculate their interests in terms of their power and in the context of the international environment they confront. While all states seek power, it is not necessary to assume that states seek to maximize power. Not every state needs or wants nuclear weapons, for example. Similarly, although security and survival are the highest priority in terms of state interest, there is no need to assume that states always strive to maximize security at the expense of other goals. States pursue an array of interests. The key point for realists is that in defining the so-called national interest, state officials look "outward," and respond to the opportunities and constraints of the international environment.

Fourth, realists assume that state behavior can be explained as the product of rational decision-making. As Robert Keohane puts it, for the realist "world politics can be analyzed *as if* states were unitary rational actors, carefully calculating the costs of alternative courses of action and seeking to maximize their expected utility, although doing so under conditions of uncertainty" (Keohane 1986: 165). States act strategically and instrumentally, in an arena in which the "noise level" is high. The problem of incomplete information is compounded because states have incentives to conceal or misrepresent information to gain strategic advantage. Consequently states may miscalculate, but for realists not with such frequency as to call into question the rationality assumption (Mearsheimer 1994/5: 9).

These assumptions constitute the starting point for realist analysis. They do not lead to a unified understanding of contemporary world politics or to a single theory of state behavior. Each realist image below embraces these core assumptions. But, by making additional assumptions and emphasizing different features of contemporary international politics, they arrive at different assessments of the emerging international order.

Model I: geoeconomic competition

The traditional realist depiction of the international system emphasizes security competition among sovereign states under the ever-present threat of war. Military force is a routine instrument of statecraft employed by states to gain territory, extract resources, or enhance prestige. Limited military conflicts among major powers can become costly and protracted, and can escalate into the all-out struggles typified by World Wars I and II. From this perspective, hegemonic wars are a reflection of and a reaction to the changing distribution of power and prestige among the great powers in the international system (Gilpin 1981; Levy 1983).

To many observers, however, contemporary world politics presents a very different picture. Developments in military technology, most obviously the nuclear revolution, have raised the costs of warfare among great powers to almost prohibitive levels (Mueller 1989; Jervis 1989). The acquisition of territory or resources by force is no longer recognized as a legitimate "right" even of the great powers. Territorial acquisition in any event may be of diminishing utility as knowledge resources overtake natural resources as the principal stimulant to national wealth and power (Rosecrance 1986).[2] Great power war no longer plays the role it once did as the primary mechanism for adjustments in the balance of power. The intense rivalry of the Cold War ended peacefully and the Soviet empire collapsed without precipitating a major international conflict. Many believe that the possibility of hegemonic warfare among great powers has become exceedingly remote.

Put differently, in the post-Cold War world the military security and survival of the major powers are not challenged as they have been in the past. Randall Schweller recently argued that the key concept for understanding great power competition is not security but scarcity (Schweller 1999). In some international environments, military security is a scarce commodity. But in others, it is not. The key question arises as to whether realism is still a useful analytical construct in an international environment in which military security is plentiful because great power warfare is unlikely.

The answer given by "geoeconomic" realists is yes. They contend that the diminution of great power *military* competition does not signify the end of great power competition. Positional competition shifts to other arenas, most importantly to the world economy. Nation-states remain the principal actors, and their competition for markets, raw materials, high value-added employment, and the mastery of advanced technology becomes a surrogate for traditional military competition. Success in geoeconomic competition brings the nation-state economic prosperity and discretion in its foreign policy. It also enables the state to remain at the cutting edge of military research and development. Geoeconomic realists believe that economic and technological competition will remain at the center of great power relations until traditional security competition reasserts itself. Military security may once again become a scarce commodity if military technology changes radically or if and when revisionist states assert themselves as great powers seeking to change the international status quo.

Numerous examples of geoeconomic realism can be found in the academic and policy-oriented literature after the Cold War. Kenneth Waltz wrote in his 1993 assessment of the emerging international order that "economic competition is often as keen as military competition, and since nuclear weapons limit the use of force among great powers at the strategic level, we may expect economic and technological competition among them to become more intense" (Waltz 1993: 59). Samuel Huntington similarly claimed that "in the coming years, the principal conflicts of interests involving the United States and the major powers are likely to be over economic issues." He went on to assert that the idea of economic relations as a non-zero-sum game "has little connection to reality," and that Japan has "accepted all the assumptions of realism but applied them purely in the economic realm" (Huntington 1993b: 71–3). Richard Samuels and Eric Heginbotham develop the latter line of argument into the concept of "mercantile realism," and associate with it the ideas that security threats are as much economic as military, that powerful states will engage in "economic balancing" and that geoeconomic interests may be pursued at the expense of traditional political and security interests

(Heginbotham and Samuels 1998: 190–4). Popular versions of these and related arguments are evident in recent books by Lester Thurow (1992), Jeffrey Garten (1992), Laura Tyson (1992), and Edward Luttwak (1993).

Proponents of the geoeconomic model of international order associate the following types of behavior with their worldview. First, they expect great powers to mobilize for international economic competition. Since that competition is vital to national security, states are likely to shape their national economic systems in a way that creates or reinforces advantages for their national firms. Partnerships between government and industry in research and development, export promotion, industrial policies, selective protectionism, and the shedding of costly military commitments are all plausible strategies depending on the competitive position of any particular nation-state.

Second, geoeconomic realists expect governments to be sensitive to relative gains or relative position in their foreign economic policies. Contemporary great powers recognize that international economic relations produce economic benefits for all concerned. But they remain wary of the fact that in any situation or relationship, some states may benefit more than others. States will therefore seek to adjust policies or minimize relationships that bring disproportionate gains to other major powers, and emphasize those that bring disproportionate gains to themselves.[3] Geoeconomic realists believe that states will be sensitive to relative gains regardless of whether the potential for military warfare is proximate or remote.[4]

Third, geoeconomic realists expect powerful states to organize their relations with their weaker neighbors in order to enhance their position in great power economic competition. This expectation usually manifests itself in the familiar projection of a post-Cold War world divided into three competing economic blocs. Thurow, for example, foresees competition among a US-led bloc centered around NAFTA, a European bloc led by Germany and extending into Eastern Europe, and an Asian bloc organized by Japan (Thurow 1992). Even though these blocs are unlikely to be completely exclusionary, geoeconomic realists expect that the dominant power in each region will assure that the bulk of economic advantages will accrue to it rather than to its economic competitors. The anticipated systemic consequence is that the forces of regionalism will gradually undermine the commitment to global liberalization in the world economy.

Assessment

The geoeconomic model has inspired considerable criticism. Economic liberals contend that at best it exaggerates the zero-sum aspects of what is fundamentally a non-zero-sum activity, and at worst it encourages governments to pursue, in the name of national security, shortsighted and ultimately destructive economic policies. Paul Krugman argues that concern over national competitiveness is a "dangerous obsession." Individual firms compete, and may or may not be competitive; nation-states do not compete or have competitiveness in the same way (Krugman 1994). Miles Kahler finds fault with the idea that the end of the Cold War necessarily leads to a destructive economic regionalism (Kahler 1995: 5). Others question whether multinational corporations retain any meaningful national identity and take issue with the image of these firms lining up with particular nation-states in international competition.[5] Still others, including Joseph Nye and Henry Nau, believe that the geoeconomic modelers have been too quick to dismiss traditional security and alliance concerns that are still prevalent after the Cold War (Nye 1992).

Debates over the analytical and policy wisdom of the geoeconomic model will continue. But to what extent does this image of international order accurately characterize great power relations after the Cold War?

The model appeared most promising in the immediate aftermath of the Cold War. The Soviet Union collapsed because it failed economically more than militarily. The rising power, Japan, was an economic rather than military superpower. Japan's success was directly associated with its national system of political economy, which equated international economic competition with war and forced government, finance, and industry to collaborate with a long-term focus on the conquest of foreign markets. The states of Western Europe, struggling to compete with the United States and Japan, developed an ambitious regional integration scheme to create a market the size of America's, joint industrial policies to emulate Japan's, and a common currency to counter the dominance of the dollar.

Europe's integration plan came on the heels of the US-Canada Free Trade Agreement which was subsequently expanded to include Mexico. These regional initiatives coincided with the stalemate and 1990 collapse of the Uruguay Round talks intended to accelerate multilateral trade liberalization. The main protagonists in the GATT conflict, the United States and European Union, indicated by their behavior that regionalism was a viable alternative.

The seeming emergence of regional blocs in Europe and North America created anxiety in Asia. One politically charged reaction came in the form of Malaysian Prime Minister Mahathir's proposal to create an East Asian Economic Caucus (EAEC) which would exclude the United States, Australia, and New Zealand. Japan's political reaction to this proposal was muted, but Japan's trade and investment patterns in any event had gradually been shifting to Southeast Asia as the yen appreciated and US-Japan trade conflicts mounted. Between 1986 and 1990, the US share of Japan's exports dropped from 38.5 to 31.5 percent and the East Asian share increased from 24.7 to 30.9 percent (United States Embassy, Tokyo 1992).

A further indicator of geoeconomic competition was the changing role of the United States. For most of the postwar era, US foreign economic policy emphasized the multilateral system and placed broad diplomatic and security interests ahead of the pursuit of particularistic economic interests. By the late 1980s, the United States had shifted to "aggressive unilateralism" in pursuit of its economic interests (Bhagwati and Patrick 1990). During the FSX crisis of 1989, the economic agencies of the US government forced the security agencies to reconsider, at considerable diplomatic cost, a military co-development agreement with Japan because it might be commercially disadvantageous to the United States (Mastanduno 1991). In 1992, President Bush turned a traditional head-of-state visit to Japan into a commercial sales mission on behalf of the US auto industry.

In its first term the Clinton administration went even further and elevated export promotion and the pursuit of economic interests to the very top of the US foreign policy agenda (Stremlau 1994/5; Mastanduno 1997). Administration officials embraced explicitly the use of industrial policy for commercial as well as military applications, and launched a series of government-business partnerships to assist US firms in international competition. The Defense Advanced Research Projects Agency (DARPA) dropped "Defense" and changed its name to ARPA as a symbol of the administration's new emphasis. The Commerce Department dedicated a "war room" to tracking the progress US firms made in competing for major export contracts around the world.

In light of these developments, it is not surprising that a flurry of books heralding the new geoeconomic order emerged in the early 1990s. Yet almost as quickly, the appeal of this model has faded. Developments at the national, regional, and global levels have undermined geoeconomic competition as a compelling vision of post-Cold War international order.

After what proved to be a brief experiment, the United States returned by the mid-1990s to its postwar norm of granting priority to international security concerns. This is apparent in US policy toward both Europe and Asia. US officials have downplayed economic conflicts and aggressive unilateralism, and instead have employed foreign economic policies to reinforce broader security concerns.[6] The United States has initiated a New Transatlantic Agenda with the European Union designed to resolve existing trade conflicts, deflect future ones, and seek out opportunities for mutually beneficial economic collaboration. The thrust of US policy toward Japan since 1995 has not been market access, but the strengthening and expansion of the US-Japan Security Treaty. US officials have viewed and responded to the Asian financial crisis less as an opportunity to make relative gains and more as a threat to regional security and global financial stability. They have sought to engage Russia and China economically, even at the risk of strengthening those states as future economic competitors. And, despite constant criticism from the US business community, the United States continues to resort routinely to unilateral economic sanctions, even though those sanctions hurt US firms in international competition (Jentleson 1998).

Two factors account for the US shift away from geoeconomic competition. First, the initial euphoria that the post-Cold War world would be stable and peaceful gave way to a realization by US policy makers of threats to regional security that required careful management. The United States almost went to war over the North Korean crisis of 1994, and faced another series challenge in the Taiwan Straits crisis of 1996 (Oberdorfer 1997). The conflict in Bosnia, which US officials initially considered Europe's problem, became America's problem as it threatened to tear NATO apart. The US response in both regions has been to strengthen existing alliances and de-emphasize disruptive economic disputes.

Second, by the middle of the 1990s the United States seemed to have regained some measure of international economic primacy. Much of the United States' aggressive unilateralism had been directed at Japan's challenge to US commercial, technological, and financial hegemony. By the late 1990s the Japan challenge seemed to have collapsed, and US officials became more concerned with bolstering a weak Japan than with beating down a strong one.

The image of geoeconomic blocs in conflict also waned by the mid-1990s. The anticipated "yen bloc" did not materialize. Japan, pressured by the United States, never signed on to the EAEC and instead supported APEC, an institution that supports economic liberalization and "open regionalism," i.e., a regionalism that includes the United States as a major player (Grieco 1999). Similarly, initial expectations (and fears) of a "Fortress Europe" proved exaggerated. The European Union has generally remained open to US and Japan trade and investment. The United States, in turn, has supported the emergence of a single European currency, even though the Euro has the potential to challenge the dominant international role of the dollar. The GATT did not collapse; the Uruguay Round was completed successfully and a more prominent institution, the WTO, replaced the GATT. Regionalism exists, but regional blocs have proved to be neither a substitute for multilateralism nor the defining feature of post-Cold War international economic interaction.

Finally, the deepening of interdependence has limited both regional blocs and the extent to which states can engage in zero-sum geoeconomic competition. The integration of global commercial and financial markets has made economic "blowback" a serious concern to major powers. Because Japan is a major player in the world economy, it is not surprising that the main concern of US officials in the 1997–8 Asian financial crisis was to prevent its spread to Japan. The United States cooperated with Japan in strengthening the yen, and prodded Japan to revive its domestic economy so that it could help to accelerate regional recovery.

Model II: a multipolar balance of power

Multipolarity characterized international politics between 1648 and 1945. Diplomatic and economic interaction among great powers was routine in this classic balance of power system. No single power dominated and alliance commitments were flexible. The bipolar system that emerged after 1945 was an historical anomaly. The United States and Soviet Union were deemed "super" powers to indicate their extraordinary rank. They were large, economically self-sufficient by historical standards, possessed weapons of mass destruction, and faced off in an ideological Cold War in which alliance commitments remained fixed.

For many realists, the collapse of bipolarity in 1989 signaled a return to a traditional and more normal multipolar system. The elimination of the Soviet Union left the United States as the sole superpower, but in realist and especially neorealist theory, a unipolar order is even more of an anomaly than a bipolar one. The reasoning, laid out most systematically by Kenneth Waltz, is that states balance power, and thus the accumulation of preponderant capabilities in the hands of any single state will stimulate the rise of new great powers, or coalitions of powers, determined to balance the dominant state (Waltz 1979). The logic of international interaction suggests that the unipolar moment is at most a brief transition to a renewed multipolar system.

The theme of incipient multipolarity is common in post-Cold War realist writings. John Mearsheimer stated in 1992 that "bipolarity will disappear with the passing of the Cold War, and multipolarity will emerge in the new international order" (Mearsheimer 1992: 227). Christopher Layne expects the same, and writes that "in a unipolar system, states do indeed balance against the hegemon's unchecked power" (Layne 1993: 13). Waltz's 1993 article explored the prospects and potential of the emerging great powers – Japan, Germany, China, the European Union, and a revived Russia (Waltz 1993). Henry Kissinger predicts that the United States will remain the most powerful but will become a "nation with peers" in the emerging international order (Kissinger 1994: 805).

Proponents of the multipolar image have stated clear behavioral expectations. Multipolarity will emerge fairly quickly because states will not tolerate preponderance over an extended period. In direct contrast to the geoeconomic model, military or security competition among great powers will remain the distinguishing feature of international politics. Relations among great powers, and in the international system more generally, will be characterized by conflict and instability rather than harmony and stability (Mearsheimer 1992: 214). This is true regionally as well as globally.[7] Nuclear weapons will proliferate, not only to less powerful states but also to Japan and Germany who will wish to avoid being blackmailed by nuclear great powers (229).

We should expect Japan and Germany to abandon their Cold War status as "trading states" and become independent great powers that are not subordinate to the United States. As Layne asserts, "a policy of attempting to smother Germany's and Japan's great power emergence would be unavailing because structural pressure will impel them to become great powers regardless of what the United States does or does not do" (Layne 1993: 46–7). Russia and China, singly or as part of a larger coalition, will balance the United States. Cold War alliance systems will collapse or fade; recall Waltz's often-quoted statement that NATO's days are not numbered, but its years are. Security alignments will become more fluid on the familiar realist premise that today's friend may be tomorrow's enemy.

Assessment

The geoeconomic model appeared most plausible immediately after the Cold War, but became less plausible as time passed. For the multipolar model, the opposite is likely to be true. Its principal expectations were not met in the first post-Cold War decade, and may not be in the next decade or two either. As more time passes, however, the international system is likely to move closer to that model.

To be sure, some expectations of the multipolar model have been borne out, at least partially. The pessimism of multipolar realists has proven well-founded in that recurrent conflict has characterized the post-Cold War world, most dramatically in the Balkans but elsewhere as well. Nuclear tests by India and Pakistan in 1998 revived concerns of inadvertent nuclear war and the specter of widespread proliferation. Japan and Germany have become somewhat more assertive. Each desires a permanent seat on the UN Security Council and both have contributed peacekeepers to regional conflicts. Government officials, particularly from France, Russia, and several Middle Eastern states, have expressed uneasiness about the dangers of a one superpower world and at times have directed their resentment explicitly at US officials or policy.

But the central expectations of the multipolar model have not been fulfilled. There has been no meaningful effort to balance the preponderant power of the United States. A fluid system of alliance commitments has not emerged. Instead, the Cold War alliance systems dominated by the United States have been reaffirmed and strengthened. Former adversaries of the United States have been more interested in integration into the US-centered international order than in challenging the legitimacy of that order.

Japan's foreign policy since the end of the Cold War has centered on the strengthening of the US-Japan Security Treaty, including maintenance of US ground forces and the US nuclear guarantee. Japanese politicians rarely question the necessity of US ground forces, and when they do they are quick to emphasize the critical importance of the bilateral alliance itself (see, e.g., Hosokawa 1998). Japan has not opted for an independent defense force, and in 1995 reaffirmed its status as a nonnuclear power by signing on to a permanent extension of the Nuclear Nonproliferation Treaty. For Germany, the US-led NATO alliance remains the cornerstone of national security strategy. Germany deflected French demands for a European defense force independent of NATO, and German officials continue to view the US military presence as essential to the security and stability of Europe (Art 1996). Other European states, France in particular, have sought to bind themselves to their powerful German neighbor rather than balance it. The vulnerable states of Central Europe, caught between Germany and Russia, have not sought to acquire nuclear weapons as anticipated by proponents of the multipolar model. Instead, they have lobbied to join an expanded NATO.

Despite having their differences with the United States, neither Russia nor China has sought to organize a balancing coalition against it. Each has flexed its power close to home; Russia in the "near abroad," and China in the Taiwan Straits and South China Sea. But neither has staked out a position of global revisionism. Each has sought recognition as a responsible member of the existing international community and integration into its economic and security institutions.

Revisionist challenges since the end of the Cold War have involved lesser powers rather than great powers. Iraq upset the balance of power in the Middle East and was struck down by a US-led coalition. North Korea defied the nonproliferation regime and was bought off with a compensation package. Serbia expanded in the Balkans in the early 1990s, but since 1994 has been contained uneasily by a US-sponsored peace plan and NATO deterrent threats.

For its part, the United States has in no way accepted the inevitable multipolar world envisioned by its realist proponents. Instead, the United States has dedicated its post-Cold War foreign policy to preserving the status quo in security relations with its Cold War allies, and to engaging and integrating its Cold War adversaries into an order that reflects the design and preserves the dominant position of the United States.

Model III: a unipolar, US-centered system

Most realists would accept that the international system since 1990 has been unipolar. They would disagree with respect to its durability. Advocates of the multipolar model anticipate the imminent collapse of unipolarity; others believe that the unipolar moment has the potential to last longer, say for a total of twenty to thirty years.[8]

Two arguments underpin the belief in the durability of unipolarity. One focuses on US capabilities. The United States emerged during the 1990s with a commanding lead in the technologies of the information revolution, in the same way that Britain dominated the new technologies of the industrial revolution at the beginning of the nineteenth century. America's "information edge" has enabled it to lead and exploit a Revolution in Military Affairs (RMA) that involves the utilization and integration of intelligence and reconnaissance, command and control, and the precision use of force (Nye and Owens 1996). Mastery of the same information technologies supports US economic dominance, particularly in computer software, telecommunications, financial services, and arms production. Technological primacy, military and economic power, and ideological appeal combine to offer the United States strong potential to remain the world's only superpower in the years ahead.

The second argument concerns threat perception. I have argued elsewhere that unipolarity can only endure if balancing behavior is a response to threat as well as to capabilities (Mastanduno 1997).[9] If balancing is a response solely to capabilities, then by now we should have witnessed other states attempting to counter US preponderance. But if balancing behavior is also triggered by threat, then whether or not states balance against a dominant state will depend on the international environment and on the foreign policy behavior of the dominant state. An international environment that is dangerous or threatening is likely to prompt potential great powers to mobilize military capabilities. Similarly, a dominant state that is aggressive or provocative is more likely to inspire balancing behavior than one that is reassuring or accommodating. A dominant power can shape the international environment in a way that reassures rather than provokes potential challengers. By its own behavior, the unipolar power can affect the calculations of other states and help to convince them that it is neither necessary nor desirable to engage in a balancing strategy.

Implications for the behavior of the dominant state follow from the logic of the unipolar model. We should observe it making a consistent effort to preserve its privileged position. Security threats to the dominant power are minimized and its foreign policy autonomy is maximized in a unipolar world. That situation is preferable to being one of many great powers in an uncertain multipolar world, or to facing off against the concentrated hostility of an adversary in a bipolar world. Unipolarity is the best of all possible positions in anarchy; it is consistent with realist logic that any great power should prefer to be a unipolar power regardless of whether or not it possesses expansionist ambitions.

We should expect the unipolar state to engage and integrate – in effect, to try to co-opt – potential great powers who do not have clear revisionist intentions. Unambiguous revisionist challengers are impervious to accommodating behavior, and thus in relations with them we should anticipate that the dominant state will adopt a confrontational stance. But, in relations with status quo states and states whose intentions are unclear, we should find that the dominant power adopts policies of reassurance, engagement, and accommodation intended to reinforce the belief that the existing international order is desirable and acceptable.[10] Specifically, we should expect the dominant state to assure that its own behavior is not threatening; to use its foreign policy to help deflect other threats to the security of potential challengers; to stabilize regional conflicts that involve other great powers; and to find opportunities to confer international prestige on other powers as a substitute for full great power status.

It is also reasonable to expect the unipolar state to rely on multilateral decision-making in its foreign policy. Powerful states are tempted to act unilaterally, and the temptation is greatest for a unipolar power. But multilateral procedures are more reassuring to other states and may help to convince them that their preferences matter and that they are not simply being directed to follow the dictates of the dominant state.

Assessment

Some would argue that US foreign policy since the end of the Cold War has lacked an overall strategy and has been indecisive and inconsistent (see, e.g., Lieber 1997). That criticism has some validity, especially if one focuses on the early years of the Clinton administration or on particular foreign policy problems such as the aborted intervention in Somalia. In general, however, the US has followed a consistent strategy of seeking to preserve its preponderant position. As Benjamin Schwarz recently put it,

"America's foreign policy strategists have hoped to keep the reality of international politics permanently at bay" (Schwarz 1996: 100). This US objective, for obvious reasons of diplomacy, has not been emphasized in foreign policy rhetoric, which has focused instead on the liberal goals of promoting democracy, individual rights, and open markets. But occasionally it does slip into public discourse. In 1992, for example, the grand strategy of preserving unipolarity leaked out in the form of a subsequently much-discussed Pentagon planning document which concluded that, following the defeat of the Soviet Union, "our strategy must now refocus on precluding the emergence of any future global competitor" (cited in Mastanduno 1997: 66).

The strategy of preserving preponderance has been clear in the US approach to other major powers. US policy has been dedicated to dissuading Japan from becoming a normal great power with full and independent military capabilities. The Asian strategy of "deep engagement" calls for the United States, over the indefinite future, to maintain the forward deployment of US forces, stabilize regional security, and strengthen the security commitment to Japan for a new era (Nye 1995). US officials took the initiative in responding to the Korean crisis of 1994. They attempted to dissuade North Korea from obtaining nuclear weapons – a step that could plausibly have led Japan to obtain them as well. In 1996, as regional and bilateral tensions mounted, the Clinton administration assured that US economic disputes with Japan were set aside so that the two governments could focus on deepening their security preparations in the event of a future crisis.

In Europe, US officials have continued the Cold War strategy of harnessing the great power potential of a now unified Germany while simultaneously providing for its security. NATO is the key element, and US officials have made clear their intention to expand the alliance into the historically turbulent zone of Central Europe and maintain it indefinitely.[11] When the United States finally took the lead in Bosnia, one crucial objective was to repair the damage to NATO caused by sharp disagreements between the United States and its major European partners over how to handle the conflict.

US policy toward Russia has been dedicated to forestalling a revisionist challenge and encouraging Russian support for the international status quo. US officials have offered the prospect of full integration into the institutions of the capitalist world economy in exchange for domestic political and economic reform. In a move designed in part to bolster its battered prestige, the G7 summits of advanced industrial states now include Russia. The Clinton administration also worked out a compromise to allow Russian forces to participate in the Bosnian peacekeeping effort under US command, when it became obvious that Russia was unwilling to serve under NATO command. Russia clearly has perceived NATO expansion as a political affront and security threat, so US officials have sought to reassure Russia by searching for formulas and institutions that might make NATO expansion more politically palatable to Moscow.

The central thrust of the Clinton strategy toward China – "comprehensive engagement" – is to offer a US-Chinese partnership, with China as the junior partner, as long as China behaves responsibly and meets its international obligations in the judgment of the United States. The United States would prefer that China be a liberal state, but appears to consider a non-liberal China acceptable as long as China accepts a subordinate role in the existing international order. President Clinton revived head-of-state summitry with China in 1997, and with great fanfare in 1998 made the first visit to Beijing of a US President since the Tiananmen Square massacre of 1989.

In relations with all major powers, the United States has tried to demonstrate that greater benefits accrue from accepting rather than from challenging the unipolar order. It has reinforced that message by punishing lesser powers, such as Iraq, who exhibit revisionist ambitions at a regional level. US officials have also relied heavily on multilateral mechanisms to promote their objectives and develop an international consensus behind them. The military and diplomatic efforts to restore international order in the Persian Gulf, Korean peninsula, and the Balkans were led by the United States but involved multilateral coalitions. The response to the Asian financial crisis of 1997–8 reflected US preferences for domestic deregulation and open markets, but was orchestrated by the IMF.

The United States has managed during the first post-Cold War decade to preserve its preeminent position in a global order that reflects its preferences. But will it be able to do so for another decade or more beyond that? The future durability of the international order depends on the ability of the United States to meet three challenges. Each will be difficult in its own right, and the three must be met simultaneously.

The first and most important is to continue to discourage the rise of states that combine formidable economic and military capability with global ambition. The task was relatively easy in the first unipolar decade. Japan and Germany showed little inclination to abandon their identity as "trading states." Europe emerged as a potential economic powerhouse, but without a unified foreign and defense policy. Russia remained devastated economically and unprepared militarily. China received considerable attention as the most likely challenger, but only on the assumption that it would maintain over an extended period the economic development, political stability, and military modernization needed to fulfill its potential. Several Middle Eastern states harbored deep resentment of US hegemony, but none was sufficiently powerful individually, and collectively Middle Eastern states have proven incapable of the political unity required to produce a great power challenger.[12]

Nevertheless, as anyone who witnessed the end of the Cold War can attest, the international system can change dramatically in a decade. Korean unification could leave Japan paradoxically feeling both more vulnerable and less willing to support the continuation of a US defense presence in the region. Russian economic recovery could be accompanied by the mobilization of nationalist sentiment and a desire to make amends for the humiliation of the Cold War settlement. China might fulfill its potential and demand the respect and influence it believes it is owed by the West. Other challengers – a nuclear-capable India or Brazil, for example – could move from the middle ranks to become major players with conceptions of international order that differ significantly from that of the United States.

The challenge for US diplomacy in this uncertain environment will be to accommodate and co-opt states that lean towards the status quo, confront revisionist states, and, most importantly, distinguish between the two. Hans Morgenthau wrote in his classic realist text that the ability to distinguish and respond appropriately to status quo and revisionist states was the "fundamental question" of statecraft, and that the answer determined the "fate of nations" (Morgenthau 1978: 67–8).

The second US challenge is to manage and minimize what has been termed the arrogance of power.[13] The dominant state in any international order faces strong temptations to go it alone, to dictate rather than consult, to preach its virtues and to impose its values. In the case of the United States, these temptations are compounded by a democratic political tradition that blurs the distinction between state and society and imbues foreign policy with the values of society.

Efforts to impose values or to "preach" to other states create resentment and over time can prompt the balancing behavior that the US engagement strategy is seeking to forestall. As the Bush administration learned, when the top officials of the world's most powerful state begin to proclaim "a new world order" after a military victory, other governments, even friendly ones, become very uneasy.

The Clinton team has had similar experiences. The President began with strident public pronouncements and a determination to place the protection of human rights at the center of US China policy. He was forced to retreat amid charges of US arrogance and with the fear that his policies were alienating a country with great power ambitions and the world's largest population. Similarly, the Clinton administration angered its closest trading partners by supporting legislation that extends American sanctions unilaterally and extraterritorially against foreign firms that do business with Cuba, Iran, and Libya. "This is bullying," complained Canada's Foreign Minister, "but in America you call it global leadership." One US official responded to the chorus of criticism in 1996 by stating that "we're America, and they'll get over it" (quoted in Erlanger and Sanger 1996). The administration apparently recognized subsequently that it was wrong to assume others have no choice but to accept their place in a US-centered order. By 1998, it found a face-saving way to diffuse the conflict and retreat without imposing any sanctions.

The third challenge is for US officials to maintain domestic support for the political and economic policies needed to preserve preponderance. This may prove to be the greatest challenge. It is difficult to mobilize and maintain public support, after the war has been won, for the task of "preserving stability" in the absence of a clearly defined, unifying threat.

Significant parts of the US Congress and public have become increasingly reluctant to bear the political risks and economic costs of the US global engagement strategy. With the Cold War over, they are skeptical of the need for US military intervention in distant lands, and intolerant of casualties when intervention takes place. They resent what they perceive as the "free ride" that America's closest allies still enjoy in military operations and economic relations. They resent free trade and globalization when it seems to lead to the loss of US employment. And they do not have the patience for a comprehensive partnership, over the long term, with a communist state that does not respect the human rights of its citizens in a way that is fundamental to the American political tradition.

Preserving preponderance requires US officials to manage the internal as well as the external environment. During the first Cold War decade, the Bush and Clinton administrations deflected the formation of a protectionist coalition and kept some momentum in the direction of freer trade. In military intervention, they sought to avoid extensive commitments, minimize costs and casualties, and develop "exit strategies" even at the risk of leaving unfinished business. They extracted resources from other major powers to assure the US public that the United States was not bearing the financial burden of maintaining international order on its own.

US officials, in effect, adopted a two-sided strategy. They attempted to accommodate foreign powers, but not in a way that provoked or mobilized potential domestic opponents. They also tried to accommodate domestic opponents, but without provoking a challenge from foreign powers. Whether this dual balancing strategy can be maintained and for how long remains to be seen.

Conclusion

The end of the Cold War has not meant the end of realism. But it has provided a worthwhile opportunity to recognize that realism, like any other rich research program, offers neither a single unified theory of state behavior nor a single vision of the emerging international order.

In this paper I have offered three realist visions of international order. The model of geoeconomic competition looked promising initially but has been overtaken by events. The unipolar model best characterizes contemporary international relations. Its durability will depend significantly on the effectiveness of US statecraft. When the unipolar order sooner or later gives way, it will most likely be replaced by multipolar world politics. But a multipolar system in which the great powers may be nuclear-armed and may at the same time be interdependent, peaceful democracies will pose new challenges of interpretation for realist and non-realist analysts alike.

NOTES

1 This discussion draws on Mastanduno and Kapstein (1999).
2 A challenge to this position is Liberman (1996).
3 Grieco (1990) argues that states are "defensive positionalists," more concerned to avoid disproportionate gains by others than to make such gains themselves.
4 See Mastanduno (1991). Traditional realists trace relative gains concerns to the ever-present threat of war. Geoeconomic realists attribute those concerns to the threat of war, but also to the desire for foreign policy autonomy or the pursuit of economic prosperity.
5 Robert Reich (1990) popularized this critique. A powerful rejoinder that stresses the distinctive national character of multinational firms is Doremus, Keller, Pauly, and Reich (1998).
6 I develop this argument in greater detail in Mastanduno (1998).
7 On Asia, see Friedberg (1993/4) and Betts (1993/4). On Europe, see Mearsheimer (1990).
8 Krauthammer (1990) expects it will be "decades" before unipolarity collapses. See also Nye (1990) and Kapstein (1999).
9 The general argument that states balance threats is Walt (1987).
10 A good discussion of this logic is Nordlinger (1995), ch. 6.
11 Barry Posen and Andrew Ross (1997: 117) argue that the United States is pursuing NATO expansion to preserve and widen its role in European affairs and to "forestall even a hint of an independent German foreign policy."
12 For the reasons why, see Lustick (1997).
13 This discussion borrows from Mastanduno (1997).

REFERENCES

Art, Robert J. 1996, "Why Western Europe Needs the United States and NATO," *Political Science Quarterly* III: 1–39.

Betts, Richard K. 1993/4, "Wealth, Power, and Instability: East Asia and the United States After the Cold War," *International Security* 18: 34–77.

Bhagwati, Jagdish and Patrick, Hugh 1990, *Aggressive Unilateralism: America's 301 Policy and the World Trading System*, Ann Arbor: University of Michigan Press.

Brooks, Stephen G. 1997, "Dueling Realisms," *International Organization* 51: 445–77.

Deudney, Daniel 1993, "Dividing Realism: Structural Realism versus Security Materialism on Nuclear Security and Proliferation," *Security Studies* 2: 7–36.

Doremus, Paul, Keller, William, Pauly, Louis and Reich, Simon 1998, *The Myth of the Global Corporation*, Princeton: Princeton University Press.

Erlanger, Steven and Sanger, David 1996, "On Global Stage, Clinton's Pragmatic Turn," *New York Times* July 29: 1.

Friedberg, Aaron L. 1993/4, "Ripe for Rivalry: Prospects for Peace in a Multipolar Asia," *International Security* 18: 5–33.

Garten, Jeffrey E. 1992, *A Cold Peace: America, Japan, Germany, and the Struggle for Supremacy*, New York: Times Books.

Gilpin, Robert G. 1981, *War and Change in World Politics*, Cambridge: Cambridge University Press.

    1986, "The Richness of the Tradition of Political Realism," in *Neorealism and Its Critics*, Robert Keohane (ed.), New York: Columbia University Press, pp. 301–21.

Grieco, Joseph 1990, *Cooperation Among Nations*, Ithaca: Cornell University Press.

    1999, "Realism and Regionalism: American Power and German and Japanese Institutional Strategies During and After the Cold War," in Kapstein and Mastanduno (eds.), pp. 319–53.

Heginbotham, Eric and Samuels, Richard 1998, "Mercantile Realism and Japanese Foreign Policy," *International Security* 22: 171–203.

Hosokawa, Morihiro 1998, "Are US Troops in Japan Needed? Reforming the Alliance," *Foreign Affairs* 77: 2–5.

Huntington, Samuel P. 1993a, "The Clash of Civilizations," *Foreign Affairs* 72: 22–49.

    1993b, "Why International Primacy Matters," *International Security* 17: 68–83.

Jentleson, Bruce W. 1997, "Economic Sanctions and Post-Cold War Conflict Resolution: Challenges for Theory and Policy," paper prepared for the Committee on International Conflict Resolution, National Academy of Sciences.

Jervis, Robert. 1989, *The Meaning of the Nuclear Revolution*, Ithaca: Cornell University Press.

Johnston, Iain 1999, "Realism(s) and Chinese Security Policy in the Post-Cold War Period," in Kapstein and Mastanduno (eds.), pp. 261–318.

Kahler, Miles 1995, *Regional Futures and Transatlantic Economic Relations*, New York: Council on Foreign Relations Press.

Kaplan, Robert 1994, "The Coming Anarchy," *The Atlantic Monthly* 277: 44–76.
     1997, "Was Democracy Just a Moment?" *The Atlantic Monthly* 280: 55–80.
Kapstein, Ethan B. 1990, "Does Unipolarity Have a Future?" in Kapstein and
     Mastanduno (eds.), pp. 464–90.
Kapstein, Ethan B. and Mastanduno, Michael (eds.) 1999, *Unipolar Politics:
     Realism and State Strategies After the Cold War*, New York: Columbia Univer-
     sity Press.
Keohane, Robert O. 1986, "Theory of World Politics: Structural Realism and
     Beyond," in *Neorealism and Its Critics*, Robert O. Keohane (ed.), New York:
     Columbia University Press, pp. 158–203.
Kissinger, Henry A. 1994, *Diplomacy*, New York: Simon and Schuster.
Krasner, Stephen 1976, "State Power and the Structure of International Trade,"
     World Politics 28: 317–47.
Krauthammer, Charles 1990/1, "The Unipolar Moment," *Foreign Affairs* 70:
     23–33.
Krugman, Paul 1994, "Competitiveness: A Dangerous Obsession," *Foreign Af-
     fairs* 73: 28–44.
Layne, Christopher 1993, "The Unipolar Illusion: Why New Great Powers Will
     Rise," *International Security* 17: 5–51.
Levy, Jack 1983, *War in the Modern Great Power System, 1495–1975*, Lexington:
     University of Kentucky Press.
Liberman, Peter 1996, *Does Conquest Pay?* Princeton: Princeton University Press.
Lieber, Robert J. 1997, *Eagle Adrift: American Foreign Policy at the End of the
     Century*, New York: Longman.
Lustick, Ian 1997, "The Absence of Middle Eastern Great Powers: Political
     'Backwardness' in Historical Perspective," *International Organization* 51:
     653–84.
Luttwak, Edward N. 1993, *The Endangered American Dream*, New York: Simon
     and Schuster.
Mastanduno, Michael 1991, "Do Relative Gains Matter? America's Response to
     Japanese Industrial Policy," *International Security* 16: 73–113.
     1997, "Preserving the Unipolar Moment: Realist Theories and US Grand
     Strategy After the Cold War," *International Security* 21: 49–88.
     1998, "Economics and Security in Scholarship and Statecraft," *International
     Organization*, 52: 825–59.
Mastanduno, Michael and Kapstein, Ethan B. 1999, "Realism and International
     Relations After the Cold War," in Kapstein and Mastanduno (eds.), pp. 1–27.
Mearsheimer, John 1990, "Back to the Future: Instability in Europe After the Cold
     War," *International Security* 15: 7–57.
     1992, "Disorder Restored," in *Rethinking America's Security*, Graham Allison
     and Gregory F. Treverton (eds.), New York: Norton, pp. 213–37.
     1994/5, "The False Promise of International Institutions," *International Secur-
     ity* 19: 5–49.
Morgenthau, Hans 1978, *Politics Among Nations: The Struggle for Power and Peace*,
     5th edition New York: Knopf.
Mueller, John 1989, *Retreat From Doomsday: The Obsolescence of Major War*, New
     York: Basic Books.

Nau, Henry R. 1995, *Trade and Security: US Policy at Cross-Purposes*, Washington, DC: AEI Press.

Nordlinger, Eric A. 1995, *Isolationism Reconfigured: American Foreign Policy for a New Century*, Princeton: Princeton University Press.

Nye, Joseph S. 1990, *Bound to Lead: The Changing Nature of American Power*, New York: Basic Books.

1992, "What New World Order?" *Foreign Affairs* 71: 83–96.

1995, "The Case for Deep Engagement," *Foreign Affairs* 74: 90–102.

Nye, Joseph S. and Owens, William 1996, "America's Information Edge" *Foreign Affairs* 75: 20–36.

Oberdorfer, Don 1997, *The Two Koreas: A Contemporary History*, Reading, MA: Addison Wesley.

Posen, Barry and Ross, Andrew 1997, "Competing US Grand Strategies," in Lieber (ed.), pp. 100–34.

Reich, Robert B. 1990, "Who Is Us?" *Harvard Business Review* 90: 53–64.

Rosecrance, Richard 1986, *The Rise of the Trading State: Commerce and Conquest in the Modern World*, New York: Basic Books.

Schwarz, Benjamin 1996, "Why America Thinks It Has to Run the World," *The Atlantic Monthly* 277: 92–6.

Schweller, Randall 1999, "Realism and the Present Great Power System: Growth and Positional Conflict over Scarce Resources," in Kapstein and Mastanduno (eds.), pp. 28–68.

Singer, Max and Wildavsky, Aaron 1993, *The Real World Order: Zones of Peace, Zones of Turmoil*, Chatham, NJ: Chatham House Publishers.

Stremlau, John 1994/5, "Clinton's Dollar Diplomacy," *Foreign Policy* 97: 18–35.

Thucydides 1954, *The Peloponnesian War*, Rex Warner (trans.), New York: Penguin Books.

Thurow, Lester 1992, *Head to Head: The Coming Economic Battle Among Japan, Europe, and America*, New York: Morrow.

Tyson, Laura D'Andrea 1992, *Who's Bashing Whom? Trade Conflict in High-Technology Industries*, Washington, DC: Institute for International Economics.

United States Embassy, Tokyo 1992, "Japan's Aggregate Foreign Trade in CY 1991," Document #220223Z, January.

Walt, Stephen M. 1987, *The Origins of Alliances*, Ithaca: Cornell University Press.

Waltz, Kenneth. 1979, *Theory of International Politics*, Reading: Addison-Wesley.

1993, "The Emerging Structure of International Politics," *International Security* 18: 45–73.

Wayman, Frank W. and Diehl, Paul F. (eds.) 1994, *Reconstructing Realpolitik*, Ann Arbor: University of Michigan Press.

2 A liberal view: preserving and expanding the liberal pacific union[1]

Michael W. Doyle

For more than two centuries liberal countries have tended (and, now, liberal democratic countries do tend) to maintain peaceful relations with each other. Democracies are each other's natural allies. They tend to respect and accommodate other democratic countries and negotiate rather than escalate disputes. This provides a positive incentive to try to preserve and expand the liberal community of peace. But liberalism has also proved to be a dangerous guide to foreign policy, exacerbating tensions with nonliberal states. Expanding liberalism hence seems to provoke danger and war. This paper addresses a large and perplexing question: can the liberal zone of peace be effectively preserved and expanded without provoking unnecessary danger and inflicting unnecessary harm (Smith, 1994; Muravchik, 1991)?[2]

Let us begin by noting that liberal strategy faces special constraints. If a concern for protecting and expanding the range of international freedom is to shape liberal strategic aims, then policy toward the liberal and the nonliberal world should be guided by general liberal principles. At the minimum, this means rejecting the realist balance of power as a general strategy by trusting the liberal community and therefore refusing to balance against the capabilities of fellow democratic liberals. At its fullest, this also means going beyond the standard obligations of general international law. Membership in the liberal community implies accepting a positive duty to defend other members of the liberal community, to discriminate in certain instances in their favor, and to override in some circumstances the domestic sovereignty of states in order to rescue fellow human beings from intolerable oppression. Authentically, liberal policies should furthermore attempt to secure personal and civil rights, to foster democratic government, and to expand the scope and effectiveness of the world market economy as well as to meet those basic human needs that make the exercise of human rights possible.

In order, however, to avoid the extremist possibilities of its abstract universalism, liberal policy should be constrained by a geopolitical budget. Strategy involves matching what we are prepared to spend to what we want to achieve. It identifies aims, resources, threats, and allies. While liberal democracy therefore can identify our natural allies abroad, we must let our actual enemies identify themselves.

One reason for this is that we cannot embark upon the "crusades" for democracy that have been so frequent within the liberal tradition. In a world armed with nuclear weapons crusading is suicidal. And in a world where changes in regional balances of power could be extremely destabilizing for ourselves and our allies, indiscriminate provocations of hostility (such as against the People's Republic of China) could create increased insecurity (for Japan and ourselves). We simply do not have the excess strength that would free us from a need to economize on dangers.

A second reason why we should let our enemies identify themselves is that liberal values require that we should reject an indiscriminate "crusade for democracy." If we seek to promote democracy because it reflects the rights of all to be treated with equal respect – irrespective of race, religion, class, or nationality – then equal respect must guide both our aims and our means. A strategy of geopolitical superiority and liberal imperialism, for example, would both require increased arms expenditures and international subversion and have little (or more likely a retrogressive) effect on human rights in the countries that are our targets.

Instead, liberal strategy for expanding the liberal community should lean toward the defensive. It should strive to protect the liberal community, foster the conditions that might allow the liberal community to grow, and save the use of force for clear emergencies that severely threaten the survival of the community or core liberal values. The strategy should first *preserve* – protecting the community and managing and mitigating the normal tensions among liberal market economies – and then *expand*. Ruling out an offensive state strategy, one should rely primarily on transnational civil society for expansion by three methods: it should begin with "inspiration," focus on "instigation," and, thereby, call upon "intervention" only when necessary.

Preserving the community

Above all, liberal policy should strive to preserve the pacific union of similarly liberal societies. It is not only currently of immense strategic value (being the political foundation of both NATO and the Japanese alliance); it is also the single best hope for the evolution of a peaceful world. Liberals should be prepared, therefore, to defend and formally ally with authentically liberal, democratic states that are subject to threats or actual instances of external attack or internal subversion. We must therefore continue to have no liberal enemies and no unconditional alliances with nonliberal states.

Liberals have taken for granted and underestimated the importance of the democratic alliance. Our alliances in NATO, with Japan, ANZUS, and our alignments with other democratic states are not only crucial to our present security; they are our best hopes for long-term peace and the realization of our ideals. We should not treat them as once useful but now purposeless Cold War strategic alignments against the power of the USSR.

They deserve our careful investment. Placing a special priority on helping developing democracies (e.g., Mexico) manage their international debts is a valuable form of discrimination, if we take into account that financial decompression in those countries might undermine their democratic governance. With the help of West European and Japanese allies, a similar political investment – the so-called "democratic difference" principle – in the economic transition of the fledgling democracies of Eastern Europe merits equivalent attention.

Managing the community. Much of the liberal success in alliance management has to be achieved on a multilateral basis.[3] The current need to redefine NATO and the increasing importance of the US relationship with Japan offer us an opportunity to broaden the organization of liberal security. Joining all the democratic states together in a single democratic security organization would secure an important forum for the definition and coordination of common interests that stretch beyond the regional concerns of Europe and the Far East. With the end of the Cold War, pressures toward regionalism are likely to become increasingly strong. In order to avoid the desperate reactions that might follow regional reactions to regional crises such as those of the 1920s and 1930s, a wider alliance of liberal democracies seems necessary. It could reduce pressures on Japan and Germany to arm themselves with nuclear weapons, mitigate the strategic vulnerabilities of isolated liberal states such as Israel, and allow for the complementary pooling of strategic resources (combining, for example, Japanese and German financial clout with American nuclear deterrence, and American, British, and French expeditionary thrust). The expansion of NATO on the European continent is one part of this security umbrella. It should include all established democratic members and then create a transitional category for all democratizing states (including Russia and the various states of Eastern Europe that have not yet experienced two democratic elections).

Much of the success of multilateral management will, however, rest on shoring up its economic supports. "Above $6000," Adam Przeworski and colleagues have noted, "democracies are impregnable and can be expected to live forever" (Przeworski et al. 1997: 297). Below that income level, steady, low-inflation economic growth is one key to protecting democratic government (298). But unilateral solutions (exchange-rate depreciation, increased taxation) may be necessary but they are not sufficient, and some (long-term protectionism) are neither. To avoid a costly economic recession calls for continued trade liberalization and expansion of demand to match whatever contractions of governmental and private spending are needed to match inflationary pressures.

Discovering ways to manage global interdependence will call for difficult economic adjustments at home and institutional innovations in the world economy. Under these circumstances, liberals will need to ensure that those suffering losses, such as from market disruption or restriction, do not suffer either a permanent loss of income or exclusion from world markets. Although intense economic interdependence generates conflicts, it also helps to sustain the material well-being underpinning liberal societies and to promise avenues of development to Third World states with markets that are currently limited by low income. To this should be added mutually beneficial measures designed to improve Third World economic performance. Export earnings insurance, international debt management assistance, export diversification assistance, and technical aid are among some of these. In the case of the truly desperate poor, such as is the condition of some of the populations of Africa, more direct measures of international aid and relief from famine are required, both as a matter of political prudence and of moral duty.

Futhermore, if measures of temporary protection are needed, liberal states should undertake these innovations only by international negotiation and only when the resulting agreements are subject to a regular review by all the parties. Otherwise emergency measures could reverberate into a spiral of isolation. The liberal community thus needs to create a diplomatic atmosphere conducive to multilateral problem-solving. A national strategy that conveys a commitment to collective responsibility in United States diplomacy will go far in this direction. (Bergsten et al. 1978; Cooper et al. 1978).

Protecting the community. The liberal community needs to be protected. Two models could fit liberal national strategy designed to protect against the international power of nonliberal states.[4] If faced with severe threats from the nonliberal world, the liberal community might simply balance the power of nonliberal states by playing divide and rule within the nonliberal camp. If, for example, Russia reverted to being an authoritarian state, the liberal community could triangulate between Russia and China as the US did during the 1970s.

If, on the other hand, the liberal community becomes increasingly predominant (or collectively unipolar) as it now appears to be becoming, it could adopt a more ambitious grand strategy, which will be discussed below under "expansion." Arms exports, trade and aid could reflect the relative degrees of liberal principle that nonliberal domestic and foreign policies incorporate. Liberal foreign policy could be designed to create a ladder of rewards and punishments – a set of balanced incentives, rewarding liberalization and punishing oppression, rewarding accommodation and punishing aggression. This strategy would both satisfy liberal demands for publicity – consistent public legitimation – and create incentives for the progressive liberalization of nonliberal states.

Expanding the community

Preserving the community is important in part because there are few direct measures that the liberal world can take to foster the stability, development, and spread of liberal democratic regimes. Many direct efforts, including military intervention and overt or covert funding for democratic movements in other countries, discredit those movements as the foreign interference backfires through the force of local nationalism.[5]

Much of the potential success of a policy designed to foster democracy therefore rests on an ability to shape an economic and political environment that indirectly supports – instigates – democratic governance and creates pressures for the democratic reform of authoritarian rule.

Politically, there are few measures more valuable than an active human rights diplomacy, which enjoys global legitimacy and (if successful) can assure a political environment that tolerates the sort of dissent that can nourish an indigenous democratic movement. There is reason to pay special attention to those countries entering what Samuel Huntington (1991) has called the socioeconomic "transition zone" – countries having the economic development that has typically been associated with democracy (see also Prezworski 1995). For them, more direct support in the form of electoral infrastructure (from voting machines to battalions of international observers) can provide the essential margin persuading contentious domestic groups to accept the fairness of the crucial first election.

Following World War II, the allied occupation and re-making of Germany and Japan, and the Marshall Plan's successful coordination and funding of the revival of Europe's prewar industrial economies and democratic regimes offer a model of how much can be achieved with an extraordinary commitment of resources and the most favorable environment (Schwartz 1991). Practically today, short of those very special circumstances, there are few direct means to stimulate democratic development from development from abroad apart from *inspiration* and *instigation*.

1. *Inspiration*. The simplest program for liberal expansion is the "City on a Hill." The success of liberalism at home stands as an example for emulation and a refuge for beleaguered liberals in oppressive countries everywhere. Liberalism, moreover, strikes deep chords of common humanity that lend confidence that all may some day follow a similar path toward liberation, allowing for the appropriate national and cultural differences. Peoples will either *liberate themselves* or *modernize themselves*. One liberal "strategy" is for them simply to protect themselves, live up to their own principles domestically, and wait.

For Locke, *liberation* is explained by successful rebellion, which in turn is explained, as well as justified, by tyranny. "Politick Society," what we would now call civil society, precedes the existence of the state and is constituted by an explicit or implicit contract among human beings whose natural equality of passion and reason makes their freely exercised choice the determinative secular source of binding authority. The legislature and executive serve to regulate the common life of the people joined together in a civil society dedicated to the preservation of life, liberty, and property. Only foreign conquest dissolves a civil society. Governments, however, are dissolved by tyrannical acts: "Whenever the Legislators (or the Supreme Executor) endeavor to take away, and destroy the property of the People, or to reduce them to slavery under Arbitrary Power, they put themselves into a state of War with the People, who are thereupon absolved from any farther Obedience, and are left to the common refuge, which God hath provided for all Men, against force and violence" (Locke 1988: para. 222).

Considered as an explanation, the limitation in the Rebellion-Inspiration thesis is obvious. Tyranny may justify but it hardly explains or promotes rebellion, as the longevity and prevalence of tyrannical regimes indicates. But the rebellion trope finds a constant echo in the words of those who do rebel. The rebels mix with striking regularity the rhetoric of justification and explanation. Like Locke, they too explain rebellions by "Arbitrary Power." Vaclav Havel, for example, stresses the exceptional character of the totalitarian regime and the arbitrariness of its power when he tries to explain to Westerners the origins of the Eastern liberations in the oppressive quality of daily life: "at the mercy of the all-powerful bureaucracy, so that for every little thing they have to approach some official or other . . . the gradual destruction of the human spirit, of basic human dignity . . . lives in a state of permanent humiliation" (quoted in Brzezinski 1989: 111).[6]

Conditions such as these, together with Locke's faith in the equality of passion and reason, which can make men see themselves as free, explain the spirit of rebellion and the extraordinary reach of the demand for freedom through place and time, including in the least promising circumstances. For what else can unite the aspirations of Jack Straw and Wat Tyler with those of the Levelers, Locke's own Glorious Revolution, the Sans Culottes, Jefferson and Paine, Lincoln and Frederick Douglass, the students of Tiananmen Square, and the desperate opposition in Burma today? So while the aspirations can help account for why citizens seek freedom (*what* a rebellion is for) they tell us little about either where or when they will succeed or how they can be appropriately assisted.

Liberal *modernization* has other roots. Hegel's philosophy of history may be the most important source of an idealist interpretation of liberal modernization.[7] But Joseph Schumpeter more clearly carried forward this tradition, focusing on the material interpretation of capitalist *economic* modernization in his essay, "Imperialism" (1955: 68). Capitalism produces an unwarlike disposition, he said: its populace is "democratized, individualized, rationalized." The people's (daily) energies are daily absorbed in production. The disciplines of industry and the market train people in "economic rationalism"; the instability of industrial life necessitates calculation. Capitalism also "individualizes"; "subjective opportunities" replace the "immutable factors" of traditional, hierarchical society. Rational individuals then demand democratic governance.

Francis Fukuyama's striking argument about the "End of History" presents a radical restatement of the liberal modernization theme, bringing together both its materialist and idealist strains. His study envisions the failure of all forms of autocracy, whether in Eastern Europe or elsewhere, and the triumph of consumer capitalism and democracy under the irresistible onslaught of modernization. He tells us that History (and not just wars – cold or hot) is over. He means not that life will stop, events will cease, but that the struggle over alternative ways of life, of identity, meaning, or purpose, will come to an end – has come to an end – because it is now clear that there are no viable alternatives to Western liberalism, no credible alternative paths to the good life. There will be plenty of archaic illiberalism, autocracy, dictatorship, stale socialism left in what used to be the "Third World" (now, presumably, the "Second World"). But no longer can they claim to be the wave of the future. They have given up the struggle. World politics will henceforth, with allowances for the backward areas, be a politics of boredom, of peaceful common marketization (Fukuyama 1989).

Fukuyama tells us that this extraordinary end has come to pass for two major reasons. First, because liberalism, by which he means political democracy and consumer capitalism, has resolved all the contradictions of life for which, throughout the course of history, individuals have been prepared to fight. With democracy, economic productivity, and the VCR, we have satisfied the cravings for both freedom and wealth. Liberalism has achieved a strikingly simultaneous combination of social and psycho-moral stabilization. And second because communism and all other rival forms of political identity are finished. They have failed to satisfy either the desire for freedom or the desire for wealth.

First let us examine his claim concerning communism. Communism, as he claims, may well be finished and it may no longer offer a viable alternative, and certainly Stalinism, Brezhnevism, Maoism, and their many imitators seem now to be rejected by the elites, even more the masses, throughout what was once the communist second world. Even in China after the Tiananmen crisis, and together with reaffirmations of the supremacy of the party and a continued loyalty to Marxism and Leninism, there continue to be promises of reform, pleas for patience, and programs of partial liberal economic development. It looks like we and, directly, China's youth are being asked to defer, not to abandon, the hope of freedom.[8]

But Fukuyama claims that all democratic and liberalizing reforms that fall short of electoral multiparty democracy and the VCR, that is of capitalist democracy, are not stable. Communism, indeed socialism itself, is on a slippery slope. The only really stable point is liberalism. The police state is therefore a desperate holding measure.

He provides us with much stimulating argument for this world historical assertion. In the process he insightfully connects and thus accounts for the historical association between capitalism and democracy in many of the Eastern European revolutions.[9] But he also leaves us with a crucial and unanswered question. Is the crisis a crisis of established or existing communism, or is it a crisis of all socialism? That is, is it a crisis just of Stalinism and Maoism, or is it a crisis of the potential of a more plural but still socialist China or a democratic socialist "Third Way"?

An insightful study by Ellen Comisso (1990) does provide the argument and evidence (Comisso 1990; and Bunce 1990). Focusing on the work of the great Austrian libertarian economist Ludwig von Mises, she too suggests that socialism in all of its forms is doomed. Neither democratic Leninism nor democratic socialism nor the historic forms of Yugoslav self-managed socialism – none of these are stopping points in the forced march, the progress of liberal modernization. None of these are alternatives to the choice between liberalism and stagnation. Socialists of all types want economic equality; some now reject the public ownership of the means of production. They think they can reform socialism through perestroika by having markets for goods, recognizing that markets make for more efficiency and thereby growth.

But reforms in commodity markets, Von Mises said, were not enough to achieve productivity. An economic system also needs real capitalism – a market for capital. An efficient economy needs to insure that resources, that is capital, will be taken away from firms that are not profitable and given to the firms that are more profitable. For if the state centralizes the ownership of capital, industrial managers will have an incentive to mislead the state planner in order to get more capital, more resources. After the centralized state planner invests in these firms, each – that is both the state planner and the firms – will acquire a bureaucratic stake in the survival of the other. Since the state cannot go out of business, then neither will the industrial entrepreneurs (until they go together). Capital will be wasted in inefficient and uncontrollable businesses, overall national productivity will fall, and therefore, Von Mises implies, socialism will not produce the VCRs for which the modern consumer hungers.

But there are good grounds for us to reject economic liberalism as a fully satisfactory explanation of the democratic liberalization of Eastern Europe. First, we have reason to question the confidence in the theory of capitalism that Von Mises and other market capitalists display. On the one hand, we can envision a credible, socialist, egalitarian form of the ownership of the means of production that nevertheless relies on capital markets for social efficiency. Pension funds, for example, can compete for the investments of workers, and these funds can invest in the productive enterprises of the economy. These pension funds will attempt to maximize the long-run profits of their contributors and therefore they will invest in the most efficient firms and take away funds from those less efficient. Thus pension funds will be able to own the economy but the pension funds will themselves be owned on an egalitarian basis by the workers and managers whose salaries go to make up their funds. This is not purely a foreign vision. The great American business guru, Peter Drucker, has described how pension funds might even bring socialism to America. But at the same time it is not a solely American vision; a whole line of scientists, theorists, and promoters of industrial democracy have envisioned how workers owning (with their managers) 50 percent or so of their firms will be able to rely on external funds such as these pension funds to make up the discretionary capital they lack.[10]

Moreover, in practice communism was *not an ineffective* mode of production, at least not until the 1980s. Communism, Charles Maier (1991) has noted, like other forms of central planning was an economic success between 1930 and 1970 (Maier 1991). In an era of large productive units and heavy industry, "Communism was the ideology of heavy metal."

East and West European growth rates in the 1950s and 1960s were comparable and both quite good by global standards as both forged ahead, rebuilding and then extending heavy and light industry destroyed by the war. But in the 1980s the East European economies entered a profound economic crisis. In the 1970s and 1980s communist states proved unable (unwilling) to shed these industrial workers and miners when their productivity fell; capitalist states of the West were able to dis-employ the workforce of heavy industry and re-employ (though sometimes only their wives and children) in the growing service sector. The ten-year gap in industrial technology, Maier argues, doomed communism in Eastern Europe.

And we have mounting evidence that free market capitalism may not even be the quintessential capitalist answer to growth under the conditions of late-late capitalism. The most striking rates of growth of the postwar period appear to have been achieved by the semi-planned capitalist economies of East Asia – Taiwan, South Korea, Singapore, and Japan. Indicative planning, capital rationing by parastatal development banks and ministries of finance, managed trade, incorporated unions – capitalist syndicalism, not capitalist libertarianism – seemed to describe the wave of the capitalist future.[11] China's current success (10 percent p.a.) with "market-Leninism" or "national corporatism" seems to confirm the non-liberal path. Yet, even here, economists have raised concerns about whether Asian capitalism can evolve from capital accumulation to "total factor productivity," which may require a loosening of indicative planning. Thus in China market forces have stimulated the formation of thousands of business and professional groups, and greater village level (democratic) self-management. The government controlled 95 percent of the Chinese press in 1979; one-third in 1988. By 2015 China should, if current trends continue, be crossing the $6000–7000 (1990s dollars) threshold at which democratic governments tend to predominate and be stable.

We can also take a more *political* approach to liberal modernization and examine the effects of economic development on social identities and political mobilization (Deutsch 1966; Huntington 1968: chs. 5–6). Significant (whether stabilizing or destabilizing) change in political institutions can be a product of social mobilization, itself stimulated by economic development. Political upheavals and transformations should thus tend to correlate with social mobilization, and societies that have experienced extensive economic development and social mobilization should thus be either inclusionary (democratic) or highly repressive ("totalitarian," perhaps, rather than merely traditionally "autocratic" or "authoritarian," which, on this view, should characterize less mobilized societies).

There are some indications that modernization may offer a democratic ratchet effect. Economically, judging from the historical evidence of the 1920s and 1930s, democratic regimes seem to be more vulnerable to economic depression than authoritarian regimes. (This is why liberals should target economic aid at the margin toward fledgling democracies.) But in periods of stable economic growth, democratic regimes seem to accommodate those diverse social groups that are newly mobilized by economic growth better over the long run than do authoritarian regimes (see Dahl 1989: 251–5). Democracies expand participation better. They also allow for the expression of non-material goals more easily, it seems, than do the more functionally legitimated authoritarian regimes. Social modernization, thus, may be the liberals' best long-run strategy.

Interestingly, this is just the pattern that describes the upheavals in Eastern Europe. Czechoslovakia (together with East Germany, the most developed economy) was forcibly demobilized from its democratic regime in 1948. East Germany suppressed an upheaval in 1953. Hungary and Poland (the next two most economically developed) rebelled in 1956. Czechoslovakia rebelled again in 1968; Hungary began to adopt "Goulash Communism" in the 1970s; and Poland rebelled again in 1981. And Rumania and Bulgaria, the least economically developed members of the Bloc, did not experience political rebellion until 1989.[12] "1989" appeared so striking, another 1848, in part, because the earlier rebellions and upheavals were not allowed to play themselves out nationally. Communist "Totalitarianism" appeared permanent to Jeane Kirkpatrick, and others, less because it was different from authoritarianism than because the communist states of Eastern Europe were part of a Soviet empire that controlled their political fate. What made 1989 so striking was that, at last, Gorbachev and his associates had arrived at a willingness to abandon the Soviet empire, thus allowing national development to proceed.[13]

Another route to democratization lies in the institutional routinization of authority, what Minxin Pei has called "creeping democratization" in the Chinese context (Pei 1995: 65–79). Even when leaders are opposed to democratization and the forces of civil society lack the power or the interest in promoting a democratization of the state, democratization may "creep" in. When leaders seek to defend their authority by recruiting allies, ceding to them competency embodied in institutional routines and government structures, the beginnings of constitutional checks and balances are set in motion. Representing diverse and sometimes extensive interests, the new institutions limit arbitrary power and begin to delegate power in their turn, further institutionalizing a regime. Step by step, the foundations of the rule of law are laid, as they are now being (albeit slowly) in China, where new clusters of authority in the National

People's Congress, the court system and the legal profession, and village councils are emerging. All these new authorities, however, are in a "race against time." They supplement and replace communist authoritarianism; but eroding communism is also leaving tendencies toward anarchy. Whether the anarchy will be adequately filled by the new rule of law or instead by hostile regionalism, warlord politics, or collapse is yet to be determined.

The democratic politics of modernization, thus, are not smooth. We should also be concerned about the compatibility between democracy and capitalism that is assumed in much of this literature. A good case can be made that in the long run capitalism provides the dispersal of social power that effective democracy presupposes, and that democracy is an especially effective mechanism with which to resolve differences within a society that is characterized by a pluralistic dispersal of social power. In the shorter run, a certain comfort can be drawn from the observation that the values of democratic participation and toleration of dissent are supported by majorities in some recent polls taken in the former Soviet Union. These same polls indicate that a large majority of Russians are willing to tolerate income differentials based on people being allowed to "earn as much as they could" (ROMIR Poll, December 1991 and January 1992, reported by Mickiewicz 1992: 8). (Is this enough to sustain a full blown form of capitalist appropriation?) But in a 1989 Soviet poll concerning the future of the economy, more than 60 percent of the Soviet sample said that they preferred the rationing of basic essential commodities to reliance upon market pricing. Concerning ownership many (more than 66 percent) favored private farming and some (more than 30 percent) would be happy to work for a multinational corporation in a joint venture in the Soviet Union. But more than half of the Soviet public rejected the private ownership of businesses – these respondents regarded private enterprise as inherently corrupt and corrupting. Adam Przeworski, reflecting on the results of Polish polls, concluded, "The one value that socialist systems have successfully inculcated is equality, and this value may undermine pro-market reforms under conditions of democracy" (Przeworski 1991: 178). We do not yet know whether democratic and consumer sovereignty are on the same course in the former communist economies.

Liberal developmentalism of both variants offers some degree of confidence in trusting to democratic liberalization: 1. It explains the overall modernity of the liberal progress, the seeming long-run economic superiority of liberalism over various forms of socialism and communism; 2. It tells us when and where – *grosso modo* – liberal society has found itself selected as the dominant modern type. Employing Maier's argument, we can use industrial selection to date the collapse of communism to the 1980s; 3. It offers an account of the underlying pattern of political development that we observe (stymied by Soviet imperialism) in Eastern Europe.

Yet none of these conclusions is altogether satisfying. Consumerist modernism, we find, had not declared itself firmly liberal until the 1970s; and now there are indications that East Asian capitalist syndicalism is winning the 1990s. The 1980s seem to be a thin decade on which to hang the march of world history.

2. *Instigation.* The Kantian tradition offers an account of how liberalization could be instigated and not just awaited. The Kantian peace train has two tracks. The first track is transnational; commerce and other transnational ties and economic developments tend to operate on societies from "below." These forces individually mobilize and pluralize the sources of power in a society and thereby put pressure on authoritarian institutions, whose release lies in political participation in liberal political institutions (see Dahl 1989; Deutsch 1966; and Huntington 1968).

Here the role of global civil society and international civil politics is particularly important. Tourism, educational exchanges, and scientific meetings spread tastes across borders. *Transnational* contacts with the liberal world seem to have had a liberalizing effect on the many Soviet and East European elites who visited the West during the Cold War, demonstrating both Western material successes (where they existed) and regimes that tolerated and even encouraged dissent and popular participation (when they did) (Deudney and Ikenberry 1991/2). The international commitment to human rights, including the Helsinki Watch process, found a reflection in Gorbachev's "universal human values." The "Goddess of Liberty" erected in Tiananmen Square represented another transnational expression of ideas shared on a global basis.

Trade can have even more powerful effects. In the modern economy, fostering growth has meant at least a minimal engagement with the world economy. Even the USSR in its later days traded for 5 percent of its GNP (Colton 1992). Trade can distribute income to abundant factors of production (often discriminated against within the domestic market) in ways that serve to pluralize and put strain on established national distributions of income and power. These effects can have political consequences that enhance democratic governance by shifting the locus of domestic resources.[14]

The second Kantian track is the *international* track of war. The pressure of war and military mobilization creates incentives for authoritarian rulers to grant popular participation as a way of increasing the power resources of the states (Nef 1968). Thus states cede representation in return for the

increased manpower or taxation (or both) they need to fight wars successfully, and republican institutions descend from above.

The incentives to internationalize and democratize are not, however,
consistent or smooth. Democratization, moreover, is a bumpy road.
There is a contingent, strategic element in both the popular and governmental process in the decisions to transform (*reforma* for Juan Linz),
replace (Linz's *ruptura*), or "transplace" an existing authoritarian regime
(Huntington 1991: 114; and Linz 1978: 35). With the right incentives,
authoritarian (and, we now know, even totalitarian) regimes can choose
either to lead a transformation, or to collapse and suffer a replacement at
the hands of a democratic opposition, or to join with a democratic
opposition in a mutual transplacement toward liberalization and then
democracy.

Are the public, collective incentives of liberal internationalism sufficient to motivate an authoritarian elite to start a transformation, an
opposition to risk a crushed replacement, or both to engage in a transplacement? Although it focuses on the need to account for incentives to
act, the new literature on democratization also suggests that we need to
consider what should be called "misincentives." Would Gorbachev have
undertaken liberalization (*glasnost* and then political *perestroika*) had he
known through a crystal ball the outcome today (not to speak of during
his dangerous incarceration during the 1991 coup)? Gorbachev, it appears, sought a reformed communism, a market socialism, and, revivified
(and politically rewarded) popular democratic communist party, led
presumably by himself, not the current stumble toward Western-style
liberal pluralism and IMF-dependent capitalism, led by his rival Yeltsin
(see Gorbachev 1987; and Goldman 1991: 128–71). The process of transformation escaped his grasp before, during, and especially after the
coup.[15]

A second process factor affecting the risks replacers are willing to bear
is the simple concatenation of events, what has been called in other
contexts the domino effect. The dominoes fell in Eastern Europe in 1989,
and these had effects in the USSR too, stimulating both the coup and
some valiant Muscovites to resist it. Actions which seem imprudent here
and now appear reasonable when everyone else is doing them, even if they
are doing them elsewhere. Thus what took ten years in Poland took ten
months in Hungary, ten weeks in East Germany, and ten days in
Czechoslovakia.

And third, simple lack of information, uncertainty, is conducive to
democratic transplacements. When societies know the lines of cleavage
and the distribution of social power, all the steps of transformations and
transplacements must be negotiated in detail in advance, short-circuiting

the open-endedness of liberal democratic contestation (Przeworski 1991: 88). The very lack of knowledge of underlying social geography, after the years of strait-jacketed communism, thus may have made for a willingness to jump into contestation in Eastern Europe, and may have the same effect in Russia and Ukraine today.

Two-track internationalism helps account for the international process of change, but here, too, it is far from a complete model or coherent strategy of democratization. Its attention to transnational forces from below and international forces from above the state parallels explanations of liberalization processes that focus on splits within the governmental elite (as in Hungary 1989), as well as on collapses of the governmental elite in the face of popular mobilization (as in East Germany 1989) (Przeworski 1991: 56). These transnational and international forces offer important incentives for democratic liberal reform. They implicitly promise the opportunity to participate more fully in the liberal world market without security restrictions (such as COCOM) and with the protection of GATT standards and access to IMF programs. They also promise membership in the liberal "zone of peace" and the consequent reduction in insecurity and, possibly, defense expenditures.

Both these sets of pressures have recently been reinvigorated and institutionalized in the United Nations expansion into *comprehensive peacebuilding* operations that pierce the shell of national autonomy by bringing international involvement to areas long thought to be the exclusive domain of domestic jurisdiction. If a peacekeeping operation is to leave behind a legitimate and independently viable political sovereign, it must help transform the political landscape by building a new basis for domestic peace.

Traditional strategies of conflict resolution, when successful, were designed to resolve a dispute between conflicting parties. Successful resolution could be measured by: (1) the stated reconciliation of the parties; (2) the duration of the reconciliation; and (3) changes in the way parties behaved toward each other (for a good discussion of traditional views, see Fetherston 1994: 11). But successful contemporary peacebuilding changes not merely behavior but, more importantly, it transforms identities and institutional context. More than reforming play in an old game, it changes the game.

This is the grand strategy General Sanderson invoked when he spoke of forging an alliance with the Cambodian people, bypassing the factions. Reginald Austin, electoral chief of the Cambodian operation (UNTAC), probed the same issue when he asked what are the "true objectives [of UNTAC]: Is it a political operation seeking a solution to the immediate problem of an armed conflict by all means possible? Or does it have a wider objective: to implant democracy, change values and establish a new pattern of governance based on multi-partism and free and fair elections?" (as quoted in Doyle 1995: 86).

UNTAC helped create new actors on the Cambodian political scene: the electors, a fledgling civil society, a free press, a continuing international and transnational presence. The Cambodian voters gave Prince Ranariddh institutional power and the Khmer Rouge was transformed from an internationally recognized claimant on Cambodian sovereignty into a domestic guerrilla insurgency. The peacebuilding process, particularly the election, became the politically tolerable substitute for the inability of the factions to reconcile their conflicts.

The UN's role, as mandated in Namibia, El Salvador, Cambodia, Mozambique, Angola, and now Guatemala, includes monitoring, substituting for, renovating and in some cases helping to build the basic structures of the state. The UN is called in to demobilize and sometimes to restructure and reform once warring armies; to monitor or to organize national elections; to promote human rights; to supervise public security and help create a new civilian police force; to control civil administration in order to establish a transitional politically neutral environment; to begin the economic rehabilitation of devastated countries; and, as in the case of Cambodia, to address directly the values of the citizens, with a view to promoting democratic education.

The liberal internationalist perspective does contribute additional understanding to the transformation of the international system. It highlights possible international sources of change – commerce and war, suggesting to us that democratic liberalization was most likely where war and commerce were most intense. There was little commerce in the Soviet Bloc, and none of it free. And this proposition does not mean that a strategy of "peace through strength" – military pressure and arms racing in order to force the collapse of the opposing regime – is a justified liberal strategy. In the short run, outside pressure tends to strengthen a regime, almost *any* regime, that holds a domestic monopoly of the means of violence. It means, however, that over the long run authoritarian regimes prove to be poor mobilizers of national resources, unless they call on representation as a means toward taxation, and the Cold War, together with Soviet domestic ambitions, imposed large burdens on Soviet society.[16]

It also contributes a twofold perspective on change, stressing both the pressures from below mounted by trade unions such as Solidarity and by intellectuals and students in Czechoslovakia, and the decisions at the top made by Andropov and Gorbachev under the strain of Cold War competition. And lastly, in the spread of the pacific union it holds forth a promise of peace to all those who would be willing to undertake the dangerous course of liberal internationalist reform.

Intervention. Liberal principles can also help us think about whether liberal states should attempt to rescue individuals oppressed by their own governments. Should a respect for the rights of individuals elicit our help or even military rescue? Historically, liberals have been divided on these issues.[17] And the US public today has no clear answer to these questions. They supported the "rescue" of Grenada and the purge in Panama: but as many rejected "another Vietnam" in Nicaragua.[18] Traditionally, and in accord with current international law, states have the right to defend themselves, come to the aid of other states aggressed against, and take forcible measures to protect where necessary their citizens from wrongful injury and release them from wrongful imprisonment (Cutler 1985). But modern international law condemns sanctions designed to redress the domestic oppression of states. The United Nations Charter is ambiguous on this issue, since it finds human rights to be international concerns and permits the Security Council to intervene to prevent "threats" to "international peace and security." Given the ambiguity of the Charter and the political stalemate of the Security Council, difficult moral considerations thus must become decisive factors in considering policy toward domestic oppression in foreign countries.[19]

Nonintervention also has important moral foundations. It helps encourage order – stable expectations – in a confusing world without international government. It rests on a respect for the rights of individuals to establish their own way of life free from foreign interference.

The basic moral presumption of liberal thought is that states should not be subject to foreign intervention, by military or other means. Lacking a global scheme of order or global definition of community, foreign states have no standing to question the legitimacy of other states other than in the name and "voice" of the individuals who inhabit those other states. States therefore should be taken as representing the moral rights of individuals unless there is clear evidence to the contrary. Although liberals and democrats have often succumbed to the temptation to intervene to bring "civilization," metropolitan standards of law and order, and democratic government to foreign peoples expressing no demand for them, these interventions find no justification in a conception of equal respect for individuals. This is simply because it is to their sense of their own self-respect and not our sense of what they should respect that we must accord equal consideration.

What it means to respect their own sense of self-determination is not always self-evident. Ascertaining what it might mean can best be considered as an attempt at both subjective and objective interpretation.

One criterion is subjective. We should credit the voice of their majority. Obviously, this means not intervening against states with apparent majority support. In authoritarian states, however, determining the wishes of the majority is particularly difficult. Some states will have divided political communities with a considerable number (but less than a majority) of the population supporting the government, a large minority opposing, and many indifferent. Some will be able to suppress dissent completely. Others will not. Widespread armed resistance sustained by local resources and massive street demonstrations against the state (and not just against specific policies) therefore can provide evidence of a people standing against their own government. Still, one will want to find clear evidence that the dissenters actually want a foreign intervention to solve their oppression.

The other criterion is objective. No group of individuals, even if apparently silent, can be expected to consent to having their basic rights to life, food, shelter, and freedom from torture systematically violated. These sorts of rights clearly crosscut wide cultural differences.

Whenever either or both of these violations take place one has a *prima facie* consideration favoring foreign intervention.[20] But even rescuing majorities suffering severe oppression, or individuals suffering massive and systematic violations of human rights, is not sufficient grounds to justify military intervention. We must also have (1) some reasonable expectation that the intervention will actually end the oppression. We need to expect that it will end the massacre or address starvation (as did India's intervention in East Pakistan and Tanzania's in Uganda). Or, if pro-democratic, that it has a reasonable chance of establishing authentic self-determination, rather than (as J. S. Mill warned) merely introducing foreign rulers who, dependent on outside support, soon begin to replicate the oppressive behavior of the previous rulers. (The US invasion of Grenada and the covert push in the Philippines seem to qualify; the jury is still out on Haiti and Panama.)

Moreover, (2) the intervention must be a proportional response to the suffering now endured and likely to be endured without an intervention. Countries cannot, any more than villages, be destroyed in order to be saved. We must consider whether means other than military intervention could achieve the liberation from oppression. And we must ensure that the intervention, if necessary, is conducted in a way that minimizes casualties, most particularly noncombatant casualties. In short, we must be able morally to account for the expected casualties of an invasion, both to our own soldiers and to the noncombatant victims.

And (3), a normal sense of fallibility, together with a decent respect for the opinions of the entire community of nations, recommends a resort wherever feasible to multilateral organizations to guide and legally legitimate a decision to violate the sovereignty of another state.

The future of a pacific union

If the liberals are successful in preserving and expanding the pacific union, they should experience a number of evolutionary advantages and disadvantages in the middle run, and an extraordinary promise over the long run.

In the middle run, liberals promise that if the next hegemonic challenger is liberal, the hegemonic transition might be peaceful. Then we will suffer neither war nor the waste of resources in a Cold War and we might then enjoy another transition such as the peaceable one between Great Britain and the Unites States in the twentieth century.

Liberalism also raises sources of real concern: what Americans tend to call the "Japan problem" or, better, the "US-Japan" problem. Japan is quasi-democratic, like the United States, but it is less purely capitalist than we are. And most importantly, culturally it is not yet (and perhaps never will be) as liberal as the United States now is – "Japan-ism" always seems more important than universal liberalism. That is, while the Japanese polity is representative, its economy is, we think, too closely integrated to be one of arms-length competition and a free and flat playing field. Its culture identifies community as something more important than individuality.

Like pre-World War I Germany, therefore, Japan may not be a full member of the liberal pacific union. While Wilhelm II of Germany and Bethmann-Hollweg were sometimes idiosyncratic in the formulation of their policy, they were not noticeably more aggressive than the other governments of Europe at the time. The problem is that the other governments of Europe – particularly Britain and France – assumed that because Germany was not a fully representative liberal state, it was bound to be dangerous. This lack of trust then made Germany feel insecure and threatened. It responded in ways that confirmed the expectations of Britain and France and thereby escalated tensions and contributed to the onslaught of World War I. We need to ask, will the same thing happen in US relations with Japan?

In short there is plenty of room for the sort of spiraling misperception and rivalry that characterized the pre-war Anglo-German antagonism. We will need institutions and multifaceted contacts to offset the economic tensions that are likely to be an increasingly important part of the relationship.

One possibility is a globally enhanced role for Japan in the UN that helps integrate Japan more closely into the liberal community of nations with a status more equal to that enjoyed by the other great liberal democratic powers. Another vital institutional support is bilateral. Defense cooperation is an especially effective place to begin, and the Kakizawa Initiative is an imaginative proposal. A leading LDP defense politician (Diet member, Mr. Kakizawa) has recommended the establishment of jointly staffed defense: joint crews on warships, air stations, army units, all assembled perhaps in a pan-Pacific peacekeeping force at the call of the UN. He wisely hopes to add intense security cooperation as a counterweight to the economic tensions that are sure to arise.

Another danger in the middle run identified by liberalism is that of hegemonic decline. The problem is not one of further absolute economic decline, the US having declined from roughly 40 percent of world GNP to 25 percent of world GNP by the early 1990s. The problem is different; US absolute and, even, relative decline has slowed since the 1970s. The real problem is the decline that took place between the late 1950s and the early 1970s. It is not that the US will decline further (though it will); it is that the US has already declined from the 45 percent it held in the early 1950s to the 25 percent of the world GNP. The "horse is already out of the barn." The danger is one of who will provide the collective goods of world trade and growth so that the world economy should continue to grow. Which country's individual interest in world development is sufficiently large that it can afford to bear the costs of managing the world economy as a whole? Once it was in the US interest. Is it any longer so? So it is not surprising that there are looming fears of regional trade blocs in the 1990s. Will there be a 1930s-style collapse bringing down democracy in its wake? Democracy needs economic security. A collapse of democracy could then erode the security that the US has enjoyed in its relationships with democratic allies.

But these general strategies of democratization do not answer the particular challenges Russia and China present. In the short run, choices must be made that avoid the extremes of appeasement and provocation. Appeasing a China or Russia that turns aggressive would be the most dangerous of outcomes. But starting a new "crusading" Cold War with China or a post-coup Russia would also constitute distinct failures of diplomacy. The cost of the forty-five-year Cold War has to be calculated in the trillions – one estimate was $11 trillion (Treverton 1992: 40). Starting an equivalent Cold War against "Market Leninism" in China will cost an equivalent sum, with even larger long-run dangers, given China's dynamism. Economically reinforcing democratization in Russia and engaging with authoritarian China in a way that encourages moderate foreign policy behavior, a growing respect for human rights, and a

Table 2.1. *The pacific union*

	1800	1800–1850	1850–1900	1900–1945	1945–1990
Number of liberal regimes	3	8	13	29	68
Transnational track	+ 5	+ 5	+ 16	+39	
International track		> 2x	< 2x	> 2x	> 2x

steady advance of popular participation are the preferable courses of action.[21] No one should underestimate the difficulties. China's claim on democratic Taiwan, its possible repression of democratic Hong Kong, its growing relationship with US enemies Iran and Iraq, its trade disputes with the US, not to speak of its treatment of domestic dissent, all these merely sketch in the current range of challenges.

Thus, the decline of US hegemonic leadership may pose dangers for the liberal world. The danger is not that today's liberal states will permit their economic competition to spiral into war, nor that a world economic crisis is now likely, but that the societies of the liberal world will no longer be able to provide the mutual assistance they might require to sustain liberal domestic orders if they were to be faced with mounting economic crises.

The promise of peace. If we stretch our intellectual horizon beyond our revolutionary and troubled past decade, liberalism is an extraordinary beacon of hope in the long run. In all likelihood, the past rate of *global* progress in the expansion of the pacific union has been a complex and inseparable combination of the effects of both Kantian tracks. But if we imagine that progress had been achieved solely by one track or the other, we can deduce the outer limits of the underlying logics of the transnational and international progresses toward peace.

Thus if we rashly assume that the transnational track alone has led to the expansion of the pacific union, we can project when all regimes will have become liberal. If we followed the past arithmetic rate of increase (spilling over from country to country), which again triples in shorter and shorter periods as it did between the nineteenth and the first half of the twentieth century and again between the first and second half of the twentieth century – and if the number of states remained fixed at roughly 200 – then all states will be liberal republican by 2050. On the other hand, we can follow the international track of war. Warlike periods, such as the first half of the nineteenth century or both halves of the twentieth century, more than double the number of liberal regimes; pacific periods, like the second of the nineteenth century, less than double the number. If we assume the future resembles the late nineteenth century, when there were no great world wars but many small petty wars (having epidemic like effects), and if the geometric rate of expansion of the pacific union is thus the same, then the union will not become global until just before 2100. If, contrarily, we assume a warlike future of great tension, akin to the early nineteenth century or the twentieth century, then all states will become republican just after 2050.

Both tracks help engender liberal regimes, and thus eventually a widening of the peace, but neither the tracks nor the trip is smooth. The transnational ties create incentives for conflict as well as cooperation; the international track of war obviously presupposes war in the first place. Moreover the future portrayed is obviously only an extrapolation of the past, a past characterized by no nuclear war, technological development that was trade- and growth-enhancing, and states with limited surveillance capabilities such that they were vulnerable to the threat and reality of popular uprisings. To put it mildly, changes in these characteristics could upset Kantian expectations.

Liberal states of the industrial world have entered a nearly unprecedented condition of international security and it appears to be significantly linked to the surge of liberalism worldwide. But that good fortune is neither guaranteed to persist nor will it necessarily involve worldwide peace. Even if a war on the scale of the US-UN Gulf War against Iraq is unlikely to be repeated soon, Grenadas and Somalias and Bosnias are likely to arise frequently in the new world order we are entering. If we want to avoid them becoming revivals of destructive imperialism or arenas of neglect, we will need to reinforce the steadying institutions of multilateral security, whether in the UN or regional organizations, ready to provide guidance and support.

Moreover, it is very much in our hands whether the years ahead do in fact become another "1931," a brief moment before the collapse of collective security into complaisance (as occurred in the Manchurian Incident of 1931) and then war. Another Cold War with China or Russia – after a next, perhaps successful, authoritarian coup – could re-enact the European crisis of liberal democracy that began with the Reichstag Fire of 1933. Or instead, will future crises resemble "1911" – a paranoid rivalry with a fellow near-liberal spiraling into extensive hostility? Will the US-Japanese relationship follow on the model of the pre-World War I antagonism between Germany and Britain? Either possibility alone or both together could radically alter our pacific prospects and make whatever investments in institution-building and development aid we now consider seem cheap in retrospect.

NOTES

1 This essay draws on parts of *Ways of War and Peace* (1997) and has benefited from comments by John Ikenberry.

2 I will not consider here the full range of liberal approaches to international order but focus, instead, on a distinctly cosmopolitan or universalist version. There are other liberal views that reject attempts to expand the liberal pacific union, as does, for example, John Rawls in *The Law of Peoples* (Harvard University Press, 1999 forthcoming).

3 Multilateral management is important and far from automatic; and liberal peace is not the same as inter-liberal cooperation. Current inter-liberal pacification is, of course, compatible with considerable competition and failure to achieve the mutually beneficial outcomes that long-term peace will require. For strategies of cooperation see the paper by Martin in this volume and the studies by Ruggie (1993) and Martin (1992).

4 For a discussion of strategy toward once-enemies now in a transition zone toward potential friends, see Allison (1988).

5 The democratic movement in Panama denounced US political aid before the invasion and today suffers at home and abroad from its overt dependence on the US.

6 For an interesting application of Lockean ideas to Eastern Europe, see Rau (1987).

7 Francis Fukuyama (1992), following Alexandre Kojeve, makes this controversial suggestion in chapter 5. Although critics have challenged Hegel's liberalism, Hegel's stature as a founder of modernization theory appears to be curiously firm.

8 Such was the plea by Ambassador Han Xu on August 21, 1989 in the *New York Times*, when he said that the course of progress was not over, after the Tiananmen incident. Instead, he pleaded for American patience, and gave in return a promise of progress and pluralism and a future of cooperation with a growing People's Republic.

9 A wider study by Bhalla (1994) finds in a survey of ninety countries between 1973 and 1990 that political freedom is positively associated with economic growth.

10 A discussion of these issues can be found in *Dissent* (Summer 1991) on Market Socialism.

11 The review essay by Wade (1992) effectively makes this case. Interestingly, Fukuyama's book also stresses this latter, more complicated perspective on development; his article lends itself to the more libertarian interpretation of economic development.

12 Valuable accounts of these crises can be found in Brzezinski (1965) and Journalist (1983) for the Cold War period. For the Polish case at the end of the Cold War, see Touraine et al. (1983).

13 Jorge Dominguez (1980) notes a similar pattern in the collapse of the Spanish empire in the Americas between 1800 and 1825. I extend this argument in *Empires* (Doyle 1986: ch. 14).

14 As Gourevitch (1986) and Rogowski (1989) have demonstrated in their studies, international trade can alter domestic distributions of power – the

"second image" reversed factor.

15 See the two part *New Yorker* series on the coup and the Yeltsin aftermath and the review essay by Draper (1992).

16 I think that this is a major assumption of George Kennan's classic strategy for eventual accommodation (not victory) in the Cold War. He relied on the "internal weakness" of Soviet power, supplemented by "international frustration," to dissolve Soviet ambitions and capacities (1947: 566–82).

17 Liberals also give mixed advice on these matters. Kant argued that the "preliminary articles" from his treaty of perpetual peace required extending nonintervention by force in internal affairs of other states to nonliberal governments and maintaining a scrupulous respect for the laws of war. Yet he thought that liberal states could demand that other states become liberal. J. S. Mill said that intervention was impermissible except to support states threatened by external aggression and by foreign intervention in civil wars. Yet he justified British imperialism in India.

18 See the *ABC/Washington Post* poll reported in *Time*, November 21, 1983 and the *Washington Post*, October 24, 1984.

19 Michael Reisman (1984) suggests a legal devolution of Security Council responsibilities to individual states. Oscar Schachter (1984) argues that such rights to intervene would be abused by becoming self-serving. And for a carefully reasoned revival of moral arguments for just war criteria, see Walzer (1977). The policy of sanctions against South Africa, designed to undermine the domestic system of apartheid, is an earlier instance of these efforts.

20 Lesser violations of human rights (various lesser forms of majority tyranny, for example) can warrant foreign diplomatic interference. The two severe abuses of liberal respect call for something more. The two severe abuses of course also tend to go together. Democratic resistance to authoritarian or totalitarian governments tends to result in the government inflicting severe abuses of human rights on the democratic resistance. Governments which systematically abuse the rights of their citizens rarely have widespread popular support. But they need not go together; hence their independence as criteria add one further constraint. Although the only popular movements for which one might justly intervene need not be democratically liberal, it would by these standards clearly be wrong to intervene in favor of popular movements committed to a political program that would involve the systematic abuse of basic, "objective" human rights.

21 Indeed, this was the strategy originally recommended by George Kennan as *political* containment. See Kennan (1967) and Gaddis (1987: 20–47).

REFERENCES

Allison, Graham 1988, "Testing Gorbachev," *Foreign Affairs* 67: 18–32.

Allison, Graham and Treverton, Greg (eds.) 1992, *Rethinking America's Security*, New York: W. W. Norton.

Bergsten, C. Fred et al. 1978, "The Reform of International Institutions" (Triangle Paper 11), in *Trilateral Commission Task Force Reports: 9–14*, New York: New York University Press.

Bhalla, Surjit 1994, "Freedom and Economic Growth: A Virtuous Cycle?" Nobel Symposium, Uppsala, August.

Brzezinski, Zbigniew 1965, *The Soviet Bloc*, Cambridge: Harvard University Press.

1989, *The Grand Failure*, New York: Scribners.

Bunce, Valerie 1990, "Rising Above the Past: The Struggle for Liberal Democracy in Eastern Europe," *World Policy Journal* 7: 395–430.

Colton, Timothy 1992, *Dilemmas of Soviet Reform*, New York: CFR.

Comisso, Ellen 1990, "Crisis in Socialism, or Crisis of Socialism?" *World Politics* 42: 563–96.

Cooper, Richard N. et al. 1978, "Towards a Renovated International System" (Triangle Paper 14), in *Trilateral Commission Task Force Reports: 9–14*, New York: New York University Press.

Cutler, Lloyd N. 1985, "The Right to Intervene," *Foreign Affairs* Fall 64: 96–112.

Dahl, Robert 1989, *Democracy and its Critics*, New Haven: Yale University Press.

Deudney, Daniel and Ikenberry, John 1991/2, "The International Sources of Soviet Change," *International Security* 16: 74–118.

Deutsch, Karl 1966, *Nationalism and Social Communication*, Cambridge: MIT Press.

Dissent 1991 (Special Issue on Market Socialism) 38.

Dominguez, Jorge 1980, *Insurrection of Loyalty: The Breakdown of the Spanish American Empire*, Cambridge: Harvard University Press.

Doyle, Michael 1986, *Empires*, Ithaca: Cornell University Press.

1995, *The UN in Cambodia: UNTAC's Civil Mandate*, Boulder: Lynne Rienner.

1997, *Ways of War and Peace*, New York: W. W. Norton.

Draper, Theodore 1992, *The New York Review of Books*, June 1.

Fetherston, A. B. 1994, "Putting the Peace Back Into Peacekeeping," *International Peacekeeping* 1.

Fukuyama, Francis 1989, "An End of History?" *The National Interest* 16: 3–18.

1992, *The End of History and the Last Man*, New York: Free Press.

Gaddis, John 1987, "The Insecurities of Victory," in *The Long Peace*, New York: Oxford University Press, pp. 20–47.

Goldman, Marshall 1991, *What Went Wrong With Perestroika*, New York: Norton.

Gorbachev, Mikhail 1987, "On Socialist Democracy," in *Socialism, Peace, and Democracy*, London: Atlantic Highlands.

Gourevitch, Peter 1986, *Politics in Hard Times*, Ithaca: Cornell University Press.

Huntington, Samuel 1968, *Political Order in Changing Societies*, New Haven: Yale University Press, chs. 5–6.

1991, *The Third Wave*, Norman, OK: University of Oklahoma Press.

Journalist, M. 1983, *A Year Is Eight Months*, Garden City, NY: Doubleday.

Kennan, George 1947, "The Sources of Soviet Conduct," *Foreign Affairs* 25: 566–82.

1967, *Memoirs: 1925–1950*, Boston: Little, Brown.

Linz, Juan 1978, "Crisis, Breakdown, and Reequilibration," in *The Breakdown of Democratic Regimes*, Juan Linz and Alfred Stepan (eds.), Baltimore: Johns Hopkins University Press, pp. 3–124.

Locke, John 1988, [1690] "Second Treatise," in *Two Treatises on Government*, Peter Laslett (ed.), New York: Cambridge University Press, pp. 45–60.

Maier, Charles 1991, *Why Did Communism Collapse in 1991?*, Central and Eastern European Working Paper No. 7, Harvard University.

Martin, Lisa, 1992. *Coercive Economic Cooperation: Explaining Multilateral Economic Sanctions*, Princeton: Princeton University Press.

Muravchik, Joshua 1991, *Exporting Democracy: Fulfilling America's Destiny*, Washington, DC: AEI Press.

Nef, John U. 1968, *War and Human Progress*, New York: Norton.

Pei, Minxin 1995, "'Creeping Democratization' in China," *Journal of Democracy* 6: 65–79.

Prezworski, Adam 1991, *Democracy and the Market*, Cambridge: Cambridge University Press.

  1995, *Sustainable Democracy*, Cambridge: Cambridge University Press.

Prezworski, Adam et al. 1997, "What Makes Democracies Endure," in Larry Diamond et al. (eds), *Consolidating Third Wave Democracies: Themes and Perspectives*, Baltimore: Johns Hopkins University Press, pp. 295–311.

Rau, Zbigniew 1987, "Some Thoughts on Civil Society in Eastern Europe and the Lockean Contractarian Approach," *Political Studies* 35: 573–92.

Reisman, Michael 1984, "Coercion and Self Determination: Construing Charter Article 2(4)," *American Journal of International Law* 78: 642–5.

Rogowski, Ronald 1989, *Commerce and Coalitions*, Princeton: Princeton University Press.

ROMIR Poll, December 1991 and January 1992, reported by Dr. Ellen Mickiewicz, *Findings of Four Major Surveys in the Soviet Union*, Emory University Carter Center, p. 8.

Ruggie, John (ed.) 1993, *Multilateralism Matters*, New York: Columbia University Press.

Schachter, Oscar 1984, "Legality of Pro-Democratic Intervention," *American Journal of International Law* 78: 645–50.

Schumpeter, Joseph 1955, "Imperialism," in *Imperialism and Social Classes*, New York: Meridian.

Schwartz, Thomas 1991, *America's Germany*, Cambridge: Harvard University Press.

Smith, Tony 1994, *America's Mission*, Princeton: Princeton University Press.

Touraine, Alain et al. 1983, *Solidarity*, New York: Cambridge University Press.

Wade, Robert 1992, "East Asia's Economic Success," *World Politics* 44: 270–320.

Walzer, Michael 1977, *Just and Unjust Wars*, New York: Basic Books.

3   Preconditions for prudence: a sociological synthesis of realism and liberalism

John A. Hall and T. V. Paul

There is a sense in which sociology has conquered a good deal of the contemporary humanities and social sciences. One hears about the social construction of just about everything, from shopping malls to natural science research laboratories, making both Peter Berger and Thomas Luckmann's *The Social Construction of Reality* (1966) and Benedict Anderson's *Imagined Communities* (1991) probably the two most cited works of recent social science. In international relations too, sociological thinking has made powerful inroads as is evident in the attention given to the new approach of social constructivism (Wendt 1994; Katzenstein 1996). Given this background, there is everything to be said immediately for highlighting the argument that will be made in two ways. First, this chapter provides a sociological theory of international order. Poincaré famously observed that natural scientists discuss their results in contrast to social scientists who argue about their methods: the plethora of concepts, all-too-often complicated and confusing, considered to comprise the sociological contribution suggests that this quip has not lost its bite. Hence the need to underscore the fact that this chapter is not a prolegomenon to a theory but the real thing; that is, an explanatory scheme as to how a key element of social and political life actually functions. This is meant to be immodest and challenging; some caveats will however be made towards the end, for the theory is by no means complete and closed.

The second preliminary point concerns the relation between sociology and realism. It is probably fair to say that the interest in sociological matters on the part of some international relations scholars results from a feeling that realism as both theory and practice is, or has become, deeply flawed. This viewpoint looks to sociology for an analysis of social forces – from domestic pressure groups to international civil society linkages – that are held to determine the way in which states behave. Whilst this chapter does offer this sort of contribution, the social linkages to be specified have had more to do historically with elite than with popular

67

behavior. More generally, realism is taken very seriously, the first claim of this chapter being that the precepts of order inherent in realism work best when certain social foundations are in place. We will turn to this immediately, but can warn the reader that a second theoretical claim – that realism is, by and large, best seen as an ally rather than an enemy of liberalism – follows naturally from the initial claim. Our general argument is that international order depends in large part on prudence – the preconditions of which we seek to lay bare.

Social foundations of realism

A consequence of the richness of the realist tradition noted by Robert Gilpin (1984) is the presence of rather different views claiming a single label. It is not the intention here to chronicle and dissect such main versions on offer as classical realism (Morgenthau 1967; Carr 1939) or structural realism (Waltz 1979; Mearsheimer 1990) or the newer versions such as offensive and defensive realism (Zakaria 1992). The argument of this chapter can best be moved forward by making a more general comparison between what can be termed hard realism and sophisticated realism. We place under hard realism realist theories that predict that states are predisposed to aggrandizement, and under sophisticated realism theories that expect agents to possess the capacity to make choices that avert self-destructive wars. To do so will lead us to an ethic, whose social underpinnings can then be brought to light. It is worth noting that our position owes a great deal to the contrast drawn by Hedley Bull (1977) between a condition of anarchy and that of a partial society of states, and still more to the unduly neglected work of Raymond Aron (1966).

We can usefully begin with the core of Clausewitz's thought, as movingly analyzed in Raymond Aron's great *Penser la guerre, Clausewitz* (1976). Clausewitz's early experience of defeat at the hands of Napoleon convinced him, as is well known, of the inevitability of an escalation to extremes. Violence in its purest form could have no limits, a viewpoint that led to Clausewitz's enormous admiration for Napoleon. This initial formulation is an exemplar of hard realism: the essence of state behavior is that of seeking power without limit. It is insufficiently appreciated that Clausewitz came to reject this early formulation. He lived long enough to witness the collapse of Napoleon's ambitions, and accordingly began to re-evaluate the career of Frederick the Great. He came to distrust the unlimited quest for power; to threaten everybody was sure to create a counter-alliance, making Frederick's strategy of limited and incremental demands more rational than that of the more extreme alternative of Napoleon. The nature of sophisticated realism can be clearly seen in

Clausewitz's final trinitarian definition of war: control by the state of the military arm and of popular passions is necessary if war is to be rational.

The contrast between escalation and moderation in international affairs can be seen at work quite as much in German state behavior in the late nineteenth and early twentieth centuries. An absolutely basic element of any realist calculation must be that of avoiding war on two fronts since the splitting of one's forces is likely to lead to defeat. Bismarck understood this, and took care to prevent the formation of an alliance between France and Russia. The neo-Darwinian atmosphere of the end of the nineteenth century became linked to "the cult of the offensive" (an element of which was adulation of the early rather than the mature thought of Clausewitz) which glorified offensive military doctrines on the assumption that attackers held definitive advantages, that wars were going to be decisive and short, and that offensive solutions to security problems were the most effective. This cult created or magnified the threat perceptions and helped to make the July 1914 crisis uncontrollable (Van Evera 1984). This did much to replace the cautious, sophisticated realism of the Iron Chancellor with the aggressive, zero-sum hard realist alternative. The consequence was of course disastrous: Wilhelmine Germany's threats ensured not just the formal alliance of France and Russia, but eventual British involvement as well. We will have more to say about this case – and about the wholly remarkable fact, so key to twentieth-century history, that Germany made the same geopolitical mistake twice within the same half-century.

The contrast drawn effectively suggests that the real logic of realism is that of prudence. Calculations properly made tend to reveal that less is more, that allowing other states room in which to exist is wise given that threatening their very existence can cause diplomatic and military forces to take a shape that ensures military defeat – even the eventual destruction of one's own state. State behavior must reflect enlightened self-interest as opposed to unbridled ambition of domination or conquest of other political entities. Military doctrines and security strategies must reflect most probable as opposed to worst-case threat assumptions (Paul, forthcoming). However, it would be a great mistake to simply leave things at this point. The history of international affairs does not depend just upon ideological developments, for all that there is a measure of autonomy within this realm.

We always need to at least ask about the circumstances that lend particular ideologies appeal at specified moments: differently put, views of ideologies which see them as forms of complete conceptual constraint forget that people manipulate their worldviews to their convenience (Hall 1993). There are exceptionally strong particular reasons for being skeptical about ideological explanations in the realm of international affairs. Ideological excess is often possible when few consequences are attached; there is no need to think things through when societies are sufficiently affluent to allow life to be lived without great consistency. But matters of life and death are supposed to concentrate the mind, leaving one to put fripperies to one side. Nowhere is this more true than when dealing with relations between states. After all, did not nuclear weapons force rationality upon states? This general consideration allows us to draw a contrast between small and large mistakes in the conduct of state policy. Small mistakes are always possible: it is often very difficult to have, say, good information about one's opponents' forces, and far harder to assess all questions to do with morale. Entering a war can thus be the result of honest miscalculation. But there is a world of difference between this, a world of wars that are purposive and which can be stopped when they prove to be disastrous, and most major uncontrolled escalations to the extremes. Germany's behavior in starting wars on two fronts on two occasions should be deeply puzzling for realism, as indeed should Napoleon's failure to compromise in 1813 when facing defeat. Let us try and explain these escalations sociologically, the reverse side of the coin being the establishment of the social conditions that allow realism to work effectively in more normal circumstances.

The first consideration is straightforward: it is much easier to calculate the intentions of another party when one feels one understands the way in which it thinks. Formally, the analytic point was well expressed by Aron in terms of the degree of heterogeneity or homogeneity within the state system (1966). These terms deserve analysis in turn.

The sources of homogeneity can vary. It was relatively easy for Britain and the United States to cooperate at the turn of the nineteenth century because both countries shared not just a language, but a huge reservoir of taken-for-granted Anglo-Saxon cultural assumptions. Extensive norms equally can be those of religion, as was true for Christianity – whose states accordingly had rules for behavior for their fellows that differed from those accorded to Muslim societies. Perhaps realism worked best in Europe – that is, became sophisticated and prudential – when upper-class solidarities were strong. In the eighteenth century, French provided a common medium, the norms of sophisticated realism were well understood (not least since they received classical statement at the hands of David Hume), and nobody was offended at the amorality of the "Diplomatic Revolution" of 1740 – when states suddenly realigned in order to reflect the newest calculation of the balance of power.

Heterogeneity is more clearly expressed as the incursion of ideology onto the political stage. There was an element of this at work at the end of the nineteenth century when Kaiser Wilhelm II refused to play the game of diplomatic rivalries as it had hitherto been practiced. But much more important are the genuine ideological innovations of the modern world. The French Revolution certainly unleashed new social forces upon the world. The exact way in which this caused escalation to the extremes is now the subject of an interesting dispute within international relations. On the one hand, Stephen Walt (1996) insists that the revolutionaries were initially pacific, being driven to expansion when attacked from the outside by old regimes – who, in his view, most certainly did not understand the new principles on which they were based. The contrasting view is that the huge energy and absolute sense of conviction of the revolutionaries was always bound to break out of the container of a particular national state (Skocpol 1994). Whatever the case may prove to be, the general principle is not in question: ideological challenge made calculations, not least about the stakes at issue in international affairs, very much more difficult for state leaders to assess correctly. The same point is obviously true of the impact of nazism and bolshevism, the two great revolutionary forces of the twentieth century.

There is a second foundation to the effective working of realism, the absence of which is again likely to cause escalation to the extremes. This foundation is quite as straightforward as the first. It is the actual ability to calculate. Obviously calculation depends upon information, and so the degree of state capacity to collect, process, and filter information becomes part of this variable. But much more important than this technical point is the ability of any particular state to set priorities. On this occasion let us consider the negative situation first, before contrasting it to a more positive scenario. In doing so we follow Aron less than before, although he made the point prescriptively when concluding his book on Clausewitz by insisting that states should *become* the agent of personified intelligence; instead, we base our argument on the remarkably similar accounts given by Snyder (1991) and Mann (1993) of the way in which German behavior led to war in 1914.

It may be useful to say at the start that German behavior is not explicable in terms of the social forces to which attention has most often turned. There is little sense either to the notion of economic imperialism in general given that the German economy was already outpacing those of its rivals, or to the more particular claim that German capitalists pressured the state into war. The thesis of social imperialism propounded by Hans Ulrich Wehler (1985) fails to convince as well: key German statesmen felt that war would more likely bring revolution than the integration of the working classes. So the puzzle remains: why start a war that was almost sure to be lost – a sentiment absolutely apparent in the weird feelings of despair and helplessness among much of the German elite in July 1914?

The best answer concerns the nature of the German state. Bismarck had controlled policy-making, famously disappearing on occasion to his estate in Prussia in order to think and to change the direction of foreign policy. Matters were utterly different after Wilhelm II "dropped the pilot." Systematic calculation was replaced by the caprice characteristic of a court. Whoever had the ear of the Kaiser or his wife could influence policy, and this led to the simultaneous adoption of two policies. The new policy of *Weltpolitik* pioneered by Tirpitz appealed to some industrialists and to the Social Democrats, whilst the traditional policy to the East appealed to the Army; the former angered Britain, whilst the latter ensured that Russia would combine with France, Germany's irreconcilable foe. Furthermore, Chancellor Bethmann-Hollweg did not attend all meetings, and so was in charge of diplomacy without having any idea – for example – that a knockout blow against France involved invasion via Belgium, something almost certain to bring Britain into the war. The analytic point is simple: the success of realism depends upon the ability to make proper calculations; sophisticated realism therefore rests upon the character of a state.

Snyder claims that the type of bandwagoning described is typical of a late-developing society in which a traditional elite is confronted by newly aroused but only half-integrated popular forces. He goes on to suggest that rather different sorts of state structures allow for the rational calculation of priorities. The chaos brought by bandwagoning contrasts with the elite cohesion characteristic both of pre-modern European states and of late, late developing states, such as the Soviet Union, in which a brutal single party dominated all alternative sources of social power. But state intelligence can be assured by more attractive means. One illustration of this point is the behavior of Britain in the years before the First World War. Here a Cabinet system helped ensure that commitments were brought into line with resources. Thus agreement with Japan meant that Britain abandoned much of its interest in Asia, whilst closer understanding with the United States similarly reduced potential overstretch; these changes allowed the fleet to be brought back to home waters to deal with the German threat. This is not for a moment to say that liberal elites have never engaged in irrational wars, as is made obvious once one recalls American escalations in Vietnam driving Johnson's administration and the imprudence of French and Dutch colonial policies in Algeria and Indonesia. To the contrary, liberal leaders can take whimsical decisions without proper deliberations, or if consultations take place they could be biased by groupthink (Janis 1982) and other psychological barriers to proper judgment. Still, a slightly different element of liberalism, that of pressure both within and without the legislative arm of the state, is often seen in the retreat from overextension.

The argument made to this point can be summarized by saying that conflict has lost intensity within an homogeneous world populated by intelligent states, whilst escalations to the extreme have been occasioned by the absence of these factors. But this position identified two variables upon each other, with the historical moments analyzed seeing them at work together: analysis has largely been marked either by homogeneity in combination with intelligent states or by heterogeneity with states made incapable of calculation by fundamental lack of social coherence. Is it possible to say which of these two variables matters most? It is by no means easy to discover historical moments when only one of the variables was present. Nonetheless, it may be argued that the ability to calculate was of greater import than ideological homogeneity (for fuller details, see Hall 1996). The character of the Napoleonic regime rather than ideological division prevented an accord being reached by 1813; too many people had come to depend upon expansion, and this meant that the notion of retreat ruled out for Napoleon an option that his hubris might anyway have foreclosed. Equally the Soviet Union's conflict with capitalism – in fact by no means total, given shared stakes in nuclear weapons – did not lead to total war since the coherent state of a late, late developer had room within which to calculate.

Liberalism as a friend of realism

But to make this point should not then entail any complete reversion to realism. To the contrary, the eclectic mixture that guides us is that of a mix of realism and liberalism. It is as well to delimit the argument to be made immediately, to prevent misunderstanding. Of course, we have in mind a particular strand within liberalism. That protean doctrine has variously suggested that normative dislike of war (whether by the people of a state or by peoples linked across state borders), economic interdependence, or liberal institutions (which, again, can be internal to a state or provide an international frame) can encourage peace. Our attention focuses on the way in which liberal institutions within a state can encourage calculation. Differently put, the other elements of liberalism, at least to this point within the historical record, have had little impact. Wars have often been popular, at least until casualties mount, whilst the solidarity of peoples has been much undermined by the caging effects of nation-states. Similarly, a high degree of interdependence did not stop European states hating each other bitterly; indeed, perhaps lack of mutual relations made for clarity in the relations of the United States and the Soviet Union. Finally, the frame of international institutions seems to us to depend upon states able to make use of the information that they provide.

The best way to make our point is to highlight the fact that liberalism and realism have traditionally been seen as mutually opposed. The opposition of liberals to war is obvious and well known. But at least as important is the incompatibility between the two doctrines seen by the other side. Both George Kennan and Henry Kissinger draw on Tocqueville's notion that the people are slow to anger but then remorseless when provoked in order to argue that democracy makes for great difficulty in the conduct of foreign policy (Tocqueville 1969: 645–51; Kennan 1951; Kissinger 1994). More specifically, they suggest that democracies are slow to threaten when threats are needed, and slow to disengage when a cessation of hostilities would be rational – in large part because the mobilization of the people necessitates a raising of stakes and passions. Kennan viewed these difficulties caused by democracy sufficiently seriously to draft in the 1930s a manuscript hostile to the very idea of democracy.

As with many things in life, there is something to this negative contention. Sir Edward Grey might well have liked to formally tell Germany that Britain would fight in order to preserve the balance of power; he could not do so without losing the pacifist members of the cabinet. This may have mattered: Germany's diplomats in London realized that Britain would enter the war if France was invaded, but Bethmann-Hollweg was not entirely sure. More generally, conducting foreign policy in a democracy requires a constant process of public education; this requires time and effort, habitually in short supply in modern conditions.

Nonetheless, the advantages of liberal democracy are much greater than the problems that it causes. First, liberalism can help rational calculation on the part of states, as we can see immediately when we review the historical episodes that we have had in mind. Wilhelmine Germany lacked this ability to assign priorities, thereby so offending its neighbors that it created the encirclement from which it then tried to escape. In contrast, the cabinet structure of the British state allowed for more rational policy-making. Perhaps the best way to make this general point, however, is to note that liberal states have avoided the disastrous adventures to which late, late-developing states have been prone; in this matter the rashness of Hitler must be set against the relative caution of the Soviet Union. None of this is to say that liberal states have perfect institutions. To the contrary, foreign policy-making within liberal democracies is still conducted with a very great deal of secrecy. But this is just to say that liberal institutions should be extended; greater openness in

American foreign policy-making would have prevented the second-rate James Bond machinations of Oliver North. Secondly, liberal states have greater capacity for self-correction. Opposition from the people and within the elite did much to end the Vietnam War, and thereby to end overextension.

Caveats by way of conclusion

We have moved from talking about the social foundations that allow sophisticated realism to work to suggesting that the institutions of a liberal state are best seen as aiding rather than opposing the logic of realism. Concentration has been on establishing a clear position, and this makes it all the more necessary to end with two caveats.

First, it is worth highlighting our concentration on the state. This should not be misunderstood. On the one hand, the fact that alternatives to the state do not as yet seem strong enough pillars on which to build should not be taken to signal state worship on our part. Circumstances may change. Some progress towards a Kantian liberal league can be seen in the insistence of the European Union that membership must entail various liberal commitments, notably to democracy and to the protection of minority rights; equally, the bonds of international civil society may be widening, in terms of both geography and social class. So our skepticism as to the present power of such links should not be equated with cynicism. Description is not prescription – and prescriptively we would welcome a greater impact of the forces identified by liberalism to which we have felt it right to pay only limited attention. If an increase in international solidarity would make the calculations of realism easier, it might equally mark the beginning of a world in which the shells of states were less necessary. On the other hand, we have not presented a complete argument. A full and rounded appreciation of the roles of war and peace would need to consider the other mechanisms of Westphalia outlined in the introduction to this volume (for such an account, see Hall 1996). Suffice it to say here that the weakness or the historical rarity of other principles justifies the concentration on liberalism and realism.

Secondly, it is worth situating our concern with prudence in relation to recent debates about agency and structure. We certainly do not think that the nature of international relations can be read off the brute structure of the power of states. But this is not to succumb to an excessively unrestricted, wholly voluntarist view of agency. Our intention for the largest part has been that of *explaining* the preconditions that allow for prudential calculations. But a precondition is a sufficient rather than a necessary condition, meaning that we do recognize a role for skill and for intelligence. This allows us to offer a final reflection. The attention given to Wilhelmine Germany should not be taken as implying any general sympathy on our part to status quo powers. Peaceful change in the international system depends in part on the skill with which established states can find room to integrate the newly powerful – so as to prevent them becoming genuine challengers. If Britain's behavior toward Germany is not open to much criticism, one notes with concern the failure of the United States to incorporate Japan by letting it lead some of what still deserve to be called its international institutions. One can increase one's power by surrendering some of its elements.

REFERENCES

Anderson, Benedict 1991, *Imagined Communities*, London: Verso.
Aron, Raymond 1966, *Peace and War*, London: Weidenfeld and Nicolson.
  1976, *Penser la guerre, Clausewitz*, Paris: Gallimard.
Berger, Peter and Luckmann, Thomas 1966, *The Social Construction of Reality*, New York: Doubleday.
Bull, Hedley 1977, *The Anarchical Society: A Study of Order in World Politics*, New York: Columbia University Press.
Carr, E. H. 1939, *The Twenty Years' Crisis: 1919–1939*, New York: Harper Torchbooks.
Gilpin, Robert 1984, "The Richness of the Tradition of Political Realism," *International Organization* 38: 287–304.
Hall, John A. 1993, "Ideas and the Social Sciences," in *Ideas and Foreign Policy*, Judith Goldstein and Robert Keohane (eds.), Ithaca: Cornell University Press, pp. 31–54.
  1996, *International Orders*, Oxford: Polity.
Janis, Irvin 1982, *Groupthink*, Boston: Houghton Mifflin.
Katzenstein, Peter J. (ed.) 1996, *The Culture of National Security: Norms and Identity in World Politics*, New York: Columbia University Press.
Keohane, Robert 1984, *After Hegemony*, Princeton: Princeton University Press.
Kissinger, Henry A. 1994, *Diplomacy*, New York: Simon and Schuster.
Mann, Michael 1993, *The Sources of Social Power, Volume II: The Rise of Classes and Nation-States, 1760–1914*, Cambridge: Cambridge University Press.
Mearsheimer, John J. 1990, "Back to the Future: Instability in Europe after the Cold War," *International Security* 15: 5–54.
Morgenthau, Hans J. 1967, *Politics Among Nations*, 4th edition, New York: Alfred A. Knopf.
Paul, T. V. forthcoming, *Power Versus Prudence: Why Nations Forgo Nuclear Weapons*, book manuscript, McGill University.
Skocpol, Theda 1994, "Social Revolutions and Mass Military Mobilization," in *Social Revolutions in the Modern World*, Skocpol (ed.), Cambridge: Cambridge University Press, pp. 279–98.
Snyder, Jack 1991, *Myths of Empire*, Ithaca: Cornell University Press.

Tocqueville, Alexis de 1969, *Democracy in America*, New York: Anchor Books.

Van Evera, Stephen 1984, "The Cult of the Offensive and the Origins of the First World War," *International Security* 9: 58–107.

Walt, Stephen 1996, *Revolution and War*, Ithaca: Cornell University Press.

Wehler, Hans-Ulrich 1985, *The German Empire 1871–1918*, Leamington Spa: Berg.

Wendt, Alexander 1994, "Anarchy is What States Make of It: The Social Construction of Power Politics," *International Organization* 46: 391–425.

Zakaria, Fareed 1992, "Realism and Domestic Politics," *International Security* 17: 177–98.

4   An institutionalist view: international institutions and state strategies[1]

Lisa L. Martin

The twentieth century has seen a major innovation in the context of international politics: the institutionalization of interactions among sovereign states. While this process has seen its ebbs and flows, successes and failures, over the last hundred years, the trend toward institutionalization now seems entrenched. If anything, experiences since the end of the Cold War suggest that states value the institutionalization of their relations ever more highly. New studies show that while many international organizations die every year, new ones are being created at an even faster rate (Shanks et al. 1996). The trend toward institutionalization is not accidental, nor is it something that is being imposed on reluctant governments; it is the result of government choice. This chapter examines the state strategy of institutionalization, asking about the causes and consequences of increasing reliance on international institutions throughout the globe.

The movement toward institutionalization has not escaped the notice of international relations theory. Some of the major theoretical debates in international relations over the last two decades have involved new attempts to understand why states turn to institutions and what effects these institutions have on patterns of state behavior. The first section of this chapter reviews rationalist theories of international institutions, an approach that has its roots in liberal theory but has developed a genuinely new perspective on the role of institutions in world politics.

The chapter next turns to some of the major research puzzles in the study of international institutions. While we observe institutionalization, many aspects of this process remain highly puzzling and demand better integration into our explanatory frameworks. The third section turns to the problem of international institutions and world order. The relationship here may seem straightforward: institutions create a status quo bias, and thus induce order of a sort in international politics. Yet this institutionalized order may occur at the expense of neglected distributional effects. The discussion concludes by focusing on some dimensions of these distributional problems, among members of institutions and between members and nonmembers. I conclude that our evaluation of institutionalization requires more attention to the problem of institutional design. Different types of institutions have vastly different efficiency and distributional effects. International relations theory, however, has neglected such questions by framing the question of institutionalization as a dichotomous problem: do institutions matter or don't they? Turning our attention to asking instead *how* institutions matter, and under what conditions, promises substantial theoretical, empirical, and practical payoffs.

Rationalist theories of international institutions

Before delving into the analysis of institutions, a brief word on definitions is in order. Those who discuss international institutions think of them in two different ways: as rules of the game and as endogenous descriptions of actors' strategies. As Duncan Snidal (1996) points out, these two ways of thinking about institutions are not as incompatible as they may seem at first glance. The rules of the game – e.g., the game of trade liberalization – must themselves be equilibria of some higher-order game. Whether we choose to treat institutions as endogenous depends on our theory and the particular problem we are trying to resolve. Those who treat institutions as exogenous recognize that at some level these institutions are the result of state decisions about how they wish to organize their relations with one another.

An influential definition of international institutions has been offered by Robert O. Keohane (1988: 383): "related complexes of rules and norms, identifiable in space and time." He differentiates between general institutions, referring to some category of activity, and more specific institutions. While pertinent, Keohane's definition is perhaps too general to be as useful as we would wish. John Mearsheimer (1994/5: 8) has offered a definition that is more specific: an institution is "a set of rules that stipulate the ways in which states should cooperate and compete with one another. [International institutions] prescribe acceptable forms of state behavior, and proscribe unacceptable kinds of behavior." I adopt Mearsheimer's definition in this chapter.

Concepts closely related to international institutions are international regimes and international organizations. Regimes, most carefully defined by Stephen Krasner (1983), emphasize the normative and often informal nature of institutions. Yet regimes may also be formalized, thus the definition seems not substantially different from our definition of institutions. I will use the term institutions, but substituting the term regime should not introduce any major confusion. International organizations are formal structures that embody and sustain many international institutions. Some institutions, such as the GATT, persist for years without the benefits of having an organization attached to them. But states typically, and increasingly, find that institutionalization works most efficiently when some level of oversight is delegated to an organization. Thus, most successful institutions also take the form of international organizations.

While the extent of institutionalization we now see in international politics is a new phenomenon, some important institutions obviously existed in earlier periods (the Concert of Europe; the gold standard). However, our understanding of the role of institutions has changed at least as radically as the level of institutionalization of world politics. The League of Nations, for example, was understood as an attempt to transcend power politics, to put international relations on a new foundation. After the failure of the League, the United Nations was established on a more pragmatic basis, for example with recognition of great-power prerogatives in the Security Council. Yet more idealist approaches to institutions remained current, for example David Mitrany's (1975) neofunctionalism, as applied by Ernst Haas (1958) to European integration.

World War II effectively undermined idealist approaches to studying institutions. Realists such as E. H. Carr (1964) and Hans Morgenthau (1948) showed the poverty of idealism and established realism as the dominant approach to the study of international relations. Yet institutions proliferated. The answer to this paradox lies in a rationalist, state-centered understanding of institutions. Current theories of institutions, which can perhaps best be dated to Krasner's edited volume on international regimes (1983), do not argue that institutions transcend traditional international politics. Instead, theorists ask about the instrumental role of institutions, from the perspective of states. Initially, analyses have taken state interests as given, treated states as units, and asked about how institutions can help states achieve their goals. This approach generally goes by the label of "functionalist" theories of institutions (Keohane 1984). More recent work begins to drop the unitary state actor assumption, asking how domestic political factors influence state preference formation and other dimensions of state policy toward institutions (e.g., Goldstein 1996). But the assumption of rational, goal-oriented behavior remains.

The assumptions underlying a functionalist theory of institutions are severe but simple. States are the central actors in world politics; they create, maintain, and abide by international institutions if such institutions further states' exogenously specified goals. Goals need not be monetary, nor even necessarily material, although non-material goals give rise to especially difficult problems of research design. The answer to why institutions can change patterns of state behavior under these sparse conditions lies in recognition of collective-action problems and market failure, as does the answer to analogous questions about institutions in other fields (Libecap 1989; Ostrom 1990).

According to functionalist theory, states often face problems like the Prisoners' Dilemma, in which individually rational behavior gives rise to outcomes that leave all unhappy. In economics, such a situation is called market failure, since a properly functioning market should prevent suboptimal outcomes. In international relations, this situation has been called a game of collaboration, drawing attention to the fact that states must collaborate with one another to reach their own, individually specified goals (Martin 1992a; Snidal 1985; Stein 1983). The motivation behind institutional creation and maintenance is to allow states to reach the Pareto frontier, the set of outcomes at which no more joint gains are available. At the Pareto frontier, any gain to one state by definition results in losses for others.

Keohane (1984) has spelled out how international institutions can help states overcome collective action and market failure dilemmas. Drawing on Coase, he argues that market failure should not occur if transaction costs are negligible and property rights are clearly defined. Under these conditions, states should be able to make and maintain mutually beneficial agreements. However, in international politics transaction costs are high and property rights often poorly defined. Thus states may often fail to overcome collective-action problems, because of fear that others will renege on deals, because they are unable adequately to monitor others' behavior or learn about others' preferences, or because they act opportunistically since inadequate punishment mechanisms are in place.

Institutions enter the picture at this point, to allow states to overcome such problems and reach mutually beneficial agreements. The primary function of institutions, in this framework, is to allow reciprocity to operate efficiently (Keohane 1986). Institutions perform this function by providing information about others' preferences, intentions, behavior, and standards of behavior. They also reduce transaction costs, which are the costs of reaching and maintaining agreements. Thus, in functionalist theory, the primary effect of institutions is an efficiency effect, in that they allow states to reach agreements that are closer to the Pareto frontier. Institutions, in this rationalist model, do not modify underlying state interests. Instead, by changing the informational environment and other constraints on states, they change state strategies in such a way that self-interested states find it easier to cooperate reliably with one another.

A number of authors have responded to functionalist theory by pointing out that collaboration problems are not the only impediments to cooperation states face. They also face distributional, coordination, or bargaining problems (Krasner 1991; Snidal 1996; Fearon 1998). All of these problems revolve around disputes over where on the Pareto frontier states will find themselves, rather than the less contentious question of how to reach the Pareto frontier. In any institutionalized pattern of cooperation, a number of ways to cooperate are available; and many of these may not be readily distinguishable from one another in terms of efficiency (i.e., they are all on the Pareto frontier). States that agree to coordinate their exchange rates will disagree on precisely what the appropriate parities are; states that cooperate with one another in a military alliance will disagree on precisely how much each should contribute to mutual defense.

Initial studies of international regimes argued that such coordination problems were easier to solve than collaboration problems, and that regimes had little to contribute to their resolution (Stein 1983). However, these arguments have come under serious attack. Bargaining problems can be just as devastating to the prospects for international cooperation as are collaboration problems. In addition, they are resolved under different conditions. Fearon (1998) has shown, for example, that while the long shadow of the future may enhance the prospects of finding mutually beneficial agreements, it also intensifies bargaining problems because any deals struck will have consequences that reach far into the future. Only coordination problems with no distributional consequences – a rare category – will lend themselves to quick resolution. In other cases, states will delay, make threats, hide or distort information, and generally engage in all the time-honored techniques of statecraft that make international politics a fascinating yet grim business.

How do bargaining problems get resolved? The general problem is one of multiple equilibria (many possible sustainable agreements), over which the actors involved disagree. Analysts have suggested a number of mechanisms by which coordination problems get resolved in the international arena. Krasner (1991) follows the traditional realist line, arguing that a straightforward exercise of state power determines which of the possible outcomes gets chosen. The most powerful state simply chooses the outcome it prefers; others have little choice but to go along. While this analysis suffers from the usual difficulties of defining and measuring power in a useful manner, it nevertheless seems a good starting point for analysis. It turns our attention to a new and potentially quite fruitful question: under what conditions will powerful states choose to institutionalize their patterns of cooperation with others? Institutionalization requires resources and locks in patterns of cooperation, denying the powerful the ability costlessly to change the terms of cooperation in the future. Thus why powerful states, like the United States after World War II, would choose to institutionalize relations with others is a puzzle. The likely answer lies in reducing the costs of oversight and establishing patterns of cooperation that will be durable even in the face of changes in the distribution of power (Martin 1992a; Ikenberry in this volume). Powerful states that can look far into the future and anticipate a relative decline in their power may choose to institutionalize beneficial patterns of cooperation while they have the chance.

Power is not the only possible solution to the multiple equilibria problem. Garrett and Weingast (1993) have pointed to the role of focal points in resolving coordination problems. The concept of a focal point dates back to Schelling (1960), and initially referred to solutions that had an "obvious," natural ring to them: meeting at Grand Central Station if one were taking the train to New York, or dividing the benefits of cooperation fifty-fifty. Garrett and Weingast extend the notion to include "constructed" focal points, those that are intentionally chosen and promoted by international actors. They concentrate especially on the European Court of Justice (ECJ), arguing that its choice of the norm of mutual recognition as a method to complete the internal market is an important example of a constructed focal point. They claim that the ECJ's ability to establish focal points explains the puzzle of why the ECJ has been so influential in the course of European integration, even though it lacks (at least until recently) any enforcement power. Thus, using the constructed focal point analogy, analysts have found that international institutions themselves can operate to resolve coordination problems.

Other mechanisms for resolving multiple equilibria problems exist, and exploring the ways in which institutions are implicated in these mechanisms is an important avenue of research. Some have suggested that culture can be understood as a solution to the problem of choosing among equilibria (Ferejohn 1991). And sometimes bargaining problems are resolved by – well, by bargaining (Moravcsik 1991). In each of these cases institutions come into the picture as a way to cement and make durable a particular equilibrium. Overall, our understanding of institutions and cooperation has been greatly enhanced by this attention to distributional problems. We now understand that states must solve (at least) two types of problems if they wish to cooperate with one another: market failure and coordination. Institutions have a role to play in each of these problems.

Rationalist approaches to international institutions assume that states turn to institutions in an attempt to solve cooperation problems. These cooperation problems are defined by patterns of state interests. Institutions change patterns of state behavior not by changing fundamental state goals in this perspective. Instead, they change two key features of rationalist models: strategies and beliefs. By changing the rules of the game, and so increasing the costs of particular courses of action and decreasing others, institutions lead states to change their strategies in the pursuit of stable underlying goals, such as wealth and power. Institutions also change the informational environment. They provide information about others' preferences, behavior, and intentions. They can also provide information about means-ends relationships, i.e., how particular policies will lead to different outcomes. Such causal knowledge is essential, for example, to an understanding of how the choice of a particular exchange-rate regime will affect key macroeconomic variables. By providing various types of information, institutions change states' beliefs. Equilibria in rationalist models are defined by a combination of beliefs and strategies (Morrow 1994). Institutions operate directly on both. Of course, we should not rule out the possibility that institutions change more fundamental state goals as well. Yet developing such a model takes us out of the realm of rationalist approaches into constructivism (Wendt 1992; Katzenstein 1996). Rationalist models take goals as given (or perhaps derive them from domestic politics) and ask why goal-oriented actors choose to institutionalize their relations with one another.

Research puzzles

What research agenda does the rationalist view of international institutions suggest? One sign of a progressive research program is its ability to generate new questions and directions for research. The rationalist approach has been quite successful by this standard, and directs our attention to a range of vital, yet only vaguely understood, questions about the causes and consequences of international institutions.

Looking back to work on international regimes, we see an ironic twist in the direction of research, one that defined research on institutions for the next decade. In *International Regimes*, the introductory and concluding chapters focused on developing typologies of the alternative roles institutions played in different theoretical perspectives (Krasner 1983). Some theories focused on regimes as determined by fundamental variables such as power and interests; others saw regimes as intervening variables or even having feedback effects on fundamental variables. Based on this framework, one might expect that the chapters in this volume would concentrate on establishing and understanding institutional effects. However, almost none of the first generation of empirical work took this approach. Instead, this work focused on regimes as a *dependent* variable, developing alternative understandings of regime change and its causes. Thus little effort went into establishing that regimes themselves could have an independent causal effect on patterns of behavior, although this question was clearly suggested by the analytical framework of the volume.

Researchers were perhaps deterred by the empirical difficulties of establishing that regimes matter. Whatever the reason, the lack of attention to institutional effects in this body of work led to an obvious objection, posed most starkly by realists. Why study institutions, they asked, if we have no evidence that they exercise an independent impact on important outcomes in international affairs? If institutions merely reflect the dominant pattern of power and interests, as much of the work in *International Regimes* suggested, are they not epiphenomenal? And if so, why devote scarce intellectual resources to studying them?

Responding to this challenge, the next generation of work on international institutions focused single-mindedly on one question: whether institutions matter. Drawing almost exclusively on the functionalist, efficiency-driven approach, empirical researchers worked to show that patterns of cooperation in the presence of institutions differed from those we would find in the absence of institutions. John Duffield (1992), for example, showed how the rules of NATO led to stability in force structures. Martin (1992b) found that the use of international institutions enhanced the level of multilateral cooperation to impose economic sanctions. Ronald Mitchell (1994) demonstrated that regime rules had a definitive impact on intentional oil pollution by ships discharging their tanks at sea.

In retrospect, this move of allowing realists to set the institutionalist research agenda may have been an error.[2] It created a false dichotomy: institutions either matter or they do not; they are either exogenous and therefore consequential, or endogenous and therefore epiphenomenal. As the discussion above about institutions as simultaneously rules of the game and equilibria suggests, this either/or approach is wrongheaded. Instead, a rationalist, equilibrium understanding of institutions suggests that they are both endogenous, because they are the objects of state choice, and consequential, because they change state beliefs and strategies. Institutions are endogenous but consequential because they have some staying power, some durability.[3] If institutions change smoothly as power and interests change, realists may be correct that we should consider them to be epiphenomenal; of perhaps passing interest, but surely not deserving of their own research program. But if we can demonstrate that institutions influence state beliefs and strategies, and that they are sometimes stable in the face of changing fundamental variables, such as power and interests, the institutionalist agenda looks highly promising.

How do we move beyond the either/or approach to institutions? I would suggest four directions for research that look particularly promising. The four central questions are: *how* institutions matter; variation in the use of institutions; institutional stability and change; and the relation between international institutions and domestic politics.

Asking only whether institutions matter has prevented more sophisticated thinking about questions such as how institutions matter, and the conditions under which they matter. In general, the point that institutions sometimes make a difference seems incontrovertible. It is hard to imagine that global trade liberalization would have pursued the course it has without the influence of the GATT; or that the end of the Cold War would have happened as it did without the moderating influence of security institutions such as NATO and the OSCE (Wallander 1997). Yet we can point to many situations in which institutions have not had the desired effect. War in the former Yugoslavia took many lives in spite of UN peacekeeping institutions; the United States places bilateral trade pressure on vulnerable states in spite of the availability of regional and multilateral institutions. Understanding variation in institutional effects is the key challenge for institutionalist theory today. To explain this variation, we require a finer-grained understanding of the mechanisms through which institutions might exert their effects, and of the conditions under which these mechanisms are effective.

A first step might be to develop a typology of institutional effects. As a beginning, I would suggest two ideal-type institutional effects. International institutions might serve as *substitutes* for domestic mechanisms and institutions; or they might *complement* the effect of domestic-level processes and structures. Of course, there are other possibilities. Institutions may have no effect at all, or a constant effect; or they may exhibit a complex combination of these various effects. Nevertheless, distinguishing between substitution and complement effects provides a convenient starting point.

Most functional theories implicitly assume that international institutions will substitute for domestic practices, perhaps by correcting failures of domestic institutions. For example, many explain the desire of high-inflation states such as Italy to join European Monetary Union (EMU) by asserting that EMU will provide the fiscal discipline that Italy's domestic politics have failed to provide. Thus EMU will substitute for Italian domestic institutions, bringing Italian inflation under control. If such a process works as planned, EMU – or even monetary arrangements short of full monetary union – should lead to convergence of inflation rates among members (Fratianni and von Hagen 1991).

If international institutions do indeed substitute for domestic institutions, they will lead to a convergence of outcomes among their members.

Monetary union is a straightforward example of this pattern, but similar outcomes should obtain in other fields as well. Environmental institutions will lead to convergence in environmental indicators, such as carbon dioxide emissions (Levy 1993); human rights institutions should lead members to adopt increasingly similar human rights practices. Even if full convergence does not occur, the major effect of an institution that is acting as a substitute will be to bring state practices more closely in line with one another. A substitution effect could thus be measured by decreased variation in the relevant indicators of state practices: inflation rates, pollution, human rights abuses, etc.

Alternatively, and in direct contrast to the functionalist view of institutions, international institutions may complement and exaggerate domestically generated practices. Perhaps those states that join free-trade arrangements are precisely those that tend toward liberalization anyway. Andrew Moravcsik (1995) has argued that human rights institutions make a difference only for those states that already exhibit strong respect for human rights. Anne-Marie Slaughter (1995) finds that democratic states replicate legalistic practices in their relations with one another. In these frameworks, the primary effect of international institutions is to complement domestic institutions. States whose initial practice falls far from the guidelines established by institutions will show little change in behavior if institutions are acting as complements. This hypothesis stands in direct contrast to substitution effects, where institutions have their greatest impact on states whose behavior substantially deviates from institutional norms. Thus, while substitution effects manifest themselves in convergence of state practices, complement effects will lead to increasing divergence of state practices. Those states that already come close to institutional norms will move further in that direction, while those that deviate from such norms will remain unchanged.

Distinguishing between substitution and complement effects is important because it allows us to begin specifying more precisely the mechanisms by which institutions can exert influence. It leads us to realize that not all institutions may work in the same manner, and so to turn our attention to variation in institutional mechanisms and effects. The distinction thus serves two important purposes, from the perspective of advancing the institutionalist research program. It turns our attention to thinking about *how* institutions matter, rather than just to the issue of *whether* they matter. Second, it allows us to begin thinking about causal mechanisms, and thus developing hypotheses that may be more susceptible to careful empirical testing.

The question of variation in institutional effects also leads directly to the second major topic on the institutionalist research agenda: the question of variation in the use of international institutions. We find substantial variation in the degree to which states rely on institutions across any dimension we wish to examine: time, region, issue-area, etc. However, we have not yet made much progress in identifying patterns in the use of institutions, much less in explaining any patterns that we find.

Thinking about the variety of potential institutional effects could provide guidance for beginning to move in this direction. If institutions are designed to act as substitutes, we would predict that states turn to them when they most desire to achieve an outcome that they cannot achieve through purely domestic measures. The factors that might give rise to such a situation are not difficult to identify: weak domestic institutions; domestic or international collective-action problems; inability to overcome time-inconsistent preferences through purely domestic mechanisms.[4] We would predict increased reliance on international institutions as substitutes when such domestic failures exist. In contrast, reliance on institutions as complements would primarily occur when a group of like-minded states, perhaps pushed by domestic or transnational interest groups, found institutionalization a convenient strategy. The conditions under which states are likely to find institutions as complements convenient are more difficult to specify than those for institutions as substitutes, since the underlying analytical framework has not been worked out as fully as has functionalist theory.

Focusing on variation in institutions provides another mechanism for overcoming the false dichotomy between institutions as independent or dependent variables. A rationalist approach to international institutions assumes that states rely on institutions when doing so will promote their interests. Thus reliance on institutions is a strategy adopted because states anticipate that it will give rise to particular outcomes. The relationship between institutions and outcomes is understood and anticipated by states; only through such anticipation can we explain state strategies toward institutions. In this framework, explaining variation in reliance on institutions forces us to recognize that questions about institutional causes and effects are really just two sides of a single coin, and cannot neatly be separated from one another. Empirical work on the conditions under which states turn to institutions would allow us to test alternative models of international politics in more powerful ways than arguing about counterfactuals that may or may not prove that "institutions matter."

A third major item on the research agenda is suggested by the previous questions of how institutions matter and when states turn to them. The functionalist approach has treated domestic politics purely as a source of state preferences, if domestic politics are considered at all. Because the goal of functionalist theory was to adopt assumptions close to those of realism but to show that realist conclusions about institutions were not valid, it accepted the approach of treating states as units. This approach has inhibited progress on understanding how domestic politics interacts with international institutions.

The notion that international institutions might serve as complements to domestic institutions, in particular, opens a path to thinking more rigorously about the ways in which domestic politics could interact with international institutions. Any model that claimed that participation in international institutions exaggerated domestic tendencies would likely rely on domestic politics as its causal mechanism. Perhaps interest groups force states to adhere to international norms, using international organizations as simply another method to pursue their agendas (see Sikkink 1993). Perhaps governments use institutions as a way to avoid blame for unpopular policies, or as a lever to gain increased control over outcomes in the face of domestic opposition. Judith Goldstein (1996), for example, finds that such domestic political incentives were central to aspects of US acceptance of provisions of the US-Canada Free Trade Agreement (FTA). In some respects, US acquiescence in the use of binding binational dispute-resolution panels is puzzling, since this procedure predictably moved outcomes in a direction preferred by Canada. Goldstein solves this puzzle by considering the president's domestic incentives. She finds that prior to the FTA, control over some key outcomes was in the hands of bureaucratic actors that were not under presidential control. The FTA transferred authority from these bureaucratic actors to the binational panels, which were likely to have preferences closer to the president's than the US bureaucracy did. In this example, only by considering a complex interaction of domestic institutions and presidential incentives to use any means available to realize his preferred outcomes can we understand the transfer of authority from the domestic to the international level.

A final key issue on the research agenda has to do with the durability and stability of international institutions. The dichotomy between institutions as causes and as effects is a false one, because in many cases the cause of an institution is precisely its anticipated effect. That is, states design institutions in order to achieve particular outcomes. In this way institutions can be endogenous yet absolutely essential to understanding the patterns we observe in international politics. However, in order for institutions to be both endogenous and consequential, they need to have some durability and stability in the face of changing underlying conditions, such as the international distribution of power. If institutions change without friction, they become less important and interesting objects of study.

In an important article, Robert Powell (1994) has shown that disagreement about institutional "stickiness" is perhaps the key disagreement between realist and institutionalist approaches to international politics. He demonstrates that the debate between relative and absolute gains is a false one, since the desire to pursue relative gains is driven by an underlying concern for absolute gains, particularly the desire to increase security. He also demonstrates that institutions influence both the pursuit of joint gains (efficiency) and the distribution of any gains achieved. They do so by identifying a particular pattern of outcomes; if efficient, a point on the Pareto frontier. Distributional politics enters the picture by specifying exactly where on the Pareto frontier an institution lies (see also Krasner 1991). The question is whether this particular institutional outcome will change smoothly as power shifts, or whether it will remain stable for some time, changing in a less continuous manner and thus exerting a more prominent independent effect on patterns of behavior. Realists answer that the movement is smooth; institutions will change as fundamental variables do. Institutionalists assert a more discontinuous path of change. Because new institutions are costly to create, because actors are risk-averse, and because of increasing returns to scale, institutions will show some staying power even in the face of changes in fundamental variables.

Because the two perspectives give such different predictions about institutional change, and because understanding institutional change is essential if we are to appreciate the role of institutions in world politics, looking for patterns of change should be a high priority on the research agenda. The realist prediction is straightforward: a direct relation between changes in power and changes in institutions. Mearsheimer (1990), for example, drew on this hypothesis when he famously predicted that NATO would disappear within months, or at most a few years, of the end of the Cold War.

The institutionalist prediction about change has not been as well specified. Beyond predicting more stability than realists, for the types of reasons listed above, theorists have not offered much precision in specifying which institutions will change relatively quickly, and which will change more slowly.[5] Potential answers to this question, however, are implicit in the reasons offered for expecting durability. For example, we might expect that the greater the expected costs of constructing new institutions, or the more risk-averse the actors involved in an existing institution, the more likely that old institutions will be relatively stable.

Another promising line of analysis might be to consider the general problem of path dependence. The more the conditions that give rise to path dependence are met, the more we might expect institutions to remain in place even once the factors giving rise to their creation have changed. While invocations of path dependence are common today in studies of international relations, few have taken note of the environmental characteristics that create path dependence. For example, increasing returns to scale can be a major source of path dependence. Increasing returns to scale mean that it is difficult for one or a few actors to turn to a new institution; they will gain more by working with others in an old institution. Thus we could predict that the more an issue-area is characterized by path dependence, the more institutional stability we should see. Other factors that could enhance institutional stability, and thus give rise to hypotheses about variation in stability, are not difficult to sketch out. Ideas might include: the scarcity of information; investment in institutional structure; or uncertainty about the outcome of moving to a new institution.

Overall, the rationalist research agenda for studying international institutions and state strategies is an exciting one. Specifying the major items on this agenda begins with turning our attention away from the simplistic question of whether institutions matter to the more intriguing and complex one of specifying how and when they matter. Thinking in these terms leads to a number of promising areas for research. The items identified here as being at the top of the agenda include developing a typology of institutional effects; explaining variation in the use of international institutions; studying how domestic politics and international institutions interact; and understanding the sources of institutional stability and change. All are important and tractable problems, where empirical and theoretical research are jointly necessary and possible.

International institutions and order

From a positivist perspective, the relation between international institutions and order is a relatively simple one. The entire point of institutions is to embody norms and rules, and thus to induce more certainty and predictability in patterns of international interactions. Institutions may be criticized for creating a status quo bias (Strange 1983), but other terms for status quo bias are order and predictability. Poorly designed institutions will be less successful at reducing uncertainty than well-designed ones. Yet there seems little doubt that the correlation between institutions and order of a sort is a positive one.

The more difficult question relating to institutions and order is the normative one: whether we approve of the order created by particular institutions. Normative questions have primarily to do with the distributional effects of institutions. As noted above, the dominant functionalist approach to institutions has focused on efficiency effects, and so has not considered in much depth distributional effects. While Keohane (1984), for example, noted that international cooperation may enhance the well-being of cooperating states at the expense of those left outside international regimes (think of OPEC), this insight has not been central to institutionalist research.

In enhancing our understanding of the normative effects of institutions, two types of distributional effects seem central: those among members of an institution; and those between members and nonmembers. Asking about distributional effects among members may seem beside the point and inconsistent with the rationalist approach. If states are free to choose whether they join an institution or not, can we not assume that all members must benefit from the institution? While in general this seems like a reasonable assumption, it needs to be qualified in at least two ways. First, Lloyd Gruber (1998) has made an intriguing argument about whether the decision to join an institution can truly be treated as welfare-enhancing. He points out that if a few powerful states decide to create an institution, that step changes the status quo. Those states not in the new institution now face a changed environment, one in which they may be worse off than they were previously. In this new status quo ex post institutional creation, they may be better off becoming members. But this begs the question whether erstwhile outsiders are better off than they were before the institution was created in the first place. Gruber studies the European Monetary System (EMS), arguing that French and German decisions had precisely this welfare-decreasing effect on other European states such as Italy. While Italy may now be better off in the EMS than outside it, it may have been even better off if the EMS had never been created.

A second internal issue has to do with how the benefits of cooperation are distributed among the members of an institution. As noted above, most instances of international cooperation are multiple equilibria problems: there are a number of possible stable patterns of cooperation. These different equilibria can have very different distributions of payoffs. We can expect, and indeed institutionalist and realist theories agree, that powerful states will select equilibria that tend to work to their advantage. Evidence that the United States behaved in this manner in establishing institutions after World War II is abundant (Ruggie 1992). If in fact institutions create a status quo bias, they will tend to lock in uneven distributions of benefits. Thus while institutions enhance order, they may do so only at the cost of creating serious equity concerns. Developing countries have raised these concerns in most multilateral institutions. This expression of concern has sometimes led to modest changes, as in the Generalized System of Preferences in the GATT. But rarely have we seen fundamental institutional changes that tilt the distribution of benefits substantially in the direction of poor and weak states.

The UN Security Council is perhaps the foremost example of this dilemma today. The restricted membership and veto power of the permanent members of the UN certainly creates an order that would not otherwise exist. But it also provides significant distributional benefits to the permanent members, such as the power to veto any economic sanctions that might be imposed against them or their allies. Because any change in membership would require the unanimous consent of the current permanent members, it is unlikely to happen. Thus the permanent members find their position highly beneficial; they have substantial influence, even if, like the United States, they do not bother to pay their dues.

As this discussion suggests, the distribution of benefits among member states of institutions, and the question whether all members of an institution are in practice made better off by the presence of the institution, are vital theoretical and practical concerns. Distributional implications form the heart of the issue when we consider the role of international institutions in constituting and maintaining the international order. They are a useful way to frame the debate, frequently joined by realists and liberals, about the relation between power and international institutions. In general, realists have argued that institutions merely reflect the distribution of power in the international system, and therefore should be treated as dependent rather than explanatory variables in our models of international politics. Liberals, while recognizing the role that power plays in the creation and maintenance of institutions, also believe that institutions provide benefits to all their members, therefore moderating if not overthrowing the practice of power politics.

The evidence on the distributional implications of institutionalized cooperation among states has not yet been systematically collected, so that we cannot definitively resolve this debate. This author inclines toward the liberal position, recognizing that some states benefit more from institutions than others, but all are in a better situation than if institutions did not exist. Institutions do reflect the power relations prevailing at the time of their creation, and tend to reinforce those relations, presumably directing a large share of the benefits they provide toward the most powerful. Yet, the very act of creating an institution binds the hands of powerful states. If they wish to gain the benefits of institutionalized cooperation, they must in most regards respect the operating principles, norms, and rules of those institutions. At times the powerful surely ignore inconvenient institutional constraints, as do all states. In these situations, institutionalized patterns of cooperation and negotiated standards of behavior allow other members of institutions to develop a response, reducing the ability of the powerful to engage in divide-and-conquer tactics. For example, while the United States is clearly taking advantage of its power in refusing to pay its UN dues, its failure to make good on its debt has increased the level of friction in dealing with other members of the Security Council, reducing the potential benefits of cooperation that the United States could be deriving from its privileged position in this institution.

Institutionalized cooperation, even if organized along lines that conform more to the preferences of the powerful than of the weak, provides a degree of predictability and stability that may be especially valuable for less powerful and poorer states. For example, those states now undergoing the trying processes of economic and political liberalization would find the going even more difficult if they were confronting a less institutionalized international environment. Existing institutions contribute to stable expectations about other states' policies and behavior that are essential if states are to undergo fundamental domestic reforms or invest in particular patterns of economic activity.

The benefits of institutionalized cooperation are reflected in the intense demands of liberalizing states to join existing institutions in every realm of activity. While they may chafe under the specific conditions and restrictions of these institutions, on balance liberalizing states anticipate that joining them will provide immense benefits. Liberalizing states are anxious to join economic institutions, such as the WTO, and security institutions, such as NATO; the benefits of institutionalized cooperation are not limited to one issue-area.[6] These institutions will continue to provide, as they have in the past, arenas for working out collective solutions to common problems and integrating liberalizing states, large and small, into the international order. Concerns about the distribution of benefits among the members of institutions are real, and are inherent in politics in a world of power asymmetries. But the appropriate response to such concerns seems to lie in more careful consideration of how institutions can be designed so as to provide benefits to the weak, rather than in rejecting the strategy of institutionalization wholesale.

Distributional concerns are more pronounced when we turn to the question of members versus nonmembers of an institution. Any well-functioning institution provides its members with substantial benefits. Most also allow current members substantial control over admitting new members. This situation can, and does, create major tensions between the haves, who are insiders, and have-nots, the outsiders. Examples of this dilemma are legion in the 1990s. NATO is perhaps the most consequential example. Central and East European states are desperate to enter, for the military and legitimacy benefits membership would provide.

The first states to become members will gain an edge over other states in the region. At the same time, their entry into NATO, and NATO's refusal to make Russia a full member, rightly causes deep-seated concern among the Russian elite. Economic institutions show the same dynamic, sometimes in even clearer form. For example, most Caribbean and Central American states are being hurt in absolute terms by the current status of NAFTA, and are clamoring for its extension. Because the US market is now more open to Mexican exports than those from other states in the region, investment naturally flows away from them and toward Mexico. This is a real, absolute loss for those states not included in NAFTA. Thus the creation of this institution has had immediate, observable negative economic effects for those states that otherwise would have been strong competitors for investment that is now directed to Mexico.

The effects of institutions on order and equity depend heavily on the specifics of institutional design. Institutions that are supposed to provide their members with information about one another's behavior can only do so if they are delegated monitoring authority. The negative distributional consequences of institutions are magnified if they give some subset of powerful states a veto, or have arbitrary rules for extension to new members. These observations suggest that institutional design should be a high-priority item on the institutionalist research agenda. However, it has not been. Because of the obsession with proving that "institutions matter," researchers have left equally important and more tractable questions about institutional variation to the realm of "policy analysis." This is a mistake. Institutionalist theory has a great deal to tell us about variations in institutional design, from both a positive and a normative perspective. Such research could have great practical payoffs. But what researchers have not yet appreciated is that it could also have great theoretical payoffs. Research in the last fifteen years has adequately addressed the possibility proof challenge: can institutions matter? We need to turn now to the issue of variation, moving beyond the demonstration that institutions can matter to showing how and when they do.

NOTES

1 My thanks for comments go to John Ikenberry, T. V. Paul, John Hall, and other conference participants.
2 It may also have been a necessary step in establishing a foothold for the institutionalist research program; only time will tell.
3 Kenneth Shepsle (1986) has made a similar point, to great effect, about the study of domestic institutions. He draws an important distinction between behavioral equilibria induced by institutions (structure-induced equilibria) and

equilibrium institutions. Both fit comfortably in a rationalist, strategic understanding of institutions.

4 In order to overcome problems of time inconsistency, states need to bind
themselves. Sometimes they can do so through the creation of appropriate
domestic institutions, such as independent central banks. But international
institutions can also provide such a binding function.

5 One important exception to this generalization is Celeste Wallander and
Robert Keohane's work on NATO's persistence (1997); see also McCalla (1996).

6 On the relation between democratization and security relations, see Michael
Doyle's contribution to this volume.

REFERENCES

Carr, Edward Hallett 1964, *The Twenty Years' Crisis, 1919–1939*, New York:
Harper and Row.

Duffield, John S. 1992, "International Regimes and Alliance Behavior: Explaining NATO Conventional Force Levels," *International Organization* 46: 819–55.

Fearon, James D. 1998, "Bargaining, Enforcement, and International Cooperation," *International Organization* 52: 269–305.

Ferejohn, John 1991, "Rationality and Interpretation: Parliamentary Elections in
Early Stuart England," in *The Economic Approach to Politics*, Kristen Renwick
Monroe (ed.), New York: HarperCollins, pp. 279–305.

Fratianni, Michele and von Hagen, Jürgen 1991, *The European Monetary System
and European Monetary Union*, Boulder, CO: Westview Press.

Garrett, Geoffrey and Weingast, Barry 1993, "Ideas, Interests, and Institutions:
Constructing the EC's Internal Market," in *Ideas and Foreign Policy*, Judith
Goldstein and Robert Keohane (eds.), Ithaca: Cornell University Press, pp.
173–206.

Goldstein, Judith 1996, "International Law and Domestic Institutions: Recon-
ciling North American 'Unfair' Trade Laws," *International Organization* 50:
541–64.

Gruber, Lloyd G. 1998, *Ruling the World: Power Politics and the Rise of Supranational Institutions*, manuscript, University of Chicago.

Haas, Ernst B. 1958, *The Uniting of Europe*, Stanford: Stanford University Press.

Katzenstein, Peter J. (ed.) 1996, *The Culture of National Security*, New York:
Columbia University Press.

Keohane, Robert O. 1984, *After Hegemony*, Princeton: Princeton University
Press.

   1986, "Reciprocity in International Relations," *International Organization* 20:
   1–27.

   1988, "International Institutions: Two Approaches," *International Studies
   Quarterly* 32: 379–96.

Knight, Jack 1992, *Institutions and Social Conflict*, New York: Cambridge University Press.

Krasner, Stephen D. (ed.) 1983, *International Regimes*, Ithaca: Cornell University
Press.

1991, "Global Communications and National Power: Life on the Pareto Frontier," *World Politics* 43: 336–56.

Levy, Marc A. 1993, "European Acid Rain: The Power of Tote-Board Diplomacy," in *Institutions for the Earth*, Peter M. Haas, Robert O. Keohane, and Marc A. Levy (eds.), Cambridge: MIT Press, pp. 75–132.

Libecap, Gary D. 1989, *Contracting for Property Rights*, New York: Cambridge University Press.

Martin, Lisa L. 1992a, "Interests, Power, and Multilateralism," *International Organization* 46: 765–92.

1992b, *Coercive Cooperation: Explaining Multilateral Economic Sanctions*, Princeton: Princeton University Press.

McCalla, Robert B. 1996, "NATO's Persistence After the Cold War," *International Organization* 50: 445–76.

Mearsheimer, John J. 1990, "Back to the Future: Instability in Europe after the Cold War," *International Security* 15: 5–57.

1994/5, "The False Promise of International Institutions," *International Security* 19: 5–49.

Mitchell, Ronald B. 1994, "Regime Design Matters: Intentional Oil Pollution and Treaty Compliance," *International Organization* 48: 425–58.

Mitrany, David 1975, *The Functional Theory of Politics*, London: St. Martin's Press for the London School of Economics and Political Science.

Moravcsik, Andrew 1991, "Negotiating the Single European Act: National Interests and Conventional Statecraft in the European Community," *International Organization* 45: 19–56.

1995, "Explaining International Human Rights Regimes: Liberal Theory and Western Europe," *European Journal of International Relations* 1: 157–89.

Morgenthau, Hans 1948, *Politics Among Nations*, New York: A. A. Knopf.

Morrow, James D. 1994, "Modeling the Forms of International Cooperation," *International Organization* 48: 387–423.

Ostrom, Elinor 1990, *Governing the Commons*, New York: Cambridge University Press.

Powell, Robert 1994, "Anarchy in International Relations Theory: The Neorealist-Neoliberal Debate," *International Organization* 48: 313–44.

Ruggie, John Gerard 1992, "Multilateralism: The Anatomy of an Institution," *International Organization* 46: 561–98.

Schelling, Thomas C. 1960, *The Strategy of Conflict*, Cambridge: Harvard University Press.

Shanks, Cheryl, Jacobson, Harold K. and Kaplan, Jeffrey H. 1996, "Inertia and Change in the Constellation of International Governmental Organizations, 1981–1992," *International Organization* 50: 593–628.

Shepsle, Kenneth A. 1986, "Institutional Equilibrium and Equilibrium Institutions," *Political Science: The Science of Politics*, in Herbert Weisberg (ed.), New York: Agathon Press, pp. 51–81.

Sikkink, Kathryn 1993, "Human Rights, Principled Issue-Networks, and Sovereignty in Latin America," *International Organization* 47: 411–41.

Slaughter, Anne-Marie 1995, "International Law in a World of Liberal States," *European Journal of International Law* 6: 503–38.

Snidal, Duncan 1985, "Coordination Versus Prisoners' Dilemma: Implications for International Cooperation and Regimes," *American Political Science Review* 79: 923–42.

1996, "International Political Economy Approaches to International Institutions," *International Review of Law and Economics* 16: 121–37.

Stein, Arthur A. 1983, "Coordination and Collaboration: Regimes in an Anarchic World," in Krasner (ed.), pp. 115–40.

Strange, Susan 1983, "*Cave! Hic Dragones*: A Critique of Regime Analysis," in Krasner (ed.), pp. 337–54.

Wallander, Celeste 1997, *Balancing Acts: Security, Institutions, and German-Russian Relations After the Cold War*, manuscript, Harvard University.

Wallander, Celeste and Keohane, Robert O. 1997, "When Threats Decline, Why Do Alliances Persist? An Institutional Approach," manuscript, Harvard University and Duke University.

Wendt, Alexander 1992, "Anarchy is What States Make of It: The Social Construction of State Politics," *International Organization* 46: 391–425.

5   Is the truth out there? Eight questions about international order[1]

Steve Smith

My aim in this chapter is twofold: first, I want to examine the prevailing assumptions about international order, and thereby engage in disagreement with many of the contributors to this volume. Secondly, I want to point to an alternative post-positivist research agenda for thinking about international order, one that disputes the concentration on world order found in the mainstream literature. I will proceed by posing eight questions about international order. These questions are inspired by my work on what can broadly be called post-positivist work on epistemology and international theory. These questions pose rather more fundamental re-examinations of the *normative* assumptions underlying the traditional literature on international order.

Positivism and international theory

I come to this subject from having spent most of my time working on international theory, most recently concentrating on the epistemological assumptions underlying contemporary theory (Hollis and Smith 1990; Smith 1995, 1996). From this vantage point some fairly obvious concerns about the literature on international order emerge. My feeling has been that most work on order ultimately reduces it to a super-structural consequence of power relations, either in structural-functional (Kaplan 1957) or in structural (Waltz 1979) mode. Nuances apart, for they are just nuances, each of these writers sees agency ultimately being reducible to structure, with no particular need to delve inside the black-box of the state to get an explanation of patterns of international order. As such it essentially treats order as something "out there," to be observed much in the same way as a natural scientist examines aspects of the natural world. The objections to this position are well known and do not need rehearsing here. The point is that there remain some rather deep ontological questions about what kind of phenomenon order is, and these, in part, depend on our epistemological assumptions since how we know something in part determines what it is that we find to be the furniture of the social world.

International theory has been dominated by positivism for the last fifty years, despite the fact that most international theorists argue that they are not now "strict" or "naive" positivists. To make my claim as clear as possible, I fully realize that few international theorists would want to sign up to the stark empiricist warrant underlying logical positivism, but I believe that most work in the field remains wedded to central features of positivism. If positivism can be defined as accepting four main features – naturalism, empiricism, belief in patterns existing in social phenomena, and the value/fact distinction – then I would argue that most North American international relations theory has happily jettisoned the last two of these, but retained the first two as foundational epistemological positions. I realize that this is decidedly not the self-image of most who write in this area, but I do maintain that it is a fair judgment. This does not mean that writers are so naive that they do not think that what goes on in the heads of actors matters, nor that there are not elements of social construction at work in international relations, only that ultimately their epistemology forces them to reduce the ideational to the material, be that in Marxist, liberal, or realist form.

I need to say something about how I see the current situation of international theory. It can broadly be characterized by three main theoretical clusters. First there is *rationalism*, containing the bulk of neorealist and neoliberal, as well as some Marxist, work on international theory (see Baldwin 1993). Second, there is *reflectivism*, which broadly consists of the post-positivist approaches of critical theory, postmodernism, and feminist and gender theory (see Smith 1997). Third, there is *social constructivism* (see Wendt 1992), which attempts to bridge the gap between rationalism and reflectivism, basically by adopting the ontology of the former and a very "thin" version of the epistemology of the latter. I think that the current state of theory is that rationalist approaches continue to dominate the mainstream, reflectivist approaches are gaining powerful sets of adherents, and that social constructivism will be "flavor of the month" theory-wise within a year or two. Geographically, I would see rationalism dominating the North American (but specifically the US) international relations community, and reflectivism being more a European interest, aided by a few geographical outliers on the North American continent. Does this tell us something both about ethnocentrism and concepts of international order and about the power-knowledge relationship within different academic communities?

My own interests have shifted from an essentially positivistic education towards a profound skepticism about positivism and about the effects of foundational epistemological positions on the social sciences. This does not mean that I prefer a slide towards relativism, only that I am concerned that statements about order or sovereignty or the like are not deceptively rooted in a (non-existent) foundational epistemology. I think that these statements are in fact ethical and irreducibly judgmental and that the resort to epistemology serves as a mask to cover the political with the technical. My basic claim in this paper will be that discussions of international order are ineluctably political and that there is no such thing as an epistemological warrant for these judgments. I hope that I can substantiate this claim by posing a series of questions about the nature of international order from a post-positivistic epistemological position.

1) What is international order?

What is the exact referent point of discussions about international order? Broadly speaking, there are two views and I want to argue that the accepted relationship between these is problematic. The two views are that order refers to a relationship between states or that order refers to a condition of humanity as a whole. This is evident in the most widely cited work on international order, Hedley Bull's *The Anarchical Society*. Bull defines international order as "a pattern of activity that sustains the elementary or primary goals of the society of states, or international society" (1977: 8). This, of course, is deduced from his prior definition of order in social life as "a pattern of human activity that sustains elementary, primary or universal goals of social life" (5). He defines these goals as "life, truth and property" (5). Note immediately how truth and order are intertwined right at the start of his analysis. Bull believes that "we" can agree on the need for international order in a way that we could not do about international justice.

Bull then distinguishes between international order and world order. The former is based on the existence of states as the "starting point of international relations" (8), and on a distinction between a system of states and a society of states. For Bull, a system of states occurs when two or more states are in regular contact with one another and thereby "make the behaviour of each a necessary element in the calculations of the other" (10). A society of states exists "when a group of states, conscious of certain common interests and common values, form a society in the sense that they conceive themselves to be bound by a common set of rules in their relations with one another, and share in the working of common institutions" (13). Crucially, an international society presumes the existence of an international system whereas the opposite does not hold. The goals of a society of states are: "the preservation of the system and the society of states itself" (16); "maintaining the independence or external sovereignty of individual states" (17); "the absence of war among member states of international society as the normal condition of their relationship" (18); and "the common goals of all social life [life, truth and property]" (19). In contrast, world order refers to "those patterns or dispositions of human activity that sustain the elementary or primary goals of social life among mankind as a whole" (20). World order is also wider, more primordial and morally prior to international order. Nonetheless "this is the moment for international relations" (22) in the absence of world order emerging from a universal political organization. For Bull, order is prior to other moral values because it is the condition for their realization. Without order in social life there can be no possibility of achieving "advanced, secondary or the special goals of particular societies" (97).

Another view is offered by Robert Cox, for whom the focus should be on world order rather than international order. For Cox, world orders refer to "the particular configurations of forces which successively define the problematic of war or peace for the ensemble of states" (1996: 100). Cox's view of order derives from his view of the social world as resulting from the intersection of three "categories of forces" – ideas, material capabilities, and institutions, linked by Gramsci's concept of hegemony. Consequently, the global historical structures of any era are the result of the interrelation between three spheres of activity – social forces ("engendered by the production process"), forms of state ("derived from a study of state/society complexes"), and world orders. These three spheres of activity are not arranged in any one hierarchy, since, for example, forms of state may both structure and be structured by world orders. The point, of course, is that Cox has a far more extensive notion of order than does Bull, since his view explicitly links the "domestic" and the "international," as well as the economic, the political, and the social. Nonetheless, note that his referent point for international order is the state, and that the motor for his analysis is firmly historical materialist. As Robert Latham has noted in his recent study of the post-war liberal order, "For Cox, capitalism is the macro-historical context for liberal order" (Latham 1997: 35).

A third view is that of Richard Falk, most clearly expressed in his 1975 book *A Study of Future Worlds*. For Falk, world order involves something far more radical than envisaged by either Bull or Cox. Falk is concerned with finding solutions to *global* (not international) problems, and focuses not on social groups or states but on people. His aim is to construct an order that deals with the problems of humanity in such a way as to be beneficial for all humans. He notes four main problems: the

minimization of large-scale collective violence; the maximization of social and economic well-being; the realization of fundamental human
rights, and of conditions of political justice; and the maintenance and
rehabilitation of ecological quality. In each case the point of reference is
the individual.

Now, my concern here is simply with the issue of what order refers to.
For Bull and Cox it refers to relations between states, whereas for Falk it
relates directly to individuals. Which of these views is "right"? I know
what the traditional answer is, but I want to know why that view is
accepted? Crucially this takes us back to the issue of what kind of
phenomenon is "order." There is a real tension in Bull's and Cox's work
between order as observable and order as construction, with each arguing
for some measure of construction, yet, I claim, in each case seeing order
as a result of underlying causal forces (the power relations between states
for Bull, and for Cox, ultimately the relations of production). The material definitely dominates the ideational in each case. For Falk the
situation is very different, with order being something we construct. The
point at issue is that there is a contradiction between treating order as an
observable and order as construct. The vast bulk of the literature talks of
order and of states as if they are natural phenomena. Order therefore
becomes something that results from the great causal forces of international history, much like notions of the rise and fall of powers. This kind
of language implies a kind of naturalism about the social world, almost, in
fact, a kind of stark structural-functionalism.

My worry is that too much of the literature on international order
presents it as something inherent in the world, as a "given." The language
of social construction is used but all too often this refers to the *processes* by
which international order is managed. This tension is evident in chapters
five to nine of Bull's analysis (1977), and in part three of Cox's recent
volume (1996). The same treatment can be found in John Hall's *International Orders* in which he proposes a "realism/liberalism mix" (1996: 25).
His mix of realism and liberalism results in patterns of international order
that treat order as the resultant of various international and domestic
forces (see particularly 29–32). Hall wants to combine realism and liberalism but in a way that places less emphasis on the social construction of
order than on the relationship between rational calculation and the international power balance.

I am not convinced that such a view captures the social world. I do not
believe that international order is "out there." It is something we construct, not something we discover. Now, I fully expect that many will
argue that this is a gross over-simplification, and that they know that the
social world is not like this. But, for example, Hall's characterization of

order does, in my view, ultimately place the ideational as secondary to the material. And I think that it is precisely this tension that lies at the heart of most of the literature on international order, and that is why Bull is more a realist and Cox more a historical materialist than a constructivist; yet note that each wants to claim a role for the ideational.

2) Why does international order privilege the state and protect sovereignty?

My second question concerns the way in which international order, rather than world order, privileges the state and sovereignty. My concern is not so much with its being the empirical focus as that it is too often the normative focus, in the sense of being taken as *the* natural political unit. As noted above, Bull, Cox, and Falk have very different views of international order, and Bull in particular sees the primary goal of international order as protecting the sovereignty of the state. I think that this is very problematic, since of course it assumes that state sovereignty is something that should be protected. I see no clear reason why the state should be the referent point for discussions of order, nor do I think that it is obvious just why we should treat states as ethically privileged. Why should we privilege the given distribution of power and the processes whereby the dominant values of the dominant groups become accepted as "natural," or the processes whereby male dominance is enhanced?

Now if this is "how the world is," that is to say if this is a feature of the social world that our theories do not create, then fair enough; but if international order is something we construct then why should we privilege the state when the state may well be more harmful to its citizens than protective of them? Although not all states are harmful to their citizens, and despite the fact that states must be converted to "good" causes for them to stand a chance of implementation, perhaps more people on the planet face a greater threat from their own state than from any other state. What then is so special and defensible about sovereignty? Maybe sovereignty is something that we should wish to dismantle in the name of constructing a better world. Critically, if order is a construct why should we accept the state as the analytical unit for our analysis and sovereignty as the primary goal to be protected? There could well be a host of other goals that we should advance, such as human rights, economic well-being, life chances, opposition to genocide, female genital mutilation, and so on.

I know the problems concerning the Western nature of these values, and I note the concerns about them being culture-bound, but I am not batting for any particular values as much as noting that a focus on protecting sovereignty as the primary goal of international order is by no means obvious or neutral. My concern is simply that in so doing either we are making a very clear (but unstated) normative choice to privilege the state and sovereignty or we are in fact reverting to a naturalistic view of the social world, one in which ultimately social construction is secondary to material forces. Either move is problematic: the first because there are obvious alternatives to the state as referent and to sovereignty as the primary value; the second because it undermines any claim to order as a construct, and accepts a view of the social world that is extremely controversial, yet which is made more palatable and less stark by dashes of social construction. As such, this appeal, in logic if not in words, to a foundational epistemological warrant for treating the state and sovereignty as the "natural" focus and the "natural" primary value to be protected, represents an attempt to paint what is an ethical and irreducibly normative choice as one dictated by "the way that the world is." In this way, the normative content of discussions of international order is either smuggled in via an appeal to a non-existent epistemological warrant or presented as in some way primary.

3) Is international order desirable?

My third question asks whether discussions about international order do not implicitly assume that order is desirable. In his characteristically lucid summary of Bull's work on international order, John Vincent (1990) notes that Bull is open to criticism because he assumes exactly that. As pointed out earlier, Bull assumes explicitly that order is somehow prior as a social good to other ethical considerations such as justice, but maintains that his study of order is not meant to imply a preference for order over, say, justice. Indeed, in the introduction to his book Bull claims that his aim is to write a detached account of international order; but Vincent argues persuasively that Bull did not manage to be detached. Vincent notes that since Bull's view of order is one which sees it as a prerequisite to "the enjoyment of any other social values . . . [then] . . . there does seem to be built in a general presumption in favour of order" (1990: 44). In this sense, order is the primary social good since without it other social goods cannot be achieved.

Vincent has another objection to Bull's view of international order, and this is basically E. H. Carr's objection to the writing about international politics (1939) in the inter-war period. For Carr, this work was simply the doctrine of the satisfied powers, so that ideas such as the primacy of peace, the sanctity of treaties, the belief in international harmony, and the obligations of the League Covenant were no more than reflections of the interests of Britain and France. Vincent notes that although Bull argued that his views on international order were not intended to sanctify it, Bull "had more time for the practical problems of those saddled with power and responsibility for policy than for those who, having neither, enjoyed the luxury of criticizing both" (1990: 46). Indeed, Bull concludes *The Anarchical Society* by admitting that it is "an implicit defence of the states system" (1977: 318).

International order legitimizes non-intervention and sovereignty, but what is the moral content of this legitimization? This, of course, gets us into the standard cosmopolitan-communitarian debate (see Brown 1992 for an excellent survey), and in so doing forces us to consider whether order is indeed desirable; desirable for whom? Are states really upholding plural conceptions of the common good, or does the concern with order, because it privileges sovereignty and non-intervention, rule out the possibility of advancing any notion of the common good? Maybe advancing the common good requires preferring other values to international order, thereby de-legitimizing sovereignty and the principle of non-intervention. At base, why is order to be preferred to disorder?

I imagine that one obvious answer to this question is that international order is to be preferred to international disorder because disorder carries with it the prospect of large-scale death through war. But this runs the risk of confusing international order with orderly change. Clearly a concern with orderly change does not mean that the given international order is to be privileged. To prefer the existing order is to make a rather more specific claim, namely that certain types of order are to be preferred to others, and this simply re-introduces the earlier question of what kind of thing is international order. Is it any order, in the sense of the order that happens to exist at any point in time, or is it order in accordance with certain criteria? In which case, note that what is being posited is that certain kinds of death are more important than others; for example, deaths as a result of politics (war) are more important than deaths as a result of economics (famine and underdevelopment). Treating international order both as a primary goal and as desirable masks the fact that a given international order may be accompanied by large-scale "economic" or "ethnic conflict" or "cultural" deaths. Precisely why is this order to be preferred *a priori*?

4) What is the relationship between international order and identity?

My concern here is with the kinds of effects international orders have on political identity in world politics. As Rob Walker has shown, the division, central to debates about international order, between the international and the domestic polities is critically important in constructing political identities. There are two main aspects to this, a temporal and a spatial. The temporal concern is that the two political settings involve very different notions of the nature of political time. For Walker, the domestic political realm is portrayed as the realm of progress, where citizenship emerges and where debates about ethics have meaning. It is also the realm where "the possibility of universalist claims to the good, the true and the beautiful is opened up to actualisation in time" (1993: 63). In contrast, in the international realm "the lack of community can be taken to imply the impossibility of history as a progressive teleology, and thus the possibility merely of recurrence and repetition" (63). This, of course, is what Martin Wight was referring to when he spoke of the impossibility of there being international theory to match the works in political theory. Or, in other words, that what happens within states is politics whereas what goes on between them is *merely* relations. Similarly, there is a spatial aspect to discussions of the division between the domestic and the international. Walker argues that sovereignty, the preservation of which was the primary goal of international order for Bull, "did not appear out of thin air. It embodies an historically specific account of ethical possibility" (62). The contrast is between life inside and life outside the political community, with universalist aspirations to the good being realizable "only within spatially delimited territory."

Together the spatial and the temporal aspects of the "inside/outside" nature of debates about sovereignty and the relationship between the domestic and the international have enormous effects on political identity, since that identity is determined by what happens within the political units that are firmly located within given international orders. As Walker puts it: "The possibility of justice is permitted within, the extreme difficulty of order is affirmed without. The danger of transferring assumptions about political life inside the state onto the analysis of relations between states becomes both a regulative principle of research and a normative prescription" (70). In other words, it is exactly this specific spatial/temporal resolution of the relationship between universality and particularity that has been taken by both political and international theory as setting the limits and the conditions for political identity. And it is precisely this very distinction between political and international theory that Walker wants to disrupt because of its limitations on the kind of political identities that can be created within its limits. This is because both the domestic and the international are constituted by the existence of each other, and because this distinction, represented as universally applicable and timeless, is in fact a very specific realization of the political problems of modernity.

International order, therefore, by protecting as its primary goal the preservation of the states system and state sovereignty, sets the limits to the kinds of political identities that are possible within world politics. Order is decidedly not neutral when it comes to the construction of political identities; indeed, it reinforces communitarian identities and undermines the possibility of cosmopolitan identities. This is the case both if order is treated as a construct and if it is treated as an observable.

But international orders do much more than merely limit the possibilities of political identity. They also construct economic, religious, social, ethnic, racial, sexual, and gendered identities. It is not simply a case of what is omitted in a focus on international political order, although as I shall argue in the next section, there is a significant amount omitted. Rather, I want to argue that given international orders have significant effects on personal identity. The division of the international realm into states has fairly obvious consequences for the construction of ethnic identity, but I would also claim that there are major effects on gender identity as well. Think of what it means to be a "man" during the Cold War, or in the current Balkan conflict. Think of how masculinities get constructed in a world of bipolarity and compare them to masculinities in a world where the armed forces of the world have to play peacekeeping roles. Similarly, what kinds of female identities are required by different international orders? Is it not the case that women in Eastern Europe during the Cold War had very different identities than in the post-Cold War world?

5) What is omitted in discussions about international order?

The last question dealt with the thorny issue of identity and order; my concern here is with those things that get left out of discussions concerning international order. There are two points to make. First, there is much to do with politics internationally that is left out of the focus by debates on international order. Second, international order tends to be written about from the perspective of the dominant powers in the international system.

As to the first point, in one sense there is no need to ram it home since it is obvious that many aspects of international life are ignored by any focus on international order. The most obvious example is gender, although I am well aware of Rob Walker's comment that we cannot simply add gender to an analysis of international relations since that discipline has been built upon gendered concepts and assumptions. Nonetheless, it is important to point out that a focus on international order represents one very specific reading of the nature of international relations, and of what matters in discussions or analyses of it. It focuses overwhelmingly on *states* and on the patterns of interactions between them. It rarely focuses on economic relations, and very rarely on notions such as "the clash of civilizations" (Huntington 1996). But questions of race, ethnicity, and gender are largely omitted, since they are not presumed to be parts of any international order.

Cynthia Enloe (1990, 1993) has probably done more than any other writer to show how international order both ignores women and their roles within it, and yet relies on women (and men) playing very specific roles for the international order to function. As she argues, the international system takes a lot more power to work than a focus on the traditional agenda implies. Women have to play a variety of roles for the system to function, so in an important sense it is not "just" a case of asking where are the women in international relations, but rather of looking to see exactly where they are and what they do. They are there, and the system would not function without them, but their roles are not deemed to be relevant to the commonsense agenda of the discipline. These roles are seen as either "economic," or "cultural," or "social" or, more commonly, as "private." Yet Enloe's work shows just how centrally involved are women and their roles in the functioning of the international system. As such, discussions on international order choose to see some sorts of relations as more important than others. Obviously this is defensible especially if one sees international order as an observable, but this defense is considerably weakened if one accepts that order is something constructed, since that means that our *analytical* choice is in fact a *normative* choice. Therefore maybe one question to pose about international order is to ask "whose order?"

As to the second point, it is clear that the literature on international order is based on a "great-power" view of international relations, but why should this view be privileged? How might international order look from the peripheries of world power? Maybe any discussion of international order will unavoidably reflect a culturally determined view of what is important in international relations, but, nonetheless, it is important to note that a "great power" focus is dependent on one reading of what matters most in international relations. A very different view of the international order would come from those scholars interested in development or in dependency/world-systems theory.

6) What is the effect of international order on patterns of exclusion and inclusion?

My concern here is with the impact of notions of international order on the practices of inclusion and exclusion in world politics. Put simply, an order that privileges sovereignty is engaged in the acts of exclusion and inclusion. For Andrew Linklater (1990, 1992), these acts should be central to social research, and a concern to resist forms of exclusion is a concern that must privilege universalism over communitarianism (Linklater 1992: 80–1). For Linklater, the work of Bull on international order, and its relationship to international justice shows the importance of inclusion and exclusion; its clearest example is the Third World's revolt against the West, where "the West's universal morality was turned against it when the non-European states struggled to gain access to the economic and political resources from which they had been excluded . . . The West was invited to create a more just world order, not relying entirely on Western values and not excluding cultural differences" (81). Indeed, Linklater argues that practices of inclusion and exclusion are as primary as the values of life, truth, and property identified as central by Bull, both because the state is itself a system of inclusion and exclusion and because "exclusionary states participate in an inclusive society of states which is held together by international legal norms and moral principles" (83). And it is international order that takes precedence for this society of states over other ethical considerations such as justice.

But what makes talk of a society of states importantly different from a pure realist approach to international relations is that whereas realists see anarchy as entailing the endless repetition of conflict, society-of-states theorists see international society and international order as a way of increasing international community. International order therefore works by expanding the shared norms of international society to different cultures, moral perspectives, and legal systems.

Yet herein lies a major problem, which is whether such an expanding community is possible, and if possible, whether it is no more than the latest form of imperialism. Linklater, of course, wants to ground this expanding notion of community by recourse to Habermas' notions of communicative competence, whereby the practice is to increase the community of those involved in the conversation. Another version is that of Richard Rorty, who, contra Habermas, does not accept the idea of a universalism, but instead seeks to expand solidarity and community by increasing the number of "we liberals." In each case the objection is that this move will not increase community to include more and more, because this cannot be achieved by such conversational moves except if they are backed by force. This has been the setting for the major disputes between Habermas and Foucault and between Rorty and Lyotard. In each case the argument is very similar: for Foucault and Lyotard, cultures are radically incommensurable so that one culture cannot convert another to its views except by the use of force. In each case both Habermas and Rorty disagree, each pointing to the possibility of, respectively, discourse ethics and the force of the better argument, and the possibility of converting another to your views by the use of persuasion (see Wheeler 1997). The problem, then, is whether any notion of an international order based on a series of norms and moral principles can ever hold for all societies and all cultures, or whether instead the language of the society of states is always a reflection of one set of political and moral values that become superimposed on the rest of international society, and all the more effectively if the leaders of other cultures can be bought into the system.

7) Is there an assumption of progress in international order?

There are clear indications that many writers about international order do indeed speak as if there is a progressive quality to succeeding forms of order. The introduction to this volume lists seven mechanisms of Westphalia, including three realist versions that seem to see the system of states remaining essentially static (balance of power, concert, and hegemonic stability theory) and three that hint at some notion of progress, namely democratic peace theory, interdependence, and liberal institutionalism. Of these the democratic peace theory of Doyle (1986) and Russett (1993) seems most clearly to involve the notion of progress and a view of history moving in a direction.

My concern here is very much Foucauldian. I have been enormously influenced by Foucault's method of genealogy (1986), and his work on prisons (1977), madness (1967), medicine (1975), and sexuality (1979, 1987, 1988). From his work a very different picture of international order emerges, and it is clear to me that there is an obvious research project here to examine the genealogy of international order. The main point to make is that Foucault is distrustful of anyone who claims progress in social arrangements. He prefers to see history not as the gradual progressive improvement of humanity but instead as a series of dominations replacing earlier dominations, in each case involving their own patterns of hierarchy, hegemony, bio-power, inclusion, and exclusion. Together these always constitute identities and always discipline subjects. Although I have also been very influenced by Derrida, and I can see very obvious ways in which the relationship between order and disorder could be examined by using his work on difference and logocentrism (see Derrida 1976, 1978, 1982), I will limit my comments to Foucault's concept of genealogy to illustrate my general concerns about the relationship between order and progress.

For Foucault, genealogy involves rejecting the claim that study reveals that which was already there (1986: 78); instead "it disturbs what was previously considered immobile; it fragments what was thought unified" (82). History is not the emergence of the essence of things but "the secret that they have no essence or that their essence was fabricated in a piecemeal fashion" (78). Nor is there a transcendental subject that exists throughout (or outside) history; rather, genealogy's task is "to expose a body totally imprinted by history" (83). Most salient for any discussion of international order are Foucault's comments about genealogy's rejection of either a teleology to history or a notion of progress. For Foucault

only a single drama is ever staged in this "non-place," the endlessly repeated play of dominations . . . Humanity does not gradually progress from combat to combat until it arrives at universal reciprocity, where the rule of law finally replaces warfare; humanity installs each of its violences in a system of rules and thus proceeds from domination to domination . . . Rules are empty in themselves, violent and unfinalized; they are impersonal and can be bent to any purpose. The successes of history belong to those who are capable of seizing these rules, to replace those who had used them, to disguise themselves so as to pervert them, invert their meaning, and redirect them against those who had initially imposed them; controlling this complex mechanism, they will make it function so as to overcome the rulers through their own rules. (85–6)

In short, to understand history is not the slow unraveling of an essential meaning but instead to record the violent appropriation of a system of rules.

Seen in this light, international order has little to do with progress since any new order imposes a series of exclusionary practices on some for the benefit of others. The fact that a new order may be more "peaceful" may simply reflect a change of means for excluding rather than a change of ends. In this sense a new great power order may be more exclusionary and exploitative if it is hegemonic and "peaceful" than if it is not. But Foucault's work also carries with it ideas about resistance, and especially it has the message that power, because it is instantiated in practices, can be resisted more than the meta-narratives may suggest. Yet a Foucauldian view of order directs attention primarily to the thought that any order may be simply another form of domination by one group over another, and that the history of international order is nothing more than one domination replacing another. This is a very different view of international order to that of the writers discussed above, and points to some serious problems for Hall's hopes for a "realism/liberalism mix."

8) What does international order mean in a globalized world?

My final question takes me from a focus on the assumptions of the existing literature on international order, and the assumptions of the other contributions to this volume, towards an alternative post-positivist research agenda for thinking about international order. If the organizing theme for this volume is the question of what will be the nature of international order in the next century, then I want to end by saying something about the relevance of past approaches for thinking about international order in the future.

My starting point is that the world of the next century will be very different to that of the last three centuries because of the effects of globalization. I will not survey the main developments that accompany globalization (see Baylis and Smith 1997) except to point to the fact that the kind of world that is emerging seems to me to be one in which *international* order of any kind will be of little relevance. I think that the next century will see a very different agenda for leaders and academics to deal with than that which has characterized both international relations and the International Relations discipline for the last century.

Ken Booth (1996) has summed up these changes very effectively. He lists 12 developments: 1) from international politics to world politics; 2) from positivism to constitutive theory; 3) from soldiers and diplomats to silenced voices; 4) from history to theory; 5) from strategy to security; 6) from micro-international history to macro-global history; 7) from the past to the future; 8) from Cold War International Relations to global moral science; 9) from romanticizing the state to problematizing it; 10) from high politics to deep politics; 11) from binaries to balance; and 12) from foundations to anchorages. To put it concretely, politics in the globalized world of the next century will be concerned with ethnic conflict, with the environment, with human rights, with migration, with large amounts of small-scale conflict, with economics, and with transnational factors such as disease and crime. In all these cases, international order will be neither effective nor relevant. The world we are moving into will be a world in which sovereignty is less relevant than it is today and in which the values of the society of states are less and less able to cope with the main problems facing humanity. Indeed these problems may require action which involves transgressing the very basis of existing international order.

All of this poses the crucially important question of what a post-positivist research agenda about international order might look like. As will be clear from the other contributions to this volume, the position adopted in this chapter is essentially one of critiquing the mainstream literature on this topic. The obvious charge that can be leveled against my position is that I do not address the research questions deemed central in that literature. Thus, I can be accused (as I was at the conference at which this chapter was first presented) of "ignoring reality." What, it was asked, can social constructivists do about empirical reality? Similarly, it can be noted that both the state and international order are necessary for any project to emancipate human beings. Would not another Cold War make it more difficult to realize any individual-centered strategies? How can I have a research agenda if I cannot give answers to these questions?

The problem of course is that if I try and answer these questions directly, in the language of the research agenda that spawns them, then I have no choice but to debate them within the language of the dominant paradigm, and this axiomatically involves me in a very specific epistemological position, one that provides a warrant for claims both about what exists in the world and about the space for moral and ethical discourse. On the other hand, if I do not deal with them, then I can be accused of failing to deal with some of the dominant issues facing world politics as the new millennium approaches.

My response then will be to make four points about what a post-positivist research agenda might look like. *First,* my point is not that states = bad and non-state actors = good. I am not arguing that it should be left to non-state actors to construct order, either domestically or internationally. I quite take the point that non-state actors can be every bit as undemocratic as state actors; they can be forces for good or for ill. Thus my argument is not that states are the problem; nor is it that international order is "bad." Instead I simply want any discussion of international order to be aware that a focus on the state *automatically* privileges the state over other kinds of actors, as well as privileging it over civil society.

Similarly, focusing on international order privileges international order over other values (such as justice or equality) and over other forms of order. Again, I am not saying that this privileging should be reversed, only that this axiomatic privileging needs to be recognized. In neither case do I think that there is any simple way of resolving this problem as if by fiat; it is ultimately a matter for empirical examination whereby various forms of order and other values can be examined. In other words, my view of the research agenda is for us to move away from overarching general theories of international order towards case-by-case analyses of how international and domestic forces impact on social relations and individuals. I am simply very skeptical of privileging international order, and of privileging order over other values, and I think that in so doing we introduce by the back door a whole set of normative commitments which we justify by pointing to the "empirical reality." It is in this way that anyone questioning the focus on international order can be portrayed as evading intellectual responsibility by being unable to deal with the policy agenda of the dominant states in the international system.

Secondly, I think that as a result of my worries about focusing on international order, we need to deal with questions about the emerging international system by examining in far more detail than hitherto the processes and structures that comprise international order. By this I mean that we need to locate debates about the rise and fall of great powers within a much wider social and historical setting (one wider than that found in John Hall's recent [1996] study), one that does not treat the social world that emerges as simply a resultant of a clash of international/domestic, economic/political forces. Again, this is something to be done on a case-by-case basis and by detailed empirical study. To take one obvious example, the Cold War can be studied as a problem of international order, but it must also be looked at in terms of how the structure of the Cold War created and sustained certain, very specific, identities and interests rather than others; that is to say that the international order of the Cold War can be analyzed in terms of its impact on domestic politics. That international order supported specific economic, social, cultural, and political interests within both the superpower states concerned and within their alliance systems. The hard empirical work comes in looking at how the various structures and processes impacted on one another, and in tracing the correlations between the construction of international order and political and economic interests.

Thirdly, from this it follows that I am not saying that we should simply overthrow all states or undermine sovereignty in every case. As noted above, states are enormously important actors in world politics, and I am saying neither that they are not, nor that other actors should take their place. It is, once again, simply that the entire research agenda on international order privileges both states and sovereignty. I want to investigate just how states and sovereignty may contribute to a worsening of human experiences in many states. In this sense I am claiming that debating international order may be pitching the debate at the wrong level of analysis if our concern is with world (as distinct from international) politics. This implies that my concern will not be with predicting future great power structures but with the constituting effects of these structures on societies, social movements, social relations, and individuals. My interest is thus not with replacing the state or denying its importance as an actor, but with the relationship between its role as the key actor and specific economic and political interests.

Fourthly, I want any discussion of international order to be broadened to involve the following four post-positivist research themes: 1) We need to ask how and in what ways a given international order constructs the identities and interests of actors (be they states, social movements, or individuals). These are usually treated as exogenous to discussions of international order, whereas they are in part constituted by the dominant order. 2) I think that the entire international order literature needs to be read as a discourse of truth, in which the rules for determining what counts as true are a construction of these rules. Thus the obvious objections to my argument from those working on international order gain their persuasive force in large measure because I am not responding to the "self-evident" empirical reality of the international system. It is not that I think it unimportant if there is an arms race in South-East Asia, nor that I am unworried if there is a rise of certain types of repressive states; it is rather that I want to deal with each case on its merits, with "merits" here referring to a range of values and actors. I simply do not want the analysis automatically to side with the powerful, either internationally or within societies. Thus I would be just as worried as the other contributors by the rise of a new Cold War, but I would not simply want to restrict analysis to the international dimension of this problem; nor crucially would I see such an event as the "product" of a set of international "causes." 3) I am particularly concerned with undermining both the "commonsense" and the "practitioners' view" of debates about international order, since I believe that such positions introduce values by an empirical warrant which demarcates the realm of the possible and thereby of the practical. I think these need to be shown as ideological constructs rather than as the "realistic" assessments that they are presented as; only then can their status as ideologies be evaluated alongside other normative commitments. 4) Finally, I want to investigate just how other values and empirical focal points are constituted by an overarching conception of international order; it is not the case that we should ask how international order relates to, say, gender, or culture, but rather how the very concept of international order is unavoidably implicated in the concepts of the international and of order. Given the tendency to present questions of international order as in some way primary, or outside our control, these implications have devastating consequences for the ways in which we think and act about world politics.

Conclusion

In summary, then, my argument is that the tension in work on international order between seeing order as a construct and order as an observable reflects two very different views of the social world. To the extent that order is something we construct, then any order must be grounded ethically, and it is not always clear that most debates about international order have much moral content, especially when their conceptions of international order privilege the state and sovereignty. Much of the time, writers on international order seek to present it as something observable, but the problem here is that this misrepresents what the social world is like, so that normative prescriptions creep in through the back door as consequences of "what the world is like." Since I believe that all discussions about order unavoidably involve normative choices and commitments, I want to point out that it is by no means obvious that a focus on *international* order is preferable to a focus on *world* order. Indeed, I believe that the globalized world of the next century will make international order less and less relevant to the main problems facing humanity and potentially more and more a partial view of order that in fact reflects dominant Western values. In this light, the discourse of international order is a discourse of ideology. Of course it all comes back to the ethical basis of our choices, and it is a matter of judgment whether international order is to be preferred in specific circumstances, but just as there is a tension in Bull's work on order between seeing it as construct and seeing it as observable, so this tension permeates all such discussions. The problem is not that debates about international order involve normative judgments but that some write as if that is not the case, and thereby try to cloak the fundamentally ethical in naturalist clothes.

The emerging international order protects one set of values and freezes the existing distribution of resources in the world. Order may indeed make it more difficult for these to be transferred more equitably, and for the striking inequalities in life chances to be equalized. If one looks at the world and sees great power rivalry and an international order that regulates that potential conflict, that is a choice. Given the dangers posed by any new Cold War it is an understandable focus but it is not self-evidently the only or the most important focus. There are others, and in the next century it is probable that for humanity's sake the existing international order needs to be undermined. This is because that political/military order holds in place an economic and cultural order that is built on exclusion and hierarchy to the detriment of the vast majority of the world's population. In this light, pretending that the "truth" about international order is out there is the ultimate act of political power, and privileging order over justice, the state as actor, and sovereignty as the basis of identity are themselves normative choices. In this light, international order may well be a major source of problems for world politics in the next century, rather than their solution.

NOTES

1 I would like to thank Tim Dunne, Steve Hobden, Nick Wheeler, John Ikenberry, Jack Snyder, and the editors of this volume for their comments on an earlier version of this paper. In particular I would like to thank T. V. Paul and

John Hall for their constructive engagement with my ideas, despite the obvious intellectual disagreements they have with my position.

REFERENCES

Baldwin, David (ed.) 1993, *Neorealism and Neoliberalism: The Contemporary Debate*, New York: Columbia University Press.
Baylis, John and Smith, Steve (eds.) 1997, *The Globalization of World Politics*, Oxford: Oxford University Press.
Booth, Ken 1996, "75 Years On: Rewriting the Subject's Past – Reinventing its Future," in Smith, Booth and Zalewski (eds.), pp. 328–39.
Brown, Chris 1992, *International Relations Theory: New Normative Approaches*, London: Harvester Wheatsheaf.
Bull, Hedley 1977, *The Anarchical Society*, London: Macmillan.
Carr, Edward Hallett 1939, *The Twenty Years' Crisis*, London: Macmillan.
Cox, Robert with Sinclair, Timothy 1996, *Approaches to World Order*, Cambridge: Cambridge University Press.
Derrida, Jacques 1976, *Of Grammatology*, Baltimore: Johns Hopkins University Press.
   1978, *Writing and Difference*, London: Routledge.
   1982, *Margins of Philosophy*, Brighton: Harvester.
Doyle, Michael 1986, "Liberalism and World Politics," *American Political Science Review* 80: 1151–69.
Enloe, Cynthia 1990, *Bananas, Beaches and Bases: Making Feminist Sense of International Politics*, Berkeley: University of California Press.
   1993, *The Morning After: Sexual Politics at the End of the Cold War*, Berkeley: University of California Press.
Falk, Richard 1975, *A Study of Future Worlds*, New York: Free Press.
Foucault, Michel 1967, *Madness and Civilisation: A History of Insanity in the Age of Reason*, London: Tavistock.
   1975, *The Birth of the Clinic: An Archaeology of Medical Perception*, New York: Vintage.
   1977, *Discipline and Punish: The Birth of the Prison*, Harmondsworth: Allen Lane.
   1979, *The History of Sexuality Vol. I: An Introduction*, Harmondsworth: Allen Lane.
   1986, "Nietzsche, Genealogy, History," in *The Foucault Reader*, Paul Rabinow (ed.), Harmondsworth: Peregrine Books, pp. 76–100.
   1987, *The Use of Pleasure: The History of Sexuality Vol. II*, Harmondsworth: Peregrine Books.
   1988, *The Care of the Self: The History of Sexuality Vol. III*, Harmondsworth: Allen Lane.
Hall, John 1996, *International Orders*, Cambridge: Polity Press.
Hollis, Martin and Smith, Steve 1990, *Explaining and Understanding International Relations*, Oxford: Clarendon Press.
Huntington, Samuel 1996, *The Clash of Civilizations and the Remaking of World*

Order, New York: Simon and Schuster.

Kaplan, Morton 1957, *System and Process in International Politics*, New York: John Wiley.

Latham, Robert 1997, *The Liberal Moment*, New York: Columbia University Press.

Linklater, Andrew 1990, *Beyond Realism and Marxism: Critical Theory and International Relations*, Houndmills: Macmillan.

1992, "The Question of the Next Stage in International Relations Theory: A Critical-Theoretical Point of View," *Millennium* 21: 77–98.

Russett, Bruce 1993, *Grasping the Democratic Peace*, Princeton: Princeton University Press.

Smith, Steve 1995, "The Self-Images of a Discipline: A Genealogy of International Relations Theory," in *International Relations Theory Today*, Steve Smith and Ken Booth (eds.), Cambridge: Polity Press, pp. 1–37.

1996, "Positivism and Beyond," in Smith, Booth and Zalewski (eds.), pp. 11–44.

1997, "New Approaches to International Theory," in Baylis and Smith (eds.), pp. 165–90.

Smith, Steve, Booth, Ken and Zalewski, Marysia (eds.) 1996, *International Theory: Positivism and Beyond*, Cambridge: Cambridge University Press.

Vincent, John 1990, "Order in International Politics," in *Order and Violence: Hedley Bull and International Relations*, J. D. B. Miller and J. Vincent (eds.), Oxford: Clarendon Press, pp. 38–64.

Walker, R. B. J. 1993, *Inside/Outside: International Relations as Political Theory*, Cambridge: Cambridge University Press.

Waltz, Kenneth 1979, *Theory of International Politics*, Reading: Addison-Wesley.

Wendt, Alexander 1992, "Anarchy is What States Make of It: A Social Construction of Power Politics," *International Organization* 46: 391–425.

Wheeler, Nicholas 1997, "Agency, Humanitarianism and Intervention," *International Political Science Review* 18: 9–25.

Part II

Contenders: major powers and international order

6   Liberal hegemony and the future of American postwar order

G. John Ikenberry

Introduction

A remarkable aspect of world politics at century's end is the utter dominance of the United States. Fifty years after it emerged hegemonic, the United States is still the dominant world power at the center of a relatively stable and expanding democratic capitalist order. This is surprising. Most observers have expected dramatic shifts in world politics after the Cold War – such as the disappearance of American hegemony, the return of great power balancing, the rise of competing regional blocs, and the decay of multilateralism. Yet despite expectations of great transformations and new world orders, the half-century-old American order is still the dominant reality in world politics today.

This durable American order is a puzzle. Its relative material power capabilities have declined to be sure, but its larger package of political institutions, economic assets, and far-flung relations makes it a resilient and singular world power. The durability of the wider democratic capitalist order is also a puzzle. The conventional view is that the Cold War was an essential "glue" that held the advanced industrial countries together, dampening conflict and facilitating cooperation.[1] Yet even without the Soviet threat and Cold War bipolarity, the United States along with Japan and Western Europe have reaffirmed their alliance partnerships, contained political conflicts, expanded trade and investment between them, and avoided a return to strategic rivalry and great power balance.[2]

The durability of American hegemony and Western order is a puzzle primarily because scholars of international relations have tended to rely on realist theories of balance and hegemony to explain it. Realist theories of balance argue that order and cohesion in the West are a result of cooperation to balance against an external threat, in this case the Soviet Union, and with the disappearance of the threat, alliance and cooperation will decline (Waltz 1979; Mearsheimer 1990b). Realist theories of hegemony argue that order is a result of the concentration of material power capabilities in a single state, which uses its commanding position to create

123

and maintain order. With the decline of hegemonic power, order will decay (Gilpin 1981; see also Krasner 1982; and Rapkin 1990). To understand the continued primacy of the United States and the continued durability and cohesion of the advanced industrial world, we need to go beyond our existing theories of hegemony and balance.

In particular, I want to make three arguments. First, I argue that the basic logic of order among the Western states was set in place before the Cold War, and it was a logic that addressed problems internal to Western capitalism and industrial society. Economic openness, reciprocity, multi-lateral management – these were, and continue to be, the organizing arrangements of a distinctively liberal Western order. Although the Cold War reinforced this liberal order, it was not triggered by or ultimately dependent on the Cold War for its functioning and stability. The "containment order" ended along with the Cold War, but the much more deeply rooted Western liberal order lives on.

Second, I argue that in the wake of World War II, American hegemony was built around decidedly liberal features. Here the problem was how to build a durable and mutually acceptable order among a group of states with huge power asymmetries. The penetrated character of American hegemony, allowing for access by secondary states, and binding economic and security institutions, provided mechanisms to increase confidence that the participating states would remain within the order and operate according to its rules and institutions. Liberal hegemony involves institutions and practices that reduce the returns to power; that is, they reduce the long-term implications of asymmetries of power. Agreement results from a trade-off; the hegemonic state gets commitments by secondary states to participate within the hegemonic order, and in return the hegemon places limits on the exercise of its power. The weaker states are not as inclined to fear domination or abandonment and the leading state does not need to use its power assets to enforce order and compliance.

Third, I argue that the American hegemonic order has actually become more stable because the rules and institutions have become more firmly embedded in the wider structures of politics and society. This is an argument about the increasing returns to institution, in this case American and Western security and economic institutions. Over the decades, the core institutions of Western order have sunk their roots ever more deeply into the political and economic structures of the states that participate within the order. The result is that it is becoming increasingly difficult for "alternative institutions" or "alternative leadership" to seriously emerge. American hegemony has become institutionalized and path-dependent – that is, more and more people will have to disrupt their lives if the order is to radically change. This makes wholesale change less likely.

Overall, the durability of American liberal hegemony is built on two core logics. First, the constitution-like character of the institutions and practices of the order serves to reduce the "returns to power," which lowers the risks of participation by strong and weak states alike. This, in turn, makes a resort to balancing and relative gains competition less necessary. Second, the institutions also exhibit an "increasing returns" character, which makes it more and more difficult for would-be orders and would-be hegemonic powers to compete against and replace the existing order and leader.

The implication of this analysis is that the American hegemonic order is a relatively stable and expansive political order. This is not only because the United States is an unmatched economic and military power today, but also because it is uniquely capable of engaging in "strategic re-straint," reassuring partners and facilitating cooperation. Because of its distinctively penetrated domestic political system, and because of the array of international institutions it has created to manage political con-flict, the United States has been able to remain at the center of a large and expanding hegemonic order. Its capacity to win in specific struggles with others within the system may rise and fall, but the larger hegemonic order remains in place with little prospect of decline.

Two postwar settlements

World War II produced two postwar settlements. One was a reaction to deteriorating relations with the Soviet Union, and it culminated in the containment order. It was a settlement based on the balance of power, nuclear deterrence, and political and ideological competition. The other settlement was a reaction to the economic rivalry and political turmoil of the 1930s and the resulting world war, and it culminated in a wide range of new institutions and relations among the Western industrial democ-racies – a Western liberal order. This settlement was built around eco-nomic openness, political reciprocity, multilateral institutions, and joint management of relations (Ikenberry 1996).

The Cold War did play a role in reinforcing Western solidarity by dampening incentives to engage in relative gains competition. Cold War threats were also useful to American officials as they sought to convince an otherwise reluctant Congress to appropriate funds for postwar recon-struction and assistance. Cold War bipolarity also gave the United States added hegemonic leverage at critical moments in the management of Western order. But the two settlements had distinct political visions, intellectual rationales, political logics, and (as has become clear lately) historical trajectories.

The containment order is well known in the popular imagination. It is celebrated in our historical accounts of the early years after World War II, when intrepid American officials struggled to make sense of Soviet military power and geopolitical intentions. In these early years, a few "wise men" fashioned a coherent and reasoned response to the global challenge of Soviet communism (see Isaacson and Thomas 1986). The doctrine of containment that emerged was the core concept that gave clarity and purpose to several decades of American foreign policy. In the decades that followed, sprawling bureaucratic and military organizations were built on the containment orientation. The bipolar division of the world, nuclear weapons of growing size and sophistication, the ongoing clash of two expansive ideologies – all these circumstances gave life to and reinforced the centrality of the containment order.

By comparison, the ideas and policies of Western liberal order were more diffuse and wide-ranging. It was less obvious that the liberal democratic agenda was a "grand strategy" designed to advance American security interests. As a result, during the Cold War it was inevitable that this agenda would be seen as secondary – a preoccupation of economists and American business. The policies and institutions that supported free trade and economic openness among the advanced industrial societies were quintessentially the stuff of "low politics." But this view is wrong. The liberal democratic agenda was built on a robust and sophisticated set of ideas about American security interests, the causes of war and depression, and the proper and desirable foundations of postwar political order. Indeed, although the containment order overshadowed it, the ideas behind postwar liberal democratic order were more deeply rooted in the American experience and a thoroughgoing understanding of history, economics, and the sources of political order.

The most basic conviction behind the postwar liberal agenda was that the closed autarkic regions that had contributed to world depression and split the world into competing blocs before the war must be broken up and replaced by an open and nondiscriminatory world economic system. Peace and security were impossible in a world of closed and exclusive economic regions. The challengers to liberal multilateralism occupied almost every corner of the advanced industrial world. Germany and Japan, of course, were the most overt and hostile challengers. Each had pursued a dangerous pathway into the modern industrial age that combined authoritarian capitalism with military dictatorship and coercive regional autarky. But the British Commonwealth and its imperial preference system was also a challenge to liberal multilateral order (see Cumings 1991; and Maier 1987). The hastily drafted Atlantic Charter was an American effort to insure that Britain signed onto its liberal democratic war aims.[3] The joint statement of principles affirmed free trade, equal access for countries to the raw materials of the world, and international collaboration in the economic field so as to advance labor standards, employment security, and social welfare. Roosevelt and Churchill insisted on telling the world that they had learned the lessons of the interwar years – and those lessons were fundamentally about the proper organization of the Western world economy. It was not just America's enemies, but also its friends and America itself, that had to be reformed and integrated.

This liberal "grand strategy" for building order within the Western world reflected a confluence of ideas and designs from a wide array of American officials and thinkers involved in making postwar policy. One group, located primarily at the State Department and inspired by Cordell Hull, was primarily interested in creating an open trading system after the war. They gave voice to the old liberal view that free trade and open economies would check tyranny and military aggression and reinforce peaceful international relations. Trade officials at the State Department saw liberal trade as a core American interest that reached back to the Open Door policy of the 1890s (see Gardner 1964; Eckes 1995). Their argument was not just that free trade would advance American interests, but that an open trading system was an essential element of a stable world political order.

Another group of thinkers was concerned with creating political order among the democracies of the North Atlantic region. This vision was of a community or union between the United States, Britain, and the wider Atlantic world. Ideas of an Atlantic union can be traced to the turn of the century and a few British and American statesmen and thinkers, such as John Hay, British Ambassador to Washington Lord Bryce, American Ambassador to London Walter Hines Page, Admiral Alfred T. Mahan, and Henry Adams. These ideas resurfaced during and after World War II, reflecting a variety of convictions and historical experiences: that the failure of the League of Nations revealed the virtues of a less universal security community; and that there was a pressing need to protect the shared democratic values and institutions that united the Atlantic world (Lippmann 1943; Streit 1939).

Another position on postwar order was animated more directly by considerations of American geopolitical interests and the Eurasian rimlands. This is where American strategic thinkers began their debates in the 1930s, as they witnessed the collapse of the world economy and the emergence of German and Japanese regional blocs. The question these thinkers pondered was whether the United States could remain as a great industrial power within the confines of the Western Hemisphere. What were the minimum geographical requirements for the country's economic and military viability? For all practical purposes this question was answered by the time the United States entered the war. An American hemispheric bloc would not be sufficient; the United States must have security of markets and raw materials in Asia and Europe. If the rimlands of Europe and Asia became dominated by one or several hostile imperial powers, the security implications for the United States would be catastrophic. To remain a great power, the United States could not allow itself "merely to be a buffer state between the mighty empires of Germany and Japan" (Spykman 1942: 195). It must seek openness, access, and balance in Europe and Asia.

Finally, a related view of postwar order was concerned with encouraging political and economic unity in Western Europe, creating in effect a European "third force." This view emerged as a strategic option as cooperation with the Soviet Union began to break down after the war. As officials in the State Department began to rethink relations with Western Europe and the Soviet Union, a new policy emphasis emerged concerned with the establishment of a strong and economically integrated Europe. The idea was to encourage a multipolar postwar system, with Europe as a relatively independent center of power.[4] The policy shift was not to a bipolar or spheres-of-influence approach with a direct and ongoing American military and economic presence in Europe. Rather, the aim was to build Europe into an independent center of military and economic power.

These various positions on postwar order reflect the diversity of agendas and problems that officials sought to address – but they shared an underlying view that the major Western industrial powers must be united and interconnected in new and fundamental ways. Several additional conclusions follow. First, it is clear that sophisticated and well-developed sets of ideas and plans about postwar order predated the rise of bipolarity and containment. Indeed, it is remarkable how late and reluctant the United States was in organizing its foreign policy around a global balance of power.

Second, most of the ideas that were proposed and debated before containment and the breakdown of relations with the Soviet Union dealt with the reconstruction of relations within the West, particularly among the Atlantic countries. American officials were clearly preoccupied with how to stabilize Europe and integrate the Atlantic world into the core of a wider postwar order. Some postwar designs were more universal, such as those concerning free trade and global governance, but they also were to be anchored in a deepened set of relations and institutions among the Western democracies. Other ideas, such as the geopolitical arguments about access to the Eurasian rimlands, saw the stability and integration of the liberal capitalist world in essentially instrumental terms. But the goals and policies would have the same result. Likewise, many who supported NATO and containment did so not simply to build an alliance against the Soviet Union but also because these initiatives would feed back into the Western liberal democratic order. NATO was partly a structure designed to reintegrate Germany into the West – partly to counter Soviet power, but also to reconstruct and reintegrate Germany as a liberal capitalist country. It was both a means and an end (Hampton 1995: 610–56; and 1996).

Third, even many of the advocates of containment and the preservation of the European balance were also concerned with safeguarding and strengthening liberal democratic institutions in the West. One virtue that Kennan saw in a multipolar postwar order was that it would help to protect the liberal character of American politics and institutions. Kennan worried that if bipolar order emerged, the United States might find itself trying to impose political institutions on other states within its sphere and that would eventually threaten its domestic institutions.[5] The encouragement of dispersed authority and power centers abroad would reinforce pluralism at home.

American postwar thinkers and planners did not wait until the Cold War clarified necessary principles and policies of American foreign policy. Those ideas and policies were already actively being formulated, debated, and implemented. The postwar liberal democratic settlement among the Western industrial countries reflected a synthesis of various intellectual, historical, and political strands of thinking and experience. But in this amalgam of ideas and agendas was a vision of America's basic postwar goal – to secure an open, stable, interconnected, legitimate, and jointly managed community of Western industrial democracies.

Limiting the returns to power

The United States had a postwar agenda to build a new structure of relations among the industrial Western powers. But how actually was agreement secured? How was it that American dominance was rendered acceptable to the Western Europeans and Japanese? Why was it that the Europeans and Japanese did not balance against American power, returning the industrial countries to a world of strategic rivalry, fragmentation, and estrangement? How were American hegemony and the great upheaval of the war turned into a widely acceptable political order?

The answer is that the United States engaged (through policy and structural circumstance) in "strategic restraint," thereby reassuring its would-be European and Asian partners that participation in the American postwar order would not entail coercive domination. In other words, the United States gained the acquiescence of secondary states by accepting limits on the exercise of its own hegemonic power. At the heart of the American hegemonic order is an ongoing trade-off: the United States agrees to operate within an institutionalized political process and, in return, its partners agree to be willing participants.

This logic is seen most clearly in the immediate aftermath of World War II, when the asymmetries in power relations between the United States and the other Western industrial countries were most extreme. At such moments, there are incentives for the victorious and suddenly hegemonic state to construct a postwar order that is legitimate and durable. That is, there are incentives for the leading state to convert its favorable postwar power position into a durable political order that commands the allegiance of the other states within it. To achieve a legitimate order means to secure agreement among the relevant states on the basic rules and principles of political order. A legitimate political order is one whose members willingly participate and agree with the overall orientation of the system (Beetham 1991). They abide by its rules and principles because they accept them as desirable – they embrace them as their own.

More specifically, the newly emerged hegemon has an incentive to move toward a "constitutional" settlement after the war – that is, to create basic institutions and operating principles that limit what the leading state can do with its power.[6] In effect, constitutional agreements reduce the implications of "winning" in international relations, or, to put it more directly, they serve to reduce the returns to power. This is fundamentally what constitutions do within domestic orders. They set limits on what a state that gains disproportionately within the order can do with those gains, thereby reducing the stakes of uneven gains (Elster and Slagstad 1988). This means that they reduce the possibilities that a state can turn short-term gains into a long-term power advantage. Taken together, constitutional agreements set limits on what actors can do with momentary advantages. Losers realize that their losses are limited and temporary – to accept those losses is not to risk everything nor will it give the winner a permanent advantage.

If agreements can be reached on constitutional arrangements after the war, the asymmetries in power are rendered more tolerable by secondary states. This is potentially an attractive outcome for weaker states for two reasons. First, if the actions of the hegemonic state are carried out (more or less) within an agreed upon and institutionalized political process, it means that competition over outcomes will not simply be determined by brute material power, which will always work to the advantage of the leading state. Second, the institutionalized settlement creates greater certainty over what the hegemonic state will do in the future. The possibility of indiscriminate and ruthless domination is mitigated. Just as importantly, the possibility of abandonment is also lessened. If the hegemonic state is rendered more predictable, this means that the secondary states do not need to spend as many resources on "risk premiums," which would otherwise be needed to prepare for either domination or abandonment.

But why would a newly hegemonic state want to restrict itself by agreeing to limits on the use of hegemonic power? The basic answer is that a constitutional settlement conserves hegemonic power, and this for two reasons. First, if the hegemonic state calculates that its overwhelming postwar power advantages are only momentary, an institutionalized order might "lock in" favorable arrangements that continue beyond the zenith of its power. In effect, the creation of basic ordering institutions is a form of hegemonic investment in the future. The hegemonic state gives up some freedom on the use of its power in exchange for a durable and predictable order that safeguards its interests in the future.

This investment motive rests on several assumptions. The hegemonic state must be convinced that its power position will ultimately decline. If it does, it should want to use its momentary position to get things that it wants accomplished. On the other hand, if the new hegemon calculates that its power position will remain preponderant into the foreseeable future, the incentive to conserve its power will disappear. Also, the hegemon must be convinced that the institutions it creates will persist beyond its own power capabilities – that is, it must calculate that these institutions have some independent ordering capacity.[7] If institutions are seen as simply isomorphic with the distribution of power, the appeal of an institutional settlement will obviously decline.

The second reason why a hegemon might want to reach agreement on basic institutions, even if it means giving up some autonomy and short-term advantage, is that is can reduce the "enforcement costs" for maintaining order. The constant use of power capabilities to punish and reward secondary states and resolve conflicts is costly. It is far more effective over the long term to shape the interests and orientations of other states than to directly shape their actions through coercion and inducements.[8] A constitutional settlement reduces the necessity of the costly expenditure of resources by the leading state on bargaining, monitoring, and enforcement.

Even if there are reasons why the leading and secondary states might favor a constitutional order, it is not obvious that they would accept the risks seemingly inherent in such an order. The leading state, in placing limits on its use of power, must be confident that it will not be exploited by secondary states, and secondary states must be confident that they are not opening themselves up to domination or abandonment by the leading state. In effect, each state agrees to forswear a range of actions that, in the absence of guarantees that the other state will also abide by the limits, it would be prudent to pursue. For self-regarding states to agree to pursue their interests within binding institutions, they must convey to each other a credible sense of commitment – an assurance that they will not abandon their mutual restraint and exploit momentary advantages.[9]

There were a variety of ways in which the United States and its prospective partners were able to overcome these constraints and create reassurances and credible commitments – all of which reflect the remarkably liberal character of American hegemony. These include America's policy of "strategic restraint" over postwar order; the "penetrated" character of American hegemony, which provides opportunities for voice and reciprocity in hegemonic relations; and the use of "institutional binding" as a mechanism to mutually constrain the hegemon and secondary states. In each of these ways, the postwar order was established in a way that served to limit the returns to power.

The first way in which the United States provided reassurances to its partners was in its basic orientation toward postwar order – that it was a "reluctant hegemon" in many respects, and that it fundamentally sought agreement among the Western states on a mutually acceptable order, even if this meant extensive compromise. It is revealing that the initial and most forcefully presented American view on postwar order was the State Department's proposal for a postwar system of free trade. This proposal did not only reflect an American conviction about the virtues of open markets, but it also was a vision of order that would require very little direct American involvement or management (Ikenberry 1989). The system would be largely self-regulating, leaving the United States to operate within it, but without the burdens of direct and ongoing supervision.

This view on postwar trade reflected a more general American orientation as the war came to an end. It wanted a world order that would advance American interests, but it was not eager to actively organize and run that order. It is in this sense that the United States was a reluctant superpower (Holt 1995; Lundestad 1986). This general characteristic was not lost on Europeans, and it mattered as America's potential partners contemplated whether and how to cooperate with the United States. To the extent the United States could convey the sense that it did not seek to dominate the Europeans, it gave greater credibility to America's proposals for a constitutional settlement. It provided some reassurance that the United States would operate within limits and not use its overwhelming power position simply to dominate.

This orientation was reflected in the compromises that the United States made in accommodating European views about the postwar world economy. The British and the continental Europeans, worried about postwar depression and the protection of their fragile economies, were not eager to embrace America's stark proposals for an open world trading system, favoring a more regulated and compensatory system.[10] The United States did attempt to use its material resources to pressure and induce Britain and the other European countries to abandon bilateral and regional preferential agreements and accept the principles of a postwar economy organized around a nondiscriminatory system of trade and payments.[11] The United States knew it held a commanding position and sought to use its power to give the postwar order a distinctive shape. But it also prized agreement over deadlock, and it ultimately moved a great distance away from its original proposals in setting up the various postwar economic institutions (Ikenberry 1991/2).

A second major way that the United States projected reassurance was structural – its own liberal democratic polity. The open and decentralized character of the American political system provided opportunities for other states to exercise their "voice" in the operation of the American hegemonic order, thereby reassuring these states that their interests could be actively advanced and processes of conflict resolution would exist. In this sense, the American postwar order was a "penetrated hegemony," an extended system that blurred domestic and international politics as it created an elaborate transnational and transgovernmental political system with the United States at its center (Deudney and Ikenberry 1996).

There are actually several ways in which America's penetrated hegemony serves to reinforce the credibility of the United States' commitment to operating within an institutionalized political order. The first is simply the transparency of the system, which reduces surprises and allays worries by partners that the United States might make abrupt changes in policy. This transparency comes from the fact that policy-making in a large, decentralized democracy involves many players and an extended and relatively visible political process. But not only is it an open and decentralized system, it is also one with competing political parties and an independent press – features that serve to expose the underlying integrity and viability of major policy commitments. The open and competitive process may produce mixed and ambiguous policies at times, but the transparency of the process at least allows other states to make more accurate calculations about the likely direction of American foreign policy, which lowers levels of uncertainty and provides a measure of reassurance – which, everything else being equal, provides greater opportunities to cooperate.

Another way in which the penetrated hegemonic order provides reassurances to partners is that the American system invites (or at least provides opportunities for) the participation of outsiders. The fragmented and penetrated American system allows and invites the proliferation of a vast network of transnational and transgovernmental relations with Europe, Japan, and other parts of the industrial world. Diffuse and dense networks of governmental, corporate, and private associations tie the system together. The United States is the primary site for the pulling and hauling of trans-Atlantic and trans-Pacific politics. Europeans and Japanese do not have elected officials in Washington – but they do have representatives.[12] Although this access to the American political process is not fully reciprocated abroad, the openness and extensive decentralization of the American liberal system assures other states that they have routine access to the decision-making processes of the United States.

A final way in which reassurance was mutually conveyed was in the institutions themselves, which provided "lock in" and "binding" constraints on the United States and its partners, thereby mitigating fears of domination or abandonment. The Western countries made systematic efforts to anchor their joint commitments in principled and binding institutional mechanisms. Governments might ordinarily seek to preserve their options, to cooperate with other states but to leave open the option of disengaging. What the United States and the other Western states did after the war was exactly the opposite: they built long-term economic, political, and security commitments that were difficult to retract. They "locked in" their commitments and relationships, to the extent that this can be done by sovereign states.[13]

The practice of institutional binding makes sense only if international institutions or regimes can have an independent ordering impact on the actions of states.[14] The assumption is that institutions are sticky – that they can take on a life and logic of their own, shaping and constraining even the states that create them. When states employ institutional binding as a strategy, they are essentially agreeing to mutually constrain themselves. In effect, institutions specify what it is that states are expected to do and they make it difficult and costly for states to do otherwise.[15] In the case of international institutions, examples of binding mechanisms include treaties, interlocking organizations, joint management responsibilities, agreed upon standards and principles of relations, and so forth. These mechanisms raise the "costs of exit" and create "voice opportunities," thereby providing mechanisms to mitigate or resolve the conflict.[16]

The Bretton Woods economic and monetary accords exhibit the institutional binding logic. These were the first accords to establish a permanent international institutional and legal framework to ensure economic cooperation between states. They were constructed as elaborate systems of rules and obligations with quasi-judicial procedures for adjudicating disputes (James 1995). In effect, the Western governments created an array of functionally organized transnational political systems. Moreover, the democratic character of the United States and the other Western countries facilitated the construction of these dense interstate connections. The permeability of domestic institutions provided congenial grounds for reciprocal and pluralistic "pulling and hauling" across the advanced industrial world.

It was here that the Cold War's security alliances provided additional institutional binding opportunities. The old saying that NATO was created to "keep the Russians out, the Germans down, and the Americans in" is a statement about the importance of the alliance structures for locking in long-term commitments and expectations. The American-Japanese security alliance also had a similar "dual containment" character. These institutions not only served as alliances in the ordinary sense as organized efforts to balance against external threats, they also provided mechanisms and venues to build political relations, conduct business, and regulate conflict (Schroeder 1976).

The constitutional features of the Western order have been particularly important for Germany and Japan. Both countries were reintegrated into the advanced industrial world as "semi-sovereign" powers; that is, they accepted unprecedented constitutional limits on their military capacity and independence (Katzenstein 1987).[17] As such, they became unusually dependent on the array of Western regional and multilateral economic and security institutions. The Western political order in which they were embedded was integral to their stability and functioning. The Christian Democrat Walther Leisler Kiep argued in 1972 that "the German-American alliance . . . is not merely one aspect of modern German history, but a decisive element as a result of its preeminent place in our politics. In effect, it provides a second constitution for our country" (Schwartz 1995: 555). Western economic and security institutions provide Germany and Japan with a political bulwark of stability that far transcends their more immediate and practical purposes.

Overall, American hegemony is reluctant, penetrated, and highly institutionalized. All these characteristics have helped to facilitate a rather stable and durable political order. American strategic restraint after the war left Europeans more worried about abandonment than domination, and they actively sought American institutionalized commitments to Europe. The American polity's transparency and permeability fostered an "extended" political order – reaching outward to the other industrial democracies – with most of its roads leading to Washington. Transnational and transgovernmental relations provide the channels. Multiple layers of economic, political, and security institutions bind these countries together in ways that reinforce the credibility of their mutual commitments. The United States remains the center of the system, but other states are highly integrated into it, and its legitimacy diminishes the need for the exercise of coercive power by the United States or for balancing responses from secondary states.

American hegemony and increasing returns

The bargains struck and institutions created at the early moments of American hegemony have not simply persisted for fifty years, but they have actually become more deeply rooted in the wider structures of politics and society of the countries that participate within the order. That is, more people and more of their activities are hooked into the institutions and operations of the American liberal hegemonic order. A wider array of individuals and groups, in more countries and more realms of activity, has a stake – or a vested interest – in the continuation of the system. The costs of disruption or change in this system have steadily grown over the decades. Together, this means that "competing orders" or "alternative institutions" are at a disadvantage. The system is increasingly hard to replace.

The reason institutions have a "lock in" effect is primarily because of the phenomenon of increasing returns. There are several aspects to increasing returns to institutions. First, there are large initial start-up costs to creating new institutions. Even when alternative institutions might be more efficient or accord more closely with the interests of powerful states, the gains from the new institutions must be overwhelmingly greater before they overcome the sunk costs of the existing institutions.[18] Moreover, there tend to be learning effects that are achieved in the operation of the existing institution that give it advantages over a new start-up institution. Finally, institutions tend to create relations and commitments with other actors and institutions that serve to embed the institution and raise the costs of change. Taken together, as Douglass North concludes, "the interdependent web of an institutional matrix produces massive increasing returns" (North 1990: 95).[19]

When institutions manifest increasing returns, it becomes very difficult for potential replacement institutions to compete and succeed. The logic is seen most clearly in regard to competing technologies. The history of the videocassette recorder is the classic example, where two formats, VHS and Beta, competed for standardization. The two formats were introduced at roughly the same time and initially had equal market share, but soon the VHS format, through luck and circumstances unrelated to efficiency, expanded its market share. Increasing returns on early gains tilted the competition toward VHS, allowing it to accumulate enough advantages to take over the market (Arthur 1995). Even if Beta was ultimately a superior technology, a very small market advantage by VHS at an early and critical moment allowed it to lower its production costs, and the accumulation of connecting technologies and products that require compatibility made it increasingly hard for the losing technology to compete. The costs of switching to the other technology rise as production costs are lowered, learning effects accumulate, and the technology gets embedded in a wider system of compatible and interdependent technologies (Arthur 1989).

American postwar hegemonic order has exhibited this phenomenon of increasing returns to its institutions. At the early moments after 1945, when the imperial, bilateral, and regional alternatives to America's postwar agenda were most imminent, the United States was able to use its unusual and momentary advantages to tilt the system in the direction it desired. The pathway to the present liberal hegemonic order began at a very narrow passage where really only Britain and the United States – and a few top officials – could shape decisively the basic orientation of the world political economy. But once the institutions, such as Bretton Woods and GATT, were established, it became increasingly hard for competing visions of postwar order to have any viability. America's great burst of institution-building after World War II fits a general pattern of international continuity and change: crisis or war opens up a moment of flux and opportunity, choices get made, and interstate relations get fixed or settled for a while.

The notion of increasing returns to institutions means that once a moment of institutional selection comes and goes, the cost of large-sale institutional change rises dramatically – even if potential institutions, when compared with existing ones, are more efficient and desirable.[20] In terms of American hegemony, this means that, short of a major war or a global economic collapse, it is very difficult to envisage the type of historical breakpoint needed to replace the existing order. This would be true even if a new would-be hegemon or coalition of states had an interest in and agenda for an alternative set of global institutions – which they do not.

While the increasing returns to institutions can serve to perpetuate institutions of many sorts, American hegemonic institutions have characteristics that particularly lend themselves to increasing returns. First, the set of principles that infuses these institutions – particularly principles of multilateralism, openness, and reciprocity – are ones that command agreement because of their seeming fairness and legitimacy. Organized around principles that are easy for states to accept, regardless of their specific international power position, the institutional pattern is more robust and easy to expand. Moreover, the principled basis of hegemonic order also makes it more durable. This is Ruggie's argument about the multilateral organization of postwar international institutions: "all other things being equal, an arrangement based on generalized organizing principles should be more elastic than one based on particularistic interests and situational exigencies" (Ruggie 1993: 32–3). Potential alternative institutional orders are at an added disadvantage because the principles of the current institutional order are adaptable, expandable, and easily accepted as legitimate.

Second, the open and permeable character of American hegemonic institutions also serves to facilitate increasing returns. One of the most important aspects of increasing returns is that once a particular institution is established, other institutions and relations tend to grow up around it and become interconnected and mutually dependent. A good analogy is computer software, where a software provider like Microsoft, after gaining an initial market advantage, encourages the proliferation of software applications and programs based on Microsoft's operating language. This, in turn, leads to a huge complex of providers and users who are heavily dependent on the Microsoft format. The result is an expanding market community of individuals and firms with an increasingly dense set of commitments to Microsoft – commitments that are not based on loyalty but on the growing reality that changing to another format would be more costly, even if it were more efficient.

The penetrated character of American hegemony encourages this sort of proliferation of connecting groups and institutions. A dense set of transnational and transgovernmental channels are woven into the trilateral regions of the advanced industrial world. A sort of layer cake of inter-governmental institutions spans outward from the United States across the Atlantic and Pacific. Global multilateral economic institutions, such as the IMF and WTO, are connected to more circumscribed governance institutions, such as the G7 and G10. Private groups, such as the Trilateral Commission and hundreds of business trade associations, are also connected in one way or another to individual governments and their joint management institutions. The steady rise of trade and investment across the advanced industrial world has made these countries more interdependent, which in turn has expanded the constituency within these countries for a perpetuation of an open, multilateral system.

What this means is that great shifts in the basic organization of the American hegemonic order are increasingly costly to a widening array of individuals and groups who make up the order. More and more people have a stake in the system, even if they have no particular loyalty or affinity for the United States and even if they might really prefer a different order. As the postwar era has worn on, the operating institutions of the American hegemonic order have expanded and deepened. More and more people would have their lives disrupted if the system were to be radically changed – which is another way of saying that the constituency for preserving the postwar political order among the major industrial countries is greater than ever before. It is in this sense that the American postwar order is stable and growing.

Conclusion

The twentieth century began as a world dominated by a handful of great powers, but it will end dominated by a single superpower. The character of that domination is as interesting and remarkable as the fact of its existence. American domination or hegemony is very unusual, and the larger political order that surrounds it is unique as well. Fundamentally, American hegemony is reluctant, penetrated, and highly institutionalized – or in a word, liberal. This is what makes it unusual, and it is also what makes it so stable and expansive.

Even with the end of the Cold War and the shifting global distribution of power, the relations between the United States and the other industrial countries of Europe and Asia remain remarkably stable and cooperative. This chapter offers two major reasons why American hegemony has endured and facilitated cooperation and integration among the major industrial countries rather than triggered balancing and estrangement. Both reasons underscore the importance of the liberal features of American hegemony.

First, the United States moved very quickly after the war to insure that relations among the liberal democracies would take place within an institutionalized political process. In effect, the United States offered the other countries a bargain: if the United States agreed to operate within mutually acceptable institutions, thereby muting the implications of power asymmetries, the other countries would agree to be willing participants as well. The United States got the acquiescence of the other Western states, and they in turn got the reassurance that the United States would neither dominate nor abandon them.

The stability of this bargain comes from its underlying logic: the postwar hegemonic order is infused with institutions and practices that reduce the returns to power. This means that the implications of winning and losing are minimized and contained. A state could "lose" in intra-Western relations and yet not worry that the winner will be able to use those winnings to permanently dominate. This is a central characteristic of domestic liberal constitutional orders. Parties that win elections must operate within well-defined limits. They cannot use their powers of incumbency to undermine or destroy the opposition party. They can press the advantage of office to the limits of the law, but there are limits and laws. This reassures the losing party; it can accept its loss and prepare for the next election. The features of the postwar order – and, importantly, the open and penetrated character of the American polity itself – have mechanisms to provide the same sort of assurances to America's European and Asian partners.

Secondly, the institutions of American hegemony also have a durability that comes from the phenomenon of increasing returns. The overall system – organized around principles of openness, reciprocity, and multilateralism – has become increasingly connected to the wider and deeper institutions of politics and society within the advanced industrial world. As the embeddedness of these institutions has grown, it has become increasingly difficult for potential rival states to introduce a competing set of principles and institutions. American hegemony has become highly institutionalized and path-dependent. Short of large-scale war or a global economic crisis, the American hegemonic order appears to be immune from would-be hegemonic challengers. Even if a large coalition of states had interests that favored an alternative type of order, to justify change, the benefits would have to be radically higher than are those that flow from the present system. But there is no potential hegemonic state (or coalition of states) and no set of rival principles and organizations even on the horizon. The world of the 1940s contained far more rival systems, ideologies, and interests than the world of the 1990s.

The phenomenon of increasing returns is really a type of positive feedback loop. If initial institutions are established successfully, where the United States and its partners have confidence in their credibility and functioning, this allows these states to make choices that serve to strengthen the binding character of these institutions.

The American hegemonic order fits this basic logic. Its open and penetrated character invites participation and creates assurances of steady commitment. Its institutionalized character also provides mechanisms for the resolution of conflicts and creates assurances of continuity. Within this liberal and institutionalized order, the fortunes of particular states will continue to rise and fall. The United States itself, while remaining at the center of the order, also continues to experience gains and losses. But the mix of winning and losing across the system is distributed widely enough to mitigate the interest that particular states might have in replacing it. In an order where the returns to power are low and the returns to institutions are high, stability will be its essential feature.

NOTES

1 As Robert Lieber argues: "In the past, the Soviet threat and the existence of an American-led bloc to contain it placed limits on the degree of friction that could develop among the Western partners and Japan for fear of diminishing common security" (Lieber 1997: 10). This point is also made in Oye (1992).

2 On anticipations of increasing conflict and fragmentation of relations within the West after the Cold War, see Calleo (1996) and Mearsheimer (1990a).

3 Churchill insisted that the charter did not mandate the dismantlement of the British empire and its system of trade preferences, and only the last-minute sidestepping of this controversial issue insured agreement. See Gardner (1994).

4 This position was articulated by George Kennan and the State Department's Policy Planning staff. See Gaddis (1987).

5 See the discussion of Kennan's speech at the Naval War College in October 1948 in Gaddis (1987: 43–4). See also Weber (1995: 241).

6 This argument is developed in Ikenberry (1998). See also Stone (1994: 441–74).

7 The argument that international regimes and institutions, once created, can have an independent ordering impact on states comes in several versions. The weak version of this claim is the modified structural realist position that sees lags in the shifts of regimes as power and interests change. See Krasner (1983: 1–12). The stronger version entails assumptions about path dependency and increasing returns. For a survey, see Powell and DiMaggio (1991).

8 The argument that hegemons will want to promote normative consensus among states so as to reduce the necessity of coercive management of the order is presented in Ikenberry and Kupchan (1990).

9 For a discussion of the general problem of credible commitment and its importance to institutional development and the rule of law, see Weingast and North (1989).

10 The strongest claims about American and European differences over postwar political economy are made by Block (1977: 70–122).

11 The 1946 British Loan deal was perhaps the most overt effort by the Truman administration to tie American postwar aid to specific policy concessions by allied governments. This was the failed Anglo-American Financial Agreement, which obliged the British to make sterling convertible in exchange for American assistance. See Richard Gardner (1969) and Eckes (1971).

12 For the transnational political process channeled through the Atlantic security institutions, see Risse-Kappen (1995). On the US-Japanese side, see Katzenstein and Tsujinaka (1995).

13 For an argument about why democratic states are particularly inclined to

engage in "binding," see Deudney (1996).

14 In other words, the assumption is that under some circumstances, institutions can be more than simply "solutions" for states seeking to reduce uncertainty and alter transaction costs. For a discussion of this more limited, "rationalistic" understanding of institutions, see Keohane (1988).

15 This view accords with our general view of what institutions are and do. As Lorenzo Ornaghi argues: "the role of institutions in politics is to give the rules of the game, in that, by reducing the uncertain and unforeseeable character of interpersonal relations, insurance is mutually provided"(1990: 27).

16 For a preliminary attempt to use this logic of binding to explain European union, see Grieco (1995: 21–40).

17 For a discussion of Japanese semi-sovereignty and the postwar peace constitution, see Tamamoto (1995).

18 On sunk costs, see Stinchcombe (1968).

19 For discussions of path dependency arguments and their implications, see Krasner (1984) and Pierson (1993).

20 This notion of breakpoint is not developed in the increasing returns literature, but it is implicit, and it is very important for understanding the path dependency of American hegemony.

REFERENCES

Arthur, W. Brian 1989, "Competing Technologies, Increasing Returns, and Lock-In by Historical Small Events," *The Economic Journal* 99 (March): 116–31.

1990, "Positive Feedbacks in the Economy," *Scientific American* February 1990, pp. 92–9.

Beetham, David 1991, *The Legitimation of Power*, London: Macmillan.

Block, Fred 1977, *The Origins of International Economic Disorder*, Berkeley: University of California Press, pp. 70–122.

Calleo, David P. 1996, "Restarting the Marxist Clock? The Economic Fragility of the West," *World Policy Journal* 13: 57–64.

Cumings, Bruce 1991, "The End of the Seventy Years' Crisis: Trilateralism and the New World Order," *World Policy Journal* 8: 195–222.

Deudney, Daniel 1996, "Binding Sovereigns: The Practices, Structures, and Geopolitics of Philadelphian Systems," in *Constructing Sovereignty*, Thomas Biersteker and Cynthia Weber (eds.), New York: Cambridge University Press, pp. 190–239.

Deudney, Daniel and Ikenberry, G. John 1996, "Structural Liberalism: The Nature and Sources of Western Political Order," *Working Paper*, Christopher Browne Center, The University of Pennsylvania.

Eckes, Alfred E., Jr. 1971, *A Search for Solvency: Bretton Woods and the International Monetary System, 1944–1971*, Austin: University of Texas Press.

1995, *Opening America's Market*, Chapel Hill: The University of North Carolina Press, ch. 5.

Elster, Jon and Slagstad, Rune (eds.) 1988, *Constitutionalism and Democracy*, New York: Cambridge University Press.

Gaddis, John Lewis 1982, *Strategies of Containment*, New York: Oxford University Press.

1987, *The Long Peace*, New York: Oxford University Press.

Gardner, Lloyd C. 1964, *Economic Aspects of New Deal Diplomacy*, Madison: University of Wisconsin Press.

1994, "The Atlantic Charter: Idea and Reality, 1942–1945," in *The Atlantic Charter*, Douglas Brinkley and David R. Facey-Crowther (eds.), London: Macmillan, pp. 45–81.

Gardner, Richard 1969, *Sterling-Dollar Diplomacy*, New York: McGraw Hill.

Gilpin, Robert 1981, *War and Change in World Politics*, New York: Cambridge University Press.

Grieco, Joseph 1995, "The Maastricht Treaty, Economic and Monetary Union and the Neo-Realist Research Programme," *Review of International Studies* 21: 21–40.

Hampton, Mary N. 1995, "NATO at the Creation: US Foreign Policy, West Germany and the Wilsonian Impulse," *Security Studies* 4: 610–56.

1996, *The Wilsonian Impulse: U.S. Foreign Policy, the Alliance, and German Unification*, Westport: Praeger.

Holt, Richard 1995, *The Reluctant Superpower*, New York: Kodansha International.

Ikenberry, G. John 1989, "Rethinking the Origins of American Hegemony," *Political Science Quarterly* 104: 375–400.

1991/2, "A World Economy Restored: Expert Consensus and the Anglo-American Postwar Settlement," *International Organization* 46: 289–321.

1996, "The Myth of Post-Cold War Chaos," *Foreign Affairs* 75 (3): 79–91.

1998, "Constitutional Politics in International Relations," *European Journal of International Relations* 4: 147–78.

Ikenberry, John G. and Kupchan, Charles A. 1990, "Socialization and Hegemonic Order," *International Organization* 44: 283–315.

Isaacson, Walter and Thomas, Evan 1986, *The Wise Men: Six Friends and the World They Made*, New York: Simon and Schuster.

James, Harold 1995, *International Monetary Cooperation Since Bretton Woods*, New York: Oxford University Press.

Katzenstein, Peter J. 1987, *Policy and Politics in West Germany*, Philadelphia: Temple University Press.

Katzenstein, Peter J. and Tsujinaka, Yutaka 1995, "'Bullying,' 'Buying,' and 'Binding': US-Japanese Transnational Relations and Domestic Structures," in *Bringing Transnational Relations Back In*, Thomas Risse-Kappen (ed.), Cambridge: Cambridge University Press, pp. 79–111.

Keohane, Robert 1988, "International Institutions: Two Approaches," *International Studies Quarterly* 32: 379–96.

Krasner, Stephen D. 1982, "American Policy and Global Economic Stability," in *America in a Changing World Political Economy*, William P. Avery and David P. Rapkin (eds.), New York: Longman, pp. 29–48.

1983, "Structural Causes and Regime Consequences: Regimes as Intervening

Variables," in *International Regimes*, Stephen D. Krasner (ed.), Ithaca: Cornell University Press, pp. 1–12.

1984, "Approaches to the State: Alternative Conceptions and Historical Dynamics," *Comparative Politics* 16: 223–46.

Lieber, Robert 1997, "Eagle Without a Cause: Making Foreign Policy Without the Soviet Threat," in *Eagle Adrift: American Foreign Policy at the End of the Century*, Robert Lieber (ed.), New York: Longman, pp. 3–38.

Lippmann, Walter 1943, *US Foreign Policy: Shield of the Republic*, Boston: Little, Brown.

Lundestad, Geir 1986, "An Empire by Invitation? The United States and Western Europe, 1945–1952," *The Journal of Peace Research* 23: 263–77.

Maier, Charles 1987, *In Search of Stability: Explorations in Historical Political Economy*, New York: Cambridge University Press.

Mearsheimer, John 1990a, "Back to the Future: Instability in Europe after the Cold War," *International Security* 15: 5–56.

1990b, "Why We Will Soon Miss the Cold War," *The Atlantic Monthly* 266: 35–50.

North, Douglass C. 1990, *Institutions, Institutional Change and Economic Performance*, New York: Cambridge University Press.

Ornaghi, Lorenzo 1990, "Economic Structure and Political Institutions: A Theoretical Framework," in *The Economic Theory of Structure and Change*, Mauro Baranzini and Roberto Scazzieri (eds.), Cambridge: Cambridge University Press, pp. 23–44.

Oye, Kenneth 1992, "Beyond Postwar Order and the New World Order," in *Eagle in a New World: American Grand Strategy in the Post-Cold War Era*, Kenneth Oye, Robert Lieber, and Donald Rothchild (eds.), New York: HarperCollins, pp. 3–33.

Pierson, Paul 1993, "When Effect Becomes Cause: Policy Feedback and Political Change," *World Politics* 45: 595–628.

Powell, Walter W. and DiMaggio, Paul J. 1991, "Introduction," in *The New Institutionalism in Organizational Analysis*, Powell and DiMaggio (eds.), Chicago: University of Chicago Press, pp. 1–38.

Rapkin, David (ed.) 1990, *World Leadership and Hegemony*, Boulder: Lynne Rienner.

Risse-Kappen, Thomas 1995, *Cooperation Among Democracies*, Princeton: Princeton University Press.

Ruggie, John G. 1993, "Multilateralism: The Anatomy of an Institution," in *Multilateralism Matters*, Ruggie (ed.), New York: Columbia University Press, pp. 3–47.

Schroeder, Paul 1976, "Alliances, 1815–1945: Weapons to Power and Tools of Management," in *Historical Dimensions of National Security Problems*, Klaus Knorr (ed.), Lawrence, KS: University of Kansas Press, pp. 227–62.

Schwartz, Thomas A. 1995, "The United States and Germany after 1945: Alliances, Transnational Relations, and the Legacy of the Cold War," *Diplomatic History* 19: 549–68.

Spykman, Nicholas 1942, *America's Strategy in the World*, New York: Harcourt, Brace.

Stinchcombe, Arthur L. 1968, *Constructing Social Theories*, New York: Harcourt, Brace and World, pp. 108–18.

Stone, Alec 1994, "What is a Supranational Constitution? An Essay in International Relations Theory," *The Review of Politics* 56: 441–74.

Streit, Clarence 1939, *Union Now: The Proposal for Inter-democracy Federal Union*, New York: Harper and Brothers.

Tamamoto, Masaru 1995, "Reflections on Japan's Postwar State," *Daedalus* 125: 1–22.

Waltz, Kenneth 1979, *Theory of International Politics*, New York: Wiley.

Weber, Steve 1995, "Shaping the Postwar Balance of Power," in *Multilateralism Matters*, John Gerard Ruggie (ed.), New York: Columbia University Press, pp. 233–92.

Weingast, Barry and North, Douglass C. 1989, "Constitutions and Commitment: The Evolution of Institutions Governing Public Choice in Seventeenth Century England," *Journal of Economic History* 44: 803–32.

Jack Snyder

States facing the prospect of relative decline have been notorious disturb-
ers of the international order, as have irredentist states trying to recoup
losses suffered during temporary declines in power. Alfred Vagts' *Defense
and Diplomacy* (1956) pointed to the preventive motive for war as one of
the main culprits of modern European history. Robert Gilpin's *War and
Change in World Politics* (1981) argued that power transitions not only
cause conflict but also shape the character of the international order
emerging from such changes. Randall Schweller (1992), however,
showed that behavior in power transitions depends to a large degree on
the domestic character of the states involved: democracies, for example,
almost never fight preventive wars, because the average voter sees them as
reckless and illegitimate. Thus assessments of the effect of power shifts on
the coming international order must take into account the interaction of
international and internal conditions confronting states in relative decline.

Russia's response to its recent relative decline is not only intrinsically
important to the future of world politics, but it may also shed light on the
more general phenomenon of relative decline and world order. For
several centuries, Russia has played the role of an autonomous great
power in the international system, despite its relative economic backwardness. Now, the collapse of Soviet power raises the question of
whether Russia can maintain its autonomous position in the balance-of-
power system and the world political economy – whether it will continue
to be one of the "makers" of the system, forcing other societies to come to
terms with Russian interests and norms, or whether it will become a mere
"taker" of norms and practices defined by others.

The loss of autonomy and great power status would not necessarily be
disadvantageous for Russia. Compare, for example, the benefits that
accrued to Germany and Japan when they became "takers" in the US-
dominated system after 1945 as opposed to the costs they incurred as
would-be "makers" of the system. Nonetheless, societies that have substantial power usually try to be system makers, at least in their own

regions, and their attempts to do so have major consequences for world order.

In past cases of great-power setbacks, such as that of the Weimar Republic, the response to relative decline has been profoundly influenced by the feasibility of mobilizing popular support for a geopolitical revival. Current trends suggest that, barring an unexpectedly intense mobilization spurred by some urgent external threat, post-decline Russia is heading for a pattern of weak social, cultural, and political popular mobilization. Theorists of atomized mass society leading to mass totalitarian or nationalist mobilization were wrong: Russia's weak civil society, in sharp contrast to that of Weimar, leaves an insufficient mass base for popular political mobilization. This outcome is in the interests of all the principal elites of contemporary Russia, whether "democrats," neo-communists, or nationalists of the variety that support General Alexander Lebed.

The present situation of weak external threats and limited internal popular mobilization, combined with Russia's considerable size, will likely leave Russia in the position of an autonomous but weak power. This is good news, insofar as it means that Russia will not be making much trouble. Nor will Russia be much help to the West's possible foes, like China; nor will it be an especially easy target for exploitation by them. In short, Russia in decline is likely to become something of a geopolitical backwater, possibly liberal in form, but not in content.

The pattern of Russian backwardness

The temporary collapse of Russian power has been a chronic theme over the past two centuries. In every instance, Russia has rebounded from those earlier setbacks by exploiting paradoxical advantages of backwardness. However, there is reason to believe that that pattern may now be broken. Consequently, it will be necessary to consider a broader range of possible responses to relative decline, as well as those suggested by Russia's own past.

Russia has experienced a substantial collapse of its military power four times in the past two centuries – at the end of the Crimean War, in 1905, at the end of the First World War, and during the collapse of the Soviet Union (Snyder 1994). The first three setbacks were reversed within a decade or two. The pattern of Russia's rebounds has been shaped by a variety of factors: its large geopolitical size; the security afforded by its geographical remoteness from the striking power of other large states; the firm control over resources and society exercised by its centralized state; and its relative independence of the world economy. These factors allowed Russia to be an autonomous player in world politics, despite its relative backwardness.

Yet to retain its autonomy – or at any rate, its military competitiveness – backward Russia repeatedly had to undertake extraordinary efforts to catch up with the power and efficiency of more advanced states. Exploiting the political and economic "advantages of backwardness," Russian autocrats from Peter to Stalin imposed top-down reforms on Russian society, employing authoritarian mobilization and centralized management of innovation as "substitutes" for the more spontaneous, bottom-up sources of innovation in Western states. These revolutions from above often yielded dramatic increments to Russian military and technological power in the short run, but in the long run top-down approaches to innovation contained the seeds of their own destruction. For example, Stalin's state-led strategy of industrialization was well suited for mobilizing fallow factors of production for the initial industrial breakthrough in a strategy of "extensive" economic growth, but it was poorly suited for maintaining innovation and allocative efficiency once the required task shifted to "intensive" growth. The hypercentralized, authoritarian approach failed to produce institutions capable of self-sustaining development, and thus ossified.

This authoritarian, boom-and-bust pattern caused difficulties for international order in two ways. One difficulty was the power fluctuations attendant on this catch-up strategy. World War I, for example, was caused in part by the perceived German incentives for preventive war due to the accelerating rise of Russian power in the decade after the 1905 revolution. Another factor exacerbating international suspicion was the reinforcement by the pattern of authoritarian mobilization of Russia's ideological distance from the advanced Western states.

Arguably, this pattern is now broken, and is unlikely to return. Backwardness may nowadays confer fewer "advantages" in an era of intensifying globalization of capitalist production. Strategies of autarky or selective participation in the world economy, based on distinctive top-down institutions, may have higher opportunity costs than ever before. Moreover, the sociological profile of Russia is now more urban and literate than it was during previous revolutions from above. Thus, top-down social reforms may be more difficult to impose, and bottom-up reforms may be more feasible.

Four strategies of adaptation to decline

If the old pattern of Russian economic and institutional backwardness is broken, what new options might be available for adapting to Russia's relative decline? Four common patterns in international politics deserve mention. I will begin with three patterns that operate mainly on the plane of international strategies and interactions. My main attention, however, will focus on the fourth pattern, which emphasizes the role of popular mobilization as a response to decline.

1) Prevention, alliance, or appeasement

The first is to resolve the problems of relative decline by means of adjustments of the state's geopolitical strategy. One typical strategic adjustment is to launch a preventive war to forestall relative decline. In the early 1980s, Colin Gray insisted that Soviet decline was likely to lead to precisely this outcome (Gray 1981). In fact, this was never even considered by Soviet leaders because of the two-way deterrent power of nuclear weapons (which rendered preventive war too reckless and also unnecessary), the new thinkers' unwarranted optimism about their re-form efforts, the aspirations of the reformist elite to join the West rather than destroy it, and their sense that the democratic West would not recklessly exploit Soviet retreats.

Another geopolitical adjustment is to offset declining power by attract-ing allies. Because Russia is not yet strongly threatened by either China or the West, it has thus far not had to make a clear alliance choice, but it may do so whenever that becomes necessary. Of course, if no allies are avail-able, a third type of geopolitical adjustment – appeasing the source of threat – may become necessary. The *peredyshka*, or temporary accommo-dation of a foe in order to gain a breathing spell, is a recurrent theme in Russian diplomatic history. In fact, Russian leaders have often preferred a *peredyshka* to a strategy of firm alliance. Russia's relative geographic isolation and potential for autarky makes temporary appeasement less dangerous than it might be for other powers, and minimizes the danger of entrapping Russia in others' quarrels. Even in the years before 1914, when Russia was most committed to a strategy of military alliance and eco-nomic integration, some Russian traditionalists correctly argued that Russia would be better advised to retain its freedom of action.

2) Dependency

Another possibility is that a declining great power may become a depen-dent or irrelevant backwater of world politics – a taker, no longer a maker. A relatively backward great power, like Spain, may have so many of its most valuable assets stripped away through decolonization as to lose its great power status entirely. At this point, the question becomes whether the former metropole will itself become part of the penetrated periphery, specializing in raw materials exports or other low-value-added economic activities, and losing much of its decision-making autonomy. By virtue of its size and latent technical capacities, Russia should surely be able to prevent this fate unless rent-seeking Russian elites find that they can profit by encouraging this outcome.

3) Supportership

A third possibility is that a declining great power can downsize and reform itself in such a way that it fits into the global division of labor and political system as a medium-sized supporter rather than as a maker or as an exploited taker. This is of course what happened to Britain in the context of the ascendancy of the US as a hegemon with compatible, liberal institutions. It also happened to Germany and Japan after their post-occupation "makeovers." These seem unlikely models for Russia's future. They were either weaker relative to the rising hegemon, more fully penetrated, closer ideologically to the hegemon in the first place, and/or better prepared sociologically to adapt to participation in a liberal-democratic international system.

4) Social mobilization

A final element in responses to relative decline is social and cultural mobilization to be able to compete better. As Charles Tilly argues, the pressure of international competition gradually led West European states to bargain with groups in society, trading the opportunity to participate in the benefits of state policy in exchange for heightened contributions to the state's military and economic enterprises (Tilly 1990). Social mobilization in order to cope with external pressure is of course one of the key triggers for the rise of modern nationalism. It is striking that virulent nationalism has so far failed to take hold in contemporary Russia, despite its relative decline. This reflects the lack of a strong external threat (NATO expansion notwithstanding), the weak tradition of Russian nationalism (always subsumed under a broader imperial identity), and the discrediting of ambitious programs for the projection of power abroad (due to disillusionment with Soviet internationalism).

Social mobilization for international competition is sometimes also a stimulus for democratization, as Olive Anderson describes for the British middle classes in the Crimean War and Gerald Feldman describes for the German working class in World War I (Anderson 1967; Feldman 1966). Statistical evidence suggests that war usually undercuts democracy in the short run, but large-scale, long-term popular mobilization for international competition may lead to expanded political participation in the longer run (Gurr 1988; Stein and Russett 1980). Fear of this outcome is one factor that led the German General Staff to prefer a short, offensive war in 1914. Once again, however, the lack of a strong immediate threat allows Russian leaders to drift along without fully mobilizing mass energies, and thus without correspondingly cutting them into the benefits of rule.

Other cultural forms of mass mobilization for international competition are possible as well: e.g., popular religious neo-fundamentalism (Juergensmeyer 1993), or cultural revival movements, as described among the Iroquois by A. F. C. Wallace (1966). In such situations, defeated cultures may undergo a crisis followed by a cultural revitalization, based on a marriage of some traditional cultural themes to new cultural elements adapted from the example of the victorious culture. There is little sign, however, that any neo-traditional synthesis of this kind could serve as a cultural basis for energizing a new burst of Russian competitiveness in the international system. Russian Orthodoxy hardly seems a dynamic ideological platform for a mass movement, and revivals of traditional Cossack identity are of only local significance.

Analytically, what accounts for this lack of mass mobilization to stem Russia's relative decline? Arguably, international and domestic factors both contribute. Internationally, the disinclination of other powers to exploit Russia's decline reduces the urgency of the elite's need to mobilize. And domestically, mainstream Russian elites of all stripes ("democrats," neo-communists, and even Lebed-style nationalists) want to avoid true popular mobilization. The Communists stuck to an inert, stodgy campaign style in the face of an impending Yeltsin victory in the 1996 Presidential election. And the Yeltsin "democrats" have consistently preferred a plebiscitary approach to short-term electoral success, through media domination to the establishment of an institutionalized party system. These elites prefer to play the game of rent-seeking in a superficially democratic system than try to ground their power in a well-entrenched mass democratic base.

Many of Russia's Soviet-era elite proved themselves able to adapt well to the post-Soviet setting of partial democracy and economic privatization. The two most powerful economic interests in the new Russia were the banking sector and the oil and gas industry, which was largely staffed by nimble holdovers from the Communist era. Russian Prime Minister Viktor Chernomyrdin's background was in the natural gas industry. Both the banking and energy sectors had a major stake in maintaining good relations with their clients abroad and with international lending institutions. Thus, these cartels had little reason to thwart Russia's system of limited democracy or to flirt with excessive imperial nationalism. They played no role in pressing for a military solution in Chechnya. On the contrary, their considerable financial and bureaucratic influence acted as a force for moderation in state policy and in the content of the news media that they owned (McFaul 1997/8).

Another important reason for the weakness of nationalist mobilization in Russia may be the underdevelopment of Russian civil society. This argument will surely sound counterintuitive to most readers, who are likely to share the common view that a strong civil society is a precondition for stable, liberal democracy rather than for belligerent nationalism. Indeed, they are half-right. It is difficult to sustain liberal democracy without a dense network of voluntary organizations, not dependent on the state, which both reflect and engender the highly developed skills in social self-organization which successful democratic participation requires (Putnam 1993). The problem is that it is also difficult to sustain mass nationalist movements without the skills and habits of voluntary mass organization. Nationalists need dense social networks and habits of large-scale coordination among like-minded citizens just as liberal democrats do. To coin a variation on Barrington Moore's formulation about dictatorship and democracy: no civil society, no mass nationalism.

The first two instances of modern nationalism are commonly held to be eighteenth-century Britain and France (Greenfeld 1992). British nationalist consciousness was largely borne by the vehicle of the urban middle classes and the increased press freedom after the Glorious Revolution (Colley 1992; Snyder forthcoming). In France, this link is even more clear-cut, because the explosion of civil society and urban newspapers occurred over a very short time during the French Revolution. It led almost immediately to a nationalism-fueled war espoused by the Jacobin clubs (voluntary organizations calling for popular sovereignty) and by a radical journalist who became France's dominant political figure, Jacques Pierre Brissot. Note also that this mobilization of nationalist feeling took place on the heels of French geopolitical setbacks in the enduring rivalry with Britain. Defeats in North America, for example, triggered reform efforts and fiscal crises which created a revolutionary situation and a need for nationalist mobilization to renovate the state (Skocpol 1979).

The story of nationalist mobilization in the late Weimar Republic has some strong similarities. Following Germany's defeat in World War I, middle-class and small-town opinion held that a revitalization of German folkish patriotism was needed to redress the injustices imposed by the Versailles Treaty and contain the rising power of the working-class enemy within Germany, which was blamed for having "stabbed Germany in the back" in 1918. This mobilization that made possible the abrupt rise to power of the Nazi Party was accomplished almost entirely through small-scale, voluntary networks. Nationalist organizers were able to piggyback on a vast array of beer-drinking veterans and choral societies. Nationalist mobilization from below was possible because Weimar's middle-class civil society was strong (Berman 1997).

This puts in a new light older theories about the link between atomized individuals in "mass society" and the rise of totalitarianism, including both fascism and communism (Kornhauser 1959). Such theories argued that rapid modernization could break down social ties and make individuals vulnerable to totalistic propaganda appealing on behalf of unmediated fealty of the individual to the state. Thus Hitler would come on the radio and rootless moderns would fall in step en masse. Unfortunately for this theory, few people heard Hitler on the radio until after he had gained power. Instead, they were responding to pro-Nazi speeches and handbills offered up by their neighbors.

It is true that, once in power, the Communist Party did atomize individuals through terror and totalistic control of nearly all social organizations. As a result, civil society remained very poorly developed in most communist societies, with the exception of Poland and Hungary, where a semi-pluralistic form of communism had created an opportunity to organize some social groups (Linz and Stepan 1996). The bad news is that this weakness of civil society in the post-communist states has hindered the development of vibrant democratic politics (Casanova 1998). The good news is that in Russia it has also hindered the development of a successful nationalist mass movement.

Conclusion

In short, post-decline Russia seems headed for a pattern of weak social, cultural, and political popular mobilization. Russia's weak civil society leaves an insufficient mass base for popular political mobilization, whether for full-fledged democracy or for mass nationalism. This outcome is in the interests of all the principal elites of contemporary Russia, whether "democrats," neo-communists, or Lebed-style nationalists. The combination of weak external threats and limited internal popular mobilization, together with Russia's considerable size, will likely leave Russia in the position of an autonomous but weak power, and thus a backwater of world politics.

REFERENCES

Anderson, Olive 1967, *A Liberal State at War: English Politics and Economics during the Crimean War*, New York: St. Martin's.

Berman, Sheri 1997, "Civil Society and the Collapse of the Weimar Republic," *World Politics* 49: 401–29.

Casanova, José 1998, "Ethnolinguistic and Religious Pluralism and Democratic Consolidation in Ukraine," in *Post-Soviet Political Order: Conflict and State-Building*, Barnett Rubin and Jack Snyder (eds.), London: Routledge, pp. 81–103.

Colley, Linda 1992, *Britons: Forging the Nation, 1707–1837*, New Haven: Yale University Press.

Feldman, Gerald D. 1966, *Army, Industry and Labor in Germany, 1914–1918*, Princeton: Princeton University Press.

Gilpin, Robert 1981, *War and Change in World Politics*, Cambridge: Cambridge University Press.

Gray, Colin S. 1981, "The Most Dangerous Decade," *Orbis* 25: 13–28.

Greenfeld, Liah 1992, *Nationalism: Five Roads to Modernity*, Cambridge: Harvard University Press.

Gurr, Ted Robert 1988, "War, Revolution, and the Growth of the Coercive State," *Comparative Political Studies* 21: 45–65.

Juergensmeyer, Mark 1993, *The New Cold War? Religious Nationalism Confronts the Secular State*, Berkeley: University of California Press.

Kornhauser, William 1959, *The Politics of Mass Society*, Glencoe: Free Press.

Linz, Juan J. and Stepan, Alfred 1996, *Problems of Democratic Transition and Consolidation*, Baltimore: Johns Hopkins University Press.

McFaul, Michael 1997/8, "A Precarious Peace: Domestic Politics in the Making of Russian Foreign Policy," *International Security* 22: 5–35.

Putnam, Robert 1993, *Making Democracy Work: Civic Traditions in Modern Italy*, Princeton: Princeton University Press.

Schweller, Randall 1992, "Domestic Structure and Preventive War: Are Democracies More Pacific?" *World Politics* 44: 235–69.

Skocpol, Theda 1979, *States and Social Revolutions*, Cambridge: Cambridge University Press.

Snyder, Jack 1994, "Russian Backwardness and the Future of Europe," *Daedalus* 123: 179–202.

    forthcoming, Voting for Violence: Democratization and Nationalist Conflict, New York: Norton Books.

Stein, Arthur and Russett, Bruce M. 1980, "The Consequences of International Conflicts," in *Handbook of International Conflict*, Ted Robert Gurr (ed.), New York: Free Press, pp. 399–422.

Tilly, Charles 1990, *Coercion, Capital, and European States, AD 990–1990*, Oxford: Basil Blackwell.

Vagts, Alfred 1956, *Defense and Diplomacy*, New York: King's Crown.

Wallace, Anthony F. C. 1966, *Religion: An Anthropological View*, New York: Random House.

8   The European Union: economic giant, political dwarf

Juan Diez Medrano

The study of international relations has focused on the contexts that facilitate or hinder cooperation between states and on the role that institutions play in international politics (for example Keohane 1984, 1986, 1988; Baldwin 1993; Waltz 1979; Axelrod 1984; Krasner 1983; and Powell 1994). More recently, scholars have begun to study the problem of coordination in cooperative behavior, that is, the choice between alternative cooperative strategies when actors have different preferences and have only limited information about the consequences of alternative courses of action (e.g., Morrow 1994; Stein 1990; Krasner 1991; and Snidal 1985). For those interested in the evolution of cooperative agreements, the problem of coordination is indeed the most important topic, but also one full of complexities that cannot always be addressed through formal-deductive models. In this chapter I study the problem of coordination of foreign affairs and security policy in the European Union. I explain the slower pace of European integration in foreign affairs and security policy when compared to the degree of integration in the economic area. Furthermore, I discuss the possible reasons for the less than excellent record of the European Union (EU) in solving post-Cold War era international crises and the role that the lack of integration in foreign affairs and security has played in explaining this mediocre performance.

Work in the area of coordination bargains has shown that even the simplest "war of the sexes" coordination game presents greater complexities than the classical "prisoners' dilemma" game used to study cooperation problems. The range of possible solutions is too broad to allow precise predictions about outcomes. One can analyze, however, the roles of structural features, such as the relative gradient of actors' preferences, the number of players, power asymmetries, and the impact of time. Research on this topic has provided hypotheses that can be applied in the context of foreign affairs and security policy in the EU. For instance, the hypothesis that the greater the number of players, the more difficult it is to reach coordination agreements; also, the hypothesis that power asymmetries modestly facilitate coordination agreements and slightly favor larger states (Snidal 1985: 935). Beyond this point, however, scholars usually refer to the need to take into account specific contextual conditions in order to explain the choice of one coordination option over another. The process of European integration is in this sense a useful case-study for the investigation of the factors explaining coordination choices.

Scholars working on European integration have often addressed the problem of coordination in cooperation between states (for instance Wallace 1992; Pierson 1996; Haas 1958; Moravcsik 1991; Fligstein and Mara-Drita 1996; and Keohane and Hoffman 1991). These discussions have proceeded, however, under the questionable assumption that the intergovernmental approach indicates less cooperation on a particular policy field than does an integrationist approach (e.g., Pijpers 1991; Weiler and Wessels 1988; and Hoffmann 1991).[1] This assumption does not take into account that how smoothly intergovernmental cooperative arrangements function depends among other things on the will of the participants to reach consensus or on their sheer number, and that non-intergovernmental political institutions, e.g., states, also show a high degree of variation in solidarity, capacity to reach decisions, and efficacy. In order to study European integration, it might be more fruitful to treat the intergovernmental and the integration approaches as two alternative forms of cooperation or coordination strategies, and to discuss issues of cooperation intensity, efficacy, and solidarity as another type of problem.

Another characteristic that describes the discussion of modes of coordination in the European Union is that it has taken different routes depending on whether the focus is on foreign affairs and defense cooperation or on economic cooperation. In general, explanations for why things do not occur show a tendency for post hoc rationalization and lack a discussion of what would be needed for things to happen. This problem pervades discussions of European foreign affairs and defense cooperation. In explanation of the lack of integration in the field of foreign affairs and security policy, four main hypotheses can be mentioned (Pijpers 1991; Hoffmann 1991). The first is that lack of integration is due to the existence of the NATO umbrella, which guarantees Europe's security. From this hypothesis follows the conclusion that an integrated European foreign affairs and security policy is not needed. The second hypothesis is that sovereignty in foreign affairs and security policy is more central to states than is sovereignty in other areas. The third one, based on the realist "balance of power" hypothesis, is that European foreign affairs and security policy is not integrated because the bipolarity that characterized the Cold War turned the NATO solution into the most rational cooperation strategy for Western European states. A stronger European foreign affairs and security policy would have disrupted the fine balance achieved by the two superpowers. It would presumably have created tension between the Western partners and increased Soviet hostility because of fear of Germany's intentions. The last hypothesis is that the interests of the European Union member states are too different from each other to permit very close cooperation, let alone integration.

The four hypotheses listed above rest on reasonable descriptions of the logic of international politics and of post-World War II security arrangements. States indeed seek to preserve their sovereignty and tend to cooperate more if they have common interests. Moreover, NATO was a security arrangement that proved to be quite successful in holding within bounds the Soviet Union's ambitions in Europe. They do not tell us the whole story, however, about why intergovernmental rather than integration cooperation has taken place. The first and third explanations, for instance, are perfectly compatible with a situation in which European foreign affairs and security policy were integrated but still subordinated to NATO. This arrangement would not have meant less security for Europe or a disruption of the balance of power during the Cold War. In fact, it was the solution that the United States insisted upon at the end of World War II, when it strongly supported plans for a European Defense Community (EDC), which would be subordinated to NATO. It is clear that the US, a most interested party, did not see the EDC as a destabilizing factor in superpower relations.

The second hypothesis is questionable on two grounds. First, it is not established that foreign affairs and security policy is more central to the sovereignty of states than is sovereignty on economic affairs. In fact, public support for a European army and a common European foreign affairs policy is very strong (well above 60 percent of respondents support these steps, with small variations around this percentage in the different EU member states), especially in Germany, where it is even stronger than support for a European currency. Secondly, an integrationist strategy does not necessarily mean a loss of sovereignty. This point has been well argued over the years by Robert Keohane and Stanley Hoffmann, for whom "the European Community can best be viewed as a set of complex overlapping networks, in which a supranational style of decision-making, characterized by compromises upgrading common interests, can under favorable conditions lead to the pooling of sovereignty" (Keohane and Hoffmann 1992: 277). Integration and the preservation of sovereignty are not a zero-sum game, as long as states are present in the integrated structures that are created and as long as integration of some spheres increases the states' control over their internal affairs.

Finally, the fourth hypothesis can be criticized because it assumes that integration takes place only when the interests of the participants converge. The contrary can indeed be the case, as long as the participants agree on an overarching goal, e.g., security or international stability. If disagreements between states on the strategies to follow in order to attain a particular goal are so strong that they paralyze cooperation between them, states may end up accepting integration as a solution, even if it somewhat reduces the states' autonomy. What needs to be studied is under what conditions this will happen.

What is missing from all these explanations of the intergovernmental character of foreign affairs and security policy is a consideration of what is needed for integration to take place. A comparison between cooperation in the economic sphere, where integration has taken place, and the foreign affairs and security area, where it has not, may provide us with a more empirically grounded explanation of the persistence of intergovernmental cooperation in foreign affairs and security policy and a better base for making prognoses.

The analytical framework I use here relies on several contributions of realist and institutionalist perspectives of international relations. It draws especially from Moravcsik's intergovernmental institutionalist perspective (1991) and Fligstein and Mara-Drita's cultural frame institutionalist approach (1996). I briefly outline some of the defining aspects of this framework. Underlying it is the assumption that cooperation is possible only if actors perceive that it will help them to attain a collective good that they would have difficulty attaining alone or in competition with other actors with whom they are in frequent interaction (Keohane 1988). Once they decide to cooperate, they have to choose between different cooperation alternatives (Snidal 1985; Morrow 1994). This problem is what is known as the problem of coordination. In this coordination game, players act rationally in order to obtain a cooperative arrangement that best satisfies their perceived interests, which are not necessarily "objectively" rational. When the actors are states, the preservation of sovereignty is one of the main interests driving their preferences for different coordination arrangements. More powerful players play a greater role than do less powerful players. Therefore, changes in power balances often translate into efforts by different actors to modify the prevailing coordination arrangement to one that better suits their perceived interests (Snidal 1985). Because of their desire to preserve sovereignty, states will rarely prefer an integration solution to alternative coordination possibilities. Periods of crisis, that is, periods in which sudden, drastic changes create uncertainty about how best to attain a collective good through cooperation, offer an opportunity, however, to political actors, individuals or institutions, interested in integrationist arrangements (Fligstein and

Mara-Drita 1996; Garrett and Weingast 1993). In order for the integration proposal to succeed, it needs to be persuasive enough to get support from politically strong groups in at least the most powerful states that participate in the coordination game. Furthermore, these groups must be in power simultaneously in order for a powerful enough interstate alliance to form that allows the integration proposal to prosper (Moravcsik 1991; Keohane and Hoffmann 1991). Therefore, ideas, domestic factors, and the convergence in power of the right groups play a decisive and independent role in the adoption of an integration solution.

The argument I make in this chapter is that European integration in the foreign affairs and security area has not moved beyond intergovernmental cooperation because it would not help solve any pressing coordination problem in the field of foreign policy. Furthermore, I argue that the relatively poor performance of the European Union in recent international crises is due not to lack of integration, but to lack of operational capability in the area of defense and divisions between the European Union member states. I explain the insufficiency of operational capabilities with reference to the West's foreign policy arrangements during the Cold War (and to NATO in particular), and show how the end of the Cold War, while not leading to the drastic reorientation of the European Union's foreign policy institutional arrangements that some had hoped for, has certainly led to a reconsideration of the preexisting ones. This reconsideration frames current debates about the strengthening of the Western European Union (WEU) and the assertion of Europe's role within NATO.[2]

The problem

If an architect were assigned the task of giving physical translation to the image that represents the European Union – a Greek temple's façade with three pillars, each corresponding to one of the EU's three dimensions, the European Community, foreign affairs and security policy, and internal affairs and justice policy – she would indeed have an odd job ahead of her. For if she were to be faithful to actual progress in European unification, the temple would have to defy the laws of gravity in order to stand up: one long pillar representing progress in economic integration (European Community) and two tiny plinths representing progress in the other two areas. This asymmetry in the degree of integration achieved in the different functional dimensions of the European Union, which could cost our architect her job and has surprised, even frustrated, many observers of the European unification process, is not so odd when analyzed through the lenses of a historian. Indeed, the history of the formation of both the United States and Germany presents some similarities in this respect, with economic integration proceeding at a much faster pace than political integration. This similarity with previous instances of state formation is of little consolation, however, for those for whom the end of the Cold War and the completion of the single market within the European Union offered a golden opportunity for the realization of the European Community's founding fathers' dream of a politically and economically integrated Europe. Soon after the dramatic historical transformations that marked the end of the 1980s, the Gulf and Yugoslavian wars were to open people's eyes to the different rhythms of European integration and to reveal the obstacles lying ahead on the road toward political unity. The performance of the European Union in these military conflicts promoted the public perception that without the United States' lead, Europeans are unable to bring conflicts to a successful end and, related to this, that Europeans lack the resolve to apply military force in order to solve international crises. Beyond organizational considerations related to the way the European Union makes decisions on foreign policy and security, it has become increasingly evident that the European Union cannot exert a role in foreign affairs commensurate to its economic strength unless it has control over military forces of its own.

In the next section of the chapter I provide a summary description of the history and current status of the European Union's foreign and security policy. Then I focus on two moments of European integration, the period of the creation of the European Coal and Steel Community (ECSC) and the failure of the plan to create a European Defense Community (EDC), and the twelve-year period of institutional reform beginning in 1986 with the signing of the Single European Act (SEA). Finally, I provide an explanation for the perceived weakness of the European Union's foreign policy.

Foreign affairs and security in the European Union

Embarrassed by the poor performance of the European Union in post-Cold War era international crises, advocates of European integration have pushed for further steps to give the European Union's foreign affairs and security policy a more supranational character and a stronger defensive component.

Efforts toward European unification in the foreign affairs and security areas are, however, as old as efforts toward European economic unification (Fabre 1996). The idea of European integration, as conceived by the likes of Churchill, Monnet, Schuman, and Adenauer soon after World

War II, was indeed intended to eradicate the possibility of another war on European soil. European Political Cooperation (EPC), already sketched in Fouchet's 1962 Plan, but made official only after 1970, was structured around periodic meetings of heads of state and government to consult on foreign policy issues. Over time, the EPC's institutional structure was fine-tuned through a series of reports and agreements. The 1974 Schmidt-Giscard initiative, for instance, created the European Council of Heads of Government. It was established that the President of the European Community act as the European Council's speaker and be made responsible for the management of contacts and relations with third countries. Later on, in the Stuttgart Summit of 1983, it was decided that heads of state and government be assisted by foreign affairs ministers and by a member of the European Commission.

Over the years, EPC habits and procedures were institutionalized into a coherent body of European values and rules that informally constrained EC member states' autonomy in foreign affairs and even changed state interests and preferences (Smith 1998). It was not until 1986, however, on the occasion of the signing of the Single European Act, that EPC was mentioned in a Treaty of the European Community. The Single European Act made official the existence and composition of the European Council, whose activities were to be complemented by periodic meetings of the foreign affairs ministers of the European Community. In addition, the SEA fully associated the Commission with the deliberations on EPC and gave it a right of initiative. Similarly, the SEA specified that the European Parliament be consulted over the main aspects and the main decisions in foreign affairs and security policy. Finally, the SEA effectively made the Western European Union (WEU), of which more below, into the secular arm of the European Community, by recognizing that foreign policy and common security include all questions of European security, including the eventual definition of a common defense policy that could also lead to a common defense.

The Maastricht Treaty and the reforms to the Treaty of European Union approved at the Amsterdam Intergovernmental Conference of June 1997 further institutionalize foreign affairs and security policy. The Maastricht Treaty turns it into one of the three pillars of the European Union. Furthermore, the Maastricht Treaty outlines the objectives of the foreign affairs and security policy and establishes the power of states to formulate "common positions" and to conduct "common actions." There is a clear division of labor between the European Council and the Council of Foreign Affairs Ministers: the former fixes the general orientations, whereas the latter determines through unanimity rule the matters to be the object of a "common action." When a "common action" is adopted and at every stage of its implementation, the Council defines the issues that must be decided on a qualified majority basis.

Defense policy naturally falls within the realm of foreign affairs and security policy. The process of European unification has been character-ized, however, by the separate development of the two policies, an anom-aly that the Maastricht Treaty and the Draft Project for the reform of the Treaty of European Union, signed at the Amsterdam Summit, have begun to correct. The strategy that has been chosen is to gradually integrate the Western European Union in the European Union's institu-tional framework.

The WEU, initiated by France and the United Kingdom, was the first cooperative defensive structure to develop at the end of World War II (Dumoulin 1995; Maury 1996). Like many other political and military initiatives of that time, its aim was to safeguard Europe from a potential new German aggression. It evolved out of the Treaties of Dunkirk (1947) and Versailles (1948) and was named as such in the Brussels Treaty (1954). The WEU was initially conceived as an intergovernmental organization to guarantee automatic military assistance in case of aggression by a third party. Thereafter, it developed independently of the European Commu-nity until the drafting of the Treaty of Maastricht, which for the first time mentions defense as an object of European foreign affairs and security policy, to be conducted through the WEU. Despite a well-defined perma-nent structure and organization (a Council of Foreign Affairs Ministers, a permanent Council, an Assembly of Parliamentarians, and several advis-ory bodies) the WEU was until the 1980s little more than a consultative forum subordinate to NATO, where security and arms production issues were regularly discussed. Since the 1980s, however, several initiatives have been taken to strengthen the role of the WEU in the process of European integration. These initiatives find expression in the Treaty of Maastricht and in the Draft Project for the reform of the Treaty of Maastricht approved at the Amsterdam Summit. In addition to including defense policy within the responsibilities falling under the foreign affairs and security pillar of the European Union, the reformed Treaty of European Union states in Article J.7 (former J.4 in the Maastricht Treaty) that "The Western European Union (WEU) is an integral part of the development of the Union."

The Western European Union thus appears to be on the road to becoming the EU's defense arm. Some obstacles need to be overcome, however, before this becomes a reality. In particular, the WEU suffers from a problem of "double jurisdiction." On the one hand, it is called upon to act as the defense arm of the EU, on the other it is supposed to be subordinated to the defense strategy outlined by NATO. Regarding this issue, Article J.7 (third paragraph) stresses that "the policy of the Union in accordance with this Article shall not prejudice the specific character of the security and defense policy of certain member states and shall respect the obligations of certain member states, which see their common defense realized in NATO, under the North Atlantic Treaty, and be compatible with the common security and defense policy established within that framework." The ambiguity embedded in Article J.7 reflects US pressures to ensure the subservience of the WEU to NATO as well as disagreement between EU members about the role of the WEU in the European defense system. It is thus not clear what the WEU would do if it received contradictory instructions from the EU and NATO.

A second major obstacle that the WEU needs to overcome before becoming the EU's defense arm is that of its operativeness. Without clear guidelines regarding the WEU's power to call on military forces and the way they should be financed and deployed, the WEU will remain a consultative body unable promptly to translate EU policy into action. In recent years, significant efforts have been made to provide the WEU with an operational capability. The creation of multinational military structures, such as the Eurocorps, the Euromarforce, and the Euroforce, are steps in this direction. Even more significant is the Declaration of Petersberg (June 19, 1992), that calls for the creation of a planning unit within the WEU and states the readiness of WEU to make military units available for eventual deployment under the WEU's authority. These military units can be used, not only to fulfill the members' mutual defense obligations, but also in humanitarian and evacuation missions, peace-keeping missions, and combat missions aimed to manage crises. Substantial ambiguity remains, however, about the obligations that the WEU has with respect to NATO when using these troops, which are often "double-hatted," in EU missions conducted independently of NATO.

Several points about the EU's foreign affairs and security policy area need to be made. First of all, foreign affairs and security policy is conducted predominantly through the intergovernmental method. The approval of both common positions and common actions requires unanimity among EU members, and so does any decision requiring the use of military forces. Qualified majority voting is reserved only for implementation of measures regarding common positions and common actions, when the Council unanimously so decides. There are certain aspects of foreign affairs and security policy, however, with supranational connotations. First, the presence of the Commission at Council meetings and the right of initiative it enjoys. Secondly, the requirement for the Council to consult the Parliament before taking any decision. Thirdly, the fact that commercial and development policy, which falls entirely within the jurisdiction of the European Community, is a major weapon in foreign affairs and security policy, which gives a great deal of leverage to the Commission. Finally, the fact that the European Parliament can control the conducting of foreign affairs and security policy indirectly, through the co-decision power it enjoys with respect to the EU's budget, source of a significant proportion of the Common Foreign and Security Policy (CFSP) resources.

A second point that needs to be made before discussing the factors explaining the intergovernmental character of the EU's foreign affairs and security policy, as well as the EU's record on foreign policy, is that most of the progress in integrating this policy sphere and the WEU within the EU's institutional framework, as well as efforts to provide the WEU with an operational structure, has taken place in the 1990s, that is, in the post-Cold War era. This, as I argue below, cannot be considered a mere coincidence.

Economic and foreign affairs and security integration: two comparisons

One useful approach to understand the EU's intergovernmental approach to foreign affairs and security policy is to compare it with the integrationist approach used in the economic realm. I will focus on two particular moments of integration, the period of the creation of the European Coal and Steel Community (ECSC) and the failed attempt to create a European Defense Community (EDC), and the period of institutional reform comprised between the signing of the Single European Act and the Amsterdam Summit of June 1997. Each comparison tells us something about the factors shaping the process of integration.

The ECSC and the EDC

The period immediately following the end of World War II was rich in initiatives to rebuild Europe's economies and polities and to prevent another war in Europe. The Treaty of Dunkirk (March 1947) and the Pact of Brussels (March 1948) set the foundation of the WEU, Truman's signing of the Marshall Plan (April 1948) prepared Europe's economic recovery, the signing of the North Atlantic Treaty created NATO (April 1949), and the creation of the Council of Europe (May 1949) constituted the first major step toward the promotion of the Western values of democracy and respect for human rights. The main objectives of these initiatives were to facilitate Europe's recovery, to secure Europe against communism, and to prevent another German aggression. It is in this context that one can understand the early efforts toward European integration. West European countries were at a critical juncture, in which they had to choose between modes of cooperation that would succeed in guaranteeing peace and prosperity. They needed to cooperate and the question was how. The game was asymmetric because of the overwhelming dominance of the United States.

The United States saw cooperation with Western European democracies as unavoidable in order to contain the Soviet Union, which emerged as the main enemy very soon after the end of the war, but its military and economic power allowed it to set the terms of cooperation. At the other end of the scale was Germany, without sovereignty and largely at the mercy of the great powers' plans for its future. The United States organized cooperation in Europe along two axes, the North Atlantic Pact (NATO), that would ensure defense against the Soviet Union, and the Organization for European Economic Cooperation (OEEC) (later Organization for Economic Cooperation and Development, OECD), that would administer the funds allocated by the Marshall Plan. Beyond this, it allowed Europeans to organize their cooperation as they wished, even encouraged European integration, as long as two conditions were fulfilled: subordination of any military organization to NATO's security plans for Europe and the reconstruction of Germany's economy and military. These requirements were needed to guarantee the permanence of Germany as part of the West and the participation of Germans in the defense of Western Europe against communism. Great Britain did not feel much threatened by this design, but France, twice invaded by Germany, did. Therefore, it was France that invested the most effort in designing a mode of cooperation between Europeans that would satisfy US demands while, at the same time, reducing the threat represented by Germany. If one looks for evidence of the role of individuals and ideas in institutional development, Jean Monnet and Robert Schuman provide a prime example. For it was they who, in a context of paralysis about how to solve the German question, proposed the plan that served, with some modifications, as the model for the organization of the European Community.

The idea of the European Coal and Steel Community did not have a precedent; it allowed simultaneously the reconciliations of France's wish to ensure that Germany not exploit the Ruhr and Saar mineral resources to rebuild a new conquering army (and France's own wish to have access to this rich source of coal and steel), and the US's desire to facilitate the rebuilding of the German economy.[3] Within the ECSC (1951), to which France, Germany, the Benelux countries, and Italy belonged, coal and steel production was put under the control and supervision of a supranational institution named the High Authority. Whatever Jean Monnet's and Robert Schuman's Europeanist ideals may have been, the success of their idea was not so much due to its embodiment of deeply felt Europeanism as to the fact that it provided a good solution to a cooperation problem, even if it involved some loss of sovereignty.

Having solved the economic aspects of German reconstruction, Europeans were left with the task of solving the more sensitive issue of Germany's rearmament. This question had become more pressing for the Americans because of the beginning of the Korean War in 1950. The French opposed, however, an independent German army, even if integrated into NATO. This is why, even before approval for the creation of the ECSC in October 1950, the French Premier, René Pleven, had put forward a defense project inspired by Monnet's and Schuman's ideas, that basically reproduced the model of the ECSC in the military sphere. The Treaty project for the European Defense Community, which meant the dissolution of national armies, was signed in May 1952, by Germany, France, the Benelux countries, and Italy, and called for the following:

1. Integration of national units at the division level into multinational military units.
2. Creation of a nine-member Commissariat with administrative duties, to be in charge of preparing equipment plans and controlling armament production, import, and export.
3. Subordination of the European defense forces in peacetime to NATO's Supreme Command, which has total discretion regarding their use.

The project got the US's backing since it solved once and for all the problem of Germany's rearmament. It proved to be a highly divisive issue in France, however, and this at a time of high government instability. The Christian-Democrats grouped around the Mouvement Républicain Populaire (MRP) were the staunchest supporters of the plan, whereas the conservatives of the RPF, close to General de Gaulle, and the Communists opposed a plan that they feared meant a very significant transfer of sovereignty. These fears were increased by new proposals that called for a political European Community to ensure democratic control of the European Defense Community. The rest of the French political forces were divided about the EDC.

In order to understand the eventual fate of the EDC, one needs to understand that the Fourth French Republic was characterized by political instability and constant government turnover. The EDC project was only one of the issues that divided the French political forces; institutional reform, economic policy, decolonization, the Korean War, and fear of the Communists marked this period, and explain the constant shifts of government. This is why approval of the EDC project by the French Assembly was a highly contingent issue. It just so happens that between the signing of the draft of the Project in 1952 and the eventual call for a vote in the French Assembly in 1954 under the Premiership of Mendès-France, the political orientation of the Assembly had shifted slightly in favor of the forces opposing the project.

The study of the history of the EDC illustrates very nicely the factors that enter into the explanation of European integration. Steps in the direction of integration would not have taken place without the existence of a coordination problem that seemed unsolvable: how to arm Germany and at the same time avoid the risks implied by this rearmament. Europeanists such as Monnet and Schuman provided the ideas, and the successful ECSC a model to imitate. The problem was one of sovereignty, however: how best to secure a state's border in the face of a potential German threat. The only constraint to an eventual solution to the dilemma was that Germany had to be rearmed. This constraint was imposed by the United States, a fact that is consistent with the hypothesis that power asymmetries make it easier for the dominant actor to play a determinant role in the choice of a coordination solution. It is important to note that the EDC project might have been approved had the composition of the French Assembly and the deputies' attitudes remained the same between Pleven's proposal and the final vote. French interests were not uniform or stable as the literature on international relations often assumes of its actors, and changes in the composition of the Assembly between 1952 and 1954 had only partly to do with debates over the EDC project. This observation reinforces Hoffmann's hypothesis about the significant role played by domestic politics in the evolution of European integration.[4]

In retrospect, one could argue that the EDC solution was not optimal if one assumes that the states' preferred choices in coordination problems are those that minimize the loss of sovereignty while providing maximum satisfaction in terms of the objective that is pursued. The most rational solution, that is the one that minimized sovereignty loss and maximized military security, was the one that was eventually reached: preservation of national armies; German rearmament; and integration of Germany into both the WEU (in 1954) and NATO. It is difficult to conceive of how Germany could have represented a real threat to Europe, given the bipolar power structure that emerged out of World War II and the partition of Germany. What is important, however, is that a large segment of the French political elite, comprising both those who proposed the EDC plan and those who rejected it, really believed in the threat represented by Germany, and their strategic choices corresponded to these beliefs. Objectively rational reasons are not necessarily those that are reached first, and it is in this sense that the persuasiveness of well-placed actors or actors representing institutions play an independent role in shaping the choice of coordination strategies.

The SEA and recent efforts toward a stronger foreign affairs and security policy

The second moment of integration that can shed light on the factors that have shaped European foreign affairs and security policy corresponds to the period between the negotiation of the SEA and the 1997 Amsterdam Summit.

The Single European Act has received more scholarly attention than almost any other event in the European integration process. The complementary contributions of different scholars provide a coherent argument for the process that led to it. In the early 1980s, the European Community was experiencing a serious crisis due to the absence of significant progress toward the completion of the internal market since the achievement of the Common Market in 1968. Trade tariffs between countries had been eliminated and a common external tariff put in place, but many other bureaucratic impediments to the free movement of goods and services, workers, and capital still remained. The practice of reaching most decisions through unanimity, especially accentuated since the Compromise of Luxembourg in 1966, and the attempt to eliminate obstacles to the completion of the internal market through harmonization measures, were dragging the process out indefinitely. The objective of reaching the internal market had become particularly urgent in the minds of European politicians. The two main reasons for this perceived urgency were the economic stagnation of the European economies in the 1970s, compounded by the relative failure of traditional Keynesian recipes in fighting inflation and unemployment, and stepped up competition from the United States and Japan (Fligstein and Mara-Drita 1996). Hoffmann has emphasized the convergence toward the adoption of neoliberal economic policy by the British, French, and German governments, which led to renewed interest in the completion of the internal market (Hoffmann 1991; Moravcsik 1991).

It is in this period of double crisis, a crisis of previous economic policy and a crisis of the efficacy of the European Community, that cultural entrepreneurs such as the newly elected President of the European Commission, Jacques Delors, were able to gather support for an innovative plan for the completion of the internal market (Fligstein and Mara-Drita 1996). This plan relied on the concept of "mutual recognition" coined by the European Community's Tribunal of Justice in the famous "Cassis de Dijon Decision" (1979), on qualified majority voting on all issues concerning the internal market, on the primacy of European Community law over national law, and on control by the Tribunal of Justice over the implementation of decisions taken by the European Community (Garrett and Weingast 1993). This revolutionary plan played an independent role in the completion of the internal market, but it would not have been formulated or considered had there not been a coordination problem that European leaders needed to solve in order to attain their goals of completing the internal market and, indirectly, of achieving higher rates of economic growth (Fligstein and Mara-Drita 1996). Integration became the solution to a problem for which no other solution of an intergovernmental nature had been found or agreed upon. States were pooling sovereignty, however, in order to strengthen their legitimacy at home rather than because of their Europeanism.

Despite the enthusiasm with which the SEA was received, which created enough momentum to carry the integration process into its next stage, Monetary Union, little of this spilled over to foreign affairs and security policy. Undoubtedly, bringing together the European Community and European Political Cooperation under one single Treaty was a major achievement, and so were the reforms of the EPC geared to giving it a decision-making dimension and the gradual integration of defense policy within the foreign affairs and security policy pillar of the European Union. CFSP remains an intergovernmental form of cooperation, however, whereas the European Community has become more and more supranational.

Both the observed changes and the limits of these changes can be explained with reference to the historical circumstances surrounding the changes and the nature of the coordination problem that needed to be solved. Historically, the decisive event that explains the strengthening of the foreign affairs and security dimension of the European Union is the end of the Cold War. The significance of this event is that it removed the main factor that explained the power of the United States to determine the broad contours of foreign and security policy in Western and Northern Europe since the end of World War II. The perceived diminution of the threat represented by the Soviet Union and then Russia for European security made Europeans less dependent on the United States' military apparatus, and this influenced power relations among Western democracies (Pijpers 1991: 22–4). Predictably, with the end of the Cold War the coordination game oriented to the goal of security became more complex and more difficult to solve because of the significant diminution of power asymmetries. The United States has tried to maintain its dominance in the coordination arrangements, while simultaneously reducing its financial and military commitment to the security of Europe, and the European Union's member states have become more assertive and sought to define their foreign policy in a more autonomous way (Ullman 1991: 150).

This new assertiveness and search for autonomy is also partly caused by the gradual divergence between the foreign policy interests of EU member states and those of the US.[5] Before the fall of the Wall, cooperation between Western Europe and the United States was justified because the security interest of Western European countries and the United States's interest in fighting communism overlapped. Since the end of the Cold War, the threat from Central and Eastern Europe to the EU's security is of a new nature (immigration, refugee crises, nuclear pollution, drug smuggling, organized crime) and does not overlap so neatly with the United States' broader interest in political and military stability.[6]

The same factors that promote a distancing of the United States with respect to its European partners could also lead to a distancing between the European partners themselves. This is what a realist perspective would predict. Nevertheless, although the military threat from the East that motivated tight cooperation between Western and Northern Europeans and between Europeans and the United States within the NATO structure has diminished, the states that form the European Union share to some extent the new problems created by the East's transition toward market economies and democratic government. This justifies further and closer cooperation in the foreign affairs and security area between the EU's member states. What is less clear is whether cooperation in this area will be intergovernmental or integrated (Pijpers 1991: 9; Hoffmann 1991: 288). The EU member states seem to think that an intergovernmental approach is more suitable, or at least this is what one can infer from their actions and public statements, despite occasional calls for more integration by French and German officials. The question is whether the logic that led to integration in the economic area applies to the topic of foreign affairs and security policy (Keohane and Hoffmann 1991: 27–8). In other words, does the integration approach provide a unique solution to pressing issues in foreign affairs and security policy that the intergovernmental approach cannot provide? I would argue that it does not, despite the marginal advantages in terms of efficacy that the supranational approach would bring. One reason for this is that unlike what happened in the economic area, there is currently no focal objective of such urgency and controversial character that it would call for a pooling of sovereignty by EU member states. Integration in many policy areas related to the economy would not have taken place were it not for the fact that the completion of the internal market was perceived to be a pressing matter, especially by the key players in the EU, the United Kingdom, France, and Germany. To be sure, the EU has outlined priorities in the foreign affairs and security area, but these are objectives which cannot be attained within a specific time period. Each of them will have to be pursued indefinitely. Therefore, there is no need to create specific arrangements that will accelerate a particular process, as was the case with the creation of the internal market.

There are, of course, other reasons that could justify supranational integration. The will to control a potentially aggressive neighbor could justify drawing integration plans such that the potentially threatening neighbor was made part of this supranational organization and thus ceased to be a threat. This was the motivation behind the EDC. Security threats such as those that characterized the Cold War could also be seen as a problem of sufficient magnitude and complexity that they would justify integration. The NATO arrangements were, however, inter-governmental, and they have functioned well enough to guarantee Euro-pean security. Moreover, security issues in coming years are unlikely to be as serious as during the Cold War. Therefore, there does not seem to be a good reason for a more integrated approach to foreign affairs and security policy (Ullman 1991). At most, one could imagine the establishment of provisions such that in emergency circumstances the EU would be able to make decisions through qualified majority vote rather than through una-nimity.

The European Union: a secondary actor?

In recent international crises, the European Union has given the impres-sion of lacking the resolve and capacity to solve them successfully (Hill 1993; Allen and Smith 1990). It is criticized for lacking the political muscle that would correspond to its economic strength, which puts it in the same league as Japan and Germany, two economic giants with little political weight on the world scene (Gnesotto 1996). Recent reviews of the European Union's foreign affairs and security policy show, however, that the European Union is hardly a passive player in world politics. What most differentiates the European Union from the United States is its lack of reliance on military force to contribute to the solution of international crises and its lack of diplomatic weight. Most of the "common positions" and "common actions" undertaken by the European Union to pursue political goals have been economic, whether in the form of economic sanctions or humanitarian aid.[7] In the case of Rwanda, for instance, the European Union was the main provider of humanitarian assistance; in Yugoslavia, the EU contributed more than 60 percent of the expenses of humanitarian aid.

One can invoke international relations theory in order to explain this mismatch between economic and political strength. Cooperation between states hinges most of all on the existence of a common interest in obtaining a particular collective good. It is doubtful, however, that there exist collective goods that justify very close cooperation between the European Union member states, outside the domain of commercial policy and collective security, in which there is indeed close cooperation.[8] And even if additional collective goods exist, the European Union member states do not seem to perceive it this way (Gnesotto 1996; Burghardt 1995).

The need to cooperate in commercial policy is inevitable because of the imperatives of the internal market, that led for example to the introduction of the common external tariff with third countries. In commercial policy, the European Union acts decisively and with some degree of success, as in GATT negotiations and in commercial disputes with the United States and other countries. Moreover, commercial policy is an exclusive competence of the European Union and thus one area where an integrationist form of cooperation predominates. Cooperation in the domain of security is also crucial and this is why it is so frequent, either through the WEU or through NATO. Outside these two domains, the payoff from cooperation is less clear, with greater gains from cooperation to be obtained with respect to bordering areas such as Central and Eastern Europe and the Mediterranean basin. One could thus argue that although the European Union failed a major test during the war in Yugoslavia because of lack of consensus on a particular course of action between the major EU players, it is not clear what the collective stakes were, besides the EU's prestige, that would have led to a more coherent foreign policy: Germany's almost unilateral decision to recognize the new self-proclaimed independent republics, which contradicted initial EU policy tending to support Yugoslavia's unity (e.g., Brioni Agreements in 1991), Greece's opposition to recognizing Macedonia, and France's and Great Britain's ambiguous attitude toward the parties in conflict, debilitated the EU's diplomatic actions but did not threaten the security of the EU or major economic or political interests. One could accuse the EU of failing a test of morality, but it is not so clear whether they failed from a Machiavellian perspective, apart from the fact that the EU lost a lot of money that might have been saved through more decisive action at the start of the hostilities.[9]

Diplomatic disunity was one factor behind the EU's poor performance during the war in Yugoslavia. The other significant factor was the WEU's lack of the operational capability to conduct military actions independently of NATO, had the will to act existed (which is not at all clear, given that France and the United Kingdom seemed, through their actions, to be somewhat sympathetic to the Serbian side). Everybody recognized that an external military solution to end the war in Yugoslavia was fraught with difficulties, because of the nature of the war and the geographic characteristics of Yugoslavia. The only viable approach seemed to be the debilitation of the Bosnian-Serb army through carefully targeted air attacks. This was an operation that only NATO could carry out.

In sum, the EU thus far has shown little diplomatic and military muscle in international crises. The explanation for this is less the lack of supranational arrangements than the fact that its members lack a common vision of how to solve the crises that arise and that they have thus far lacked the military capacity to intervene. In the near future, it is unlikely that this situation will change very much. First, because of a lack of commonly perceived interests in crises whose implications for Europe's security and economic well being are far from clear (Allen and Smith, 1990). Secondly, because even if it develops its military capabilities, the presence of neutral, anti-militaristic, countries in the EU will make it difficult for the EU to agree to use force for anything other than peace-keeping purposes. Thirdly, because it will be difficult for the EU to act independently of the US's wishes, even if the EU has already developed its military capacity. European Union member states will probably continue to try to assert their autonomy vis à vis the US, by further integrating the WEU into the institutional structure of the EU and developing the WEU's operational structure. Simultaneously, they will try to counterbalance the power of the United States within NATO itself. The integration of France and Spain into NATO's military structure, at first glance an indication that they see it as the most appropriate forum for organizing Europe's defense, may in this sense turn out to be a Trojan Horse.

Conclusion

The previous pages provide an explanation for the form of cooperation within foreign affairs and security policy in the European Union and for the unsatisfactory role played by the European Union in recent international crises. This argument rests on a clear conceptual distinction between forms of cooperation (coordination strategies), of which intergovernmentalism and integration are the two poles of a continuum, and the degree of efficacy in a particular policy area. Moreover, the comparison between the integration processes in the economic and political spheres permits a more balanced analysis of the European Union's foreign affairs and security policy, one that focuses as much on factors that slow down integration as on factors that would accelerate it. The first conclusion of this comparison is that integration in the foreign affairs and security policy area has proceeded more slowly than it has in the economic area because no foreign affairs and security policy objective has arisen that was of such urgency that the EU member states, unable to find a commonly agreed intergovernmental solution, would be open to persuasion by advocates of an integrationist solution. The closest Europeans came to having an integrated defense system was at the end of World War II, when the EDC was proposed. The EDC project was primarily the victim, however, of shifting government coalitions in France. The second conclusion of this comparison is that the efficacy or role of the European Union in international politics is hampered not by the lack of integration in the foreign affairs and security area but by a lack of common interests and by low operational capability. In areas where European Union states agree that they have a common interest, such as commercial policy, development aid, and security, they have been quite effective, but in other areas, where a perceived common interest did not exist or a very sophisticated military capability was needed, they have been less effective. The main predictions that follow from this analysis are that steps toward integration in European foreign affairs and security policy are unlikely in the short term and that the EU will try to assert its military autonomy vis à vis the United States, both by strengthening the WEU and by penetrating the NATO structures. Meanwhile, the role of the EU in international affairs will in all likelihood remain hostage to the differences of interest that exist between its major states.

NOTES

1 For a clearer conceptual distinction, see Hill (1993) and Allen and Smith (1990).
2 In this sense Ikenberry's optimism (this volume) about the harmony existing in NATO after the Cold War, and his dismissal of realism, are perhaps exaggerated. It is true that the US has exerted a particularly successful form of hegemony but it was and is not devoid of tension. Current debates within NATO (e.g., who will command NATO's southern flank) and attempts by the EU to gain more autonomy vis à vis NATO reveal this tension.
3 Robert Schuman would say (translated from the French): "The solidarity of production that will be so achieved will guarantee that any war between France and Germany will become not only unthinkable, but also materially impossible" (May 9, 1950).
4 And it totally contradicts Pijpers' assertion that domestic factors did not play any role in the development of a common European foreign affairs policy (1991: 28).
5 Allen and Smith (1990) trace these changes to the 1970s.
6 On American, British, French, and German positions with respect to foreign affairs policy, see Moens and Anstis (1994) and Masclet (1994).
7 If Brawley's prediction (1997) about the declining dissuasion of economic

sanctions resulting from globalization proves true, the European Union may lose one of its most significant weapons.

8 Thus, for David Allen and Michael Smith, "Western Europe is neither a fully-fledged actor nor a purely dependent phenomenon in the contemporary international arena. Rather, it is a variable multi-dimensional presence, which plays an active role in some areas of international interactions and a less active one in others" (Allen and Smith 1990).

9 Manuel Marín (EU Commissioner) (September 15, 1994, addressing the European Parliament) (author's translation): "In Rwanda we have spent 350 million Ecus. If one adds what the member states have spent individually and the contributions of non-governmental organizations (NGO) and specialized agencies, the sum of expenditures that we committed in Rwanda in the three months was over 500 million Ecus. This year we have spent only 158 million Ecus in Yugoslavia . . . [W]ith 500 million Ecus, couldn't we have sent capable people to prevent the conflict from happening?"

REFERENCES

Allen, David and Smith, Michael 1990, "Western Europe's Presence in the Contemporary International Arena," *Review of International Studies* 16: 19–39.
Axelrod, Robert 1984, *The Evolution of Cooperation*, New York: Basic Books.
Baldwin, David A. (ed.) 1993, *Neorealism and Neoliberalism: The Contemporary Debate*, New York: Columbia University Press.
Brawley, Mark R. 1997, "Globalization, Democratization and the Paradoxical Future of Economic Sanctions," paper presented at Conference on International Order in the Twenty-First Century, Montreal, May 16–17.
Burghardt, Gunther 1995, "Politique étrangère et de sécurité commune: garantir la stabilité à long terme de l'Europe," *Revue du Marché Commun Européen*, Paris: Clément Juglar.
Dumoulin, André 1995, *L'UEO et la politique européenne de défense*, Paris: Documentation Française.
Fabre, Dominique 1996, *La politique étrangère et de sécurité commune (PESC)*, Paris: Documentation Française.
Fligstein, Neil and Mara-Drita, Iona 1996, "How to Make a Market: Reflections on the Attempt to Create a Single Market in the European Union," *American Journal of Sociology* 102: 1–33.
Garrett, Geoffrey and Weingast, Barry 1993, "Ideas, Interests, and Institutions: Constructing the EC's Internal Market," in *Ideas and Foreign Policy*, Judith Goldstein and Robert Keohane (eds.), Ithaca: Cornell University Press, pp. 173–206.
Gnesotto, Nicole 1996, *La défense européenne au carrefour de la Bosnie et de la CIG*, Paris: Institut français des relations internationales.
Haas, E. B. 1958, *The Uniting of Europe: Political, Social, and Economic Forces, 1950–1957*, Stanford: Stanford University Press.
Hill, Christopher 1993, "The Capability-Expectations Gap or Conceptualizing Europe's International Role," *Journal of Common Market Studies* 31: 305–28.

Hoffmann, Stanley 1991, "Balance, Concert, Anarchy, or None of the Above," in Gregory F. Treverton (ed.) *The Shape of the New Europe*, New York: Council on Foreign Relations Press, pp. 194–220.

Keohane, Robert K. 1984, *After Hegemony*, Princeton: Princeton University Press.

1986, *Neorealism and its Critics*, New York: Columbia University Press.

1988, "International Organizations: Two Approaches," *International Studies Quarterly* 32: 379–96.

Keohane, Robert and Hoffmann, Stanley 1991, *The New European Community*, Boulder, CO: Westview Press.

1992, "Conclusions: Community Politics and Institutional Change," in *The Dynamic of European Integration*, William Wallace (ed.), London: Pinter Publishers, pp. 276–300.

Krasner, Stephen D. (ed.) 1983, *International Regimes*, Ithaca: Cornell University Press.

1991, "Global Communications and National Power: Life on the Pareto Frontier," *World Politics* 43: 336–66.

Masclet, Jean-Claude 1994, *Où en est l'Europe politique*, Paris: Documentation Française.

Maury, Jean Pierre 1996, *La construction européenne: La sécurité et la défense*, Paris: Presses Universitaires de France.

Moens, Alexander and Anstis, Christopher (eds.) 1994, *Disconcerted Europe: The Search for a New Security Architecture*, Boulder, CO: Westview Press.

Moracvsik, Andrew 1991, "Negotiating the Single Act: National Interests and Conventional Statecraft in the European Community," *International Organization* 45: 19–56.

Morrow, James D. 1994, "Modeling the Forms of International Cooperation: Distribution versus Information," *International Organization* 48: 387–423.

Nuttall, Simon 1992, *European Political Cooperation*, Oxford: Clarendon Press.

Pierson, Paul 1996, "The Path to European Integration: A Historical Institutional Analysis," *Comparative Political Studies* 29: 123–63.

Pijpers, Alfred E. 1991, "European Political Cooperation and the Realist Paradigm," in Mike Holland (ed.), *The Future of european Political Cooperation: Essays on Theory and Practice*. London: Macmillan, pp. 8–35.

Powell, Robert 1994, "Anarchy in International Relations Theory: The Neorealist-Neoliberal Debate," *International Organization* 48: 313–44.

Smith, Michael E. 1998, "Rules, Transgovernmentalism, and the Expansion of European Political Cooperation," in *European Integration and Supranational Governance*, Wayne Sandholtz and Alec Stone-Sweet (eds.), Oxford: Oxford University Press, pp. 434–77.

Snidal, Duncan 1985, "Coordination versus Prisoners' Dilemma: Implications for International Cooperation and Regimes," *American Political Science Review* 79: 923–42.

Stein, Arthur A. 1990, *Why Nations Cooperate: Circumstance and Choice in International Relations*, Ithaca: Cornell University Press.

Ullman, Richard 1991, *Securing Europe*, Princeton: Princeton University Press.

Wallace, William (ed.) 1992, *The Dynamic of European Integration*, London: Pinter Publishers.

Waltz, Kenneth 1979, *Theory of International Politics*, Reading, MA: Addison-Wesley.

Weiler, J. H. H. and Wessels, W. 1988, "EPC and the Challenge of Theory," in *European Cooperation in the 1980s: A Common Foreign Policy for Western Europe?* E. Pijpers, E. Regelsberger, W. Wessels, and G. Edwards (eds.), Dordrecht: Martinus Nijhoff, pp. 229–58.

9 Unsteady anticipation: reflections on the future of Japan's changing political economy

T. J. Pempel

For the past several years, Japan has been in the midst of a fundamental regime shift domestically. First, the long-standing dominance by the Liberal Democratic Party (LDP) ended with the party's internal fragmentation and its loss of executive control in July 1993, as well as the introduction of a completely new electoral system for the House of Representatives and party system realignment. Second, Japan's endless string of economic achievements came to a crushing halt with the puncturing of the economic bubble; the simultaneous collapse of both stock and land prices (Noguchi 1992: 25); years of torpid growth; the collapse of a number of major financial institutions; and a substantial loosening of the country's long-standing mercantilism. Third, the once fraternal relationship with the United States, solidified by their common Cold War opposition to the USSR and China, has given way to increased economic competitiveness and technonationalism.

The international conditions facing Japan changed as well. The end of the Cold War meant a drastic reduction in the likelihood of nuclear war and superpower confrontation. It also eliminated much of the logic behind Japan's tight military alliance with the US as well as Japanese security concerns about Russia and China. Economics consequently became an increasingly important currency of international relations. Meanwhile, until the Asian financial crisis of 1997–8, the entire Asian region enjoyed remarkable economic growth and was thereby catapulted into enhanced international significance, even as it continued to house many of the world's most nettlesome trouble spots.

The central question that Japan poses for international relations at the turn of the century is the extent to which these new domestic and international conditions will in fact compel Japan to alter its previous foreign policies in any fundamental way. For virtually the entire postwar period, Japan practiced an international relations best described as low posture. It was closely linked to cooperation with the United States and driven by economic rather than military ends and means (Katzenstein and Okawara 1993; Sato 1989). For many, this seemed to change in a strategically insignificant, but ideologically monumental way, when Japan agreed to send military troops to participate in United Nations Peace Keeping Operations (PKO) in Cambodia and Mozambique. Ultimately the question for the future is whether Japan is more likely to continue its relatively passive and highly economic approach to international relations or whether it will take a far more active and interventionist posture in world affairs. Rather than try to predict how domestic and international conditions will evolve in the abstract and then to build even more tenuous predictions on how Japanese policy will develop as a consequence, I suggest that Japan's future behavior will emerge as an outgrowth of three central tensions. It is their interaction that will be primarily shaping Japan's future.

Three central tensions

The first tension is that between domestic and international forces. What works well for domestic Japanese politics and economics is frequently at odds with what is conducive to an improved position for Japan internationally. This tension was one of the major issues dividing Japanese conservative and progressive forces throughout the postwar period. It was also particularly acute within the ranks of the LDP before the party split in 1993; it was even more widespread during the coalition between the LDP and the socialists, as debate ranged across a wide ideological gap on such issues as participation in PKO, the constitutionality and mission of Japan's Self-Defense Forces, how to deal with Japanese military activities in Asia during the Pacific War, and other issues. It remains alive in different form in intra-conservative debates over US troops and bases on Okinawa ("Cracks Form" 1994: 1). This tension is critical to understanding the extent to which domestic politics will lead to an enhanced Japanese role internationally or whether domestic politics will constrain any such moves.

The second tension is between regionalism and internationalism. Despite China's size and population and Japan's economic slowdown throughout the 1990s, Japan remains the most powerful economy in Asia. At the same time, Japan's preeminence in the region is far from unquestioned. Simultaneously, however, as a member of the G7 and an economic power with extensive international interests beyond Asia, Japan has powers and interests that extend far beyond the region. Quite frequently, Japan's broader international orientations conflict with those inherent in any emerging regional role. The central question to examine is the extent to which Japan will focus its attention on a regional Asian role as opposed to being a much more internationally oriented player throughout the world at large, possibly with negative consequences for any potential regional role.

The third and final tension concerns the different mechanisms through which Japan will act. Three central dimensions are relevant: economic, diplomatic, and military. The lines separating these three are somewhat blurry; yet the tendencies associated with each pole remain quite distinct. Since 1945, Japan has relied principally on economic rather than on diplomatic or military means to achieve its foreign policy goals. Whether that pattern will continue in the future remains unclear.

This chapter explores the interaction of these three sets of tensions in an effort to apprise the likely directions for future Japanese foreign policy. While the three are examined separately, it should be obvious that the linkages among them are strong. A few illustrations should make this fusion clear. For example, as a country, Japan has been far more responsive to the international pulls of economics than to those of diplomacy or security. Phrased differently, Japan is a serious "international" contender economically; yet it has been terribly parochial, introspective, and barely regionally significant in its diplomatic or military activities. Similarly, Japan's government was aggressively international at various times in areas involving technology, administrative reform, and in the overseas investment policies and production processes of many of its manufacturing corporations. Yet a completely contradictory image of insular protection emerges in areas like the selective rewriting of Japanese history by the Ministry of Education or the xenophobic immigration procedures followed by the Ministry of Justice; the embedded corruption, electoral pandering, and nationalistic blusterings so readily found within the nation's political parties; the inefficiencies of its mom and pop retailers and many of its service sector firms; national tardiness in internet usage; longtime insulation from world capital markets, protectionism for its numerous "troubled industries" (Uriu 1996), as well as its heavily subsidized and well-protected farmers who tend their rice plants more like bonsai plants than mechanized cash crops.

Japan's preeminence in Asia is striking when one examines the concentration of Japanese foreign aid, the expansion of Japanese production networks into Southeast Asia, the concentration of Asian foreign labor in Japan, or the frequent hand-wringing about "resurgent Japanese militarism" by Chinese or South Korean government officials. Many Asian countries are also highly dependent on Japan for investment, technology, and markets. Certain Japanese "cultural" exports such as karaoke, *Popeye* or *Brutus* magazines, and disco styles also permeate the Asian region. Yet Japan's regional activities pale compared to the broader internationalism of Mitsubishi Trading or Japanese bond holdings, Japan's dependence on US markets or Middle Eastern oil, or the list of concert artists booked into Kumamoto or Roppongi.

Nevertheless, for analytic purposes the three tensions can be examined independently. Only then can one begin to explore their possible future interactions.

Domestic versus international pressures

Perhaps the most widely accepted axiom of modern politics is that "all politics is local politics." This has been at least as true in Japan as in almost any other country. Indeed, as a country devoid of the ethnic, religious, linguistic, or racial divisions so prevalent in most other industrialized democracies, and as a country that has been stripped of its former colonial outposts, Japan lacks many of the most important domestic constituencies that spur increased international activism in other countries. Consequently, Japanese political elites have undoubtedly been even more locally fixated than their counterparts in many other democracies. This local focus has become even more acute as a result of the country's economic problems in the 1990s.

The two major parties of the postwar period, the LDP and the Japan Socialist Party (JSP), were radically divided in their foreign policy orientations. But long-term LDP hegemony assured that Japan followed policies closely linked to those of the United States. The party had its periodic internal disputes over foreign policy direction. But for most of its reign, the LDP was fundamentally a locally oriented, patronage-driven, electoral machine. Party backbenchers in particular fixed their eyes perennially on issues that animated constituents in their local districts, rather than those that dominated the headlines on the international pages of Japan's major newspapers. Local biases also had a rural and non-metropolitan proclivity enhanced through gerrymandering, pork barrel subsidies, and the party's links to the construction industry (Kobayashi 1990: 152–60; Ishikawa 1988).

Some internationalist leadership did emerge from elected politicians, despite the localist bias of the party as a whole, since senior politicians from safe seats were "freed" to take such initiatives. Yoshida ended the Occupation and set the stage for the alliance with the US; Hatoyama entered into peace talks with the USSR in 1956; Kishi led the revision of the US-Japan Security Treaty; Sato achieved the return of Okinawa; Tanaka normalized relations with China; Nakasone sought to project the image of being a foreign policy innovator (Nakasone 1995: 7); Hashimoto oversaw the 1996 adjustment of defense guidelines between the US and

Japan. For the most part, however, these initiatives were first taken and then presented to a generally tolerant, if not openly accepting, public; rarely were they the outgrowth of electoral politics or public debate.

Very seldom in postwar Japanese history have international concerns gained high salience among voters and this trend has become more apparent over time. Indeed, Japanese domestic politics was far more concerned with international issues in the 1950s and 1960s than it was two or three decades later. In the earlier years, foreign policy and particularly bipolar relations with the United States were highly relevant to Japanese voting behavior. Confrontations between the two Cold War camps and their surrogates catalyzed various interest groups, demonstrators, and politicians in Japan in ways that often influenced domestic political decisions. This was true, for example, of the debates over the 1952 Peace Treaty, the use of Japanese military bases by US forces, the attempted normalization of Japan's relations with the USSR, the 1960 Security Treaty revision, and the reversion of Okinawa. But from the end of the war in Vietnam (or at least the quadrupling of world oil prices in 1973) until the debates within Japan over participation in the Gulf War and the peace-keeping operations in Cambodia and elsewhere, international events and Japan's world role were rarely of great relevance to Japanese domestic politics. A quiet international context allowed domestic political concerns to dominate the political agenda. The end result was that electoral politics rarely drove foreign policy or had major foreign policy consequences.

The 1990s brought changes. The debate over Article IX of the Constitution and Japan's Self-Defense Forces, the legitimacy of sending Japanese troops abroad as part of United Nation's peacekeeping operations, and debates over US bases in Okinawa provided a wedge behind which individual conservatives resurrected long dead debates over whether the 1947 Constitution should be revised, the US-Japan Security Treaty should be continued, and Japan should move toward a more activist foreign policy. Ironically, it was the socialists who revised their once sanctified positions and surrendered their entire ideological agenda. Consequently, Japan now can consider international options that would have been domestically unacceptable only a decade or so earlier. At the same time, however, current debates have engendered no particular clarity in favor of an enhanced international role. Certainly, none of the governments through 1998 showed any movement in such a direction. Quite the contrary: while there have been some "internationalist" voices, the predominant thrust has been continued "localism." A case might be made for some shifts under Hashimoto, particularly as regards the articulation of more explicit security cooperation with the US, but this hardly involved any radical national repositioning; it was simply a rearticulation of past policies with a slightly enhanced role for the Japanese military. Japanese domestic politics remains strongly biased against any serious expansion of Japan's foreign policy activities.

The 1993 split in the LDP did culminate in part from tensions related to localism versus internationalism. The LDP had, since its foundation, comfortably housed a collection of economically diverse interests – most notably big and small business as well as agriculture. High growth allowed public policies that were economically inefficient, but which were politically critical to keeping the LDP together. Slower growth and the post-1990 recession unmasked these underlying incompatibilities unveiling the different interests of "protectionist" and "internationalist" groups. Similarly, starting in the mid-1970s but accelerating after the end of the Cold War, pressure from the US for the opening up of Japan's internal markets on a variety of products further exacerbated these tensions. The result was the emergence of a division between internationalist, anti-protectionist, and deregulatory advocates on the one hand, and domestic, protectionist, and re-regulatory advocates on the other.

The first group links, among others, Japan's international businesses, unions employed in export industries, and those who would benefit from a more open Japanese market such as urban consumers and, increasingly, Japanese savers. The second involves groups more narrowly nationalistic, including Japan's small shopkeepers, farmers, and those threatened by foreign direct investment and foreign imports. This division was temporarily institutionalized at the party political level in the somewhat disproportionate "internationalist" orientation of many New Frontier Party (NFP) members, and the conversely more "protectionist" biases and constituencies of those in the LDP, but this division was hardly clear-cut. And it became more blurred at the electoral level with the splintering of the NFP. Yet some such nationalist-internationalist realignment is likely to reemerge in future party alignments.

Despite journalistic predictions to the contrary, the introduction of a new electoral system before the 1996 election, and the numerous party realignments of the early- to mid-1990s are unlikely to alter the local orientation of most politicians. Indeed, the new single member districts will be considerably smaller and more compact than those they replace, providing an even greater spur to electoral localism. Furthermore, Japan's most powerful individual politicians will continue to be those with strong local constituencies grounded in well-established personal support groups (kôenkai). Many of these are so well institutionalized that they are passed on from father to son (or other heir apparent) very much like a family heirloom. These will remain key elements in future constituency competitions, and there is no reason to think that they will engender much increased internationalism in electoral politics.

Japan's elected officials have not been alone in their localist biases, and this too is unlikely to change. Most of Japan's bureaucratic ministries also focus inward. The exception of course is the Ministry of Foreign Affairs, whose principal mission is Japanese diplomacy and foreign relations, and this agency has been among the most cautious in pressing for any increased role for Japan internationally beyond generic commitments to peace, tranquillity, and a greater formal role for Japan in international organizations. Constituent-oriented ministries such as Agriculture, Forestry and Fisheries; Education; Construction; Home Affairs; and Transportation are all fundamentally oriented toward domestic issues. They are likely to remain so in the near future (Muramatsu, Itô and Tsujinaka 1986, chs. 4, 5). So, until the late 1980s, has been the Ministry of International Trade and Industry (MITI), when its primary constituents were domestic industries undergoing reorganization. MITI's overseas activities were directed largely at expanding market opportunities for Japanese manufacturing firms rather than at encouraging foreign-domestic mergers, bringing foreign products into Japan, allowing Japanese consumers the opportunity to enjoy lifestyles equal to those of North Americans or Western Europeans or in any other way "internationalizing" the Japanese home market. Only in the late 1980s did MITI's bias shift toward opening Japan somewhat and helping foreign firms penetrate the hitherto closed Japanese market. In the future, MITI is likely to be more a force for internationalism than for localism, but this will clearly be in the economic arena and within Japan, rather than in the diplomatic arena and overseas. Interestingly, the Ministry of Finance (MOF) has also been a non-internationalist force. MOF has long had the domestic budget and regulation of domestic financial institutions as its principal concerns. It worked to insulate Japanese capital markets from those of the rest of the world, leaving them largely uncompetitive. Localism and protection have dominated MOF's response to the financial and banking crises of the 1990s, the *jûsen* debacle, the exposure of trading scandals by Daiwa bank officials in New York, and revelations of links between stockbrokerages and organized crime throughout the 1990s.

The most likely source of any substantial pressure for greater internationalism by Japan is its most sophisticated and internationalized businesses. Many, such as Sony, Toyota, Canon, and the like have developed clear corporate interests in a more internationalized Japan and a Japanese economy more closely integrated with that of the rest of the world. Similarly, international currency flows, the power of international ratings agencies such as Moody's and Standard and Poor's, the increasing number of corporate alliances between Western and Japanese firms – particularly within the financial sector – and the promised de-regulation of Japanese financial markets are all exerting powerful press-ures for a more internationalized Japanese economy. As a consequence, domestic banking, insurance, and brokerage activities in Japan are being forced to develop enhanced sensitivity to international pressures. To that extent MOF, like MITI, and quite possibly even one or more of the major political parties, will almost certainly be forced to become an even greater voice for international integration than they have been in the past. The primary manifestation of those shifts is most likely to be economic in character.

Hence, at the turn of the century, future governments in Japan will confront somewhat greater pressures to become more internationally proactive than were earlier governments. Yet within conservative party circles and within the national bureaucracy, as well as within many of Japan's less competitive corporations and industrial sectors, numerous powerful groups and organizations clearly prefer to keep things more or less the same and to retain the focus on what are seen to be local problems, rather than to open Japan dramatically to greater foreign influences or to deal preemptively with what is going on elsewhere in the world. Dramatic changes in the external conditions Japan confronts might well alter this domestic bias. So might certain party reorganiz-ations. But neither seems likely to be of such proportions as to catalyze the nation toward a dramatically more activist international role. Ab-sent some dramatic shift, the principal bias of Japan's domestic politics and economy is toward a retention of the status quo with a reluctant and gradual movement toward tentative expansion of foreign policy activism.

Regional versus international

That Japan will play a larger international role in the century to come than it did from the 1950s through the 1980s is probable. But the extent to which that role will be truly international or primarily regional is less clear. Japan has the most powerful economy in Pacific Asia and stands as an economic Gulliver in a region of Lilliputians (Pempel 1997). Its gross national product (GNP) is about six times greater than the combined GNPs of Taiwan, South Korea, Singapore, and Hong Kong. Although China has been growing fast and is projected to have the region's largest GNP by 2015, Japan easily surpasses the Central Kingdom in per capita income, finance, trade, advanced industrial production, and research, and will do so for many decades to come.

Many would even suggest that Japan is also the most powerful military presence in the region, even though in sheer arms, there are many more serious contenders. China has three million troops; India and North Korea each have over one million, Japan has only 245,000; it also has relatively few combat aircraft and limited force projection capability. But, except for the US, Japan has by far the most technologically sophisticated military force in Asia Pacific.

As Europe has moved to create a unified economic zone, and as NAFTA has gained momentum as a North American trade unit, many pundits have suggested that Asia, with Japan at its center, would emerge logically as a third regional bloc, quite possibly the most economically dynamic of the three. In this way the world's three most powerful national economies (the US, Germany, and Japan) would each be at the core of a regionally based trade and investment bloc – all three highly competitive with one another, a scenario vaguely reminiscent of George Orwell's nightmarish dystopia, *1984*.There is considerable evidence to support such a scenario. Approximately 70 percent of Japanese foreign aid is directed toward Asia, and virtually all major recipients of Japanese aid are Asian. As labor costs have risen in Japan, Japanese firms have invested vast sums in search of cheap labor. Initially this involved South Korea, Hong Kong, and Taiwan; subsequently the money moved to Thailand, Malaysia, Indonesia, and Singapore. Numerous Japanese firms have begun integrated worldwide production with Asian factories as key components (Hatch and Yamamura 1996). Japan is the largest foreign investor in Indonesia, Malaysia, and Thailand, and the second largest investor in Singapore and the Philippines. The amount of Japanese money moving into all of these economies has been ratcheting upwards annually. Kumagai Gumi (HK) developed China's first free trade zone (Yangpu). And the integration of the Russian Far East into such a bloc is also possible, with Narita airport much closer to Siberia than is Moscow.

Intra-Asian trade has also been on the rise, offering further evidence for the development of Asian regional ties. Japanese exports to Asia rose from 31 percent in 1970 to 38 percent in 1980 to 45.7 percent in 1995 (Tsûshô Sangyôsho 1994: Vol. II, 6–7; Kokuseisha 1996: 357; Asahi Shimbun 1996: 108). Significantly, in 1991, for the first time in decades, total Japanese exports to Asia were greater than Japanese exports to the United States. Meanwhile, imports from Asia to Japan rose from 29.6 percent in 1970 to 41.9 percent and 46.1 percent in 1990 and 1995 respectively (Tsûshô Sangyôsho 1994: Vol. I, 176). Furthermore, nearly 50 percent of Pacific air cargo now moves between Asian destinations. The port of Singapore handles more shipments than any other destination on the globe, and about half arrive from its immediate neighbors – Malaysia, Thailand, Hong Kong, and Taiwan.

Nearly one-half of all Japanese tourists still pick Asian countries as their primary destination (Keizai Koho Center 1992: 92). Japanese yuppie magazines tout the merits of Asian discos, karaoke bars, and cinemas. Asians are increasingly learning Japanese as their second or third language; others are taking advantage of Japan's perceived labor shortage to seek illegal employment within the country in construction, entertainment, and factories. Japan's economic preeminence in the region is exacerbated by the relatively shrinking presence and leadership of the United States. The US has begun to move troops out of the region and has also pared nonmilitary aid to Asian nations to virtually nothing. Japan's aid to the region, by way of contrast, totaled $4.4 billion in 1989 and by 1995 was up to $7.9 billion ("Japan's Spreading Regional" 1990: 96; for 1995, Asahi Shimbun 1996: 115). The US was far slower than Japan to normalize relations with China after Tiananmen, and also to improve relations with Vietnam.

Private sector US investment in Asia continues to grow, but at a pace far slower than that of Japanese corporations. In the mid-1990s, Japanese FDI outstripped that of US corporations by about three to one. Japanese investment was up five times over that of 1985 while that of the US barely doubled. Furthermore, about one-half of US investment in Asia is for natural resource extraction, especially oil and natural gas, and is particularly concentrated in Indonesia and Malaysia; Japan's broader and manufacturing-based dominance is thus even more conspicuous. With the US foreign policy and business focus seeming to shift away from the Pacific, Japan has become a more preeminent regional player if only by default.

Nevertheless, despite Japan's strong Asian presence, counter-pressures are also strong. Much of the rest of Asia, mindful of earlier expansionist efforts in the name of the Greater East Asia Co-Prosperity Sphere, remains wary of Japan. Japan, unlike Germany, has done little systematically to come to grips with the horrors of its military expansion and activities during the 1930s and 1940s. The result is that many Asian leaders, particularly in China and Korea, despite their desire to attract Japanese aid, capital, technology, and management, feel compelled to criticize any Japanese actions that seem to them to reflect myopic parallels with Japan's past. Still, while Chinese, Korean, and Philippine leaders are quick to draw attention to the negative legacy of Japan's military activities during the Pacific War, the mood in Southeast Asia is more ambivalent. There, memories of the harshness of Japanese military conquest are counterbalanced by the recognition that Japan also helped to catalyze nationalist independence movements against the European colonial powers. This is particularly true in Indonesia and Burma, while Thailand was actually allied with Japan for part of the war. Furthermore, the Asian adolescents who fought against Japan in 1945 and are now company chairmen and cabinet ministers are near the end of their careers. Today, only one in six Asians was born prior to 1945. Most are too young to have particularly adverse reactions to contemporary Japan's much milder and principally economic presence. Resistance to an increased role for Japan from among future Asian elites is almost certain to diminish, albeit cautiously.

Nonetheless, any growing role for Japan in Asia is unlikely to be unilateral or uncomplicated. Japan's predominance in Asia will confront at least three other competing trends: first, the US military's continued presence in Asia; second, the growing role of Asian powers not so dependent on Japanese capital or technology; and third, the strong non-regional, broadly internationalist pressures and aspirations felt by Japan. Such pressures work, less against Japan being a preeminence in Asia, and more against Japan's definition of itself primarily as "the" regional power, or even as "a" regional power. If Japan becomes a regional power it will do so primarily with an eye toward ensuring an open, rather than a closed, Asian regionalism.

On the first point, while US companies may not be investing in Asia as rapidly as are their Japanese and other Asian counterparts, the US military has hardly been anxious to close its Japanese or Korean bases or to pull back the Seventh Fleet. The so-called Nye Initiative suggests that a strong US presence in Asia will continue.On the second point, trade patterns in Asia have become far less Japan-centric than they were in the early 1950s. Earlier patterns of trade saw Japan in a series of bilateral relations with most of Asia. In effect, Japan was the number one or number two trade partner of virtually every other Asian country and there was relatively little other intra-Asian trade. Growth in the economies of Taiwan, South Korea, and the ASEAN-4 meant that Japan's prior dominance became vastly more intricate and less bipolar (Bernhard and Ravenhill 1995: 171–209). Simultaneously, trade and investment ties among many of the other Asian economies are increasing independent of any Japanese role as a trade or capital hub. Particularly important is investment capital from Korea, Taiwan, and Hong Kong (Pempel 1997). Japan is likely to remain an economic powerhouse in Asia, but economic dynamism in Asia increasingly involves a highly complex interdependence that will serve as a check on any Japanese unilateralism – economic or political.

Third, Japan's trade and investment patterns are moving away from any particularly Asian focus. Japanese FDI remains critical to Asia, but at the same time Asia is becoming less centrally a site for Japanese FDI. In 1975, over one-third of all Japanese FDI went to Asia; since fiscal 1985, the figure has been only 10–15 percent annually ("Drop in the Bucket" 1990: 48). Japanese investment monies have been flowing more predominantly to North America and Europe.

In terms of trade, the pattern is more complicated. In 1980, Japan's trade with Asia represented 31.3 percent of its total, while the US and EC figures were 20.8 percent and 9.8 percent respectively. In 1990, Japan's trade with Asia was up slightly to 34.3 percent, but that with the US and the EC was also up to 27.5 percent and 17.1 percent respectively (International Monetary Fund annual). Thus Asian trade has become a larger proportion of total Japanese trade, but only slightly, while that with the more advanced industrial democracies went from 30 percent to nearly 45 percent of Japan's total. It is these latter countries that provide the inputs and markets for the most sophisticated and high-value-added products of Japan's most sophisticated manufacturers. Asian markets cannot fulfill that role, as became even more apparent during the regional economic crisis of 1997–8. Japan's economic linkages with the other advanced democracies are expanding far more rapidly than are its ties with the rest of Asia. Boldly stated, Japan has far more to lose by being primarily an Asian regional power than it has to gain by keeping open its economic and political links to North America and Europe.

Furthermore, Japan's activities in a host of international economic and political organizations also work against its limiting its perspective to that of "first among Asian equals." By focusing extensively on its potential political and economic role in Asia, Japan runs the risk of losing sight of its far broader linkages with the rest of the industrialized world. Indeed this is increasingly true of the Asian NICs as well. There is no question but that all are solidly linked to Japan, but all are fundamentally dependent on US markets as well. And in the case of Japan, the linkages extend even further to Europe. The US market remains four and a half times larger than Japan's number two export market. In addition, Japan is vitally dependent on US companies for critical products such as food supplies and oil. Thus, Japan is a "world economic superstar" mostly in terms of its GNP, capital holdings, and per capita income. It is far less a world economic power in terms of diversified market capabilities.

When the question turns to security, Japan's dependence on the United States and Western Europe is even more stark. The US-Japan Security Treaty can in no way be replaced by any intra-Asian security agreement. Indeed, the 1996 reinterpretation of that treaty reaffirmed for both Japan and the United States the continued importance of security linkages between the two countries, and guaranteed a continuation of US bases in Japan. Hitherto reluctant to take any independent military actions, Japan has recently begun to rely on United Nations resolutions as the justification for a minimal expansion in its overseas activities. These too rely far more heavily on US and European (including Russian) agreements than on anything agreed to within Asia. Any remaining Japanese hopes for a seat on the UN Security Council will be similarly biased against an excessively close reliance on Asian ties. For such reasons Japanese leaders have been extremely interested in keeping the US involved in any Asian regional economic organizations, such as APEC, and working against any closed economic regionalization of the world.

Yet Japan need not choose between these two roles. Japan is a de facto economic power in Asia. Moreover, former Prime Minister Miyazawa's January 1993 speech in Bangkok made it clear that Japan intends to take a leading role in establishing an Asian regional security framework for the future. These are likely to continue regardless of the character of changes in Japan's domestic politics. But such positioning must be seen as an add-on, not as a substitute for Japan's broader international role in the United Nations and in conjunction with the US and Europe. Japan cannot afford the luxury of any pure Asian regionalism.

Economics, politics, and security

A more active world role for Japan is likely to continue to reflect glaring imbalances among its economic, diplomatic, and security dimensions. Generally speaking, Japan has been at its most international and regional economically, while it has been least international and regional in security matters. Its political and diplomatic activities fall in between, but have been much closer to the relatively passive position it has taken in security affairs.

During the 1990s, Japan looked nothing like the economic colossus that had outstripped all other industrialized democracies for the previous four decades. The bursting of the "economic bubble" brought a sharp collapse in real estate and stock prices. On December 31, 1989 – perhaps a fitting end to the decade of the go-go eighties – the Nikkei Dow, which had tripled from around ¥13,000 in January 1986, hit an all-time high of just below ¥40,000. By mid-August of 1992, the market was more than 60 percent below that peak. In about two years, some ¥300 trillion in assets had disappeared. By early 1999, the index was stagnating in the ¥13,500 range. Asset deflation also took place in land prices, which were also ratcheted down from the astronomical levels they had achieved during the real estate boom of the late 1980s. A rough tripling had taken place in the land price index from about 200 in 1985 to nearly 600 at the end of 1989; by 1992 this had shrunk to about 350. With the exception of

1975, this was the only year in which land prices had actually recorded a decline. In Tokyo alone, some ¥100 trillion in assets were wiped out (Noguchi 1992: 23–5). This dual bursting of Japan's asset bubble led to a drastic alteration in the balance sheets of financial institutions, corporations, and individuals.

Meanwhile, money supply had stopped growing and bank lending was rising at the (for Japan) torpid rate of less than 3 percent annually (Yoshitomi 1992: 44–50). Annual growth in GNP had averaged 4.4 percent from 1977 to 1991. The 1990s in Japan, in contrast, were marked by the deepest and most prolonged recession in the country's postwar history. Decades of uninterrupted profitability gains by major Japanese corporations were reversed; there was a dramatic slowdown in overseas investment; and long-standing commitments to "permanent employment" were abrogated by numerous corporate giants. Without a doubt, many Japanese firms, particularly in the real estate, banking, and brokerage sectors were hard hit. Corporate profits fell dramatically for most of Japan's giants and were slow to recover. Vast sums were lost to speculation. Corporations found it extremely difficult to recover. Within the financial sectors in particular, the disaster was profound and deep. Those institutions that only a few years earlier had looked to be the most powerful players in world capital markets were suddenly facing ¥600 billion in bad loans, a widely imposed "Japan premium" tacked on to standard interest rates when they borrowed abroad, difficulties in meeting Bank of International Standards capital requirements, and regular downgrading of their debt ratings by international agencies.

Nevertheless, parts of Japan's macro-economic picture remain comparatively bright. Japan's government is the industrialized world's smallest, and the government has gone through major retrenchments in social welfare programs, all of which suggests that the public sector should be in a good position to ride out the downturn without being forced to become a major competitor in private capital markets. Even if recovery is not immediate, the Japanese economy has deeply rooted strengths that are likely to enable the country to overcome many of its most pressing problems once a clear political direction is established. In the private sector, many of Japan's firms, particularly in manufacturing, have reached a level of sophistication in production and penetration of world markets that allows them to retain high levels of competitiveness. Many Japanese manufacturers remain among the most technologically sophisticated and internationally competitive firms in the world. Japan's particular advantages are most notable in electronics and mechanical equipment. Japanese firms employ nearly four times as many robots as firms in the US and Germany combined.

Financial institutions, as has been noted, were clearly far less internationally competitive. Long insulated from international competitiveness, Japanese banks, brokerages, and insurance firms showed little ability to function effectively in head-to-head international competition with US, British, or German institutions. Similarly, a number of other industries, such as paper, textiles, shipbuilding, computer software, and aircraft manufacture show little sign of being true world competitors. Japan is also one of the industrialized world's slowest countries to embrace the internet. Competitiveness by Japanese firms in these sectors is likely only after massive restructuring, the political and corporate will for which remains weak. Thus the economic reorganization of Japan is likely to remain a long-term, complex, and conflict-ridden process and one that is almost certain to impede any Japanese efforts at playing a substantially larger international role. Nonetheless, to the extent that Japan has any likelihood of exerting greater regional or international leadership, the sphere of economics is most likely to provide the country with its greatest comparative advantage.

Politically, Japan has been far less visibly present in either the Asian region or in the world at large. At least since Prime Minister Ikeda (1960–4), Japan has sought to "separate economics from politics" in its foreign policy. Indeed, into the early 1980s, Japanese foreign policy involved largely lockstep imitation of US actions. Independent consideration of Japan's foreign interests and political or diplomatic means to achieve those ends was comparatively rare.

By the 1990s, Japan was showing a greater willingness to pursue more autonomy in some areas of its foreign policy. The country was not willing to follow the US in imposing economic sanctions against either Vietnam or China. Rather, it pursued more independent policies in both countries. Similarly, Japanese diplomats have been far less willing than either their US or German counterparts to worry about internal Russian political or economic stability (at least until the four Northern Islands are returned or at least promises of their return are secured). Unlike virtually all of the other industrialized democracies, in deference to Japan's Arab oil ties, Japan did not send a high-level political delegation to the funeral of Menachem Begin. In such areas, Japan during the 1990s showed an increased ability and willingness to separate many of its foreign policy interests from those of the US and to use diplomatic, and not just economic, means to achieve these ends. At the same time, Japan's independent actions remain largely at the margins of international significance. They hardly pose any major challenges to the overarching political directions pursued by the US, for example. Moreover, Japanese ends were rarely purely strategic or political (with the possible exception of the

Northern Islands issue). Far more frequently, manifestations of Japanese autonomy have been largely in the pursuit of its long-standing economic interests.

In this light, Japan showed only limited interest in taking independent positions on several problems crucial to international order, particularly when there were suggestions that Japan should provide military assistance. Nowhere was this more evident than in Japanese reactions to Iraq's August 1990 invasion of Kuwait. Following the invasion, it took Japan four days to do what the United States did in ten hours – impose a trade ban on Iraq. Facing a choice between Iraq, the oil producing country from which Japan received some 12 percent of its oil, and America, the country to which Japan sent some 36 percent of its exports and on which it relied for its overall security, Japan really had no choice but to line up with the United States. Subsequently, the Japanese government stumbled through a series of indecisive and contradictory moves regarding financial aid and the dispatching of personnel. Japan eventually emerged as a major economic contributor to the US-led actions under the UN mandate, but its actions were those of a country buying off the US rather than pursuing a thought-out foreign policy strategy.

As *The Economist* noted at the time (September 22, 1990: 35), "It is Japan's fluffing of its first – and maybe most telling – chance to show that in the new world order it will occupy something more than a narrow economic niche. Less abstractly, Japan's behavior has for now laid to rest the idea that it deserves the permanent seat on the UN Security Council it so covets." Whether or not Japan's overall policies eventually shift from "economics" to "security" or its foreign policies take on a non-economic dimension, there was little evidence of such movement in fall 1990. Nor was Japan's use of its economic prowess of a non-nationalistic, global character. Thus the country showed little willingness to play a serious leadership role in resolving the agricultural disputes that threatened to derail the Uruguay Round of GATT negotiations. Even the minimally symbolic step of formally opening up Japan's rice market behind high tariffs was rejected until the very last minute, and then it was passed under the cover of the need to import foreign rice to make up for Japan's bad harvest of 1993–4.

All the same, the eventual dispatch of Japanese minesweepers to the Middle East, the sending of troops to Cambodia, Mozambique, and the Golan Heights, as well as the wide-ranging debates over the possible revision of Article IX of the Constitution all hint that a watershed might have been passed in 1990. Furthermore, Japan's agreement to share military technology with the US, its apparent willingness to play a role in creating a framework for Asian regional security, and its expanded role under the US-Japan defense cooperation guidelines suggest that the hitherto sacrosanct barriers against even hinting at a greater military role for Japan are slowly being dismantled. In addition, the Japanese government played a major role in settling the nuclear issue in North Korea, proposing and then delivering on many key parts of the bargains whereby North Korea will renounce any nuclear military capabilities in favor of peaceful access to energy sources. And Japan proved to be a hard bargainer over food aid to North Korea in 1996–7.

Such actions, relatively minor as they might appear in the context of behavior by the US, France, Britain, or Germany, suggest that Japanese leaders and the Japanese public were, by the late 1990s, in the process of reconsidering prior taboos against diplomatic and military actions. Still, Japan's moves have been extremely incremental; the technology-sharing agreement with the US was driven more by economic than strategic considerations (Pempel 1990), and the dispatch of Japanese troops and other uses of Japanese military forces have been quite limited. Indeed, when Japanese troops were to replace Canadian peace-keepers in the Golan Heights, it took weeks of domestic wrangling to resolve the issue of whether the Japanese troops should be allowed to bring two rifles or three. Yet with China's military budget expanding, and with tensions high on the Korean peninsula, there will continue to be strong external pressures for Japan to increase its involvement in Asian security matters, and eventually to expand these to an even broader arena. Nevertheless, the first tool of diplomacy for Japanese officials remains economics. This is unlikely to change quickly even as Japan explores the use of greater diplomatic and strategic influence. Furthermore, most Japanese actions in these latter fields have continued to be closely coordinated with the United States and/or various international bodies. Japan has given little indication that it is anxious to move independently or aggressively in most international problem areas.

Conclusion

This chapter has outlined what I believe are the three major tensions that will shape Japan's future role in the world's evolving political economy. In working their way toward the twenty-first century, Japan's leaders are likely to have to steer among these three in their efforts to construct a cohesive policy direction for their country. Given the competing pulls of all three, cohesiveness is far less likely than a series of inconsistent zigs and zags. Clarity on national goals will be difficult to achieve and big initiatives are improbable. The strongest pulls for Japan to play a more international role, to internationalize its domestic economy, and to shape behavior in Asia, are likely to come from economic, rather than from diplomatic or military forces. Japan's economy has reached a stage of development where it is increasingly difficult for the country's political and bureaucratic leaders to resist the tremendous international impact of currency flows, overseas investment, the needs of Japanese and other multinational corporations, and the technological and labor market imperatives of an increasingly integrated world economy.

Similarly, Japan is likely to play an increased role, economically and (perhaps) politically and militarily, in Asia. But the country can do so successfully only to the extent that it does not ignore the far more compelling pull for it to be a major world player – reflecting its clear interests beyond the Asian region. In this way, although Japan will remain extremely critical to the countries of Asia, they are likely to diminish in inherent value to Japan. Japan might, for a variety of reasons, move to enhance its overall national influence over international and regional events. But there is little evidence so far to suggest that these moves will involve becoming a "contender" for significantly greater international influence, if being such a "contender" means seeking to rewrite the major rules and directions of international relations.

Rather, in groping toward any new role over the next decade or so, Japan is unlikely to move precipitously, unless major external threats force such action. Moreover, it is most likely that Japan will continue to resist acting autonomously. Instead it will act primarily through collective frameworks. In the past, Japan has been most comfortable operating within the collective framework of the United Nations, and other international organizations such as APEC, OECD, the World Bank, the IMF, and GATT. One of its major goals is to gain a permanent seat on the Security Council, although largely in an effort to show that it is recognized as "a major international actor" than to pursue some particular international agenda. Japan has historically sought to avoid international isolation, particularly after the disaster of World War II. Working through the collective security apparatus of the UN, as well as other international organizations, would be congruent with Japan's reluctance to stand alone, as well as with Asian reluctance to see the resurgence of a strong, independent-minded, and potentially bullying, Japan.

REFERENCES

Asahi Shimbun 1996, *Japan Almanac 1996*, Tokyo: Asahi Shimbun.
Bernhard, Mitchell and Ravenhill, John 1995, "Beyond Flying Geese and Product Cycles: Regionalization, Hierarchy, and the Industrialization of East Asia," *World Politics* 47: 171–209.
"Cracks Form in Newly Forged Opposition Party," 1994 *The Nikkei Weekly*

December 5.

"Drop in the Bucket," 1990, *Far Eastern Economic Review* December 20, 48–9.

Hatch, Walter and Kozo Yamamura 1996, *Asia in Japan's Embrace*, Cambridge: Cambridge University Press.

International Monetary Fund, annual, *Direction of Trade Statistics: Yearbook*, Washington, DC: IMF.

Ishikawa Masumi 1988, *Sengo Seiji Kôzôshi* [A Structural History of Postwar Politics], Tokyo: Nihon Hyôronsha.

"Japan's Spreading Regional Power," *Fortune*, "Pacific Rim" special edition, 1990.

Katzenstein, Peter J. and Nobuo Okawara 1993, *Japan's National Security*, Ithaca: Cornell East Asia Series.

Keizai Koho Center 1992, *Japan, 1992: An International Comparison*, Tokyo: Keizai Koho Center.

Kobayashi Yoshiaki 1990, *Gendai Nihon no Senkyô* [Contemporary Japanese Elections], Tokyo: Tokyo Daigaku Shuppan.

Kokuseisha 1996, *Nihon Kokusei Zue, 1996/97*, Tokyo: Kokuseisha.

Muramatsu Michio, Itô Mitsutoshi and Tsujinaka Yutaka 1986, *Sengo Nihon no Atsuryoku Dantai* [Pressure Groups in Postwar Japan], Tokyo: Tôyô Keizai Shimposha.

Nakasone, Yasuhiro 1995, "Pitchers and Catchers: Politicians, Bureaucrats, and Policy-Making in Japan," *Asia-Pacific Review* 2: 5–14.

Noguchi Yukio 1992, *Baburu no Keizaigaku* [The Economics of the Bubble Economy], Tokyo: Toyo Keizai Shimbunsha.

Pempel, T. J. 1990, "From Trade to Technology: Japan's Reassessment of Military Policies," *Jerusalem Journal of International Affairs* 12.

  1997, "Trans-Pacific Torii: Japan in the Asian Region," in *Network Power: Japan and Asia*, Peter J. Katzenstein and Takashi Shiraishi (eds.), Ithaca: Cornell University Press, pp. 47–82.

Sato Hideo 1989, *Taigai Seisaku* [Foreign Policy], Tokyo: Tokyo Daigaku Shuppan.

Tsûshô Sangyôsho 1994, *Tsûshô Hakusho, 1994* [Economic White Paper, 1994], Tokyo: Tsûshô Sangyôsho.

Uriu, Robert M. 1996, *Troubled Industries: Confronting Economic Change in Japan*, Ithaca: Cornell University Press.

Yoshitomi Masaru 1992, "Fukyô o Osoresugiru Seisaku ga Kuni o Horobosu," [A Policy of Overreacting to the Recession Could Ruin the Country] *Shûkan Tôyô Keizai* November 14.

10 Chinese perspectives on world order

Steve Chan

World order can mean several things. First, it can refer to an empirical state of affairs, describing an existing arrangement of status distribution among some state and/or nonstate actors. Second, it can present a normative vision, prescribing a system of preferred relations among these actors. Third, the term is sometimes used in association with a particular state to describe its policy behavior (such as when one refers to country x's approach to world order). Naturally, there can be considerable analytic and policy slippage among these alternate views of world order as de facto patterns, normative ideals, and strategic conduct. Nevertheless, these views are also certainly interrelated in the sense that their articulation suggests the deliberate pursuit or promotion of certain collective values based on a particular understanding of empirical reality and approach to managing or altering it.

To attribute such views on world order to an entire national entity implies a certain degree of coherence and homogeneity in the outlook of the relevant policy community or mass public. Such attribution is therefore likely to underestimate the extent to which significant tension can arise from disagreements about facts, values, and strategies among leaders, institutions, or groups belonging to the same state – tension which often gives rise to sharp shifts in policy lines (as they say in China) that surprise outside analysts. Concomitantly, this attribution can sound like national stereotyping. It calls attention to, and perhaps even exaggerates, the differences in national views, while overlooking possible similarities in pattern recognition, normative preferences, and policy conduct among the officials of different states.

These analytic hazards are especially pertinent in the study of Chinese views on world order. The relative inaccessibility of Beijing's policy processes seems to render the rational, unitary-actor approach to policy analysis a matter of making virtue out of necessity. The powerful authority of individuals such as Mao Tse-tung and Deng Xiaoping further encourages this analytic proclivity, which often personifies Chinese foreign policy in terms of the views and wishes of the current top leader.

This highly centralized, homogeneous, and personalized portrayal is periodically contradicted by major policy reversals and leadership purges such as the Cultural Revolution and the Sino-Soviet dispute. Beijing's tendency to engage in ideological propagation and moralistic posturing has the additional effect of inclining foreign scholars to dwell on the analysis of verbal rhetoric – often as a substitute for studying other kinds of policy behavior. For career reasons, Western Sinologists are prone to emphasize China's uniqueness – a claim with which Beijing is quite happy to concur for its own reasons (such as when it proclaims the building of "socialism with Chinese characteristics"). Rarely are China's policy rationale and conduct systematically compared with those of other countries.

How do these remarks relate to the topic of this chapter, China's conception of and role in world order? To anticipate the following discussion, I advance these general arguments – propositions that should be applicable to most other states. First, China's views on world order have been shaped by a combination of its historical conditions, physical milieu, and political fortunes. This argument reflects the basic premise of the perspective of "environmental probabilism" (Sprout and Sprout 1957). Second, these views have not been universally shared by all Chinese nationals nor have they been entirely consistent or static over time. Indeed, as one would expect in the case of any large, complex, and resilient culture such as China's, there are bound to be substantial diversity and flexibility in its components to enable it to adapt to regional differences and changing times. Third, and moreover, significant discrepancies can exist between form and content, belief and ritual, and professed ideals and actual practice. This phenomenon should again be hardly surprising in an historical or comparative context, and it does not necessarily mean hypocrisy, bad faith, or deliberate obfuscation. Indeed, a ritualistic conformity to proper form (orthopraxy) – coexisting with a practical acceptance of divergent beliefs (heterodoxy) – has been a hallmark of traditional Chinese culture. This feature contrasts with the European tradition of orthodoxies (especially in the religious realm) that emphasized content over form and belief over practice. It has facilitated the spread and preservation of Chinese culture over a vast geographic area by accommodating local variations and situational adaptation within a set of generalized rules governing rites (Watson 1993). Finally, Chinese views on international order have been closely tied to, and indeed inspired and motivated by beliefs about the nature of proper domestic order. The intimate relationship between these two realms of Chinese thinking explains the reference in this chapter to Chinese treatment of *world* order.

Imperial China

The formation of a pre-modern state in China is conventionally dated from the era of the Three Dynasties of Xia, Shang, and Zhou (circa 2205–256 BC). The core of the Chinese civilization was a common ideographic script (Ng-Quinn 1993), which enabled the propagation and canonization of shared norms and values despite significant regional variations. Until the mid-1800s, these norms and values sustained a national identity that was defined more in terms of cultural assimilation than political affiliation. The very idea of nation-state or nationalism came late to China as a result of its encounters with the West.

The Westphalian system of sovereign territorial states derived from early modern Europe. It gave de facto recognition to Europe's political fragmentation and presented a diplomatic code of conduct for regulating relations among its constituent states. Until 1945, these relations were marked by a series of intense and continuous rivalries – a chronicle of "armed peace" punctuated by the recurrent outbreak of actual warfare. Military mobilization, foreign conquest, and balance-of-power statecraft were constant features of European history. The consequent "security dilemma" and the competitive dynamic that it engendered helped to launch industrialization, entrepreneurship, and the modern state (Tilly 1990; Weber 1964). War preparation and war fighting necessitated a strong military establishment and an arms industry – and since these were expensive, they in turn stimulated the organization of central bureaucracies to collect tax. These institutions strengthened the European monarchs' position relative to the nobility. Concomitantly, the competition among these monarchs for capital and entrepreneurship favored the power and status of the bourgeoisie.

Unlike this system of interstate rivalry in Europe, imperial China was preeminent in East Asia. Although there were periods of political fragmentation and regional contention in imperial China, it did not face the same constant pressure for war mobilization, competitive industrialization, and balance-of-power politics that was characteristic of the European system. Local authorities were given considerable autonomy in implementing imperial edicts, and diverse customs and heterodoxical traditions (e.g., polytheism) were tolerated as long as they conformed to general Confucian precepts and popular rituals. Moreover, in contrast to European monarchs who often took a direct and active role in policies, Chinese emperors typically reigned rather than ruled.

The "universal pacification" of the Chinese empire produced a conception of world order based more on culture than on politics. Confucian ideology assigned the lowest social status to merchants and especially soldiers, and gave the greatest prestige to the gentry, literati class. The distinction between "civilized" and "barbaric" – indeed, the definition of "Chineseness" – hinged on assimilation into the Chinese culture, which for the masses in imperial times involved primarily "the performance of key rituals in the accepted manner" (Watson 1993: 93). For the elite, this cultural transformation entailed acceptance of the Confucian canons and the mastery of the written script. It is not hard to grasp why the traditional Chinese did not develop a conception of world order based on a system of legally sovereign, contending territorial states.

Instead, imperial China propagated a world order of hierarchies among unequals who were, however, integrated into a system of reciprocal relations. Underpinning this system was the Confucian idea of harmony, which would be realized when all parties perform the obligations of their assigned role. In the domestic realm, the four cardinal relations consist of those between the monarch and his subjects, husband and wife, parent and child, and elder and younger siblings. In each case, proper role performance requires the internalization of the value of benevolence from above and especially the imperative of obedience from below. This idea was extended to the foreign arena in the form of the tributary system. The court in Beijing received emissaries from neighboring territories in ceremonies designed to symbolize the latter's submission to Chinese suzerainty. In exchange, the vassal states were granted trade privileges and military protection. Armed force was not seen as the most important means for securing the vassals' allegiance. Rather, China's cultural appeal was believed to be the most effective source of its influence. The ideal of *Da Tong* – or universal community – would be realized when all people joined a union of common norms and values.

This imperial Chinese conception of world order was expansive in scope, and its legitimacy rested more on proclaimed moral virtue than compelling military power. The distinction between virtue and power was such that "in fact, one could argue that in traditional China 'right' defined 'might,' not the other way around, and that national power was viewed as the reflection of national virtue" (Kim 1979: 24). The relevant characters and categories in this traditional thinking were not racial, territorial, or political. Rather, the world order was defined in terms of and buttressed by the emperor's cosmic virtue ("mandate of heaven") and the co-optive influence of Chinese culture. This conception is remarkable in its anticipation of several major themes in recent Western scholarship pertaining to security community, soft power, and the end of history (Deutsch et al. 1957; Nye 1992; Fukuyama 1992). At the same time, it offers an "inside out" view of politics – suggesting that domestic norms and structures serve as a proper model for international relations.

These norms and structures were supposed to reflect certain universal and timeless ethical standards and moral principles. These views were propagated at a time of supreme confidence when China faced few rivals. Even when the country suffered from foreign conquest or domestic turmoil, cultural unity and continuity were taken for granted. This sense of complacency and even arrogance changed after China was rudely shaken in its encounters with Western and Japanese imperialism in the nineteenth century (Hunt 1993).

Republican China

As citizens of international topdogs, it is perhaps difficult for Americans and Britons to appreciate how the traumas of national setback have shaped other countries' worldviews. After all, very few other countries can claim the distinction of not having been occupied or ruled by a foreign power in recent memory.

China's world order was shattered by a series of humiliating defeats during the 1800s. The rise of nationalism, the quest for a strong state, the initiation of industrialization, and the search for a new ideology could all be traced to the collapse of national authority and the encroachment of foreign interests. Domestic disintegration and foreign aggression provided the impetus and justification for a new conception of world order. This new conception recognized a state-centric system in which China, because of its national weaknesses, was subjugated to various unequal treaties that robbed it of its political sovereignty and territorial integrity. As a "hypo-colony," China was being carved up for control and exploitation by various imperialist powers. The lesson of national vulnerability and unequal treatment was dramatically underscored when China was excluded from the deliberations leading to the Treaty of Versailles, and was in fact forced to accept the transfer of German possessions in China to other foreigners – even though China had fought on the side of the victorious allies.

A Hobbesian world of structural anarchy became the dominant Chinese view of world order; an order that was buttressed by might rather than right. The traditional view of China as the center of a global Confucian order became obsolescent, and was replaced by a gradual but inexorable turn to the ideas of classical realism. International structure was still seen as a hierarchy but the differentiated national capabilities determining the pecking order were now defined primarily in military and industrial (rather than cultural) terms. Balance-of-power calculus and especially a powerful military were imperative for survival in a predatory world. National strengthening required a strong centralized state and the rapid development of strategic industries. They were justified on grounds of national security and even national survival. Laggards such as China could not afford the luxury of *laissez-faire*. State capitalism, a vanguard Leninist party (both the Kuomintang and the Chinese Communist Party followed this model), and a unifying ideology for the mobilization of national effort were important for playing the game of catch-up. Chinese officials and intellectuals looked to Japan, Germany, and the Soviet Union for possible policy lessons. Many were attracted to the Soviet Union because it had renounced Tsarist privileges in China and because the Bolshevik revolution seemed to offer a promising model for transforming quickly an underdeveloped country.

The Chinese believed that domestic decay and foreign aggression were mutually exacerbating. These processes produced a downward spiral in China's international status during roughly the century between the mid-1800s and the mid-1900s. This decline in turn provided a profound transformation in Chinese views of world order. A predominantly cultural orientation to international order was replaced by one now based on territorial and legal emphases. Communitarian notions – albeit embodying highly hierarchical and authoritarian elements – yielded to perceptions of an international system of juridically independent but materially unequal states. The ideal of universal harmony, even frequently belied by the earlier history of occasionally devastating strife, was abandoned. It was supplanted by concerns with systemic anarchy and imperialist predation. Likewise, a celebration of cultural integration was jettisoned in favor of an emphasis on armed coercion (as reflected in the well-known Maoist dictum, "power grows out of the barrel of a gun").

These changes show how China's internal and external conditions interacted to alter views of world order. These views were hardly stagnant. Moreover, their empirical, normative, and strategic contents formed a synergistic system so that it would be difficult to treat each of these components in isolation from the others. As is true for all countries, China's views on world order necessarily reflected its position in this order and its attempts to improve this position. As well, these views were not somehow naturally given. Rather, they were – and are – a matter of transaction, negotiation, construction, and mobilization by elites and masses.

Early Maoist China

With the communist victory in 1949, Mao Tse-tung announced a policy of alignment with the Soviet Union. In his words, all Chinese "must lean either to the side of imperialism or to the side of socialism. Sitting on the fence will not do, *nor is there a third road*" (quoted in Kim 1979: 75). To some extent, this policy declaration reflected a matter of making virtue of necessity; the US had supported the Nationalists in the Chinese civil war and had declined to recognize the People's Republic even after the communist victory. Washington's intervention in the Korean War, followed by Beijing's counter-intervention, ensured that a two-camp view of world order would prevail in both capitals for about the next two decades.

A world divided into two uncompromising camps of East and West signaled a sharp break from the traditional view. This new conception was based on a dialectical reasoning emphasizing the so-called law of contradictions (Bobrow, Chan and Kringen 1979). The principal contradiction was defined as the confrontation between the progressive forces of socialism and the reactionary forces of imperialism, led by Moscow and Washington respectively. Thus the traditional Chinese focus on integration was supplanted by an emphasis on contention, and the ideal of harmony was replaced by the virtue of struggle. According to this new Maoist view, compromise and cooperation in international relations are relative, conditional, and temporary, while conflict and competition are absolute, basic, and protracted. It is a "zero-sum" characterization of world order: either East wind prevails over West wind, or vice versa.

The Maoist formulation departed from traditional views in other significant respects. The traditional views abhorred disorder and chaos, and placed a social and political premium on deference to authority, conformity to ritual, and the preservation of the status quo. Maoism, on the contrary, presented an ideology for overthrowing the status quo. There was, for example, the well-known endorsement during the Cultural Revolution that "to rebel is justified." Moreover, Chinese officials often drew favorable implications from their oft-quoted observation that "there is great disorder under heaven." Hence, there was a distinct shift from a preference for stasis in the traditional conception to an agitation for change in the Maoist ideology. A topdog's perspective was replaced by that of an underdog.

Traditional Chinese culture was elitist, and it stressed ritual form while seeking to control emotional expression. Maoism also altered these predilections. This new ideology emphasized the efficacy of mass mobilization, and argued that human spirit was more important than material conditions. Popular support and revolutionary zeal would offset inferiority in conventional capabilities. These views explained a Maoist penchant for mass movements, people's war, and "redness over expertise." They also justified an unshakable optimism in the long-term victory of the Chinese cause despite short-term setbacks. Soft-power assets rather than hard-power assets were decisive in shaping human history and determining national status (thus, even though imperialists had nuclear weapons, they were still "paper tigers," doomed to defeat).

The two-camp theory propagated during the first years of the People's Republic did not admit an intermediate zone between socialist and imperialist blocs. Yet Chinese foreign policy was always quite attentive to the nonaligned countries. The 1954 Sino-Indian Trade Agreement enunciated the Five Principles of Peaceful Coexistence, pledging mutual respect for sovereignty and territorial integrity, mutual non-aggression, mutual non-interference in each other's internal affairs, equality and mutually beneficial exchanges, and peaceful coexistence. These principles were further endorsed in the 1955 Bandung conference of nonaligned nations, where China played an active role. Nikita Khrushchev's de-Stalinization campaign (1956) and the emerging Sino-Soviet split (circa 1958) gave impetus to the recognition of an important third force in China's conception of world order.

A strategic reformulation was reached after Beijing's open break with Moscow. It followed China's decision to chart an independent policy course that opposed both US imperialism and Soviet revisionism. Defense Minister Lin Piao's 1965 article, "Long Live the Victory of People's War," presented an authoritative account of the new views. The world was divided between, figuratively speaking, cities and countryside. An overwhelming majority of people lived in the latter area, and they held the key to the cause of world revolution. Drawing from the experience of China's civil war and its war against Japan, Lin proclaimed a strategy whereby the countryside (Asia, Africa, and Latin America) would encircle and prevail over the cities (Europe and North America). Instead of being considered an intermediate zone, the Third World was now seen as a vast and pivotal area with tremendous revolutionary potential.

Lin's formulation retained a dichotomous view of world order – except that the struggle was now defined to involve all the world's "have nots" against its "haves." Countries belonging to the Third World shared a common fate of economic dependency and political subjugation, and could be mobilized in a "united front" to oppose their oppressors. Common plight rather than common ideology provided the unifying force, and the quest was not so much for world *order* as for world *justice* (Kim 1979: 92). Yet despite Beijing's rhetorical promotion of people's wars and national liberation movements during this period, the extent of its actual support for foreign revolutions was rather limited and cautious (Van Ness 1971). Indeed, Chinese leaders repeatedly stressed the importance of self-reliance in each country's campaign to gain justice and independence, arguing that revolution could not be exported or imported. In Lin's essay mentioned above, he explicitly argued that "the liberation of the masses is accomplished by the masses themselves – this is a basic principle of Marxism-Leninism. Revolution or people's war in any country is the business of the masses in that country and should be carried out primarily by their own efforts; there is no other way" (quoted in Kim 1979: 71).

The urban-rural view of world order underwent another change in the mid-1970s, when the theory of three worlds was initially articulated by Mao in a 1974 interview with Zambian President K. D. Kaunda (Kim 1979: 80–1). It was formally presented by Deng Xiaoping in his address to the UN General Assembly later in the same year. This new formulation took note of the disintegration of *both* the socialist and imperialist camps, and called attention to the tension between the leaders of these camps and their allies. Its trichotomy assigned the US *and* the USSR to the First World; Japan, Canada, and Europe to the Second World; and the remaining countries (including China) to the Third World. This categorization stressed two important themes. On the one hand, it warned against the hegemonic ambitions of both superpowers; on the other hand, it recognized the potential for aligning with the secondary powers (such as Japan, France, and Canada) in a joint effort to oppose American and Soviet domination. Significantly, Marxist ideology was being eclipsed by *realpolitik* statecraft.

Late Maoist and Dengist China

It already became clear by the late 1960s that China's decision to oppose simultaneously the US and the USSR was placing it in a very precarious strategic position. Clashes with Soviet troops along the Ussuri River and rumors of a Soviet preemptive strike led to Chinese overtures for a rapprochement with the Americans. Richard Nixon and Henry Kissinger were similarly concerned with Moscow's rising power, and were interested in playing the "China card" to check Soviet expansionism (and to negotiate a gracious exit from Vietnam). "Hegemonism" – a codeword for Soviet dominance – became the new focus of Beijing's foreign policy. By the 1970s, the main threat to world order was increasingly defined as Moscow's social imperialism (socialism in form, imperialism in substance). All countries, including the capitalist ones, should be mobilized to oppose this threat. While Beijing eschewed formal alliance ties, it undertook parallel policies with Washington in a concerted effort to contain Soviet influence as well as that of its surrogates (Vietnam and Cuba). A strategic Sino-American alignment against the USSR became even more salient after the latter's invasion of Afghanistan in 1979. Verbal deference to Marxism and rhetorical support for a New International

Economic Order gave way to the reality of balance-of-power considerations among the triad. In 1986, Chinese Premier Zhao Ziyang declared that "China does not determine its closeness with, or estrangement from, other countries on the basis of their social systems and ideologies" (quoted in Wang 1994: 487). Henceforth, Beijing's focus would be on opposing the hegemonic *behavior* of any country seeking international domination. The "strategic triangle" of Sino-Soviet-American relations dominated Beijing's foreign policy agenda (Dittmer 1981). An earlier disposition to engage in a transnational people-to-people united front gave way to government-to-government diplomacy aimed at the creation of a grand coalition to balance the Soviet threat (Walt 1987).

With the conclusion of the Cultural Revolution, a concomitant de-emphasis of ideology also occurred in Chinese domestic politics. In late 1978, Deng Xiaoping launched a program of Four Modernizations. Economic reform was the primary focus of this program. It entailed the liberalization of market conditions, the contraction of state enterprises, the creation of export-processing zones, the promotion of exports, and the import of foreign capital and technologies. In this endeavor, the newly industrializing economies of East Asia (especially Singapore with its authoritarian government but vigorous economy) provided a model for China to emulate. Beijing's economic reform was highly successful, with its gross national product increasing about 10 percent per annum during the subsequent decade or so. Although China had emphasized the virtue of national self-reliance as a means of economic development during the 1960s and 1970s, it now actively sought foreign trade and investment.

Economic dependence on foreign markets, capital, and technologies carried the danger of political interference. Unlike countries in Eastern and Central Europe, economic reform had not been accompanied by political liberalization in China. Foreign, especially US, objections to Beijing's treatment of human rights mounted after the Tiananmen Square crackdown in 1989 and after China's strategic value declined precipitously with Mikhail Gorbachev's reforms and the subsequent disintegration of the Soviet empire. Rising economic interdependence and the end of the Cold War provided foreigners the leverage to pressure Beijing to democratize.

In an ironic twist of role reversal, China's response to this foreign pressure was to resort to the Westphalian conception of world order. This pressure, it has been argued, is a violation of China's sovereignty and interference in its domestic affairs. The West, especially the US, should not impose its political system on others, acting as if *its* norms and values were universal principles. The propagation of Western norms and values would therefore be tantamount to cultural imperialism. While lacking the grand design of earlier Chinese formulations of world order, these arguments are not without a certain resonance among many developing countries whose officials are concerned about the erosion of their sovereignty and autonomy due to the penetration of foreign influences. While these developing countries continue to emphasize a state-centered system, the West has begun to promote a value-based community in which sovereignty is to be checked and frontiers surmounted. Post-1949 China has undergone a metamorphosis from being a radical challenger to becoming a status quo proponent of the traditional state-centric order.

Yet it would be unwarranted to dismiss China's role change as completely unprincipled. One consistent emphasis in China's foreign policy ever since the founding of the People's Republic has been its resistance to foreign attempts to influence its domestic conditions and to compromise its decision autonomy on political and especially security matters. As already noted, even during the height of Maoism, Beijing had insisted that revolutionary struggle was each country's internal affair. Recent US pressure on Beijing to improve its human rights performance is seen as a clear and deliberate violation of both the implicit understanding and explicit agreement reached with Washington earlier. Thus, for example, Chinese officials point to the 1982 joint communiqué in which the US formally pledged and reiterated that "it has no intention of infringing on Chinese sovereignty and territorial integrity, or interfering in China's internal affairs, or pursuing a policy of 'two Chinas' or 'one China, one Taiwan.'"

While China remains an illiberal and repressive country, its record on human rights has improved since the height of Maoist radicalism. Ironically, as Harding (1992: 198) has noted, Sino-American rapprochement began during a time (1969–70) when the Cultural Revolution was responsible for the deaths of several hundred thousand and the persecution of tens of millions of Chinese. Strategic considerations, however, inclined Washington to attach only secondary importance to human rights at that time (Harding 1992: 200). The collapse of the Soviet Union changed Washington's agenda. Shambaugh (1991: 301) reported that Chinese officials and intellectuals now view the US "as an aggressive and arrogant power that throws its economic and military might around the globe." In their view, the US is seeking global domination and is increasingly turning against China because it opposes US hegemony.

Policy implications and prognosis

Unlike Russia, which has undergone a sharp decline in its national status, China is widely perceived as an ascending power. The growth of China's economy and the modernization of its military have become a source of open concern for some people (e.g., Bernstein and Munro 1997), because these increasing capabilities are believed to provide Beijing with the wherewithal for attempting regional domination. In this respect, a mirror image operates across the Pacific – with both Beijing and Washington suspecting that the other has hegemonic ambitions. Surprisingly, there seems to be an agreement by both sides that the US is suffering a relative decline while China is in the process of catching up. This mutual sense fuels speculation about power transition, which is supposed to increase the danger of war (Organski and Kugler 1980). This danger has been hypothesized to be especially great when the challenger is an undemocratic or illiberal state (Schweller 1992). According to this formulation, democracies are generally satisfied powers, which are unlikely to challenge the international status quo. Because other democracies are presumed to also support this order, changes in the relative power among democracies are not seen to be especially alarming. A power transition in favor of an undemocratic challenger, however, is likely to be treated as more threatening to this order, and hence to induce a more belligerent response from the democratic leader and its associates.

China is not a democracy, but the above characterization offers a poor empirical fit in other key respects. Although China's economy has been growing rapidly, it is still a developing country. According to one estimate (Scalapino 1993: 219), even assuming China achieves its economic goal, its per capita income in the year 2000 will only be about US$900. China still lacks significant capabilities to project its forces abroad. Its military technologies lag seriously behind those of the US and Japan (Ross 1997). Therefore, China is not about to overtake the US in either economic or military terms. There is no impending power transition.

Equally significant, while it might have been true at one time, the characterization of China as a revisionist power is no longer valid today. As already noted, China now supports the Westphalian system and seeks to guard its domestic system from foreign influence. Its current policy orientation is primarily inward-looking, with economic modernization as its top priority – a goal that requires conducive conditions from a peaceful and stable external environment. Indeed, even at the height of Maoist revolutionary rhetoric, Beijing was rather cautious in its military conduct and its use of force was primarily defensive in its intent to deter others from changing the prevailing status quo (Chan 1978; Whiting 1972). The resort to foreign intervention with the intent of affecting developments abroad has been a much more frequent occurrence in the post-1949 British, French, and American statecraft than in Chinese practice. As implied by the earlier remark about role reversal, the US rather than

China has been behaving more like a revisionist power. From the expansion of the North Atlantic Treaty Organization to the promotion of economic and political liberalization in the developing world, Washington has led the campaign to promote a new world order.

With respect to US policy toward China, one analyst observed forthrightly that it has "been a conscious purpose of many US government and private programs to foster change in China," and *both* proponents of engagement and containment "seek to undermine the Chinese Communist Party's hold on power and to accelerate the trend towards the pluralization and marketization of the Chinese polity and economy, respectively. The debate has been over methods not purpose" (Shambaugh 1994: 211). These US efforts often encounter Chinese retorts pointing to Washington's own domestic situation characterized by racial discrimination, income disparities, rampant crime, and the world's largest prison population.

China's capabilities have indeed increased recently and at a rather fast pace. These increases, however, reflect expansion from relatively modest bases, and become comparatively small when considered in per capita terms. Moreover, whether considered in terms of their economic, technological, or military dimensions, these capabilities tend to be more impressive quantitatively than qualitatively. Even in aggregate quantitative terms, the US economy was in 1994 three times larger than the Chinese economy, and Washington's military spending 5.45 times higher than Beijing's (USACDA 1996). In the same year, Japan's economy was over two times larger than China's, although its military spending was only 86.7 percent of Beijing's level. Similarly, while China has been increasing its economic ties with the outside world, its regional trade and investment still lag behind those of not only the US and Japan, but also some of the newly industrializing countries. For instance, while the US and Japan accounted for, respectively, 36.2 percent and 29.2 percent of their major APEC (Asia Pacific Economic Cooperation) partners' exports in 1992, China was responsible for only 12.7 percent (Bobrow, Chan and Reich 1997). Thus, although China is clearly an important regional actor, some distance still separates its capabilities and those of the US and Japan. And, just as statements about the ongoing or impending demise of US hegemony seem premature (Russett 1985; Strange 1987), predictions of an imminent Chinese challenge appear to be alarmist. Perceptions about regional threats can undergo remarkable transformation in the absence of significant capability changes. Most of us can recall how US evaluation of Iran's status underwent such a dramatic change in the early 1980s from being a friendly bulwark guarding against regional instability to a hostile source of instability in itself.

It is, of course, also not so long ago that Beijing was characterized by Washington as a valuable strategic ally against Soviet expansionism. The changing perception of China can, at best, be only partially accounted for by China's increasing capabilities – and certainly not by a change of its regime. If anything, Beijing's foreign relations with its neighbors are more cordial today than at any other time since the establishment of the People's Republic. And, as already mentioned, domestic treatment of human rights has in fact improved since the Cultural Revolution, when Washington and Beijing began the process of rapprochement.

Rather than relying on unwarranted images of power transition, we need a more informed understanding of how past systems of multipolarity have managed to maintain peace or have broken down to produce war. A recent study of this question led Kegley and Raymond (1994) to conclude that three factors tend to influence the stability of multipolar systems. First, fluidity in the identity and relative position of great powers seems to have a negative effect on this stability. Rapid changes in the membership and rank order of great powers tend to create uncertainty and anxiety, which in turn increase the prospects of international conflict. Second, multipolar systems characterized by both a high and a low degree of polarization appear to have been associated with frequent conflict. Both very tight and very loose alignment patterns, but especially the former, tend to be conflict-prone historically. Third, whether a multipolar system is characterized by a restrictive or a permissive normative order seems also to matter. When great powers agree to limitations on (1) the use of force in their foreign conduct, (2) their freedom to renege on treaty commitments, and (3) the geographic scope of their competition, a restrictive order tends to promote peace and stability. Conversely, when the great powers refuse to acknowledge constraints in these areas, the consequent permissive order tends to produce war and instability.

The first condition mentioned by Kegley and Raymond seems to augur more tumultuous international relations in general as we stand poised to enter the twenty-first century. Ongoing trends are altering relative national positions. Moreover, rising status discordance due to the command of different asset classes and due to real or imagined discrepancy between reputation and accomplishment is likely to be a destabilizing factor in this view. Nevertheless, the passage of the Cold War should help to lessen international polarization (the second condition mentioned above), and should therefore present a countervailing influence that favors greater systemic stability.

Whether a restrictive normative order (the third condition) is in ascendance is less clear. While underpinning ties among the developed democracies, the relevant constraints are clearly much less visible in the relations between these countries and their less developed and less democratic counterparts and among the latter countries. Whether the normative constraints noted above – regarding the use of force, respect for treaty commitments, and observance of spheres of influence – should apply to the latter relations is a source of debate in the West and especially in the US. Although established democracies adhere to these codes of conduct in dealing with each other, they are not necessarily equally scrupulous in their relations with those outside the democratic camp (Chan 1997). Whether a restrictive normative order can be extended and consolidated in the latter case impinges on the prospects for world order – defined at least in terms of stability if not also justice – as we enter the twenty-first century.

REFERENCES

Bernstein, Richard and Munro, Ross H. 1997, *The Coming Conflict with China*, New York: Alfred A. Knopf.

Bobrow, Davis B., Chan, Steve and Kringen, John A. 1979, *Understanding Foreign Policy Decisions: The Chinese Case*, New York: Free Press.

Bobrow, Davis B., Reich, Simon and Chan, Steve 1998, "Trade, Power, and APEC: Hirschman Revisited," *International Interactions* 24: 187–223.

Chan, Steve 1978, "Chinese Conflict Calculus and Behavior: Assessment from a Perspective of Conflict Management," *World Politics* 30: 391–410.

1997, "In Search of Democratic Peace: Problems and Promise," *Mershon International Studies Review* 41: 59–91.

Deutsch, Karl W., Burrell, Sidney A., Kann, Robert A., Lee, Maurice, Jr., Lichtenman, Martin, Lindgren, Raymond E., Loewenheim, Francis L. and Van Wagenen, Richard W. 1957, *Political Community and the North Atlantic Area*, New York: Greenwood.

Dittmer, Lowell 1981, "The Strategic Triangle: An Elementary Game-Theoretic Analysis," *World Politics* 33: 485–516.

Fukuyama, Francis 1992, *The End of History and the Last Man*, New York: Free Press.

Harding, Harry 1992, *A Fragile Relationship: The United States and China since 1972*, Washington, DC: The Brookings Institution.

Hunt, Michael H. 1993, "Chinese National Identity and the Strong State: The Late Qing-Republican Crisis," in *China's Quest for National Identity*, Lowell Dittmer and Samuel S. Kim (eds.), Ithaca: Cornell University Press, pp. 62–79.

Kegley, Charles W., Jr. and Raymond, Gregory A. 1994, *A Multipolar Peace? Great Power Politics in the Twenty-First Century*, New York: St. Martin's.

Kim, Samuel S. 1979, *China, the United Nations, and World Order*, Princeton: Princeton University Press.

Ng-Quinn, Michael 1993, "National Identity in Premodern China: Formation and Role Enactment," in *China's Quest for National Identity*, Lowell Dittmer and Samuel S. Kim (eds.), Ithaca: Cornell University Press, pp. 32–61.

Nye, Joseph S., Jr. 1992, *Bound to Lead: The Changing Nature of American Power*, New York: Basic Books.

Organski, A. F. K. and Kugler, Jacek 1980, *The War Ledger*, Chicago: University of Chicago Press.

Ross, Robert S. 1997, "Beijing as a Conservative Power," *Foreign Affairs* 76: 33–44.

Russett, Bruce 1985, "The Mysterious Case of Vanishing Hegemony: Or, Is Mark Twain Really Dead?" *International Organization* 39: 207–31.

Scalapino, Robert A. 1993, "China's Multiple Identities in East Asia: China as a Regional Force," in *China's Quest for National Identity*, Lowell Dittmer and Samuel S. Kim (eds.), Ithaca: Cornell University Press, pp. 215–36.

Schweller, Randall L. 1992, "Domestic Structure and Preventive War: Are Democracies Pacific?" *World Politics* 44: 235–69.

Shambaugh, David 1991, *Beautiful Imperialist: China Perceives America, 1972–1990*, Princeton: Princeton University Press.

Sprout, Harold and Sprout, Margaret 1957, "Environmental Factors in the Study of Politics," *Journal of Conflict Resolution* 1: 309–28.

Strange, Susan 1987, "The Persistent Myth of Lost Hegemony," *International Organization* 41: 551–74.

Tilly, Charles 1990, *Coercion, Capital, and European States, AD 990–1990*, Oxford: Blackwell.

US Arms Control and Disarmament Agency (USACDA) 1996, *World Military Expenditures and Arms Transfers, 1995*, Washington, DC: author.

Van Ness, Peter 1971, *Revolution and Chinese Foreign Policy*, Berkeley: University of California Press.

Walt, Stephen M. 1987, *The Origins of Alliances*, Ithaca: Cornell University Press.

Wang, Jisi 1994, "International Relations Theory and the Study of Chinese Foreign Policy: A Chinese Perspective," in *Chinese Policy: Theory and Practice*, Thomas Robinson and David Shambaugh (eds.), Oxford: Clarendon Press, pp. 481–505.

Watson, James L. 1993, "Rites or Beliefs? The Construction of a Unified Culture in Late Imperial China," in *China's Quest for National Identity*, Lowell Dittmer and Samuel S. Kim (eds.), Ithaca: Cornell University Press, pp. 80–103.

Weber, Max 1964, *The Religion of China*, New York: Macmillan.

Whiting, Allen S. 1972, "The Use of Force in Foreign Policy by the People's Republic of China," *Annals of the American Academy of Political and Social Science* 402: 55–66.

11 India as a limited challenger?[1]

Baldev Raj Nayar

Notwithstanding the usual homage to the doctrine of the sovereign equality of states, the international system is in essence an oligarchy based on differentiation in power. For much of the postwar period, the fate of the world rested in the hands of the two superpowers, the United States and the Soviet Union. As the Vietnam War weakened it in the late 1960s and reduced its earlier primacy in the bipolar system, the US articulated through Henry Kissinger the design for a new world order as a function of a concert of five great powers: the US, Soviet Union, Japan, Europe, and China. Some two decades later, in the early 1990s, the disintegration of the Soviet Union radically transformed the international system. The US emerged as the sole state deserving of the appellation "great power" as a possessor of system-wide capabilities and influence. The other possible contenders for the role are simply either incomplete powers (Russia, Japan), or subordinate military allies of the US (Japan), or not yet in existence (Europe), or yet only regional powers even though ascendant (China). Their strategic significance for now lies in their possible emergence in the not too distant future as great powers.

Ought the number of possible contenders in the future, however, be limited to just China, Japan, Russia, and Europe? Has history closed the door against the entry of any others? Are there other possible contenders? Whether intended seriously or not, Kissinger himself talked in 1989 of a group of great powers which would include India: "You will have the US, Soviet Union, China, India and Europe. All of which will be simultaneously economic, political and military powers" (Nye 1990: 235). Since then, Kissinger has repeated a similar formulation of the vision of a future world order, including India as a major center of power. In a more serious study, even though limited to Asia, an Australian scholar, Paul Dibb (1995), discusses a future balance-of-power system in Asia among five great powers: US, Russia, China, Japan, and India. India's position, however, seems rather ambiguous; it is, of course, not among the first tier of powers below the US, but it would seem rather odd on the other hand to simply consign it to the vast number of minor powers.

Some thirty years ago, a British scholar underlined the ambiguity of India's role by asking the significant question: "Is she the last and least of the great Powers, or is she the first of the lesser Powers?" (Lyon 1968: 287). That ambiguity arises from the fact that India is a middle power. India has not belonged to the group of great powers which command a subject role in international politics and constitute the dominant power structure that makes, in cooperation or contention, the vital decisions about the fate and destiny of the international system. Nor is it, however, one of the minor powers which, with limited foreign policy autonomy, are the objects of the decisions of the great powers. In contrast, middle powers, while they do not have the leverage to influence the course of the international system as a whole, possess enough capabilities to resist the application of unwelcome decisions, especially in the realm of security; usually dominant or preeminent in their own regions, and therefore often referred to as great regional powers, they constitute relatively independent centers of power. Given the anarchic nature of the international system, there is a built-in conflict between great powers and middle powers. A great power typically resists the emergence of new great powers, since to accommodate others to a similar role is to diminish one's own power. As a consequence, demonization of middle powers by great powers is quite natural. On the other hand, for those middle powers who have the potential, entrance into the exclusive club of subjects is also a compelling goal for elemental reasons of national survival and welfare. These contrary impulses of great powers and middle powers often set them on a collision course, and the story of the graduation of a middle power to the status of great power has usually, at least in the past, been written in blood and fire.

Not surprisingly, as a middle power, India's state behavior has fluctuated between that of an aspirant great power and a minor power. State behavior is often influenced not only by a country's objective status but also by its leadership's perception of the desired role for it. In India's case, the perception of a possible role as a great power is not just a vain hope but apparently stems from a sober appreciation of its substantial potential for the role. True, the leadership has not been able to fully actualize the potential and transform India into a great power in the five decades of independence, but neither has it let the country be pushed into the ranks of minor powers.

Although largely avoiding confrontation with the great powers, India has, even as a middle power, provided over the last half-century a more or less limited challenge to the great powers in their attempts to organize the world according to their own designs. It did so, first, through the mechanism of nonalignment, which it pioneered, by refusing to join up as a subordinate member of either bloc. Then it did so through its resolute resistance to the imposition of discriminatory regimes by the present nuclear powers which, while requiring nuclear self-abnegation on the part of others, legitimize their own nuclear monopoly. Finally, it did so through the daring nuclear tests in May 1998 as a clear demonstration of the unacceptability of the shrewdly organized regimes.

This chapter seeks to analyze both the sources of the challenge India poses and the reasons why the challenge has been only episodic and limited. Its central argument is that, even as India has aspired to an eventual great power role on the basis of its large size and potential, internal constraints forced it to remain moderate and restrained in the pursuit of this aspiration until compelled to a more defiant and determined response by the growing perception of threat, evidenced in the China-Pakistan collaboration with the apparent connivance of the US. At the same time, India has been constrained by external powers who have acted to keep it preoccupied with local affairs in the region and to foreclose the acquisition of such capabilities as are essential to achieving great power status. Nonetheless, India has shown remarkable tenacity in keeping open the possibility of accession to great power status, and thus provides a challenge to those engaged in the construction of a new hegemonic world order. The discussion of this theme is divided into four parts: (1) the geopolitical elements in India's role aspirations; (2) the internal constraints; (3) the systemic constraints during the Cold War; and (4) opportunities and constraints after the end of the Cold War.

The geopolitical mainsprings of a challenger role

India is located in the Indian subcontinent, also referred to as South Asia, which constitutes a single geopolitical fortress, bounded on the north by the mountain ranges of the Himalayas and on the south by the Indian Ocean and its two branches, the Arabian Sea and the Bay of Bengal. It is a geopolitical unit of massive size, comparable to Europe. Lying astride the Indian Ocean and flanking the Persian Gulf and the Straits of Malacca, it has a considerable inherent strategic significance. The subcontinent also constitutes in some measure a single civilizational complex which, regardless of its shortcomings, has endured over some three millennia.

In more recent times, Western colonialism established a nascent modern state in the subcontinent, albeit limited and exploitative. In turn, colonialism gave rise to its nemesis, nationalism. Though non-violent, the freedom struggle constituted a genuine mass-based national liberation movement. Its final victory was partial, however, because of the partition of the subcontinent. Nonetheless, it bequeathed the legacy of a spirit of national independence as a core value of the nation and state. It is this thrust for autonomy that underlay India's nonalignment, for alignment was regarded as compromising independence. Both the spirit of independence and India's geopolitical condition also led to a heavy emphasis on self-reliance, for the lack of civilizational or ethnic ties with any other centers of power made uncertain the availability of resources from outside; India could not count on being bailed out by others in security or economics.

Within the geopolitical region, India is the hegemonic power in terms of the size of its territory, population, and resources (as distinguished from being hegemonistic, which has to do not with a state's position but its behavior). That hegemonic position is given by its very existence, and the Indian leadership is convinced that there is no way that the offence it causes to some can ever be appeased except through India's fragmentation. The region as a whole is patently Indocentric, not only in the sense that India is located at the center of the region, but also because India almost constitutes the region, holding three-quarters of its territory and population. Besides, India is singularly central to the geopolitics of the region, as all of the other countries in the region border on it but not on each other.

Even in absolute terms, India is the seventh largest country in the world; with an area of 1.3 million square miles, it is about two-thirds the size of Europe (excluding the territories of the former Soviet Union). With almost a billion people, it is the second most populous country in the world, larger than that of all the permanent members of the Security Council combined minus China, and larger than that of all the Americas put together. Sometime during the first half of the twenty-first century, India will outpace China in total population. The large population makes it difficult for India to accept a situation in which much smaller nations continue to hold a monopoly of power in the international system. Given its size, population, strategic location at the head of the Indian Ocean, and its civilizational background, it would seem that India cannot but aspire to a great power role in international politics, however distant the prospect.

Because of its hegemonic position in a largely well-defined and self-contained Indocentric geopolitical region, the threat to India's security emerges not from the other regional powers as such but from outside major powers that collude with them. As a consequence, India is led – much as the US in the Western hemisphere – to a conception of national security which requires the *exclusion of external powers* from the subcontinent. Its conception of national security is thus not simply national, but *geopolitical* and *regional*. However, such a conception necessarily entails interaction with other regions as a major power; *role extension* on the world scene is thus built into India's hegemonic position in the subcontinent.

These vital geopolitical and civilizational features have not been without implications for the perceptions of India's national leadership. For one thing, they led to the policy of nonalignment in order to exclude the Cold War – and therefore the superpowers – from the subcontinent. But that policy was also intended as saying that the country could not be subordinate to external powers. As one foreign minister declared, "Our size, our potential strength, our traditions and heritage do not allow us to become a client state" (*Times of India*, June 17, 1976). Underlying the policy of nonalignment, however, was also a perception of a future great power role. Here, the architect and exponent of nonalignment, Nehru, had himself articulated the vision of such a role long before independence. The partition of the subcontinent should have induced greater caution, but Nehru (1961: 305) was convinced that India was destined to be the fourth major power after the US, Soviet Union, and China.

Such a perception of a future role for India may seem quixotic in the context of its economic backwardness, with a per capita income in 1995 of US$340. However, while India has not fully actualized its potential, it has not squandered it either; indeed, it has made considerable advances towards it. Its aspiration to a larger role is backed by some substantial material capabilities. Even with its low per capita income, it has the fifth largest GDP in terms of purchasing-power parity. Besides the second largest army, a sizeable navy with blue-water aspirations, a strong air force, and substantial nuclear and missile capability, most noteworthy is the complex and sophisticated industrial base with a vast capital goods industry. Even more remarkable are the technological capabilities; with the skills and talents of its manpower, it has demonstrated the capacity to build nuclear reactors and missile systems, all on its own, and to emerge as a major exporter of computer software. These industrial and technological capabilities are not the result of happenstance or accident, but of deliberate design. National self-reliance was at the heart of Nehru's development strategy, and India chose to bear heavy costs for it.

To aim for great power status casts India in a revisionist role, for the underlying assumption is not only that India should eventually emerge as a great power, but also that the present global structure of power monopoly is to a certain degree unacceptable because it impinges on India's independence. This assumption is firmly held, even if often unstated, by his successors as it was by Nehru. This was certainly manifest in nonalignment and in building a self-reliant industrial base and an arms industry, and it continues to be obvious in its stand in the more recent period on nuclear issues and on restructuring the UN Security Council.

Despite the underlying revisionist strain in its foreign policy posture, India has not pushed it to assuming the role of a full-fledged rebellious power. Its posture has been modest and low-key, except for (1) the initial period of activism on nonalignment in the early 1950s, (2) the early 1970s when it was defiant of the US over Bangladesh, and (3) in the late 1990s when it developed an intransigent posture against the nuclear monopoly of the nuclear powers. India has basically been reformist and middle of the road, whether at home or abroad. Its revisionism has pertained to what are perceived to be vital security interests, and its pursuit of them has largely partaken of the practice of "passive resistance" rather than confrontation. It is significant that two of the three wars with Pakistan were initiated by Pakistan even though it was the weaker party (Paul 1994). In the war with China, India was partially culpable, but more for its initial neglect of the borders and then for its unrealism in providing provocation while unprepared for the consequences. The question arises as to what is the explanation for the predominant divergence between ambition and behavior. Two sets of factors seem to have been at work in constraining its drive to power, one relating to the country's internal characteristics and the other to the policies of external powers.

Internal constraints

Four aspects of India's internal set-up have tended to act as constraints on its state behavior in international affairs: weak economic capabilities; cultural-ideological orientation; extreme pluralism; and political democracy.

Weak economic capabilities

The sharpest feature of the subcontinent at independence was its weak capabilities, rooted in the economic underdevelopment and extreme poverty that were a legacy of two centuries of colonial rule. There was little industry, even as India was unable to feed its population. Relatedly, it had no autonomous base for military capabilities. In realistic terms, India at independence was simply an economic and military appendage of the West.

Several consequences followed from this condition. First, the conventional path to participation in world affairs on the basis of capabilities was closed until such time as India had modernized her economy – a task for the long haul. In the meantime, Indian participation was directed along channels that depended on ideas and diplomacy, but this soon encountered severe problems as it came face to face with the realities of power.

Second, the economic condition forced priority for internal economic development. This did not mean abdication from international affairs, for economic development seemed to require an international environment free of war and conflict. As a consequence, India chose nonalignment to avoid foreign entanglements, emphasizing instead themes of peace and cooperation, which ran counter to the Western preoccupation with Cold War preparations.

Third, both weak capabilities and economic development made for dependence on Western powers, principally the US. Washington justifiably felt that Indian pretensions to foreign policy independence were incompatible with its economic dependence, while India tended to operate as if economic cooperation and foreign policy activism belonged to separate arenas. Differences over conditions in respect of food aid in the early 1950s arose out of the issue of nonalignment, and again in the mid-1960s out of Indian criticism of the American intervention in Vietnam. India attempted to use the US-Soviet rivalry to balance off the United States with a friendship with the Soviet Union but, as détente developed between the two superpowers, the utility of this tactic declined. While India defied both superpowers on the NPT and on its nuclear test in 1974, it refrained from making an overt entry into the club of nuclear weapon states for a long quarter-century. For most of the 1990s, the expressed concern of the G7 countries over India's missile program underlined the risks to continued economic cooperation. Understandably, then, weak economic and military capabilities induced caution in India's assertion of power. But the question arises as to why India remained lukewarm about building its capabilities.

Cultural-ideological orientation

Weak capabilities alone are perhaps an adequate explanation for Indian restraint, but the country's values also have relevance. In ancient India, two rival approaches were contenders for state policy: the Arthasastra tradition, with its emphasis on realpolitik; and the Asokan tradition, which drew on Buddhism and focused on non-violence and peace. Mahatma Gandhi – who with his doctrines of passive resistance and non-violent civil disobedience led the national liberation movement – enshrined the Asokan tradition as the appropriate ideology for independent India. His ideological preference for it was apparently rooted in Hinduism's general skepticism of dogma in religion and philosophy, in its conviction that there are many paths to the divine and salvation, and in its consequent aversion to proselytization and missionary activity. Interestingly, there are few instances of Indian expansion outside the geopolitical region, while all decisive battles with foreign forces over India's destiny took place within its borders. Again, it is significant that the political leadership that took over state power, while excelling in skills of symbol manipulation, had no skills in the use of violence.

Nehru was the inheritor of the Gandhian legacy, and translated it into nonalignment in the realm of foreign policy, stressing peaceful coexistence rather than power politics and war, international cooperation rather than conflict, peace through diplomacy rather than peace through strength, and nuclear disarmament rather than nuclear weapons. These themes are close to liberal internationalism, except that Nehru turned them in considerable measure into state policy and state ideology. In line with cognitive dissonance theory, the constant reiteration of pacifist themes psychologically inhibited Nehru and his successors from the overt exercise of power. However, since India had perforce to function in a power-driven international system, which it did not create, and at times had to resort to power in the defense of vital interests, that only invited charges of hypocrisy. Yet there is a vital difference between actions that seek to preserve one's territorial integrity and political independence and those that arise out of expansionist ends. India's behavior remained remarkably reactive and restrained. Ideology is one important factor in such behavior. India refrained from arms exports, believing that they ran counter to its principles. It would take a half-century before the cumulative realization that national security had suffered as a result of the particular ideology would lead India under a new government, unconnected with that ideology, to make the leap to a different power-based posture.

Extreme pluralism

India stands out as perhaps the world's most heterogeneous society, with some one dozen major languages, four major religious groups, and some 2,000 caste groups. The numbers involved are vast, however; Muslims constitute some 12 percent of the population, but with 120 million people they make India the second largest Muslim country. The rampant diversity often raises the specter of disintegration and, in combination with India's cultural-ideological traditions, it has encouraged among the elites a culture of bargaining and accommodation and a centrist orientation. India is one of a few countries in the developing world with a genuine federalism.

It is the accommodationist thrust, born out of social diversity, that has resulted in the founding of the Indian state on an inclusivist and nonsectarian or secular basis. In this India stands in sharp contrast with Pakistan, and indeed all the major states in the subcontinent, which are organized on an exclusivist, monoethnic or confessional basis. To that extent, India represents by its very existence a sharp ideological challenge to the other states of the subcontinent. On the other hand, for India its foreign policy is but a natural expression of its culture of bargaining and accommodation and is simply an externalization of its domestic experience. In recent years, the secular state at home has been under siege from various directions, inspired in the first instance by the rise of fundamentalism abroad.

Diversity does create severe problems of political coordination and management; the threat to India's integrity from it need not be exaggerated. While a little diversity is a dangerous thing, an abundance of it is less corrosive of the prospects for unity since it diffuses disputes away from a single sharp axis of conflict. The presence of several kinds of diversity in India results in the cross-cutting of cleavages so that all groups are, in effect, rendered into minorities. The most dangerous situation for political unity is that where there is a single axis of conflict which pits in a bipolar situation a dominated group against a dominant group, as was the case with Pakistan before 1971. In this light, the unity of India, demonstrated over the last half-century, is not an accident but is structurally based. However, its maintenance requires that there be no precedent of any part breaking away, hence the state's stern position on secessionist movements. At the same time, the downside of the extensive diversity is that it weakens national institutions and leads to frequent stalemates in politics and government.

Democracy

India is remarkable among the less developed countries in having sustained the political framework of democracy over the last half-century. However, distortions are to be expected from the installation of democratic institutions in an economically backward and traditional society, and there has, of course, occurred considerable deterioration in these institutions over the years. Nonetheless, the contrast with Pakistan and Bangladesh is dramatic; for much of their history, the two have been under military rule or military-controlled governments. All three countries had been under British rule, so that that experience alone cannot explain the contrast. The combination of the exposure to British ideas of liberalism with India's own cultural-ideological values and its abundant diversity offers a more adequate explanation. Noteworthy is the Indian elite's insistence on the subordination of the military to civilian authority, and its reluctance to expand the army except in balance with the general development of society. While these elements reduce the efficacy of its military instruments (Rosen 1996), India has been able to avoid military intervention in politics.

With its emphasis on consensus-building and gradualism, democracy has acted as a moderating force in building economic and military capabilities and pursuing an overly activist foreign policy. In the context of democracy in a poor country, there has been a predisposition to risk-aversion and cost-avoidance except in the event of a crisis. India's reformist rather than radical posture in economic and political affairs is related precisely to its democratic system, as has been its restraint in building military and nuclear capabilities.

Systemic constraints during the Cold War

It is not only internal factors that explain the limited nature of India's challenge, but also external systemic factors which have tied down India to the affairs of the region. The reason for the latter relates to the conflict dynamics of the region, which tend to set India's smaller neighbors against it and to invite intervention by external powers to balance it. This has less to do with India's behavior than its very hegemonic position, reinforced by the particular position, interests, and belief systems of the neighboring countries, particularly Pakistan. As one American scholar (Wilcox 1971: 257–8) noted: "Most India-Pakistan interstate conflict since 1947 has been generated by Pakistan. The weak party in this situation is also the revisionist power and at times it has pursued what Boulding could characterize as 'rational aggression,' 'the deliberate, planned conflict or game of ruin' against India in the calculated hope of *relative* benefit." Whereas India's conception of security has been a geopolitical and regional one, requiring the exclusion of outside powers, that of its neighbors, particularly Pakistan, has been strictly *national* and *counter-regional*, seeking to neutralize India through counter-balancing by foreign intervention. The incentive for a great power to intervene lies essentially, in line with realist theory, in that the claim to regional preeminence on the part of a middle power serves to reduce the global reach of its influence and power. This is particularly noteworthy in respect of the US which, even though it retains the Western hemisphere as its own sphere of influence, insists doctrinally that there be no exclusionary spheres of influence elsewhere in the world, meaning that it must have unhindered influence in all regions. The benign attitude of the US towards others (see Ikenberry, this volume) is premised on their prior acceptance of its hegemony.

The realist scholar George Liska (1973: 226) has outlined a typology of three policies that great powers typically pursue in relation to a middle

power, preeminent in a region: containment, satellization, and accommodation. In respect of containment, he noted: "Great powers can treat and
have reason to treat individual middle powers as regional rivals, and be
led to help still lesser states to contain them under the pretence of
restraining, unilaterally or cooperatively, all Third World conflict." The
intent, of course, is to reduce the influence of the middle power, to
subordinate its foreign policy to the requirements of the great power, to
raise the costs for it of foreign policy autonomy, and thus to prevent its
rise to the status of a major power. The key mechanism in containment is
balancing against middle powers through alliances, either tacit or explicit,
with some local or extra-regional power. Containment is thus a broader
policy than the one specifically aimed by the US at an ideologically
antagonistic great power, such as the Soviet Union. Under the policy of
accommodation, in contrast, great powers devolve regional responsibility
to "loyalist" or "apparently constructively disposed middle powers,"
while under the policy of satellization they subordinate the foreign policy
of the middle powers to their own through the acquisition of an interventionist capability, such as aid dependence.

Would it be appropriate to consider the US-Pakistan military alliance
from 1954 onwards, with some intermittent breaks, as a policy of containment aimed at India? There are two views on the subject. One view
contends that the containment of India is merely an unintended byprod-
uct of a policy of containment directed against the Soviet Union, and that
there is little evidence to interpret it otherwise (McMahon 1994: 177). If
by evidence is meant declassified government documents, that may well
be true. On the other hand, sole reliance on such documents for evidence
of motivation is problematic, for not everything is recorded or revealed
(as in the case of the US role in the 1953 coup in Iran). The containment
of the Soviet Union may have been an important impulse for the US-
Pakistan military alliance, but the second view suggests other motives as
well and offers convincing evidence on the issue of containment aimed
specifically at India (Nayar 1991).

More than three decades ago, Harrison (1966: 67) pointedly underlined
the two-pronged approach of American decision-makers, where "For the
record John Foster Dulles defined the new military pact as part of the
global collective-security pattern . . . Off the record, Vice President Nixon
defined the objectives of some elements in Washington *more candidly* in
briefings with newsmen. Pakistan's readiness to enter into a military pact
offered an opportunity, the Vice President felt, *to build a counterforce to
Nehru's neutralism* in the Indian leader's backyard" (emphasis added).
Similarly, Nixon's early biographer, Ralph de Toledano (1956: 164), to
whom Nixon opened his files, wrote that in his memorable speech before

the National Security Council, Nixon argued that "Nehru was contemptuous of flattery and respectful of strength," and forcefully urged military aid to Pakistan "as a counterforce to the confirmed neutralism of Jawaharlal Nehru's India." Nixon had revealed his thinking even earlier to the *New York Times* (December 9–10, 1953), wherein he sharply underlined the basic opposition between the global power and the middle power: "His [Nehru's] major rival for influence in South Asia is the United States." Nixon then asked Washington to "determine whether India, a country often opposed to the United States in vital international dealings, is to obtain unquestioned dominance over this entire area, plus Africa, or is to remain merely the strongest individual power in an Asia-Arab-Africa bloc." Advocating a firmer course against India, he recommended that "an early practical step in that direction would be to strengthen the friendlier nations in this orbit, beginning with Pakistan."

Nixon thus laid out sharply the inherent conflict between the US as the hegemonic global power and India as the rebellious middle power as also the means to be employed by the global power to counter middle power pretensions to greater influence. The stance taken by Nixon was, however, true of Dulles as well, for "Dulles, exasperated by Nehru's refusal to sign the Japanese Peace Treaty that he (Dulles) had negotiated or to modify India's nonaligned foreign policies, was in favor of the proposed build-up of the Pakistan military" (Bowles 1971: 478). Senator Fulbright was thus correct when he warned that the military pact with Pakistan was basically an anti-Nehru tactic "designed to force his hand" (Harrison 1959: 21). India's friends among American liberals could not stem the tide against nonalignment, which was seen as inimical to US interests. Interestingly, American Ambassador George Allen, within less than a month after the decision on military aid, directly linked it to the intended setbacks to Nehru and his foreign policy; in a secret cable to Washington, he confided: "This decision has been a *serious defeat for Nehru*. I hope with time *it will undermine his entire concept of neutralism in this region*. If this develops *it will be a major victory for US policy*" (US 1983: 1350–2, emphasis added). However, one need not rely simply on verbal testimony to discern US intentions. Equally important is the actual pattern of state behavior of the US, where it is noteworthy that the weapons-mix provided to Pakistan left no doubt that it was directed against India, with the equipment fit for use only in the plains of the Punjab. The Indian government brought this to the attention of the US, but to no avail (Bowles 1971: 480). After the military coup d'état in Pakistan in 1958, the US deepened its military relationship, reaching a new agreement with it in 1959, thus emboldening a military dictatorship in its course of confrontation with a democracy.

India's response to the stern lesson in realpolitik, so forcefully delivered by the US, was moderate and measured; it refused to be stampeded into an arms race, fearful of its impact on economic development. Indeed, it kept its defense expenditures as a proportion of GDP at an irresponsibly low 2 percent – an open invitation to its adversaries to exploit its vulnerabilities. However, it moved quickly to balance the military aid to Pakistan by moving closer to the Soviet Union, but only politically, as if indicating that it was still open to competitive bidding by the US. This move was later followed by economic cooperation, which inspired the US to increase economic aid to India for fear that it would otherwise be driven even closer into Soviet arms.

Once established, the US-Pakistan military relationship created pillars of support in both countries to perpetuate it. For its part, India viewed the relationship to be at its cost and to have been so intended. But the US was not the only power causing concern. After the brief conflagration with India in 1962, China entered into a de facto alliance with Pakistan. Convinced of its military superiority because of its technologically superior American weaponry, Pakistan attempted in 1965 to grab Kashmir. In the short war that followed, India was content with reaching a stalemate in view of its limited war aims, but was distressed at the silence of the US on Pakistan's use of American arms against India. In the wake of the war, a closer relationship developed between Pakistan and China, with the latter emerging as a major arms supplier to Pakistan. As China developed its nuclear capabilities after its first test in 1964, India sought security guarantees from the US and UK but was turned down by both.

The disillusionment of the US with Pakistan over its growing cordial relationship with China was short-lived, however. It soon gave way to a three-way collaboration among them as the US, in its weakened state because of the Vietnam War, wished to balance a seemingly ascendant Soviet Union by a de facto alliance with China. Meanwhile, as Pakistan's military dictatorship massively crushed the popular autonomy movement in its eastern wing in 1971, and forced 10 million refugees into India, the US remained quiet about human rights violations. On the other hand, when tensions escalated in the subcontinent as a result, the US disabused India of any expectations of American help if China intervened in the event of a war between India and Pakistan. This warning only drove India into a closer security relationship with the Soviet Union. When Pakistan declared war, Nixon ordered the administration "to tilt in favor of Pakistan." Despite formal suspension of military aid, American arms shipments continued to flow to Pakistan. Later, the US itself intervened in the war by sending a nuclear task force headed by the USS *Enterprise* into the Bay of Bengal, aimed at India. A violent confrontation between the US and India was avoided only because India, having accomplished its war aims, brought the conflict to a quick end. With the Bangladesh crisis also ended the bilateral aid relationship between the US and India.

After the Bangladesh war, Kissinger told Henry Brandon (1973: 252–3) that the US had merely followed, in the tradition of Great Britain, a balance-of-power policy against India by allying itself with the weaker party. Subsequently, Kissinger maintained that the US took the course that it did to rescue a military ally because its credibility was at stake with China. The Indians then drew the appropriate lesson that the US would readily sacrifice their interests for its own in relation to China. Even before the crisis, the US had, as part of its design for restructuring the world on a five-power basis, conceded the legitimacy of China's role in South Asia at the cost of India, sharply reminding India that the only role fit for it was as an object, and of all the great powers at that (Nixon 1971: 341). The Indians did not relish that prospect, and it is understandable that they set in motion around that time the plans for the nuclear explosion in 1974 as an assertion of their independence. However, after the explosion they relapsed into nuclear hibernation and abstinence for a quarter-century, undoubtedly because of fear of economic reprisals.

During much of the 1970s the US adopted a posture of symbolic accommodation towards India, but in fact combined it with concrete containment through a more far-flung alliance arrangement that encompassed China, Pakistan, and Iran, the last one now chosen as an American surrogate in the region. At the end of the decade, as Iran underwent a revolution by Islamic militants, and as the Soviets intervened in Afghanistan, the US once again directly provided a major package of military and economic aid to Pakistan during the 1980s. The US also let it be pointedly known that it had imposed no conditions on Pakistan about usage of its arms against India, even as it maintained that the large supply of arms was essential for removing any incentive for Pakistan to go in for nuclear weapons. Ironically, it is precisely during this period of reinvigorated alliance that Pakistan rapidly pushed forward its nuclear weapons program. In effect, the US presided over the transformation of Pakistan from a non-nuclear to a nuclear-capable state. Only in 1990, after the Soviet withdrawal from Afghanistan, did the US finally acknowledge that Pakistan had already achieved nuclear status. Interestingly, during the 1980s and 1990s, China also took a more active role in transferring nuclear and missile technology and equipment to Pakistan, apparently supplying it with M-11 missiles, but the US refrained from invoking sanctions against Beijing.

Opportunities and constraints after the Cold War

The end of the Cold War confronts India with new challenges in the economic and strategic arenas. In the economic sphere, the collapse of the Soviet Union as a result of the relative decline of its economy, underlined not only the untenability of rigid economic controls in an era of increasing globalization and the importance of reaching out to new and expanding markets. Coincidentally, India's liquidity crisis in 1991 forced it to accelerate deregulation and move to a closer integration with the global economy. The economic policy reforms in 1991 were dramatic, even though the process of economic liberalization had begun earlier in the 1980s. Economics now assumed an enhanced salience in India's diplomacy.

As India made a quick recovery from the economic crisis of 1991 and reached an average annual economic growth rate of over 6 percent, and as its expanding market became an attractive site for foreign investors and exporters, it acquired a greater degree of self-confidence in turning it into a major economic player. The confidence was more generalized beyond economics. Even though there was concern over political stability as India entered in 1996 a period of weak coalition governments, there was the realization of the basic resilience of the Indian state. The state had survived the severe internal challenges, often aided by external forces, to territorial and political integrity in the Punjab and Kashmir. It had prevailed, defeating one insurgency and bringing the other under control, and by 1997 the democratic process had been restored in these areas.

With the increased self-confidence, India had already begun to see its large and expanding market as the foundation for encouraging regional economic cooperation in the subcontinent and beyond. In 1996 it replaced the concept of reciprocity in economic cooperation with its neighbors with "more than reciprocity" so as to foster closer economic relationships and mold SAARC into a genuine common market. Agreements soon followed with Bangladesh, Nepal, and Sri Lanka. India was ready to cooperate similarly with Pakistan, which instead held back by making economic cooperation conditional on a prior resolution of the Kashmir dispute. However, India's aspirations extended beyond the South Asia region, and it was an active promoter in 1997 of the Indian Ocean Rim Association for Regional Cooperation (IOR-ARC). Meanwhile, it became a "full dialogue partner" with ASEAN and a member of the ASEAN Regional Forum. Although these moves were primarily economic in orientation, they are likely to have strategic implications over the long term. More generally, as if determined to resolve its status inconsistency, India objected to being equated with the much smaller Pakistan, as the US had been wont to do; rather, it now demanded that it be treated on par with China and laid claim to a permanent seat on a future restructured Security Council. At the same time, India showed remarkable restraint in its defense expenditures, which at 2.8 percent of GDP in 1996 are very low compared to the relevant neighbors (Pakistan and China, 5.7 percent), testifying to its generally defensive posture.

In its emphasis on economic liberalization and cooperation, India found the US to be an active partner. Both American business and government regarded India as one of the more important among the ten "big emerging markets" in the world, with a vast middle class ranging from 150 million to 250 million, and thus an attractive market for foreign investment and goods. The 1990s saw several American economic and other missions travel to India. Although its investment in India is small relative to that in China, the US ranks as the top foreign investor in India, with several important brokerage houses and other firms gaining considerable visibility, among them Bechtel, Ford, GE, and IBM. The growing India-US economic ties created expectations that they would spill over, as had happened in the case of China, into generating some restraint on American actions that India felt were inimical to its security interests. In this, the Indians were profoundly mistaken and therefore greatly disappointed as the US seemed to draw a distinction between the economic and strategic arenas, at least in so far as India was concerned. Regardless, as India enters the twenty-first century it will continue to focus on economics because of its importance for national security and welfare.

The strategic arena presents India with much more formidable challenges. The collapse of the Soviet Union and with it of the special India-Soviet relationship removed an important security insurance in times of crisis and more generally a useful countervailing force against possible domination by other major powers. Presently, the key powers of concern to India are China and the US, whether in competition or collaboration. With a long and disputed border, India has genuine security concerns in relation to China, especially in view of China's collaborative relationship with Pakistan on its western flank and with Myanmar on its eastern flank. Besides, because of its large size and location, India is a natural rival to China in Asia. Even if relations were to improve substantially, India would focus on Chinese capabilities, not intentions, particularly given the uncertainties associated with China's combination of economic pluralism and political centralism. Security concerns therefore make it imperative for India to correct the power asymmetry with China by augmenting its nuclear deterrent capability and building effective delivery systems. China's rise to great power status in the twenty-first century is unlikely to lead India to either bandwagoning with or balancing against China, at least overtly, for both policies would be seen as inconsistent with India's foreign policy tradition and interests. Rather, it would fortify India in its determination to build a self-reliant defense, especially in view of its own great power aspirations.

However, it is precisely this very combination of defense self-reliance and great power aspirations, to which India is perforce driven by its geopolitical circumstances, that leads India into serious problems with the US, notwithstanding the apparent eagerness of the two countries to advance economic ties. There are, no doubt, convergent interests between India and the US in several areas, such as stability in the Persian Gulf region, prevention of terrorism, and the spread of democracy. However, the very different structural location of the two in the international system as great power and middle power places them at odds with each other.

Analysts point out four different policy options for the US in its newfound situation of power supremacy in a unipolar system: (1) neo-isolationism; (2) selective engagement; (3) cooperative security; and (4) primacy. Examining both policy statements and state behavior, Posen and Ross find that the US during the Clinton years has pursued a policy of selective (but cooperative) primacy. More accurately, it emerges that, rather than such a triple-headed amalgam of a policy, primacy alone has served as the ordering framework for US policy, for selective engagement and cooperative security are simply means to that end. The implication of this policy of primacy for middle powers such as India is that it requires the great power hegemon to oppose the rise or existence of any independent centers of power anywhere unless they are subordinate to it. Of course, this intent had been explicitly previsioned and set out by the Bush administration, whose draft Defense Planning Guidance paper stated in a no-nonsense fashion that "Our first objective is to prevent the reemergence of a new rival, either on the territory of the former Soviet Union or elsewhere . . . and requires that we endeavor to prevent any hostile power from dominating a region whose resources would, under consolidated control, be sufficient to generate global power . . . Our strategy must now refocus on precluding the emergence of any potential future global competitor" (cited in Posen and Ross 1996/7: 33).

That strategy was not simply addressed to all and sundry regional powers, however; the same paper made it clear that India was a specific target, declaring: "We should discourage Indian hegemonistic aspirations over the other states in South Asia and on the Indian Ocean." In contrast, it recommended the rebuilding of "a constructive US-Pakistan military relationship." At the same time, ignoring how India's security would be affected by such a military relationship or by China's increasing nuclear capabilities, the paper affirmed: "We will seek to prevent the further development of a nuclear arms race on the Indian subcontinent" (*New York Times*, March 8, 1992: A14). For the Indian leadership, the draft Defense Planning Guidance paper only confirmed its perception that Indian strength had been unacceptable to the US in so far as it provided New Delhi defense and foreign policy autonomy. American policies in regard to the initial denial of a supercomputer, the forced cancellation of the Soviet contract to supply cryogenic technology for India's space program, and the imposition of sanctions against its space and electronics industries were simply manifestations of the basic American strategic posture towards India. Most striking of all for it in this respect was the forceful American drive to deny India the nuclear option. While maintaining the public atmospherics of increasing India–US economic cooperation, the US attempted to close off India's nuclear option by skillfully navigating in 1995 the indefinite extension of the unequal and discriminatory NPT and in 1996 forcefully pushing through, over India's objections and protests, the even more unequal and discriminatory CTBT. In effect, the US was able to marginalize and isolate India on the global scene. Meanwhile, when, in April 1998, Pakistan tested an IRBM missile, built with obvious Chinese assistance and provocatively named after a foreign invader and conqueror of northern India, there was only a minor rebuke from the US to Pakistan and silence on China.

Little wonder that India saw the US as conniving at the China–Pakistan nuclear and missile cooperation; worse, the US was seen as augmenting China's own nuclear missile capabilities through technology transfers. The Indians saw encirclement in the growing collaboration ("engagement") between the US and China alongside the de facto alliance between China and Pakistan. Coinciding with a change in government in New Delhi, these developments compelled India to review its strategic situation, which led to the nuclear tests in May 1998. The tests immediately brought forth the imposition of severe sanctions by the US against India, even as White House press adviser Mike McCurry threatened, in the language of containment, a series of measures to ensure regional balance in the wake of the tests (*Times of India*, May 22, 1998). Meanwhile, as was to be expected, Pakistan responded with its own nuclear tests within three weeks. Thus was torn the veil of ambiguity behind which nuclear competition had so far been conducted in the subcontinent. It is obvious that the contradictory imperatives of India's security and the US drive for global primacy have placed the two powers fundamentally in conflict with each other.

India's preference, like China's, is for a multipolar or polycentric world, but national security in its neighborhood is its more immediate concern as it enters the twenty-first century. Although India articulated no strategic doctrine earlier in facing its security challenges, an implicit strategy seemed evident. One, nuclear weapons are not likely to be actually used because of the "nuclear taboo," especially in view of unpredictable ecological consequences. Therefore, there is no urgency to actually deploy a vast arsenal of such weapons, wasting in the process precious economic resources. Two, as long as other states have nuclear weapons and believe that they are usable instruments in war and diplomacy, India must continue to hold on to its nuclear option, even if not weaponized, as an insurance against intervention or political blackmail. However, the combination of the pressures of the growing collaboration between China and Pakistan and between the US and China, and the US-orchestrated international regimes, which would divest India of a viable nuclear option, finally led India in 1998 to nuclear testing and to proclaiming itself a nuclear weapons state. Hereafter, its strategic doctrine will likely rest on nuclear deterrence and, as a non-expansionist power, on the no-first-use principle.

Conclusion

As in regard to many other aspects of India, ambiguity has surrounded its search for an international role. The contrast with China is obvious; regardless of whether it is to be engaged or contained, China has already arrived as a candidate great power (see Chan, this volume). For India, however, the struggle to achieve great power status still lies ahead. Interestingly, China serves both as a model for India in its aspiration for great power status and as a strategic stimulus for that aspiration. China's capacity to confidently engage and, indeed, manage the US evokes admiration even as the American differential treatment of India on the same or similar issues is taken to be a case of double standards.

While the gap between the aspirations for great power status and the actual movement towards their achievement is manifest, and the contrast with China is stark, the notion of the gap need not be overdone. Since the early 1960s, there has been under way a slow-paced and low-key but nonetheless determined drive to acquire the wherewithal of a credible autonomous deterrent capability, which is a prerequisite for great power status, and to undergird that capability with a dynamic economy. Notwithstanding all that, for a long time India did not proceed in an emphatic and forthright manner to match China's capabilities so as to confront the world with a fait accompli. However, the strategic costs of this self-containment began to loom large in its calculus in recent years. The direct consequence of the nonproliferation regime was seen by India not only as freezing the power distribution in the international system, in the process reducing India to the position permanently of a minor power, but more crucially as putting India's security at risk in relation to China and China-aided Pakistan. It is this situation that compelled India to defy the US and its allies and engage in nuclear testing in May 1998. This act of defiance received massive public support in India. However, it is yet to be seen how resilient India is in withstanding the fury of the US by way of harsh economic sanctions. Seemingly ideology and the nature of India's political system have mattered little in the American posture, for the US has accepted as legitimate the possession of nuclear weapons by China but opposes their acquisition by India. There is deep irony manifest in the American collaboration with China's communist dictatorship and its adversarial relationship with India's political democracy.

The final outcome of the contest between the US drive to disarm others in nuclear terms and the Indian determination not to be so disarmed in perpetuity, if the present nuclear powers continue to retain their capabilities, remains to be seen. Meanwhile, it is apparent that India has come to represent more than a limited challenge because it puts in jeopardy the entire edifice erected by the hegemonic power. There is no doubt that, in the contest between the two democracies, it is within the power of the US to penalize India for its pursuit of national autonomy, for Indian power is limited compared to that of the US. So far, the US as the hegemonic leader of the Western alliance has followed only the policies of containment and satellization, but these have not proven particularly productive in relation to a country that refuses, perhaps justifiably, to be treated as that which it is not – a minor power. Some (Babbage 1992: 166–7) therefore see merit, instead, in a policy of accommodation in approaching the issue of India's status inconsistency, and this for some sound reasons: "there would be advantage in not obstructing the gradual achievement of these aspirations. This is not only because they are largely inevitable but also because many of India's fundamental values and interests are broadly compatible with those of the West. India's deeply entrenched democratic heritage, its successful market economy, its open culture and English language and its role as a rising, strong but essentially status quo power provide a basis for enhanced relationships."

NOTES

1 I am grateful to Professor J. Handa and the editors for their most helpful comments.

REFERENCES

Babbage, Ross 1992, "India's Strategic Development: Issues for the Western Powers," in *India's Strategic Future*, Babbage and Sandy Gordon (eds.), Houndmills, UK: Macmillan, pp. 153–69.

Bowles, Chester 1971, *Promises to Keep: My Years in Public Life 1941–1969*, New York: Harper & Row.

Brandon, Henry 1973, *The Retreat of American Power*, New York: Doubleday.

de Toledano, Ralph 1956, *Nixon*, New York: Henry Holt.

Dibb, Paul 1995, *Towards a New Balance of Power in Asia*, Adelphi Paper 295 London: International Institute for Strategic Studies.

Harrison, Selig S. 1959, "India, Pakistan and the U.S. – II," *New Republic* 141 August 24: 20–5.

1966, "America, India, and Pakistan," *Harper's* 233 (July), 56–68.

Liska, George 1973, "The Third World: Regional Systems and Global Order," in *Retreat from Empire*, Robert E. Osgood et al., Baltimore: Johns Hopkins University Press, pp. 279–343.

Lyon, Peter 1968, "The Foreign Policy of India," in *The Foreign Policies of the Powers*, F. S. Northedge (ed.), New York: Praeger, pp. 253–88.

McMahon, Robert J. 1994, *The Cold War on the Periphery: The United States, India, and Pakistan*, New York: Columbia University Press.

Nayar, Baldev Raj 1991, *Superpower Dominance and Military Aid: A Study of Military Aid to Pakistan*, New Delhi: Manohar.

Nehru, Jawaharlal 1961, *Indian Foreign Policy: Selected Speeches, September 1946–April 1961*, New Delhi: Publications Division.

Nixon, Richard M. 1971, *United States Foreign Policy for the 1970s: Building for Peace* (February 25, 1971), in *Weekly Compilation of Presidential Documents*, 7 (9), pp. 305–770.

Nye, Joseph S., Jr. 1990, *Bound to Lead: The Changing Nature of American Power*, New York: Basic Books.

Paul, T. V. 1994, *Asymmetric Conflicts: War Initiation by Weaker Powers*, New York: Cambridge University Press.

Posen, Barry R. and Ross, Andrew L. 1996/7, "Competing Visions for U.S. Grand Strategy," *International Security* 21: 5–53.

Rosen, Stephen Peter 1996, *Societies and Military Power: India and its Armies*, Ithaca: Cornell University Press.

United States 1983, *Foreign Relations of the United States, 1952–1954: Volume XI: Africa and South Asia*, Washington, DC: Department of State.

Wilcox, Wayne A. 1971, "India and Pakistan," in *Conflict in World Politics*, Steven L. Spiegel and Kenneth N. Waltz (eds.), Cambridge, MA: Winthrop Publishers, pp. 240–60.

Part III

Challenges

12 Has globalization ended the rise and rise of the nation-state?[1]

Michael Mann

Introduction

The human sciences seem full of enthusiasts claiming that a new form of human society is emerging. The most enthusiastic compare today with the eighteenth century, whose Industrial Revolution, whose "modernism" and whose "Enlightenment" supposedly revolutionized human society. They say we are in the throes of a comparable transition to a "post-industrial" or "postmodern" society. Other terminologies imply rather less revolutionary change. Terms such as "late capitalism," "late modernity," or "radical modernity" are used to suggest varying degrees of continuous versus disruptive change. "Globalist" words also invoke varying degrees of enthusiasm: "global capitalism" may refer only to a major extension of an old economy, while "global society" usually implies a radically novel phenomenon in the history of human society.

The enthusiasts comprise a very varied group of *littérateurs*, *philosophes*, historians, sociologists, political and business economists, geographers, and environmentalists. They agree about very little – especially about whether the changes are to be welcomed. But on one point they do agree: contemporary changes are weakening the nation-state. From postmodernists like Baudrillard or Lyotard or Jamieson, to geographers like Harvey or Taylor, to sociologists like Giddens or Lash and Urry, to the business economists well-represented by *The Economist*, come similar statements about the "undermining," "undercutting," "outflanking," or "marginalization" of the nation-state (for recent exemplars, see Taylor 1996; Lash and Urry 1994; Featherstone 1990; Harvey 1990; "The World Economy" 1995). Some qualify this in one respect. Since "ethnicity" looms large in scenarios of "postmodern fragmentation," these often see nationalism as resurgent in the world today. But for the old nation-state, we find largely epitaphs.

Many enthusiasts are Western Europeans – not surprisingly, since this particular region of the globe offers most political support to their epitaph for the state. Many (both Marxian and neo-classical) are materialists who point to the great changes underway in capitalism and believe these will necessarily transform the rest of the social structure. The core of most arguments rests on the technological-informational innovations of our times. Transport and information systems providing rapid (often instantaneous) access to the world furnish the infrastructures of a global society. I accept that this potential infrastructure of globalism exists: the logistics of communication and so of power have indeed been revolutionized. Persons, goods, and especially messages circulate the globe so that the enthusiastic vision of a single global society is a technologically possible one. But is it actuality? To suggest that it is, various groups of enthusiasts advance four main theses.

(1) Capitalism, now become global, transnational, post-industrial, "informational," consumerist, neo-liberal, and "restructured," is undermining the nation-state, its macroeconomic planning, its collectivist welfare state, its citizens' sense of collective identity, its general caging of social life.

(2) Other aspects of "globalism," especially environmental and population threats, producing perhaps a new "risk society," have become too broad and too menacing to be handled by the nation-state alone.

(3) "Identity politics" and "new social movements," using new technology, increase the salience of diverse local and transnational identities at the expense of both national identities and those broad class identities which were traditionally handled by the nation-state. For this and for the previous reason we are witnessing the stirrings of a new transnational "civil society," social movements for peace, human rights, and environmental and social reform which are becoming truly global.

(4) Post-nuclearism undermines state sovereignty and "hard geopolitics," since mass mobilization warfare underpinned much of modern state expansion yet is now irrational. Martin Shaw's (1996) perception of the emergence of a "World State" is perhaps the most measured version of this thesis. It is very much a minority view in the discipline of International Relations, most of which remains attached to the study of the sovereign state.

So the empirical part of this chapter will investigate whether these four nation-state-weakening theses are correct. Since they downplay political power relations, it also considers two political counter-theses. (A) State institutions, both domestic and geopolitical, still have causal efficacy because they too (like economic, ideological, and military institutions) provide necessary conditions for social existence:[2] the regulation of aspects of social life which are distinctively "territorially-centered" (Mann 1986: ch. 1). Thus they cannot be the mere consequence of other sources of social power.

(B) Since states vary greatly, if (A) is true, these variations will cause variations in other spheres of social life. Even within Europe states differ in size, power, geography, and degree of centralization. Across the globe, variations dramatically increase: in degree of democracy, level of development, infrastructural power, geopolitical power, national indebtedness, etc. They also inhabit very different regional settings. Can contemporary capitalism, even if reinforced by environmental danger, "cultural postmodernity," and demilitarization, render all this variation irrelevant, and have the *same* effects on all countries? Or will these variations cause variation among these forces, and so limit globalization?

Only the most breathless of enthusiasts would deny all validity to these counter-theses – or to the survival of the nation-state as wielder of some economic, ideological, military, and political resources. The task is to establish *degrees* of relative causality: to what extent is the nation-state being transformed, to what extent is it declining – or even perhaps still growing?

But to establish this we must also make some conceptual distinctions. We can roughly distinguish five socio-spatial networks of social interaction in the world today.

(1) *Local* networks – which for present purposes just means subnational networks of interaction.

(2) *National* networks, structured or (more neutrally) bounded by the nation-state.

(3) *Inter-national* networks, that is relations between nationally constituted networks. Most obviously, these include the "hard geopolitics" of interstate relations which center on war, peace, and alliances. But they also include "soft geopolitics" between states – negotiations about more peaceable and particular matters like air transport communications, tax treaties, air pollution, etc. And they include relations between networks that are more nationally- than state-constituted: for example, the emergence of "national champions" playing on a broader playing field – whether these are football teams or giant corporations.

(4) *Transnational* networks, passing right through national boundaries, being unaffected by them. These might not be very extensive – perhaps a religious sect organized across two neighboring countries – or they might be continent-wide or even worldwide. Many transnational arguments about contemporary society rest on a "macro-regional" base. Examples are the frequent distinctions between "Liberal/Anglo-Saxon," "Nordic/

Social Democratic," or "Christian Democratic/corporatist" forms of contemporary social organization

(5) *Global* networks cover the world as a whole – or, perhaps more realistically, they cover most of it. But we should distinguish between networks which radiate universalistically or particularistically across the globe. The feminist movement may spread through almost all countries, but usually only among rather particular, smallish groups. The Catholic Church has some presence in all continents but has only quite a narrow base across Asia, while being near-universal across Latin America. The capitalism evoked by many of the enthusiasts is a universal global network, evenly diffusing through economic and social life just about everywhere. Thus global networks might be formed by either a single universal network or a more segmented series of networks between which existed rather particularistic relations.

Over the last centuries local interaction networks have clearly diminished in relative weight; while longer-distance networks – national, international, and transnational – have become denser, structuring more of people's lives. Genuinely global networks have emerged relatively recently. Note that global networks need not be the same as transnational networks, though many enthusiasts equate them. Nor are they necessarily economic in nature. Global networks may be constituted by geopolitics (as Shaw [1996] argues) or by ideological movements like a religion or socialism or feminism or neo-liberalism – the combination amounting perhaps to a new transnational civil society.

Since national and international networks are constituted or fundamentally constrained by the nation-state, the future of the nation-state thus turns critically upon answering two questions: *is the social significance of national and international networks declining relative to some combination of local and transnational networks? And to the extent that global networks are emerging, what is the relative contribution to them of national/international versus local/transnational networks?*

The "modest nation-state" of the North

I start with the most familiar and dominant form of state in the world today. In the "West," or more precisely the "Northwest" of Western Europe and its white colonies, arose a state claiming formal political sovereignty over "its" territories and a legitimacy based on the "people" or "nation" inhabiting them. This is what we mean by the nation-state. The regulatory powers of such states expanded through several centuries. First, from the end of the Middle Ages they increasingly plausibly claimed a monopoly of judicial regulation and military force. Then, in the eighteenth and especially the nineteenth century they sponsored integrating communications infrastructures and basic control of the poor. The twentieth century saw welfare states, macroeconomic planning, and the mobilization of mass citizen nationalism. All the while more states legitimated themselves in terms of "the people," either "representing" the people (liberal democracies) or "organically embodying" it (authoritarian regimes), with varying degrees of civil, political, and social citizenship. To a degree, therefore, Northwesterners became "caged" into national interaction networks, and these became supplemented by the inter-national relations between nation-states which we know by the term "geopolitics."

This is the now-familiar story of "the rise and rise" of the nation-state and the nation-state system – to which I myself have contributed (Mann 1986, 1993a). Yet we should note that the expansion of these national and inter-national networks always proceeded *alongside* the expansion of certain "transnational" power relations, especially those of industrial capitalism and its attendant ideologies (liberalism, socialism), plus the broader cultural networks provided in the Northwest by European/Christian/"white" senses of collective identity. National and international interaction networks thus grew much more at the expense of local than of transnational networks. For example, in the very period in the late nineteenth century when European states were deepening their national education and public health infrastructures, raising tariffs, and beginning to drift nearer to war against each other (examples of national and international caging), transnational trade was rocketing to form the same proportion of world production as it now forms, and the Northwestern powers were acting together, with a smug sense of cultural superiority, to Christianize, exploit, and drug the Chinese. Indeed nation-state growth *presupposed* a broader global expansion, most obviously to finance it, but also perhaps because a sense of nationhood may have presupposed the sense of European/Christian/White superiority which endowed *all* the classes and both sexes of the Northwest with a sense of their own moral worth and equality. Indeed, the last great expansionist surge of the nation state, from 1945 to the 1960s, may have also involved both. States were flush with funds from massive economic expansion and they possessed the war- and reconstruction-generated institutions to spend them; and Northwestern nations, having taught their colonials the values of "civilization," now "granted" them independence in their own European form, as nation-states. Thus the past saw the rise of transnational capitalism and cultural identities alongside the rise of the nation-state and its inter-national system. They have always possessed a complex combination of relative autonomy and symbiotic inter-dependence.

Most Northwestern states also *lost* certain functions during the period of their expansion. As they became more "secular," they relinquished powers over moral regulation, which they had in principle possessed in association with Churches (though Church rather than state infrastructures had usually enforced such moral regulation in earlier centuries). Remember also that most of economic life had never come into the realm of the state: we call it "private" property. Thus much of social life remained or became *more* private, outside the sphere of competence of the nation-state, even during its great period of expansion. Property remained private; gays remained in the closet. Capitalism and morality were substantially autonomous of the state. I suggest later that moral autonomy is now declining.

Thus only a "modest nation-state" became dominant in the Northwest. In the course of the twentieth century it defeated three rivals. One was the "multi-national Empire": the dynastic empires of the Habsburgs, Romanovs, and Ottomans, with weaker states and little national identity – a less "nation-statist" alternative. But the other two defeated states were actually far more nation-statist. Fascism sought a much stronger, authoritarian state which would supposedly embody the essence of a more rigidly and more ethnically defined nation. By 1945 fascism was discredited – at least for the two generations which have followed. State socialism also sought a stronger state (supposedly only in the short run). Though not strictly nationalist, its increasing tendency to equate the proletariat with a broader "people" or "masses" gave it a similar principle of legitimation. And its economic autarky and rigid surveillance greatly intensified its "national" caging. Its discrediting lasted longer and seemed finished (for the present) by 1991. Both of these defeated regimes also claimed a monopoly of morality, which the "modest nation-state" never did. It was the responsibility of the state to cultivate "Soviet Man" or what was "consciously German." Had these more ambitious "nation-states" both triumphed and the world then globalized, its global society would have been constituted by a segmental series of global networks between which the most particularistic, and probably warlike, relations would have existed. Since they did not, any subsequent globalism might be expected to be rather more universal in character.

Since 1945 the modest victor further diffused across almost all the rest of "the North," i.e., the whole European continent and increasing regions of East and South Asia. Its formal trappings have also dominated "the South," while all states meet in a forum called "The United Nations." The modest nation-state might seem to dominate the entire globe. In some limited senses it actually does. Only a few states do not base their legitimacy on the nation or lack a monopoly of domestic coercion or real territorial boundedness. Almost all manage to implement policies oriented toward basic population control, health, and education. Plunging mortality and rising literacy have multiple causes, but some lie in the realm of effective public policy. For these reasons I will go ahead and describe contemporary states as nation-states. Yet most of them actually possess rather limited control over their territories and boundaries, while their claims to represent the nation are often specious. For much of the world a *true* nation-state remains more aspiration for the future than present reality. The nation-state's rise has been global, but modest and very uneven. The modest nation-state came to dominate the "North," has been part of its expansion, and represents a desired future for the bulk of the world's people. Is all this now threatened?

The capitalist threat

The enthusiasts have correctly identified many important transformations of capitalism. It is not necessary here to document capitalism's use of new "informational" and "post-industrial" technology to expand through much of the world and penetrate more of social life. But how great is its threat to the nation-state? And just how "global" and/or "transnational" is it?

In a formal geographic sense capitalism *is* now more-or-less global. Two great geopolitical events permitted massive extension. First, decolonization largely ended the segmentation of the world economy into separate imperial zones. Second, the collapse of Soviet autarky opened up most of Eurasia to capitalist penetration. Only Iran, China, and a handful of smaller communist countries now maintain partial blockages, and these are declining or may be expected to soon start declining. China retains distinct property forms (mixing private with varieties of public ownership and control), and there still also remain (declining) areas of subsistence economy scattered through the world. Yet capitalist commodity exchange clearly dominates. With no confident adversary in sight, capitalism is becoming – at least minimally – global. That was not so in 1940, nor even in 1980. It is obviously a major transformation.

But are its global networks "pure" in the sense of being singularly universal, or do other more particularistic principles of social organization also help constitute them? An economy may be global, but this may be conferred by help from national and inter-national networks of interaction. After all, more than 80 percent of world production is still for the domestic national market. Since economic statistics are gathered at the level of the nation-state, it is unknown what is the relative contribution to this of truly national exchanges compared to the contributions made by multiple local interaction networks. The national economy is presumably considerably less integrated than the statistic suggests – especially in backward countries and bigger advanced countries like the US or Australia. Yet the nation-state clearly does systematically structure many economic networks. The ownership, assets, and R&D of "multi-national" corporations (including banks, mutuals, and insurance firms) remain disproportionately in their "home" state, and they still lean on it for human capital (education), communications infrastructures, and economic protectionism (Carnoy 1993; Castells 1993). Nonetheless, even among the more fixed multi-nationals, their sales reach, organization of production, and investment flows are also substantially transnational. Strategic alliances with corporations of other "nationality" are now proliferating, weakening the national identity of property – though many of these arrangements occur to evade protectionism and might decline if it did.

Finance is far more transnational – as evidenced by the growing complexity of financial markets and of the models supposed to be capable of explaining them – from Random Walk to Chaos theories! Yet its institutions continue to exhibit bureaucratic regularity, much of it with a pronounced national character. The employees of Nikko Europe start their London workday before the Tokyo stock market closes. They relay the latest information first to their European-based customers, who are actually mostly Japanese corporations. Then, as Wall Street awakes, the information is transmitted westward and London shuts down for the night. Financial markets also reveal a national/transnational duality. On the one hand, trading in government bonds, in currencies, in futures, and in wholesale dealing between banks, is largely transnational, often distinctively "offshore," slushing through the boundaries of states subject to very few controls. On the other hand, company shares tend to be fixed to particular national stock markets and to national corporate laws and accountancy practices (Wade 1996).

Of course, Western Europe has gone more transnational, sponsoring a unique degree of continental economic integration. Here lies a genuine single market, a movement which will probably end in a single currency within two years (at least in its core), and predominantly "Euro-" rather than national attempts at protectionism. Here "national champion" corporations are becoming "Euro-champions," assisted as much by EU government as by the nation-state. Obviously, such economic complexities should be explored at much greater length than I can attempt here. But two points emerge: Europe is extreme (and will be explored more later), and real capitalist interaction networks remain profoundly mixed. Symbiosis between the national and the transnational remains.

A third point also emerges: most "transnational" economic relations cannot be necessarily equated with a global universalism. The bulk of capitalist activity is more "trilateral" than global, being concentrated in the three regions of the advanced "North": Europe, North America, and East Asia. These contain over 85 percent of world trade, over 90 percent of production in advanced sectors like electronics, plus the headquarters of all but a handful of the top hundred multi-nationals (including banks). This does not necessarily mean capitalism is not global. It may only indicate that the North is rich, the South is poor – and that both are locked together in a global network of interaction. But it does suggest that capitalism retains a geo-economic order, dominated by the economies of the advanced nation-states. Clusters of nation-states provide the stratification order of globalism. Among other consequences, this protects the citizens of the North: the poorly educated child of an unskilled worker in Britain or the United States will enjoy far better material conditions of existence (including twenty more years of life) than will his/her counterpart in Brazil or India. True, inequalities within most nation-states are widening, yet it is almost inconceivable that the bulk of the privileges of national citizens in Northern countries could be removed. That would cause such social disorder as to be incommensurate with a stable and profitable capitalism. The nation-state provides some of the structure, and some of the stratification structure, of the global networks of capitalism. If the commodity rules, it only does so entwined with the rule of – especially Northern – citizenship.

The global economy is also subject to loose and predominantly "soft" international regulation in the shape of organizations like G7 or GATT or the World Bank or the IMF. These are also Northern-dominated. Some of these are involved in seemingly endless negotiations of trade liberalization – and are likely to drag on a lot longer since national governments have been recently raising non-tariff barriers. We are nowhere near global free trade, but we may be moving a little closer and this is at present ideologically dominant. But is this just another liberalization phase in the normal historical oscillation around the middle zone between the free trade and protectionist poles? That depends on the resolution of other tendencies discussed in this paper.

So, at the moment and probably also for the near future, a rapidly globalizing economy does not only acquire its character from transnational networks of interaction. What adds up to the global is a very complex mix of the local, the national, the international (represented in my discussion mostly by Northern trilateralism) – and the truly transnational. The *transnational* commodity does not rule the globe. Over time some of these national and international structurings may decline.

Northern domination of the world economy may diminish because of the pressures of comparative advantage. Apart from very high-tech activities, much productive enterprise may migrate to the lower costs of the South, producing more globalization (though not necessarily much reducing inequality). But so far migration has operated not by some "transnational" logic (of random walk?) but by some combination of four other principles: the possession of useful natural resources; geographical propinquity (neighboring countries); geopolitical alliances (friendly countries); and state and civil society stability (predictable countries). Whereas the first factor is found fairly randomly through the world – and so oil alone can develop rather backward, distant countries – the last three factors are generally interconnected. The historical development of the major Northern economies emerged amid broader regional settings, from which neighboring states and societies also benefited. Thus expansion has mostly been to the Koreas and the Mexicos, friendly neighbors with relatively developed nations and states, rather than, say, to most African countries. Nor does most growth take a regional, "enclave" pattern within states (except where raw materials matter, or where extension is over a border and the neighboring government sponsors "enterprise zones"). Development then tends to diffuse across the core territories of these states, aiding the development of their overall civil societies and their drift toward becoming nation-states. Thus extension of the North – and so globalization – has depended upon, and in turn reinforced, the nation-states benefiting from it. This form of globalization reinforces national networks of interaction.

Since finance capital seems more transnational than industrial capital, its constraints upon the nation-state are usually those most emphasized by the enthusiasts. Its mobility and velocity produce financial movements which dwarf the fiscal resources of states and which constrain two of the three props of postwar state fiscal policy – interest rates and currency valuation (taxation being less affected). Yet it is difficult to assess the overall significance of this, for two reasons. First, the numbers do not offer real precision about power relations. Since currencies, shares, futures, etc. can be traded many times over in a single day, the paper value of "financial flows" vastly exceeds that of world trade, and continues to grow. But power cannot be simply read off such sums. What are being traded are property rights to raw materials, manufactured goods, and (increasingly) services, almost all of which have much greater fixity of location and therefore presumably a degree of national identity.

Second, it is not clear how effective macroeconomic planning ever was in the Northwest. It *seemed* effective while massive growth was occurring and governments had access to surpluses. Many were able to be mildly interventionist (though selective incentives were generally more effective than physical controls). But since then we have seen the collapse not only of Keynesian economics but also of economic theory in general. Economists now more-or-less admit they have no explanation for any of the great booms or slumps of the twentieth century (or at least none that does not depend on singular events like great world wars). Macroeconomic planning was a general ideology surrounding some highly abstract concepts, from which were precariously derived some technical tools (including, most fundamentally, national accounting) and policies (which in fact also depended on contingencies). Macroeconomic planning still contains such a mixture, though its emphasis has changed. The ideological pretensions and the ability to expand spending have certainly declined. Thus we may expect looser and fiscally more cautious national/inter-national (i.e., trilateral) macroeconomic policies; a proliferation of G7 and GATT (WTO) guidelines and piecemeal liberalizing agreements; MITI-style collaboration and incentive programs more than nationalization or direct state investment; central banks more than politicians; less the pretense of controlling markets than of signaling intentions to them; and, above all, no increases in taxation masquerading as grandiose economic theory.

Nor are the reasons for these less-than-dramatic power reductions easy to interpret. As the economy has internationalized, real living standards have stagnated and inequalities widened (except in East Asia). If national governments are increasingly constrained in their economic planning and welfarist pretensions, this might be due to either transnational tendencies or recession – transformations such as "restructuring" may be a response to both. For example, Latin American "import substitution" policies throve on the regional economic expansion made possible by World War II; it collapsed under the mountain of indebtedness accumulated by easy credit during the 1970s followed by the stagnation and inflation of the 1980s. "Restructuring" is now extreme across much of the region, virtually eliminating national macroeconomic planning and trimming welfare states. But this may result less from transnationalism than from the power conferred on finance capital and its major institutions by the burden of debt: the creditors can enforce repayment terms. The creditors comprise the usual mixed bag: banks with national identities but transnational activities, inter-national and predominantly Northern agencies like the World Bank and the IMF, and the US government with the dual motive of protecting American investors and making the region more geopolitically and geo-economically friendly/subordinate to itself.

Similarly, the fiscal crisis afflicting most states of the North and South alike may be more the product of recession than of transnational capitalism. My previous works (Mann 1986, 1993) give me the confidence to say that, at least since the thirteenth century, citizens have only consistently agreed to pay a higher proportion of their incomes in taxes during wartime. Their reluctance to stump up during the peaceful 1970s and later, in a period of recession (when their real incomes were stagnant or falling), is hardly surprising. It is the historical norm, not the unique product of "postmodernity" or "globalism." Political movements resting traditionally on the nation-state, like Social Democracy, Christian Democracy, and the US Democratic Party, have indeed entered something of a crisis. They have stalled and entered modest decline (more in terms of their ability to devise radical policies than to attract votes). Again, it is not entirely clear why. Did it result from the new powers of transnational capital (plus perhaps Euro-institutions in Europe) or from citizens refusing to support "tax and spend" policies amid stagnant or declining real incomes? Probably both, but I have not yet seen the research which could clearly differentiate these rival hypotheses. Of course, if growth does not resume, or if its unevenness continues to widen inequality and deepen unemployment, some of its political effects in weakening the center-left might be similar to those identified by the enthusiasts. Social citizenship seems to have peaked in the North and it may now be in moderate secular decline. Yet this could be reversed by a variety of future trends: economic recovery, changing demographics (i.e., an aging or a better-educated population should reduce unemployment and so inequality), or political backlashes.

Yet national economies also vary considerably – in their prosperity, their cohesion, and their power. Consider first the three main regions of the North. North America is dominated by its superpower, the US. This has an unusual state, dominated by its unique war-machine and (a rather meager) social security system. Most other governmental activities, which in most other Northern countries are mainly the province of the central state (criminal justice, education, and most welfare programs), are the concern of fifty separate "states" or local governments in the US. Three major industries are closely entwined with the Federal government – agriculture, the military-industrial complex, and health care – and may be said to be somewhat (if particularistically) planned. They are likely to remain so – though the military is being downsized by just under a quarter over two decades. Many other industries have closer relations with "state" and local governments, for example property development and construction. Federal legislation has been traditionally tight in the area of labor relations and monopolies – especially restraining the growth of US unions and banks. But there has been little macroeconomic planning by any level of government. The principal "planning" agency (over interest rates) is the Federal Reserve Bank, which is largely autonomous of government. There is no serious American industrial policy, which is left to the postwar powerhouses of the US economy, the large corporations. Much of this is due to the radical separation of powers enshrined by the US Constitution. A coordinated political economy cannot easily be run by a President and his Cabinet, two Houses of Congress, a Supreme Court, and fifty "states" (which are also fragmented by the same separation of powers) – especially when they belong to different political parties. Thus it is difficult to see much of a weakening of US government powers, since these were never exercised very actively. Of course, recession lessened the spending capacity of the state, while recent budget surpluses have increased it slightly. On the other hand, in certain other respects, it might be said that the American nation-state is actually tightening. Organizations as diverse as banks, TV stations, and newspapers are becoming more nationally integrated, and the recent absorption of staggering numbers of immigrants (immigration is back to the pre-1914 level) by the school system and the labor market indicates formidable national solidarity.

Of course, the US has been influenced by capitalist transformations. Competitive pressures from the two other Northern geo-economies have been most visible in the creation of NAFTA, a free trade area embracing the US, Canada, and Mexico, with some prospects for its eventual extension to other stable economies in Central and South America. Though the Canadian and US economies were similarly advanced and already partially integrated, the combination of "southern" Mexico and the "northern" US has led some to view NAFTA as a microcosm of the new global economy. Yet Mexico exemplifies those "principles of orderly extension" I noted earlier. It is a neighbor, a friend, and a very stable state: ruled for seventy years by a single party, mildly coercive but so far capable of responding institutionally to pressure. It provides quite good infrastructures and a fairly literate and healthy labor force, and is a nation beset by no general civil conflict.[3]

US hegemony in the continent also makes NAFTA unique – and very different to the European Union. Canada is an advanced but small client economy with a weak state – perhaps shortly to disintegrate. Mexico is much poorer, and has recently become more debt-ridden and a little less politically stable. But the US is itself wavering, beset by doubts about free trade and Latino immigration, and its political fragmentation makes coordinated decision-making difficult. Thus NAFTA embodies three distinct power processes: it *is* a kind of "mini global economy"; yet it is also geopolitically dominated by one nation-state; and this nation-state has a peculiarly fragmented polity and political economy. The combination of the three is unique in the world, but – as we are seeing – the entwining of transnational capitalist transformation with political and geopolitical institutions is quite normal.

East Asia is at present also dominated by a single nation-state, though Japan is not a military superpower. Japanese political economy differs from both North American and European, with far more coordination between the state and capitalist corporations (and, in a more dependent role, the labor unions) – "governing the market." Wade (1990) calls it "governed interdependence." Such national coordination has been adapted in varying forms across the smaller economies of East Asia. These include active industrial policies centering on selective tax rates or conditional subsidies for key or export sectors, public absorbing of risk for innovation, and government coordination of inter-firm collaboration for technology-upgrading (Weiss 1995). These countries also have political stability and an advanced civil, i.e., "national," society which is stable, literate, and broadly honest. They have also experienced phenomenal growth at least up until the mid-1990s.

These East Asian governments have had until very recently the growth to support debt and their countries were attractive to foreign investors. They can maintain most of their levels of welfare and they can bargain with foreign business. They have fairly equal income distribution and they provide extensive public services like education and housing. They protect their domestic industries, if in different ways. Korea and Malaysia have their own automobile industries behind protectionist markets. Thailand takes a different East Asian tack. Japanese automobile plants are already there; the American majors are now negotiating to move in plants. The Thai government offers no tax breaks and requires substantial local component ratios. The Philippines offers a much bigger domestic market, big tax concessions, and no strings. Yet the auto manufacturers prefer Thailand. Why? They say it is because the Thai government is both more honest and more stable. American and Japanese accountants can calculate future profit and loss much more precisely there (*USA Today*, March 5, 1996). Thai society probably also embodies more literacy, more discipline, more honesty. But these are *all* characteristics of a national network of interaction, of the nation-state. East Asia offers different combinations of capitalist transformation and nation-states.

Europe is the only one of the three regions to have experienced significant political transformation.[4] This has reduced what we might call the "particularistic" autonomy of its member states. They can no longer do their own peculiar things across many policy areas – from the labels on products to the torturing of suspected terrorists. In the long run this may impact on major constitutional variations. The increasing lobbying pres-sure on both Euro- and national government (which must now represent more interests more effectively than it did in the past), combined with the EU's regional policy (offering many financial resources), seems likely to produce more uniform distribution of power between central and local government. Constitutional rights of citizens and minorities are also converging. The states are both converging and losing powers to Brussels.

The original impetus for all this was mainly geopolitical and military: to prevent a third devastating war in the continent, more specifically to bind Germany into a peaceful concert of nation-states. The United States had its own, primarily geopolitical, reasons for encouraging it. Thus the "Six" and the "Nine" were being bound together before much of the capitalist transformation had occurred. But since the chosen mechanisms of binding were primarily economic, they were then intensified by this transformation. The economy of Europe has thus been substantially transnationalized.

Yet the European Union also remains an association between nation-states, an inter-national network of interaction. Specific geopolitical agreements between Germany and France, with the support of their client Benelux states, have always been its motor of growth. Germany and France, like the other states, have lost many particularistic autonomies. But, when allied, they remain the masters on most big issues. Ask Germans what economic sovereignty, ask the French what political sovereignty they have lost, and they are hard pressed to answer. The minor and economically weaker states may seem to have lost more, but their sovereignty on the big issues was more limited in the past. Britain has stood to lose most, because of its historic geopolitical independence of the rest of Europe. And they vote and acquire ministries based on a combination of their population size and economic muscle. "They" are states and national economies, represented by statesmen (and women) and national technocrats and business leaders. This is not traditional "hard" geopolitics, since the agenda is primarily economic and the participants believe war between them is unthinkable. It is "soft" geopolitics structured by much denser inter-national (plus the remaining national) networks of interaction.

Thus Europe has been politically and economically transformed, with a substantial decline in the particularistic autonomy and sovereignty of its nation-states. Though the mechanisms for negotiating these transfers of powers have been largely geopolitical (supplemented by the enthusiasm of Euro-wide federalists), they are institutionalized through rules, institutions, and practices that become fairly transnational, transforming social expectations right across Europe. Yet all this coexists with a far denser, if "softer," set of inter-national networks. Since the density of both is historically unprecedented – no Delian or Hanseatic League or Confederacy ever penetrated so transnationally or inter-nationally into social life – we have no political term to describe it. The political legacy of the Greek language is finally superseded! Maybe the best term is just "Europe." If so, it may not be the future of the world.

It would be unwise to generalize about "the South," given its variety. Some of it may well follow East Asia into the North. A genuine transnational penetration would integrate bits of territory here, there, and everywhere, by "random walk," almost regardless of state boundaries. But this seems rather unlikely, since stable government, social order, and education and health systems still seem the minimum of what substantial foreign investment and economic development require, and geopolitical alliances retain some, though lesser relevance (unless some new world tension replaces the old Cold War). These all require social organization coordinated at the national or state level – what other agency can provide them? If Chile is making it into the North, then it will be because its already fairly stable state and civil society was reinforced by a firm anti-leftism, a state-imposed order, and a state-imposed economic neoliberalism which were attractive to foreign investors, especially to the US. If the richer Arab countries make it, it will be because of their oil – but this has also been accompanied by formidable states. China and India – one-third of the world's population – offer different combinations of massive economic resources, strong civil (i.e., "national") societies, and ambitious state regulation. Will the sense of national citizenship in such countries be diminished or strengthened by economic success? Surely it will be strengthened.

At the other extreme, deeply troubled states in Africa seem to be fragmenting for pre-modern rather than post-modern reasons. Their claim to modernity, including the constitution of a nation-state, proved paper-thin. International capitalism would like to prop them up, not to fragment them. But it has insufficient local power or attention span to do so. There are more attractive areas, with stronger states and civil societies.

Thus the vital issue for the nation-state across most of the world is the level of development – of the economy narrowly considered, but also of two of the preconditions of this: the "civility" of the country and the infrastructural capacity of the state. The entwined expansion of all three produced the nation-state in the Northwest and its extension to a broader North. If world development stalls then so will the extension of the nation-state – indeed, some "paper" nation-states may collapse. But if development is possible, it will occur in those countries which most resemble nation-states and it will in turn enhance them.

But supposing the drift of the economy is towards more and more transnational globalism, that free trade is largely achieved as the EU, NAFTA, the Asian and Pacific Conference countries, and other trade groups merge under the loose umbrella of GATT, that multi-nationals become more cosmopolitan, that development of the South becomes more diffuse, less nation-state-centric. Would this amount to a single transnational/global economy in which the commodity and the single market ruled universally? The answer is both yes and no. All goods and services would then have a price on a single market, and capitalist enterprises would organize their financing, production, and exchange. "Consumerism" already dominates, some of the enthusiasts say; business accountancy practices spread through previously insulated institutions like civil services or universities; and athletes sell their skills to the highest bidder on free and relatively new markets. Such commodity penetration would broaden.

But even so, the rules of those markets might still have their particularities, some being the effects of national and international networks of interaction. Though a far broader range of goods is now bought and sold, many of the most important ones are not actually sold as commodities on free markets. None of the three biggest industries in the US economy, defense, health care, and (probably) illicit drugs, are simply dominated by commodity production, though all involve considerable transnational networks. In defense the government is a monopolistic customer for hi-tech weapons systems and it decides what other states (friendly ones) will be allowed as customers; supply is not very competitive (sometimes only one manufacturer will "tender" and sometimes profit is calculated on a cost-plus basis). The weapons embody more "use" than "exchange" value – the US *must* have them, almost regardless of cost, and the corporation can produce them without much thought of market risk. The health care industry offers its wares more competitively, though the industry has a peculiar multi-tiered structure, involving considerable bureaucracies (of insurance companies, HMOs, etc.), organizationally differentiated according to the customer's ability to pay. And again, for customers who can afford to pay, the product is more of a use than an exchange value. Health preservation (defined by current medical practices and power) is desired almost at any price. Of course, both these industries involve massive multi-national corporations and the global finance networks involved in their investment. But these are funneled into organizations with distinctive national and (in the case of defense) international organization. In the third industry, illicit drugs, the delivery to the consumer seems largely commodity exchange. But the industry is also structured by the intersection of law and state policing of its boundaries with distinctively criminal organization of secrecy and violence. Addiction also produces consumers for whom the product is a use value, to be obtained at almost any price (including crime). Thus the commodity need not rule, even through an eminently capitalist-seeming economy. The economy involves diverse social practices and values, which provide their own "blockages" to the rule of commodity exchange. Though the capitalist economy is now significantly global, its globalism is "impure," a combination of the transnational and the international. The potential universalism of the former is undercut by the particularisms of nation-states – and indeed also by the particularisms of human social practices at large.

Environmental danger, new social movements, and a new transnational civil society

Through population growth, soil and plant erosion, water shortages, atmospheric pollution, and climate change, we encounter a second form of globalism – reinforced by the dangers of biological, chemical, and nuclear warfare alluded to later. We are indeed living in Beck's "Risk Society" (though this is not the only society we are living in) and have only done so in the second half of the twentieth century. On some of these issues the traditional "solution" of letting the South or the poor starve can endure. But on other issues, humanity together faces severe risks. These are not identical to the risks of capitalism, though the two are deeply entwined (since capitalism is now the dominant form of economic production). The "mastery" and "exploitation" of nature, and the enormous increase in human potentiality to do so throughout the globe are also attributable to industrialism and to the other modes of production developed in the modern period. State socialism (and fascism too) was even more destructive of the environment, while the petty commodity production of small peasants has also been forced into many destructive practices. Nation-states, scientific establishments, and (until the last few years) virtually all modern institutions contributed their piece of destruction. And rampant population growth also has sources other than capitalism – for example military, religious, and patriarchal practices. To deal with these risks, responses must go beyond the nation-state and capitalism alike.

Present responses on environmental issues seem mainly two-fold. First, organizations are already in action embodying variant forms of the famous environmental maxim "Think globally, act locally." These are mainly mixed local-transnational pressure groups and NGOs, some of them formal pressure groups (like Greenpeace), others carried by professional and scientific networks (of soil scientists, ornithologists, demographers, etc.). They are more "modern" than "postmodern," since they reject scientific-material exploitation of nature on primarily scientific and social scientific grounds. Though their elites originated in the North, they have increasingly spread globally, among both highly educated Southern elites and among diverse, and rather particular, groups threatened by real material problems. Such networks use the most modern and global means of communication. In exploiting these, they sometimes outflank national government and international capital alike – as when consumers mobilized through Western Europe to boycott Shell, humiliate the British government, and force the towing back of the Brent Spar oil platform in 1995. We may expect more of this.

Is this a "global civil society"? Its structure is not entirely new: in the early century socialists (and, to a lesser extent, anarchists, pacifists, and fascists) also generated extensive transnational networks covering much of the globe, using similarly advanced technology (printing presses, immediate translation, dictaphones, etc. – see Trotsky's remarkable study in Mexico City). The socialists launched a wave of revolutions, some successful, most unsuccessful. Many of the more idealistic proponents of the notion of a new civil society expect its scale to eventually dwarf such historical analogies.

Second, however, there is also increasing deployment of inter-governmental agencies: macro-regional and continental agencies, UN conferences etc. Their key participants, those who could implement coordinated policy decisions, are representatives of nation-states. "Soft geopolitics" is becoming denser in this arena too. The other main delegates are the "experts" mentioned above, who lead a double life. Though nurtured in transnational professional associations, they must adopt the perspective of the nation-state, persuading governments that global concerns are actually in the national interest. Some hit on excellent wheezes. Some American ornithologist managed to persuade the State Department to insert into its aid program to Belize a requirement to protect a rare bird of which the Belize planners had not previously heard. More significantly, feminists involved in development agencies are pressuring reactionary dictators in the South to put more resources into the education of women since this will reduce the birthrate (one of the primary goals of almost all Southern governments).

Thus environmental issues mainly encourage dual networks of interaction, one a potentially local/transnational civil society, the other international, in the form of "soft" geopolitics. The former may transcend the nation-state, the latter co-ordinate states more tightly together, though perhaps in partly consensual terms which are not incompatible with a gradual spread of a civil society. Again it is a mixed story. And this is also the case with others among the "new social movements." It is usually argued that those concerned with the "new politics" of identity – of gender, sexuality, lifestyle, age-cohort, religion, and ethnicity – weaken national (and nationally regulated class) identities, replacing or supplementing them with local-cum-transnational sources of identity. Ethnic politics are too variable to be dealt with in a few paragraphs; one sentence will do here. Ethnic politics may fragment existing states, but – given the defeat of alternative multi-national and socialist states – they fragment them into more, supposedly more authentic, nation-states. But for other social movements based on identity politics, I wish to argue that on balance they strengthen existing nation-states.

I argued earlier that the "moderate nation-state" began by staying out of areas of social life considered "private." The household was especially sacred, and states stayed outside the family life of all but the very poor. Secular states generally lacked their own moral concerns, taking over moral conceptions from religion. Their legislation might firmly prohibit forms of personal behavior, yet government relied more on citizens' internalizing morality than on enforcement. Where citizens did not wish to comply, they privately evaded – and states usually lacked effective infrastructures of enforcement. Apparent exceptions – child and female labor prohibitions were the main nineteenth-century instance of new legislation being enforced – resulted because they were believed to violate the patriarchal household and Christian sexual conduct.

The twentieth century changed this, through new political movements and the penetration of the welfare state into the private realm. States are now asked to legislate and enforce moral conduct in what had been hitherto private arenas. I can no longer pollute the public environment by smoking; my dog's defecations are also more restricted. I can no longer beat my wife or children. If I leave them, I must make due provision for their well-being. Much of the new legislation is paradoxically framed not in the spirit of restrictiveness, but of extending personal freedoms. Gays may practice their lifestyle openly; women may abort unwanted fetuses. But this results not in a neo-liberal absence of state regulation – it would only if there could be some consensual final resting-post for definitions of what is public and what is private. Instead it produces a continuous, highly contentious political debate and legislative stream. May gays get married, rear children, join the military, run Scout Troops? For how long, for what reasons, in what ways, and in what type of clinic can women abort fetuses? Does the presumptive father have any say? We need laws on all these issues and for the complicated welfare entitlements they imply. Thus passionate pressure groups organize and "culture wars" appear. The US is extreme – both its main political parties partially hijacked by these "new social movements." But most countries across the world are now politicized by such moral issues.

These culture wars do involve some transnational and some global interaction networks. Feminists, gays, religious fundamentalists, etc. use emerging global networks of communication and NGOs and they focus energies on the UN as well as their own state. However, most contending actors demand *more* regulation by their own nation-state through its legal or welfare agencies: to restrict or liberalize abortion, pre-marital conception and single parenting; to clarify harassment, child abuse and rape and the evidence needed to prosecute them; to guarantee or restrict the rights of those with unorthodox sexual preferences or lifestyles. Since authoritative social regulation remains overwhelmingly the province of the nation-state, the emergence of new identities may ultimately reinvigorate its politics and broaden its scope. New social movements claim to be turned off by class politics. Perhaps class politics will decline – but not national politics in general.

Post-militarism and a new world order

As Martin Shaw argues, it is in the realm of hard geopolitics that the Northern nation-states have experienced the most radical transformation – because this is where they learned the bitterest lessons. In the two Great Northern Wars (more commonly called the World Wars) they suffered perhaps seventy to eighty million dead – as a direct consequence of the nation-state system.[5] Through those wars they also pioneered weapons so devastating that they could no longer be actually used for any rational "hard geopolitical" purpose. Northern states are now less willing to engage themselves in wholesale war than almost any states in history. The original backbone of the nation-state is turning to jelly.

But again our three regions vary. None are more reluctant militarists than the Europeans, the guilty perpetrators of both wars, reliant for their defense for the last fifty years on the US and presently faced by no serious threat to their security. Though the EU contains two nuclear powers, its Franco-German brigade and its curious Western European [Defense] Union, all this is less significant than the unprecedented virtual absence of serious "hard geopolitics" within Europe. Germans remain the most constrained of all by anti-militarism. The determination to break with the terrible character of European history is probably the most causally determining modern transformation of all, and the one which is most encroaching upon traditional national sovereignties.

But to make European history the general pattern of the world would be ethnocentric in the extreme. And if it were, then the analogy would require more than just a restructuring of capitalism reinforced by a "cultural turn." The analogy would require future wars killing many millions of people in other regions of the world, before they too cried "enough." Yet most Japanese may also have cried "enough." They are at present reluctant militarists. Some Japanese politicians are bolder than their German counterparts in expressing nationalism, but they still get slapped down. Yet East Asia is potentially an insecure region. The United States differs again. It suffered little during the two Great Northern Wars – indeed its economy greatly benefited. It is a military superpower, still projects a standing armed force of 1,200,000 into the next century, and still modernizes its hardware. It remains the global policeman, a role which European and Japanese governments are keen to see continue and may even help finance. But even in the US, defense cuts have been sizeable and it is doubtful the American electorate has the stomach for warfare in which many American lives would be lost. In any case these Northern regions dominate the world without war.

The world nonetheless remains conflict-ridden, with a substantial place for "hard" geo-politics. Consider this list: rising ethnic separatism; conflict between new nuclear states like India and Pakistan or the two Chinas; China's geopolitical role incommensurate with its real strength; the instability of Russia and some smaller well-armed powers; the prevalence of military regimes in the world; the likely proliferation of nuclear weapons; and the largely uncontrolled current spread of chemical and biological weapons through the world. Who knows what eco-tensions, resulting from water shortages, foreign-dominated exploitation of a country's habitat, etc. might lurk around the corner? It is unlikely militarism or war will just go away. All these threats constitute serious obstacles to the diffusion of transnational and universal global networks.

The threats could conceivably be contained by a global geopolitical order, though this would be partially segmented. It must center for the foreseeable future on the US, flanked perhaps by greater coordination with the bigger Northern states and with the United Nations. Shaw sees their combination as providing an emerging global order, though acknowledging that it is not a true "state" and that it remains dual, torn between what he calls its "Western" and "World" components. Actually, it seems a triad, since its core is not Western but American – adding a further level of unreliability. The American electorate may not wish to provide the "mercenaries" to police the world. It may agree to police its neighbors, a few strategic places and vital resources like oil, but not most of the world – or the more powerful rivals. It seems a long way to either a transnational or a geo-political order for the world as a whole.

And even the more warlike scenarios mentioned above would not actually be on a par with the nation-state's horrendous past. "Hard" geopolitics – that is, terrible wars – caused its initial growth and remained one-half of it until recently. Hard geopolitics are now in relative decline in the North, though not everywhere. Though the dangers presented by weapons of war have increased, these actually reduce the mobilizing power of states. If states have lost some of their traditional core, are they therefore in general decline? The argument seems most plausible in Europe, least across large swathes of the South. Moreover, we have seen that "soft" geopolitics may be rising to complement the hard variety, buttressed by the new national mobilizations described above.

Conclusion

This chapter has analyzed four supposed "threats" to contemporary nation-states: capitalist transformation, environmental danger, identity politics, and post-militarism. We must beware the more enthusiastic of the globalists and transnationalists. With little sense of history, they exaggerate the former strength of nation-states; with little sense of global variety, they exaggerate their current decline; with little sense of their plurality, they downplay inter-national relations. In all four spheres of "threat" we must distinguish (a) differential impacts on different types of state in different regions; (b) trends weakening *and* some trends strengthening nation-states; (c) trends displacing national regulation to inter-national as well as to transnational networks; (d) trends simultaneously strengthening nation-states *and* transnationalism.

I have hazarded some generalizations. Capitalist transformation seems to be somewhat weakening the most advanced nation-states of the North, yet successful economic development would strengthen nation-states elsewhere. The decline of militarism and "hard geopolitics" in the North weakens its traditional nation-state core there. Yet the first three supposed "threats" should actually intensify and make more dense the international networks of "soft geopolitics." And identity politics may (contrary to most views) actually strengthen nation-states. These patterns are too varied and contradictory, and the future too murky, to permit us to argue simply *either* that the nation-state and the nation-state system are strengthening or weakening. It seems rather that (despite some postmodernists), as the world becomes more integrated, it is *local* interaction networks that continue to decline – though the fragmentation of some presently existing states into smaller ethnically defined states would be something of a countertrend, i.e., the reduction of the nation-state to a more local level.

Global interaction networks are indeed strengthening. But they entwine three main elements. First, part of their force derives from the more global scale of transnational relations originating principally from the technology and social relations of capitalism. But these do not have the power to impose a singular universalism on global networks. Second, global networks are also modestly segmented by the particularities of nation-states, especially the more powerful ones of the North. Third, that segmentation is mediated by international relations. These include some "hard" politics, and if these turned again to major wars or international tensions, then segmentation would actually increase. Yet at present the expansion of "soft" geopolitics is more striking, and this is rather more congenial to transnationalism. Is this a single "global society"? Not in the strongest sense often implied by the more enthusiastic theorists. These global networks contain no singular, relatively systemic principle of interaction or integration. My own view of "society" is less demanding, since I conceive of human societies as always formed of multiple, overlapping, and intersecting networks of interaction. Globalism is unlikely to change this. Human interaction networks are now penetrating the globe, but in multiple, variable, and uneven fashion.

NOTES

1 Reprinted with permission from *Review of International Political Economy*, May 1997.
2 Clearly, stateless societies existed (indeed they dominated much of human existence on earth) and they still exist in the world today. But states seem necessary to advanced social life – though anarchists disagree.
3 Chiapas is the only province where ethnic conflict can plausibly arise, since *mestizos* dominate everywhere else. This is because Chiapas was acquired from Guatemala in the 1920s.
4 I have discussed this in more detail, and with some comparisons with other regions, in an earlier article (Mann 1993b). As this chapter indicates, however, my views have since modified in certain respects.
5 Obviously, these wars had complex causes. However, as I have tried to show in the case of the First War (see Mann 1993a: ch. 21), they center on the institutions of the nation-state more than they do on any other power organization (such as capitalism).

REFERENCES

Carnoy, Martin 1993, "Whither the Nation-State?" in *The New Global Economy in the Information Age*, Carnoy (ed.), College Park, PA: Pennsylvania State University Press, pp. 44–96.

Castells, Manuel 1993, "The Informational Economy and the New International Division of Labor," in *The New Global Economy in the Information Age*, Martin Carnoy (ed.), College Park, PA: Pennsylvania State University Press, pp. 15–43.

Featherstone, M. 1990, "Global Culture: An Introduction," *Theory, Culture and Society* 7: 1–14.

Giddens, Anthony 1990, *The Consequences of Modernity*, Cambridge: Polity.

Harvey, David 1989, *The Condition of Postmodernity*, Oxford: Blackwell.

Lash, Scott and Urry, John 1994, *Economies of Signs and Space*, London: Sage.

Mann, Michael 1986 and 1993a, *The Sources of Social Power, Vol. I: A History of Power from the Beginning to 1760 AD, Vol. II: The Rise of Classes and Nation States, 1760–1914*, Cambridge: Cambridge University Press.

　1993b, "Nation-States in Europe and Other Continents: Diversifying, Developing, Not Dying," *Daedalus* 122: 115–40.

Shaw, Martin 1996, "The Global State: Perspectives on the Globalization and Fragmentation of State Power," paper presented to the "Directions of Contemporary Capitalism" Conference, University of Sussex, April 26–8.

Taylor, Peter J. 1996, "Embedded Statism and the Social Sciences: Opening Up To New Spaces," *Environment and Planning A* 28: 1917–28.

Wade, Robert 1990, *Governing the Market: Economic Theory and the Rise of the Market in East Asian Industrialization*, Princeton: Princeton University Press.

　1996, "Globalization and Its Limits: Reports on the Death of the National Economy Are Greatly Exaggerated," in *National Diversity and Global Capitalism*, Suzanne Berger and Ronald Dores (eds.), Ithaca: Cornell University Press, pp. 60–88.

Weiss, L. 1995, "Governed Interdependence: Rethinking the Government-Business Relationship in East Asia," *The Pacific Review* 8: 589–616.

"The World Economy: Who's in the Driving Seat?" 1995, *The Economist*, October 7.

13 Stateless nations and the emerging international order[1]

Hudson Meadwell

Introduction

This chapter examines the relationship between nationalism and international order. It is in particular concerned with stateless nations in international society. Stateless nations are of particular consequence whenever they actively seek statehood. When they do seek statehood, they challenge the prevailing order while reproducing its central feature. Stateless nations that seek statehood are structure-preserving at the same time as they challenge the identities of some of the central political units of international society. They confirm the importance of states to international order but stateless nations can change existing territorial boundaries.

The issue of nationalism is not simply related to its sway as an ideology or cultural system. The future of nationalism, and of stateless nations, is tied closely to the future of the state as a principle of political organization. Non-statist solutions to problems of order and regulation, which would operate by breaking down the distinction between domestic hierarchy and interstate anarchy, would dramatically alter the context of nationalism. Making the political and the national congruent – the goal of political nationalists – might not require statehood, or at least statehood would not be as salient and conspicuous a solution to the problem of non-congruence. Nationalism, however, continues to be about territory, and territorial politics presupposes states in the modern era. The importance of statehood to so many political nationalists in so many places is evidence for the continuing relevance of states as political organizations. As long as politics is organized on a territorial basis, states will likely dominate politics, and substate nationalists will prefer territorial states of their own.

There is still an important ambiguity in this argument. It is silent about the number of nation-states that might be expected to make up international society in the future. We should expect more rather than fewer. State-making via unification is unlikely to be as important as it has been in the past. In general, despite important regional variations, the security and economic arguments for unification in the past are not as pressing today. The two dominant exceptions are the Koreas and the continuing push for a larger Serbian nation-state in the Balkans. The occasion for the former will be regime change in the North, but unification may still be contingent on the agreement of China. The Balkans are still a long way from settling out and change to existing territorial boundaries is possible. There is no effective regional balance of power, no outside international organization has the will to enforce a territorial settlement, and there is no regional hegemon.

Imperial collapse will not be a cause of new state-formation. The waves of state-formation associated with imperial decline are over. The exception is multi-ethnic China. It will likely break up into smaller units if regime change occurs. Most new state-formation will arise not out of empires, however, but within states that are not nation-states.

For the structure and identity of international society to remain static – that is, for the number and identity of states to remain unchanged – its constituent states must be strong. I will define a strong state behaviorally: The boundaries of a strong state remain intact during and after a period of regime change. This statement is, by design, strictly a tautology. It follows that if the boundaries of a state are reordered independently of regime change, that state is weaker still. To say that there will be more rather than fewer states in the future is to say that there are cases in which processes of regime change will precipitate the formation of new states and not simply the formation of new regimes, and to say that there are states that are vulnerable to breakup independently of regime change.

The chapter proceeds in three parts. I begin with some comments about the political accommodation of stateless nations, linking these comments to a definition of political nationalism. Second, I make some observations about historical cases of secession, on the assumption that lessons can be learned about the future. Third, I assess some of the implications for the future composition of international society.

Political accommodation

States and nations, I will assume, are arranged in three possible ways. A state and a nation are congruent or, if a nation is stateless, that nation is either repressed or accommodated. When members of a nation actively seek their own state, it is by definition the case that repression or accommodation has failed. If a nation is stateless, and repression has failed, only accommodation is left as a mechanism by which to maintain this nation as a stateless nation.

I have two criticisms to make about those arguments that recommend accommodation and that propose that accommodation resolves the political problem of stateless nations. The first criticism is that these arguments actually underestimate the importance of nationalism. It is not necessarily the case that accommodation eliminates nationalism. And as long as the flame of nationalism burns, accommodation may be vulnerable. Second, these arguments underestimate the importance of a very different kind of political actor than a committed nationalist – the political entrepreneur. Arguments about the viability of accommodation rest on rather benign assumptions about the distribution of individual dispositions within a stateless nation.

I will argue that accommodation is particularly vulnerable to conditions exogenous to the terms of the political exchange between groups that underlie intergroup accommodation. More specifically, accommodation is vulnerable to the feasibility of alternative arrangements between states and nations. As the feasibility of new state-formation increases, nationalists are more likely to actively support independence. And as feasibility increases, the incentive structures of political entrepreneurs will be changed and they will see political advantages in threatening independence. As long as there are political profits to be made, someone will rise to the occasion. In short, as long as there are nationalists or entrepreneurs, the stability of accommodation is dependent on feasibility. If there are neither nationalists nor entrepreneurs, then the stability of accommodation is not dependent on feasibility, but we could then wonder why accommodation was deemed politically necessary in the first place. If an increase in feasibility does not have this effect, it is not because accommodation is stable and insensitive to changes in feasibility; rather, it is because accommodation no longer describes intergroup relations. The stateless nation has become integrated.

Others have argued differently. Lijphart (1990) has proposed that the feasibility of separation should have a moderating effect on intergroup bargaining. This means that the leaders of one nation will demand less and the leaders of another nation will concede more than they would otherwise, if separation were not feasible. Others, including Kaufmann (1995: 285, 75) and Herbst (1995: 387–8), agree. As feasibility increases, these authors imply, secession becomes less likely and political accommodation becomes easier to accomplish and/or maintain.

I will emphasize two results, associated with feasibility, that are not compatible with these arguments. First, feasibility should increase sincere support for secession. Why should a substate nationalist who has a real preference (see below) for secession not take advantage of the feasibility of secession and pursue independence? Second, feasibility should also increase insincere support for secession. Why, for example, should political entrepreneurs in one group demand less, when they expect that they can achieve more by threatening to secede? These results are consistent with the proposition that, as feasibility increases, agreements produced through power-sharing are less likely to be self-enforcing.

By nationalism, I mean "the political principle which holds that the political and the national should be congruent" (Gellner 1983: 1). This definition of nationalism is neutral between competing theories of nationalism. Gellner (1983) and Mann (1992), for example, use essentially the same definition, but Mann is critical of Gellner's theory of nationalism. Political nationalism is dependent on nationhood but it is also related to statehood. As long as states are the dominant form of political organization, political nationalists will want one of their own.

Nationalism is not about winning inclusion. Nations are not analogous to classes and, contrary to Hall's argument (1995), nations cannot be included like classes. Substate nationalists do not seek to change the regime, while holding constant the boundaries of the state. The nationalist goal of independence involves the taking of territory. The systematic differences between secession and revolution undermine the analogy between the accommodation of stateless nations and the inclusion of classes. Socialists could and did hold out the hope of a peaceful transition to socialism through access to political institutions and political power in the center, and the transformation of economic relations through the instrument of political power. Substate nationalists do not hold out the hope of a peaceful transition to independence via equivalent participation in political institutions. There is no other way within nationalism to achieve nationalist goals than to preserve differences. The commitments of nationalists are to separateness and autonomy. Political inclusion modeled on class inclusion would not recognize these differences because separateness and autonomy are precisely what communitarian socialists gave up in the process of inclusion (Przeworski 1985). The analogy between the accommodation of stateless nations and class inclusion is mistaken.

Political nationalism causes members of a stateless nation to seek their own state. A nationalist does not prefer accommodation to independent statehood. A political nationalist has a *real* preference unconstrained by external circumstances. It is that the state and nation be congruent. Anything else is second-best, including political accommodation (via consociational or federal arrangements, for example). Nationalists with this preference cannot be integrated into the institutions of another nation. Nationalists *prefer* accommodation as an alternative to fuller integration, and they *accept* accommodation, whenever independence through new state-formation is not feasible. Nationalists agree to accommodation when they fear the costs and risks of going it alone as a member of a small state. A strategic nationalist will work hard to change those parameters (that shape the boundaries of the feasible set of alternatives) that appear manipulable, and will attempt to take advantage of any exogenous changes to the full set of parameters. When the real preference is not satisfied, however, nationalists are neither integrated nor independent. Accommodation is a second-best compromise; there is nothing intrinsically positive about accommodation for political nationalists. Accommodation is a self-enforcing outcome only if independence is not feasible. If and when independence becomes more feasible, accommodation is not self-enforcing. It should follow that, all else being equal, anything that increases feasibility destabilizes the political accommodation of stateless nations.

Those forces gathered together as "globalization" sometimes are argued to be the causes of a forthcoming watershed in world politics. Transnational dynamics, it is proposed, weaken the capacities and competences of states, both from within and from without. When these states contain stateless nations, these forces lower the opportunity costs of new state-formation. There is an important element of truth to these arguments, although I will suggest several qualifications.

First, the forces may be global in some sense, but their more specific effects are at the level of subsystems. Subsystems are bounded networks and, as long as we can talk meaningfully of different subsystems, the effects of globalization are limited. Second, it is not clear that the relevant forces are accurately identified as transnational. I believe that the most important developments that modify the opportunity costs of members of stateless nations are changing economic and military economies of scale. These are parameters that are largely outside the control of members of substate nations. These have changed the feasible size of states. These changes are not only subsystem-specific (we will not find them everywhere), they are also international rather than transnational. Third, the effects of these subsystem-level forces are filtered by structures at the level of state and society. Here I emphasize the institutional capacity of stateless nations, measured relative to the institutional capacities of the states of which they are a part. The relative institutional capacity of stateless nations, unlike economies of scale, is (partially) endogenous to the actions of members of the nation.

My earlier argument takes this third point into account in one other way. Whatever the causes of regime change, democratization – the most widely anticipated form of regime transition in the foreseeable future in international society – should be specified at the level of state and society.

Democratization opens up opportunities for nationalists and entrepreneurs to carve out a new state. A moment's reflection will indicate why these structures must also influence those cases of new state-formation that occur without regime change. Economic interdependence and interstate peace characterize the environment of many states, for example; not all of them are equally likely, at any particular point in time, to break up. Variations in unit-level structures should explain differences in the likelihood of secession, when the environment is roughly the same.

Now suppose an endpoint is consolidated after a democratic transition that resembles the type of regime that makes the democratic peace possible (Russett 1993; Doyle 1983). Is all now stable? Not necessarily. The literature on the domestic politics of the democratic peace says little about how liberalism is secured domestically. There is no consideration of the relationship of a liberal regime to internal sovereignty. It is simply implicitly assumed that internal sovereignty has been achieved and that there are no threats to the territorial integrity of the liberal regime.

Internal sovereignty may have to be established through the use of force. One of the clearest instances was the decision by Lincoln to oppose the secession of the South and to use force to do it, a decision which not only contributed to the consolidation of liberal republicanism, but also changed a union of states into a federal state. A liberal regime must rest on more than simply liberal toleration if it is to maintain its boundaries. This is so because, if the virtuous circle of liberal regimes, economic interdependence, and peace is achieved, the feasible size of states has been modified. There are no security threats and markets are open. These conditions make states vulnerable to new state-formation via secession *without* regime change, unless they have established internal sovereignty and a reputation that deters would-be secessionists in the future. This is what the Civil War accomplished.

If liberalism, or democracy, or some combination of the two, has worked to limit secession in some parts of the world (Dion 1996; Newman 1996; Hall 1995), these effects are dependent on a process of state rationalization. Where this process of rationalization has been incomplete, liberalism or democracy will not have these effects.

The historical record of secession

I want to draw attention, first, to the importance of regional subsystems and, second, to the relationship of secession to security within regional subsystems. Anarchy, strictly defined as the absence of an overarching sovereign in a subsystem, is consistent with zones of war and zones of peace. In zones of war, the failure of a state to supply security can contribute to secession. In zones of peace, the absence of interstate warfare can also contribute to secession. The cases of Bangladesh and Quebec illustrate this argument. The first has been called the only pure case of secession since 1945 (Mayall 1990: 61). The case of Quebec is of interest because of the virtuous circle of peace, interdependence, and liberalism that characterizes North American society.

Bangladesh

The subsystem that produced Bangladesh had several distinctive features. Interstate violence was one of them. Armed separatist movements and ethnic conflict also have been an endemic feature of the subsystem, although only the armed movement for secession in Bangladesh has been successful and only after intervention by India. The Indian subcontinent was a regional subsystem that had not yet settled out before 1971, and it was characterized by high levels of militarized violence. "The crisis of 1971 in South Asia brought to a close the first phase of modern interstate relations in this region of the world" (Sisson and Rose 1990: 280). The causal structure of Bangladesh independence was shaped by features of the regional subsystem, and Sisson and Rose are probably correct to mark off the crisis of 1971 as a watershed in the history of interstate relations in the region. There have been no more Bangladeshes, despite the movements for independence in Kashmir, the Punjab and Assam in India, the movement for an independent Sindhudesh in Pakistan, the insurgency of the Chakma tribes, and the civil war in Sri Lanka. The Indo-Pakistani rivalry continues, but without war

The inability of autocrats to effectively supply security in this subsystem before the watershed of 1971 weakened the rationale for the Pakistani state. Security issues had a substantial impact on patterns of state-formation from partition onwards. West Pakistan and East Bengal (East Pakistan after 1956) had substantially different interests in the rivalry with India. Pakistan and India fought two wars over Kashmir, and East Bengalis had little interest in Kashmir. Moreover, in each war, East Bengal was cut off from West Pakistan. The wars, especially in 1965, demonstrated that West Pakistan could not secure East Pakistan.

Within this subsystem, the peculiar structural position of East Pakistan contributed to the success of the forces supporting independence. East Pakistan was physically isolated, some one thousand miles from West Pakistan. Pakistan, moreover, was divided by hostile territory, and one premise on which Bengali Muslims had joined Muslims from Northwest India had been that, together, they might add to each other's security. Yet during the 1965 war (Paul 1994: 107–25), although not a theatre of war, East Pakistan was cut off from West Pakistan. In the negotiating phase that concluded the conflict, Bhutto, Pakistan Foreign Minister, stated that a third country would have to guarantee East Pakistan's safety. "Mr. Bhutto, Ayub's foreign minister, proudly claimed in the National Assembly that East Pakistan had been protected by China. If that was so, the Bengalis began to argue, why do we not settle our own diplomatic and external relations? Why depend on West Pakistan, which could give no relief to East Pakistan?" (Choudhury 1974: 8).

This turn of events weakened the security rationale of the Pakistani state. "[F]ear of India served to increase the divisiveness rather than to cement the two sections, for it intensified the Bengali sense of insecurity and inaccessibility. After the Indo-Pakistani conflict, separation returned more strongly to East Pakistan than for many years" (Brines 1968: 233). The end of hostilities was followed in early 1966 by Sheikh Mujibur Rahman's (then secretary-general, soon president of the East Pakistan Awami League) six-point "charter of survival" program for East Pakistan, which he linked to the problem of security. "The question of autonomy appears to be more important after the war. Time has come for making East Pakistan self-sufficient in all respects" (quoted in Maniruzzaman 1973: 258).

Quebec

Most comparative analysis of nationalism argues that separation is difficult in the developed West. Quebec, however, has advanced farther toward independence than any other case. Political entrepreneurs and nationalist activists in other regions such as Scotland, Wales, Brittany, Catalonia, Flanders, Wallonia, or northern Italy have not organized movements that match the success of the independence movement in Quebec. Although independence has not been gained even in Quebec, this case threatens to break the historical mould. The Canadian state has been differently designed than other states in the developed West and these differences account for the anomalous status of Quebec.

The fact that Quebec has advanced so far along the path to independence rests on the pattern of state rationalization in Canada which, over time, blurred the hard distinction between domestic hierarchy and interstate anarchy via the institutional arrangements of consociational power-sharing and federation, and which did not settle the issue of statehood through civil war, as in the United States. These features of the institutional design of the Canadian case were related to features of its regional subsystem. State-formation in North America did not occur in the same sort of anarchy as original state-making in Europe. There was some room for variation from the canonical form of state predicted by the literature on state-making. The Canadian path to democratic, advanced capitalism was distinctive, and was shaped by its history as a settler society in this regional subsystem. The dynamics of North American society have not produced the security dilemmas that might have discouraged further decentralization or power-sharing.

The institutional design of the Canadian state has provided the infrastructure to shape the substate identities that contribute to a sense of national difference, and makes it easier also to politicize these differences. This process of identity-formation increases the likelihood that the baseline level of support for nationalism will be higher than in circumstances where this design is not present, or no substitutes exist for it. The same institutional design also provides political entrepreneurs and activists the opportunity to mobilize a greater degree of support for independence for any given level of nationalism than could be mobilized were this design absent.

There is no current equivalent in Europe, despite recent constitutional changes in cases such as Belgium or Spain, or the changes in the United Kingdom. No substate nation in the developed West will precede Quebec in making a transition to independence. Put differently, a substate nation other than Quebec may be the first to make this transition in the West *if* political collapse occurs. Since there is little evidence that domestic regimes in the developed West are unstable, this precondition is unlikely to be present, and therefore no other substate nation will precede Quebec. In Canada, a transition is possible without political collapse or regime change. Other cases in the developed West lag behind Quebec because there is currently no functional equivalent to consociational federalism in Europe. There are no overarching supranational political institutions in North America that might compensate for the centrifugal tendencies of territorially decentralized power-sharing in Canada. The design of the Canadian state encourages secessionist challenges, and is not nested in a larger design that could encourage cohesion. The future of stateless nations in Europe depends very much on the stability of these overarching institutions in the European Union.

Some implications

Too little security or too much security can contribute to secession. Secession can occur in these diametrically opposed conditions. In the first case, however, it was a period of regime change that provided an opportunity for change to the territorial status quo. In the second case, secession is possible, even without changes to political regime. I explore some of the broader implications in this section.

The case of Bangladesh illustrates a more common problem associated with regime transitions. For the system of states to remain stable, changes to domestic political regimes must occur while holding constant the territorial boundaries of states. In the late 1960s, Pakistan had begun a transition to democracy from the military regime established in 1958. The transition was to be managed by Yahya Khan, to whom power had been handed in 1969 by Ayub Khan. This transfer of power followed the formation of the Pakistani Democratic Movement and the Pakistan People's Party in 1967 and demonstrations in urban areas in East and West Pakistan in 1968 and 1969. The combination of the decision by Yahya to institute a primarily majoritarian electoral system for the National Assembly in 1970 and the decision to leave the issue of the autonomy of East Pakistan to be addressed after the election produced incentives for a political entrepreneur to run on an autonomy program in East Pakistan. If the problem of Bengal autonomy had been dealt with in some fashion (not necessarily meeting all of the Six Points), the Awami League would have lost its political platform. If Yahya had been able to leave the electoral system alone, the Awami League would not have been able to control the Assembly, even if it had dominated the election in East Pakistan. In facilitating a campaign by the Awami League on the issue of autonomy in an electoral system that for the first time allowed East Pakistan representation by population, Yahya produced political deadlock during an anticipated transfer of power from an authoritarian regime to a democratically elected assembly. Even if he did not want to force the issue of independence, Mujib was in a position in which his campaign and the commitment to independence of his most radical supporters in the election constrained his choices. In the process of democratization, the territorial boundaries of the state could not be held constant and the interstate system in the region was reordered. Democratization failed and the state broke apart. Of course, the boundaries of Pakistan were already peculiar. Nevertheless, the outcome was essentially a local variant of a larger problem.

The problem does not always appear whenever democratic transitions occur. The territorial boundaries of the states in the other subsystems of the Americas, Latin and Central America, are not threatened by secession. Despite the modern historical cycle of democratic transitions and breakdowns in some of its cases, it has not fragmented into a larger number of smaller states, aside from the very early failure at attempts at political union. And this breakdown did not create new states so much as confirm the original territorial basis of the breakup of the Spanish-American empire.

It is also striking, in the contemporary period, that Sendero Luminoso, despite its regional origins in the southern Andes and its local system of taxation and protection (Zirakzadeh 1997: 167–223), was not a separatist movement. It sought to capture the political center and change the political regime. The rebellion in the Chiapas, while different from Sendero Luminoso, is similar in one way. The goods it demands (e.g., land reform) are not *yet* framed as nationalist demands. In other parts of this subsystem, entrepreneurs do not need to form a new state. The sway of existing states is limited enough to allow them to establish parallel governments and to pursue trade, particularly in drugs, such as in Peru or Colombia. They have no intrinsic interest in secession or regime change, but they can continue to operate even after a change in regime. They are too powerful to be bucked by popular forces at the local level or national level.

This subsystem had a different history of state-formation than North America, although there is one important similarity that makes this subsystem more like North America than the developing world. The republics that were created after independence, north and south, were settler societies. Later waves of decolonization in blue sea empires generally did not produce states that were led by a stratum of settlers after independence. This feature distinguishes Latin American states from states in other subsystems of the developing world. But other differences distinguish the Latin American pattern from the North American pattern.

These *creole* societies were not organized in a larger union. Unlike the Spanish-American colonies, the Thirteen Colonies had signed one Declaration of Independence (Masur 1948: 592). In the south, as Bolívar had pointed out, "Republican governments [the new governments of the independent states] are based on the frontiers of the former vice-royalties, captaincies-general or presidencies" (quoted in Salcedo-Bastardo 1986: 89), and attempts to organize larger political unions or compacts of these governments failed (Gran Colombía [in 1830], United Provinces of Guatemala [in 1840]). These failures, which occurred only a few years after independence, removed the problem of secession of a state from a larger union. This removed from the historical agenda of Latin America the formative moment for the United States – a Civil War that consolidated the territorial foundations of the state. These states have had long and relatively unbroken histories. When secession did occur in the remnants of the Spanish-American empire (the secession of Texas and the Yucatán from Mexico [1836], led, significantly, by Anglo-Americans), it occurred also just after independence, unlike the secession of the American South, one hundred years after the Declaration of Independence (Anderson, 1991: 64).[2] Regime change has been possible, while holding constant the boundaries of states. Latin America is not a liberal subsystem, however, and this suggests that it is not liberalism or liberal political regimes that hold back secession, but characteristics of states.

For a system of states to be stable, preserving not only its structure but also the identity and boundaries of its constituent states, regime transitions must be possible without destabilizing the territorial boundaries of states. States have to have histories independent of the histories of their regimes. Most states in the world have had relatively short histories. Many have never established internal sovereignty. They are, following Jackson and Rosberg (1982; Jackson 1990; Mazuri 1995), juridicial states but not empirical states. This description has been proposed for sub-Saharan Africa. It is more difficult to distinguish regimes and states here, because these states do not have independent histories. It is true that boundaries have been more stable than the level of state rationalization in Africa would suggest. Territorial stability was argued to have been caused by self-enforcing agreements between local strongmen ensconced in public office. It is not clear from these arguments, however, why these agreements were self-enforcing, why, once they were agreed to, conventions about territorial boundaries were maintained. There should be an incentive to be the first to violate such conventions. What may have removed this incentive and produced the appearance of self-enforcement were external sanctions and rewards. Further, there could not truly be a continent-wide or OAU-wide single convention. The convention must be local because it stabilizes relations between states with contiguous borders, and no single state is contiguous to all other states. Thus there must be more than one convention. The caveat that is implied by such cases is not surprising. States without internal sovereignty that are not buttressed by external support are more prone to territorial breakup than states that enjoy some external support.

The larger point is that external support is not a thoroughgoing substitute for internal sovereignty. For example, in contexts where true states have not been established, kinship can continue to be a relevant, even dominant, principle of social and political organization. Where kinship continues to be important, clans and tribes, rather than nations, are the constitutive units of the polity and society. One dimension of clans and tribes is that they are organized forms of self-help where self-help includes physical survival. These segmentary societies are not politically centralized. Tribes and clans, by definition, do not seek a state. While segmented societies may be prone to breakup, this process of fragmentation is not secession.

There are two distinctive and related features of these societies – fission and feuding. Fission is a typical mode of conflict-regulation within stateless societies that are primarily organized by segments. It is as common in segmented societies as secession is rare in the fully developed modern territorial state. "All political systems except true states break up into similar units as part of their normal process of political activity" (Cohen 1978: 4). The feud, moreover, is the primary mechanism of segmentary opposition (Black-Michaud 1975) in these societies. Feuding societies also are characterized by the absence of centralized government (Black-Michaud 1975: 146–7). The feud is an "outward sign of imminent fission" (Peters 1967, quoted in Black-Michaud 1975: 23). And the feud has a further characteristic. It is extended through time much like the gift relationship. "The mnemonics of vengeance may provide a record of individual acts, but are better seen as statements of account, or if it is preferred, of the score at a given stage of the game" (Black-Michaud 1975: 81). The feud instantly recalls the past for kindred.

Much of the conflict in Africa is not ethnic or national; it is, rather, tied to kinship and to the social and political organization of more-or-less militarily self-sufficient clans. Conflict is endemic to lineage systems of the clan and tribe, which is a demonstration of state failure in Africa. At the first opportunity, the corporate organization of the clan dominates the state. One illustration is Somalia, where the clan is the largest body that acts corporately (Black-Michaud 1975: 50). With the collapse of the colonially created state, the "political geography of the Somali hinterland, consequently, resembled that reported by European explorers in the late nineteenth century, with spears replaced by Kalashnikovs and bazookas" (Lewis 1994: 233). The 1990–2 conflict in Mogadishu was not ethnic, nor "recently-manufactured – it is, on the contrary, endemic to the Somali lineage system" (Lewis 1994: 235, n.5).

It is worth recalling that the clan also continued to be important to social and political organization in parts of the Balkans, the Caucasus, and Central Asia during most of the twentieth century, although it did decline through the exercise of central government control. The effects of clan and lineage may be weaker here than in parts of Africa such as Somalia. But governments in the Balkans and Asia did not have the infrastructural capacity of modern states and did not effectively eliminate the corporate organization of clans, nor the relevance of kinship, nor the associated mechanisms of segmental conflict and regulation – fission and feud. I believe there are unmistakable signs of clan-related patterns of conflict in all of these regions during and after the fall of communism, although I do not examine them here.

There was one state that approached a true state in Africa. This was the only positive legacy of Afrikaner rule – the political expression of the *volkstaat* of the Afrikaners. Democratic transition in South Africa was able to occur without territorial fragmentation. This legacy can be measured in the preferences of the political actors in the negotiation of the transition. There was support for majoritarian institutions for the transitional constitution among most of the representatives during CODESA (Sisk 1995). Right-wing actors, on the other hand, supported secession, in some instances unilateral secession, in order to form an exclusively white polity and avoid permanent minority status (Sisk 1995: 173–4). The party that had played the ethnic card to strengthen its position in the runup to and during the negotiations, the Inkatha Freedom Party, supported consociational arrangements and Buthelezi has demanded federalism (Tucker 1996: 78). He has claimed the restoration of the Zulu kingdom as it was in 1834, and threatened secession to bolster his demand (Mare 1996: 36). The ANC rejects federalism. As it stands, the transitional constitution is unitary, and the provincial legislatures enjoy only concurrent competence with the National Assembly (Tucker 1996: 93). To this point, Sisk's (1995: 248ff.) optimism about South Africa may be warranted. As the transition is consolidated, power-sharing may be replaced by "institutions that stress incentives for moderation in place of entrenched minority vetoes" (248). If federalism is introduced down the line, however, it should be embedded in a larger institutional design that ensures internal sovereignty. Consociation joined to federation does not, as a very different case demonstrates.

Quebec is theoretically interesting precisely because it is located in a liberal subsystem. This case recalls the original justification for secession, often forgotten in the contemporary debate about self-determination in international society. A right to secede was claimed in the American South as a state's right. This, Quebec nationalists believe, justifies their demands for independence. Canada is not a state, but a union or compact. This is what Lucien Bouchard, leader of the Parti Québécois and the premier of the province of Quebec, means when he states that there is no such thing as Canada. With the arrangements of consociational federalism, Quebec is already an embryonic state. The breakup of the USSR and Yugoslavia indicates that a much weaker form of nominal federalism (Roeder 1991) and a much more attenuated form of consociational federalism (e.g., Schöpflin 1993) can contribute to secession. However, these effects were contingent on political crises within unstable regimes that had causes independent of nationalist mobilization. Secession in Quebec is not dependent on these prior processes of regime crisis and democratic transition. Liberal democracy has had an uninterrupted history in Canada. This case illustrates that, even where liberal democracy is stably entrenched and economic interdependence is high, a regional subsystem can still be prone to new state-formation. A liberal subsystem in which the internal sovereignty of states is weakly established is still subject to the problems associated with secession.

As the Canadian federal government sought closure on its constitutional relationship with the mother country, in effect seeking to achieve full constitutional independence in 1982, it became clear that the stability of consociational federalism had depended on the maintenance of the last vestiges of the imperial relationship with Britain. Fuller political self-determination appears incompatible with two centers of internal sovereignty lodged in Ottawa and Quebec City respectively. The Canadian dilemma, then, rests on the incompleteness of its transition to independence and the timing of this final phase of constitutional closure in the late twentieth century.

The dynamics of the European subsystem of the developed West are different from the dynamics of North American society. Geopolitical competition was an important determinant of the differences between the political experiences in Europe and North America, even if it does not explain all of the variation in forms of political association in Europe (Spruyt 1994; Ertman 1997). Regimes in Western Europe tended to be associated with Westphalian states. For example, a case like France (admittedly, perhaps a limiting case) could weather several changes in political regime in the nineteenth and twentieth centuries without any real internal threat to its boundaries. Its internal sovereignty was well established.

It remains to be seen whether increasing integration of independent European states within a truly supranational European constitution will produce as deep a form of decentralized power-sharing, or the occasion for substate nationalists and entrepreneurs to destabilize consociational federalism that withdrawal from the imperial constitution provided in Canada. This point summarizes some of the differences in the dynamics of North American and European society. There is no continental equivalent to the European Union in North America. The larger imperial constitution of which Canada was a part was a product of colonialism. I conjecture that a true supranational constitution in Europe would facilitate power-sharing among substate nations within member states such as Belgium or Spain, but that this power-sharing is more likely to be self-enforcing, short of new state-formation. I do not address the likelihood that such a constitution will emerge.[3]

I speculate that a true supranational constitution in Europe will raise the barriers to secession. In practical terms, peaceful secession would not depend merely on the agreement of the "national" state but also on other states in the Union. Further, the political arrangements of the Union introduce advantages in scale in bargaining that shape the incentives of substate nations. Consider the regions and communities in Belgium which, since 1993, exist within a very decentralized federal system. They may be better off working within the Belgian state within the Union. Officials from the regions and communities now can represent Belgium in the Council of Ministers on selected issues related to their competencies as assigned in the Constitution, thus controlling all of the votes that Belgium has on the Council, and they can bind Belgium as a whole to the outputs of the Council (Kerremans and Beyers 1998). They would control fewer votes as a completely independent state. Nor as an independent state could they bind those other parts of Belgium that they now can bind to Union directives.

The observations in this section suggest one final set of comments. There are limits to the kinds of internal differentiation that are consistent with liberalism. Mill, for example, recognized that liberal society depended on a principle of nationality. He argued that, as a necessary condition of free institutions, the boundaries of governments should coincide with those of nationalities. To develop this point about internal differentiation, consider together Gellner's definition of nationalism and Mill's proposition about nationality. *Definition*: nationalism is the principle that the national and political should be congruent. *Proposition*: that the boundaries of governments should coincide with those of nationalities is a necessary condition of free institutions. It should follow, after a simple substitution of the definition into the proposition, that nationalism is a necessary condition of free institutions. Or to put it differently, free institutions depend on congruence between nation and state. Liberalism, Mill argued, is incompatible with multinational society.[4] Not all nationalism is liberal, but liberalism depends on solidarity for the workings of its institutions. And it is splitting semantic hairs, normative theorists of liberal nationalism argue, to deny that this solidarity is nationalism.

This is another way of pointing out the modern power of nationalism. Even a liberal regime in which nation and state are not congruent is vulnerable to breakup. In Mill's argument, free institutions were "next to impossible in a society made up of different nationalities" because "the united public opinion necessary to the working of representative government can not work" (Mill 1991 [1862]: 310). Mill, however, also sanctioned the assimilation of those nations in multinational societies that were backward and inferior to other more civilized nations (for example, the Highland Scots, the Bas-Bretons, the French Basques, the Welsh). In making this distinction between civilized and barbaric nations, Mill implied that civilized nations, if trapped in a multinational society, should have legitimate recourse to independent state-formation. Moreover, the duties which civilized nations owed to the independence and nationality of each other were not owed to barbarous people (Mill 1867 [1859]: 167). Among civilized peoples, foreign intervention was justified when a nationality was revolting against despotic rule, whenever that rule was foreign or maintained by foreign support. The option of revolt, and of countervailing foreign support in the event of an attempt to make congruent nation and government, was not legitimately open to backward nations.

It is not necessary to go as far as Mill and sanction thoroughgoing assimilation. Nor is there any need to denigrate other cultures as barbaric or uncivilized. However, he captured something important about liberalism. Not all kinds of solidarity are conducive to liberalism, but liberalism depends on sufficient solidarity to make its institutions workable. The agreement that is implied by this solidarity is likely to be difficult to reach in a multinational setting. It will be particularly difficult to reach if nations have their own legislatures with non-concurrent competencies and independent fiscal bases. This point is important in the European context, since recent arrangements in Belgium and the United Kingdom, and the constitutional changes of the democratic transition in Spain, have created local legislatures (of varying competencies). If European integration is stalled, therefore, there is no return to the status quo ante. The substate nations of these states are now more institutionally complete.

Consider the status quo in Scotland before the recent referendum. The United Kingdom has been historically a composite, but still a unitary, state. It was internally differentiated but there was one center of political sovereignty – the King-in-Parliament. Scotland retained distinctive institutions in education, law, and religion after the Union of 1707, but gave up its legislature and accepted the Hanoverian succession. Scotland has now been granted a Scottish Parliament. Scotland is more complete institutionally than it has been in the status quo ante. New Labour expected that this version of Home Rule would kill off the nationalist movement and the SNP. It is more likely that the Scottish Parliament will provide an arena of contestation and a locus of power for nationalists, that they will move to enlarge its competences once they control it, and that they will use referenda as a bargaining tool. Indeed, unless Scottish Labour is merely an agent of British Labour, it also will move to enlarge its competences. The addition of a local parliament eventually will raise the issue of multiple sovereignties.

Nationalists with a sufficiently long-term horizon (and there is no reason to believe that nationalists cannot think in the long term) will bargain, first, for a legislature where one is absent, and then use this institution as a locus of political mobilization for a complete state. This strategy also changes the incentives of entrepreneurs, who also may make political claims using the institutions of the nation. Whether or not they have a sincere preference for independence, they will threaten it in order to win concessions, and their threats are more credible, all else being equal, the higher the institutional capacity of the substate nation.

Thus the trajectories of stateless nations within the European Union are not yet clearly defined. In general, accommodation in the form of self-government is likely to encourage rather than restrain or satisfy substate nationalists in an era of peace, interdependence, and liberal regimes. Scotland is one instance, the historic nations of Spain perhaps another, since the choices of substate nationalists, particularly in Catalonia, were time-dependent. They can demand more now than they did during the transition because the liberal democratic transition is well consolidated. As the other regions of Spain also demand more, the historic nations can also bargain for more as well – in order, they will argue, to preserve the principle of asymmetry in territorial politics. It is not clear that the institutions of the Union are, as yet, a sufficient capstone to compensate for the centrifugal tendencies associated with accommodation. It may prove to be the case that accommodation in liberal democratic regimes, rather than lowering the likelihood of new state-formation, increases the likelihood that transitions to new statehood will be relatively peaceful.

Liberal regimes are vulnerable because liberal tolerance can be exploited, but liberalism is less vulnerable if it has secured and enforces agreement about those conditions that make free institutions possible. Multiple sovereignties within a single political community make that agreement difficult to maintain. In these circumstances, there are likely to be several political communities. If the political communities are several, why not conduct inter-community relations as international relations? If the community is so divided that no single citizenship is possible, acts of inclusion and enclosure cannot be stably performed (Walzer 1983: 62). Distributive justice could not govern relations between these divided societies; the only moral principles that would govern relations are those that govern relations within international society – mutual aid and humane treatment, and these are not relations of justice (Walzer 1983: 33–5; 1995: 293). It is not obvious that a liberal regime that is committed to the recognition of differences is sufficient to hold together multinational communities, and the practical difficulties should point to problems in the normative justification of liberal multinationalism, which seeks to reconcile liberty and equality among substate nations without conceding to substate nationalists their own state (Kymlicka, 1995).[5]

Some of the most stable liberal regimes are not multinational or, if they are, have depended on institutional arrangements that have emphatically limited the accommodation of stateless nations. Great Britain may be multinational, but Scotland and Wales were incorporated without retaining independent legislatures. The political accommodation of these nations has been very limited; crucially, they have not controlled independent, elected territorial assemblies. (While Ireland also gave up its legislature in union, it was never as politically integrated as Wales or Scotland because it was governed imperially as a quasi-colony.) The United States is liberal and it is stable. Federalism in this case, however, was not a device to accommodate different nations but was part of a larger political project to reconcile republicanism and modernity, and Americans have not experienced any threat of territorial fragmentation since the Civil War. Australian federalism is also not a consociational device, despite the movement for secession in the 1930s in Western Australia. Switzerland is multilingual, not multinational. In other words, some of the oldest liberal states in the world are among the most stable either because they are not multinational or because they have institutional arrangements that limit the degree of self-government available to stateless nations.

Conclusion

Accommodation is second best for political nationalists and it is sensitive to the feasibility of alternative arrangements. Regime change is an opportunity for nationalists and entrepreneurs, but new state formation is still possible without regime change. Suprisingly, this holds for liberal regimes, which can be vulnerable to secession despite (or perhaps because of) their liberal character. More nation-states are expected, and also enduring regional networks. The effects of globalization will be segmented by regional subsystems. The arguments of the chapter reinforce the importance of institutional design for the trajectories of stateless nations.

NOTES

1 The author acknowledges with thanks the financial support of the Social Sciences and Humanities Research Council.
2 There is as well the formation of Panama from Colombia in 1903–4, an outcome closely tied to American foreign policy. The constitution of 1904 allowed the United States to intervene in domestic politics in order to protect private property and to secure peace.
3 For a detailed analysis of the European Union, see the chapter in this volume.
4 There are other versions of liberalism on offer, including a version consistent with multinational communities, another with multiculturalism and another with universalism. There is a discussion in Kymlicka (1995: 50–69).
5 For Kymlicka's recognition of the difficulties, see 1995: 181–91.

REFERENCES

Anderson, Benedict 1991, *Imagined Communities*, rev. edition, London: Verso.

Black-Michaud, Jacob 1975, *Cohesive Force: Feud in the Mediterranean and the Middle East*, London: Blackwell.

Brines, Russell 1968, *The Indo-Pakistani Conflict*, London: Pall Mall Press.

Choudhury, G. H. 1974, *The Last Days of United Pakistan*, Bloomington: Indiana University Press.

Cohen, Ronald 1978, "Introduction," in *Origins of the State*, Ronald Cohen and Elmer R. Service (eds.), Philadelphia: Institute for the Study of Human Issues, pp. 3–20.

Dion, Stéphane 1996, "Why is Secession Difficult in Well-Established Democracies? Lessons from Quebec," *British Journal of Political Science* 29: 269–83.

Doyle, Michael 1983, "Kant, Liberal Legacies and Foreign Affairs," *Philosophy and Public Affairs* 12: 205–35, 323–53.

Ertman, Thomas 1997, *Birth of the Leviathan*, Cambridge: Cambridge University Press.

Gellner, Ernest 1983, *Nations and Nationalism*, Ithaca: Cornell University Press.

Hall, John A. 1995, "Nationalisms, Classified and Explained," in *New Nationalisms of the Developed West*, Sukumar Periwal (ed.), Budapest: Central European Press, pp. 8–33.

Herbst, Jeffrey 1995, "Responding to State Failure in Africa," in *Nationalism and Ethnic Conflict*, Michael E. Brown, Owen R. Coté, Jr., Sean M. Lynn-Jones and Steven E. Miller (eds.), Cambridge: MIT Press, pp. 374–98.

Jackson, Robert H. 1990, *Quasi-Sovereignty*, Cambridge: Cambridge University Press.

Jackson, Robert H. and Rosberg, Carl G. "Why Africa's Weak States Persist: The Empirical and the Juridicial in Statehood," *World Politics* 35: 1–24.

Kaufmann, Chaim 1995, "Possible and Impossible Solutions to Ethnic Civil Conflict," in *Nationalism and Ethnic Conflict*, Michael E. Brown, Owen R. Coté, Sean M. Lynn-Jones and Steven E. Miller, (eds.) Cambridge: MIT Press, pp. 136–75.

Kerremans, Bart and Beyers, Jan 1998, "Belgium: The Dilemma Between Cohesion and Autonomy," in *Adapting To European Integration*, Kenneth Hanf and Ben Soetendorp (eds.), London: Longmans, pp. 14–35.

Kymlicka, Will 1995, *Multicultural Citizenship*, Oxford: Oxford University Press.

Lewis, Ioan M. 1994, *Blood and Bone: The Call of Kinship in Somali Society*, Lawrenceville, NJ: Red Sea Press.

Lijphart, Arend 1990, "The Power-Sharing Approach," in *Conflict and Peacemaking in Multiethnic Societies*, Joseph V. Montville (ed.), Lexington, MA: Lexington Books, pp. 491–509.

Maniruzzaman, Taldir 1973, "Radical Politics and the Emergence of Bangladesh," in *Radical Politics in South Asia*, Paul R. Brass and Marcus F. Frana (eds.), Cambridge: MIT Press, pp. 223–77.

Mann, Michael 1992, "The Emergence of Modern European Nationalism," in *Transitions to Modernity*, John A. Hall and Ian C. Jarvie (eds.), Cambridge: Cambridge University Press, pp. 137–65.

Mare, Gerhard 1996, "Civil War Regions and Ethnic Mobilization: Inkatha and

Zulu Nationalism in the Transition to South African Democracy," in *Reaction and Renewal in South Africa*, Paul B. Rich (ed.), London: Macmillan, pp. 25–46.

Masur, Gerhard 1948, *Simon Bolivar*, Albuquerque, NM: University of New Mexico Press.

Mayall, James 1990, *Nationalism and International Society*, Cambridge: Cambridge University Press.

Mazuri, Ali 1995, "The African State as a Political Refugee," in *African Conflict Resolution*, David R. Smock and Chester A. Crocker (eds.), Washington, DC: United States Institute of Peace, pp. 9–25.

Mill, John Stuart 1867 [1859], "A Few Words on Non-Intervention," in *Dissertations and Discussions*, Vol. III, London: Longmans, Green and Dyer, pp. 153–78.

  1991 [1862], *Considerations on Representative Government*, Buffalo: Prometheus Books.

Newman, Saul 1996, *Ethnoregional Conflict in Democracies*, Westport, CT: Greenwood Press.

Paul, T. V. 1994, *Asymmetric Conflicts: War Initiation by Weaker Powers*, Cambridge, Cambridge University Press.

Peters, E. 1967, "Some Structural Aspects of the Feud Among the Camel Herding Bedouin of Cyrenaica," *Africa* 37: 261–82.

Roeder, Philip 1991, "Soviet Federalism and Ethnic Mobilization," *World Politics* 43: 196–232.

Russett, Bruce M. 1993, *Grasping the Democratic Peace*, Princeton: Princeton University Press.

Salcedo-Bastardo, J. L. 1986 [1973], *Bolivar: A Continent and Its Destiny*, Atlantic Highlands, NJ: Humanities Press.

Schöpflin, George 1993, "The Rise and Fall of Yugoslavia," in *The Politics of Ethnic Conflict Regulation*, John McGarry and Brendan O'Leary (eds.), London: Routledge, pp. 172–203.

Sisk, Timothy D. 1995, *Democratization in South Africa*, Princeton: Princeton University Press.

Sisson, Richard and Rose, Leo E. 1990, *War and Secession: Pakistan, India and the Creation of Bangladesh*, Berkeley: University of California Press.

Spruyt, Hendrik 1994, *The Sovereign State and Its Competitors*, Princeton: Princeton University Press.

Tucker, David 1996, "Some Reflections on the Interim Constitutional Arrangements," in *Reaction and Renewal in South Africa*, Paul B. Rich (ed.), London: Macmillan, pp. 73–97.

Walzer, Michael 1983, *Spheres of Justice: A Defence of Pluralism and Equality*, Oxford: Blackwell.

  1995, "Response," in *Pluralism, Justice and Equality*, David Miller and Michael Walzer (eds.), Oxford: Oxford University Press, pp. 281–97.

Zirakzadeh, Cyrus Ernesto 1997, *Social Movements: A Comparative Study*, London: Longmans.

14 The coming chaos? Armed conflict in the world's periphery

K. J. Holsti

The title of this essay betrays a certain ethnocentrism that has afflicted many recent analysts of the nature and sources of international order.[1] It suggests a spatial dichotomy between centers and peripheries and a sociological dichotomy between areas of peace and areas of chaos. We should therefore begin this prognosis of armed conflict in the peripheries by acknowledging that virtually all analyses of world order have been written from European or North American perspectives and that those perspectives have traditionally relegated the remaining areas of the world to a special – meaning lower – status. Analysts have usually argued or assumed that the elements of order in the world emanated from European civilization while the rest of the world was exotic and mysterious at best and a zone of cruelty and perpetual chaos at worst. It seldom helps to point out that during the past three hundred years the worst arenas of systematic carnage, whether interstate wars, civil wars, politicides, or genocides, have been predominantly located in the ambit of European civilization and not in the so-called peripheries.

In an analysis of world order, it is important to get things right. And to do this, we must acknowledge historical biases before we examine what some have predicted will be a scenario of the "coming anarchy" or "chaos" in the peripheries. I want to emphasize the historical-perceptual background so that we can better understand the difficulties and dilemmas of the Third World (or South, or peripheries – more on this below) and its role in world order.

Concepts of world order

The concept of world order has as often muddied understanding of international politics as clarified it. The most common usage in diplomatic rhetoric is the idea that typical patterns of power, conflict, domination, and subordination are changing. But since change is a constant of most social contexts, difference is hardly an indicator of a new order. If

283

difference is the only criterion, then we can hardly expect to generate any sort of consensus, for one person's significant change can be someone else's marginal alteration. One sensible way to think of an international order is to identify the foundational principles upon which it rests. This was Hedley Bull's (1977) approach and is as helpful today as it was almost a quarter-century ago when he proposed the fundamental distinction between systems of states and a society of states. A system of states is comprised of independent political entities that interact and must take each other into consideration in their strategic decisions. Conflict and war are the typical forms of interaction in a system of states. A society of states, in contrast, is composed of political entities that have some recognition of common interests in maintaining the system and base their interactions upon fundamental norms and institutions that help sustain patterns of relations. The norms and institutions are not based on force, compulsion, or deterrence, but have widespread legitimacy and hence authority and effectiveness (Hurd 1997). That states behave with these norms on a daily basis is further evidence of their importance. Through common practice norms become institutionalized, and hence a fundamental source of order.

The foundational principle developed by Europeans for ordering the relations between communities was sovereignty. Sovereignty was originally an emancipatory idea, a license for freedom of political communities, and a strong support, if not guarantee, of their security. It was a radical idea because it subverted the hierarchical principles that previously had underlain relations between communities in Europe and elsewhere. Empires and suzerain systems often provided order and security of a sort, but the price was lack of autonomy. A system of sovereign states dilutes security and order, but provides autonomy. An example of a system of states was in Chou China during the "Spring and Autumn" period (771–483 BC), where insecure polities warred incessantly against each other and made conquest (and thereby obliteration) of neighboring states the ultimate political goal (Holsti 1967: ch. 2). In contrast, the European sovereigns more or less adhered to fundamental norms that provided some semblance of order and even security. These included non-interference, legal equality, reciprocity, territorial sanctity, and domestic heterogeneity. Together these and other principles have come to be known as the Westphalian system, or to use Robert Jackson's (1990) nice term of brevity, "the sovereignty game."

The literature on the sovereignty game is vast and not entirely relevant to problems of violence in the peripheries today. But it is important to underline the significance of this game for states, contrasting it either to empires or to systems of states. Historically, empires were moving entities. Their borders were constantly in flux and always subject to revision by invaders and those who refused to accept the paramountcy of imperial centers. In systems of states, as in the Chou example, the life expectancy of an independent political unit seldom exceeded a century. In contrast, the main contemporary European states and most of the lesser ones have a pedigree that extends at least one-half millennium. Their South American and North American progeny have survived as independent entities for about two centuries. And, again in contrast to the Chou (or Greek or Italian city states), the territorial configurations of these states have become firmly established and are rarely the object of dispute (Jackson and Zacher 1997). Since 1945, no internationally recognized state has lost its independence through armed conquest, although North Yemen, South Vietnam, and East Timor provide marginal exceptions to the generalization.

It is fashionable these days to lament the role of sovereignty in international relations. But from a historical perspective, sovereignty has provided more security, protected more diversity (particularly religious), and constructed a context for more human progress and improvement than any other political principle or arrangement. It has not been an unblemished record. Poland was obliterated as a state for more than a century. Territorial adjustments through armed force were commonplace throughout the eighteenth and nineteenth centuries. Wars were a regular feature of the diplomatic landscape, and order in the sense of long periods of peace was a rare commodity.

The great wars in Europe were not, however, the *result* of the sovereignty game. They were, rather, the result of those who attempted to create orders or systems based on *alternative* principles. The Habsburgs in the seventeenth century dreamed of a unified Europe under their hegemony. One result was the Thirty Years War, the most devastating carnage on the continent until World War I. Louis XIV also dreamt of a Paris-based hegemony under the united French and Spanish crowns, leading to the next great pan-European war of the Spanish Succession. Napoleon believed he could unite Europe under French hegemony, centered around his upstart family dynasty. Germany's ultimate objectives in 1914 remain a matter of dispute, but the Treaty of Brest-Litovsk (1918) was not consistent with Westphalian ideas of the sovereignty game. Hitler also sought to create a new order. Its foundational principle of racial hierarchy was fundamentally incompatible with the Westphalian game. World War II was ultimately a war to save the Westphalian international society as much as a war against the principles and practices of fascism.

The Westphalian system has provided a great degree of order. If played according to its essential rules, it has also provided political emancipation, national freedom, and a context within which economic, scientific, and technological progress with no historical precedent has taken place. The progressive elements of the order have been under-appreciated because of the great wars, a permanent blot on Europeans' claims to talk about order to non-Europeans. But that is the wrong story. The great wars are a blot indeed, but their authors were those who did not want to play the Westphalian sovereignty game, not those who adhered to its fundamental principles. If we could erase the Habsburgs, Louis XIV, Napoleon (and the French revolutionaries), Wilhelmine Germany, Adolf Hitler, and Joseph Stalin, Europeans could take the moral high ground and claim that, whatever their shortcomings, Westphalian principles have brought order, security, autonomy, and welfare, values that transcend political systems, religious beliefs, or "identities." The system, in brief, has worked.

But where do the peripheries fit in? When we speak of a "new world order" – a prominent academic growth industry since 1989 – is this construct relevant to the problems of the periphery? And if so, have spokespersons from the peripheries helped to define the contours of a new order? The answer to these questions is predominantly negative. I argue that the exercise is primarily the latest version of what was originally the imperial project. The same patterns of thought, the same limited perspectives, and the same paternalism reappear. A new vocabulary of world order does not successfully hide old ideas emanating from the imperial experience.

Periphery in concepts of world order

The areas of the world collectively termed the peripheries today were also the peripheries of yesteryear. In the original spurt of European explora-tion, conquests, settlement, and exploitation, there was never any idea that the rules of the Westphalian system – most particularly the rule of respect for religious and political diversity – should extend beyond the continent. During the first great wave of conquest in the sixteenth and seventeenth centuries, the local populations were exterminated, turned into slave labor (e.g., the Spanish *encomienda* system), or assimilated. A colony was to be a home only for a few settlers and commercial agents, not for the natives. Conquest was deemed a right justified by the concept of *territorium nullius*, conveniently overlooking the fact that most of the territories conquered were already inhabited. By the nineteenth century, Europeans had done some anthropological sorting – helped by visual displays of "natives" at world fairs (Wan 1992) – and fashioned the official status of colonies and other political units according to whether they judged the peoples concerned to be pagan, barbarian, or savage. The former were to be admitted ultimately to the club of sovereign states once they had met the "standards of civilization" (Gong 1984) and all the European rules of the diplomatic game. The South American colonies were admitted to the club within a decade after achieving independence because they were ruled by Catholic Spaniards and Portuguese. The first pagan polity, the Ottoman Empire, joined in 1856, followed by Japan and Siam later in the century. Coherent political units that did not quite meet the qualifications of pagan polities had different statuses, such as colonies, condominia, protectorates, dependencies, and the like. Colonies were not created to become states, so there was never any assumption that their denizens were to play any role except that of servants in the game of nations. The famous Berlin Conference (1884–5), which sorted out the territorial boundaries in Africa and set up new rules that the Europeans would apply to each other in their colonial-territorial competition, did not include a single black face.

The learning curve of those who did meet the "standards of civilization" and joined the club of states was rapid. The Japanese sent out dozens of delegations to learn how to create and run a modern state and armed forces, and by 1895 surprised the world by defeating China. The biggest shock came in 1905 when the Japanese defeated a European great power. European tolerance for such *parvenus* was limited, however. In Paris in 1919, the drafters of the League of Nations Covenant refused to include a Japanese-sponsored principle condemning racial discrimination. By the 1930s, the Japanese, having been denied access to Western markets and often to sources of vital raw materials, sought to create their own regional order. It was to be based on Confucian hierarchies rather than Westphalian egalitarian principles, and to be achieved through military prowess. The United States and its European allies terminated the alternative order-building enterprise with two atomic bombs in August 1945. Both Hitler's racial order and Japan's non-European Confucian order had challenged the Westphalian sovereignty game and lost. As in 1648, 1713, 1815, and 1919, the victorious coalition proved that only the Westphalian conception of order would be tolerated. The peripheries had no say in the matter, although hundreds of thousands of troops from the colonies died for the Allied cause.

The sovereignty game after World War II

The contradiction between Westphalian norms and colonial realities began to appear during the war. If the Westphalian system was emancipatory in the sense that sovereignty and autonomy were prime values, in contrast to hierarchically based systems, then was there any reason to believe that colonies were to be permanently parts of the vast European-based imperial system? If World War II was fought ultimately to maintain the Westphalian system and one of its main ideological underpinnings, the doctrine of national self-determination, was there any justification other than racism for perpetuating imperial rule in the peripheries? The idea that colonies might ultimately enjoy some form of self-government if not independence was already made explicit in the League Mandates system, in the British Colonial Development and Welfare programs of the 1930s, and in the Atlantic Charter. By the 1940s the imperial system and all the ideological props upon which it had been created and sustained, began to crumble. By the 1960s, despite the claims of many colonial authorities that the natives were not ready even for self-rule, de-colonization had become almost ritual – except for the Portuguese who clung to the myths well into the 1970s. The United Nations registered its main successes in helping to "liberate" colonies and then welcoming them to the international community even if they did not have the stuff of sovereign states. The UN thus added to its function of protecting states the burdens of helping to give birth to them and later to sustain them through multilateral aid and other means. In the half-century after 1945, there was an unprecedented explosion of statehood. By the 1970s, the sovereignty game had become universal. Today we have a world of political homogeneity, with only a few feudal and imperial leftovers. The last great empire – the Soviet Union – has collapsed (some would argue that China remains the last empire); Andorra, Liechtenstein, Monaco remain distinct but inconsequential; and the last great colony, Hong Kong, has reverted to China. The diversity of the late middle ages, featuring empires, emirates, khans, tribes, city states, principalities, church territories, leagues of cities, colonies, tributary states, and the like have all boiled down to a single political format: the sovereign state.

It thus makes sense to speak of *world* order because we are speaking of a domain populated by similar political entities, all operating under the foundational norm of sovereignty and its derivatives, including legal equality, territoriality, reciprocity, and *pacta sunt servanda*. While international peace and security are mentioned in the Charter's preamble, the predominant purpose of the organization is less to eliminate war – an instrumental question – than to preserve the sovereignty and independence of its members, a question of ultimate goals. It does this by outlawing the aggressive use of force to alter territorial configurations or to eliminate states, by de-legitimizing colonial-type relationships, and, in general, by sustaining the major Westphalian principles. To the extent that the behavior of states is consistent with these essential rules of the

Charter, we can say that there is some type of world order. The ordinary changes that accompany the growth and decline of nations are not so important as these fundamental rules. We have a Westphalian system or order whether there are two or four great powers, whether there are fifty or 150 states, whether we have more wars or fewer wars, or whether there is more or less "globalization."

A post-1989 new world order?

The collapse of communism brought forth a barrage of hyperbole about a new world order. The frozen thought patterns and duplicating diplomatic practices of forty-five years seemingly needed readjustment in light of the "new realities" (Holsti 1994). President George Bush provided a fillip for the academic industry by proclaiming in 1991 that the Gulf War had proven that we do indeed live in a new world order. In light of the sudden discovery of "ethnic wars," however, cynics proposed the competing concept of a new world disorder. Now we have the optimists and pessimists arrayed against each other. Triumphalists such as Francis Fukuyama (1989) announced the universal victory of liberalism and the free market, while the journalist Robert Kaplan (1994) warned, from the grass-roots Third World perspective, of the "coming anarchy." Take your pick. Since there is no consensus on a conceptual framework upon which to evaluate the multiplicity of ideas about a new order, it is impossible to say that one is correct and the other incorrect. One author's order is another author's disorder. But clearly we have not transcended the Westphalian order. The fundamental rules and institutions underlying international relationships have not changed with the end of the Cold War. Indeed, they have been strengthened. The events of 1989–91 formally put to rest the only serious challenger to the Westphalian order, the old Bolshevik idea of a world socialist state, or Stalin's later idea of a commonwealth of socialist states based exclusively on fraternal relations between working-class parties. Some Muslim activists promote the old idea of communities of faith rather than communities of nations, but most Muslim states have eagerly joined the sovereignty game and no longer adhere to the creed of *jihad* against the European conception of the state (cf. Armstrong 1993).

But the continuity of the Westphalian sovereignty game has not completely erased old, hierarchical patterns of thought. The ideas and perceptual equipment that launched and sustained imperialism remain with us. They are implied in the title of this paper, "The coming chaos." It suggests that the Third World is a different type of world. It is one prone to conflict and violence, to a never-ending source of items for the United

Nations agenda. For Max Singer and Aaron Wildavsky (1993), the *real* world order is dichotomized between "zones of peace" and "zones of turmoil." For James Goldgeier and Michael McFaul (1992) the new international relations are to be a "Tale of Two Worlds," a story of liberal consensus, growth, and peace in the industrial world, and chronic conflict and war in the Third World and post-socialist states. Stanley Hoffmann (1991: 6) has written of a New World Disorder located in the Third World, characterized by a "situation far more chaotic than the world of the Cold War." Many others have drawn the same or similar dichotomies. Where do these ideas come from? Are there not similarities between the world as seen by the *conquistadores*, by nineteenth-century racial theories, by the defenders and ideologues of imperialism, and by these contemporary authors' dichotomies? Before we confront the prospect of a "coming chaos," we should first examine the perceptual lenses through which the Third World is seen among Western academics and policy-makers, and then look at the record of war and conflict in this area of the world and see how it fits the stereotypes.

Cold War perspectives on the peripheries

The term "tiers monde" was coined in the 1950s by a French analyst of international affairs. Despite the immense variety of political, social, and economic conditions that existed in the former colonial world, the idea of a "third world" soon caught on because most of the territories and societies in question shared a common attribute of relative poverty and economic "underdevelopment." Dependency theory, the first analytical theory about international relationships to come from the South, helped sustain the dichotomy. It used the center-periphery rather than the developed-underdeveloped nomenclature and imagery, but the bases of the dichotomy – differences in living conditions – were essentially the same. In both strategic and economic analyses, the Third World was homogenized, de-cultured, and rendered a-historic. Western knowledge of these areas tended to reflect what the outside observers wanted to know rather than what the local peoples do know (cf. Escobar 1995). These images had earlier precedents.

In the late nineteenth century, for example, an elaborate system of racial and cultural classifications came into use to help justify the new imperial conquests of Africa, the Pacific, and the Middle East. The popular literature contrasted the progressive and peaceful character of "advanced" civilizations to the violent, cruel, and mysterious colonial domains (Wan 1992). Distinctions between levels of civilization were also incorporated into the League of Nations mandates system. By the 1930s, the imperial discourse had shed much of its racist overtones, to be replaced by distinctions based on capacity for self-rule. The idea of self-rule was of course based on European/American political concepts, conveniently forgetting that pre-colonial societies had ruled themselves, often with considerable success, many for centuries before they had been conquered. The question, then, was not really one of capacity for self-rule, but capacity for ruling within Western-style institutions. There could be no expectation of self-rule until "they" had become like "us." Acts of violent resistance or the organization of wars of national liberation were proof that the societies in question were not ready for self-rule.

During the Cold War, the dichotomization of rich and poor, center and periphery, developed and underdeveloped fitted in well with prevailing strategic concepts. The Third World was essentially an arena where great power rivalries and competition could be played out, not an area of intrinsic interest with problems unique to each region or country. American Secretary of State John Foster Dulles fulminated against the likes of Nehru, Nkrumah, and Nasser for their refusal to choose between godless communism and freedom, for their insistence that Indian, Ghanaian, and Egyptian national interests were not the same as those of the United States specifically or of NATO more generally. The non-aligned movement did not fit comfortably within Dulles' dichotomized worldview where the only meaningful division was between communism and democracy. It fit only slightly better with Soviet conceptions of the world. In the communist view, the Third World was an area of great revolutionary potential. But many of its players voted too often with American-led majorities in the United Nations, and some regimes were outright puppets and lackeys of imperialism. Once the colonies had gained independence, many of them reverted to the ways of Western states, notwithstanding their use of the term "socialist" to describe their economies.

Both Western and communist analysts ignored local dynamics and local problems. Wars in the peripheries, they believed, were inevitably caused by the machinations of the adversary. Ronald Reagan saw the problems of Nicaragua and El Salvador in the 1980s just as the Dulles brothers had seen the problems of Guatemala in 1954: the results of Soviet-sponsored subversion and conspiracy. The strategic studies literature of the 1960s focused on communist-led insurgencies. Malaya, Vietnam, and the Philippines were the wars to study, while wars in Burma, Sri Lanka, or Sudan were ignored because there was no way to link them to communism. It did not occur to most analysts that there were local and often structural sources of these conflicts.

Little wonder, then, that after 1989 American and European analysts suddenly discovered "ethnic wars," and argued that a *new* phenomenon, a *new* zone of turmoil, and a *new* periphery of violence and chaos were appearing. Nothing could reveal more clearly Western conceits and post-imperial perspectives than the idea that the end of the Cold War un-leashed a whole new set of security problems in the Third World and that only Cold War competition had kept the Third World from exploding into chaos.

War in the Third World: a zone of chaos?

If we mean by "chaos," "anarchy," and "turmoil" a high incidence of international conflict in general and interstate wars in particular, analysts who have employed these terms reflect old imperial thought habits more than careful analysis. On a comparative basis the record of aggression and war-making in the peripheries has been similar to the record of European wars between 1648 and 1945. If we exclude the chronic Israel-Arab armed conflicts in the Middle East – a legacy of *European* politics – there have been only twenty bilateral or multilateral wars between Third World countries since 1945. A significant proportion of these began as domestic conflicts but were internationalized by great power intervention. (We exclude wars of national liberation since they, too, are legacies of colonial-ism rather than reflections of the behavior of independent states.)[2] We can cite the truly costly Iran-Iraq war, three wars over Kashmir (but the last was an intervention occasioned by the collapse of Pakistan), the China-India border war, some low-intensity conflicts such as Indonesia's campaign against Malaysia, and a few others, but the overall record of interstate war in the peripheries does not provide a foundation for predict-ing "coming chaos" or "coming anarchy."

Analysts who saw the Cold War as a restraining system on Third World states and who predicted that with its demise a whole raft of old scores would be settled by armed force have also been proven wrong (cf. Acharya 1997). The ratio of interstate wars per Third World state since 1945 is comparable to that of several periods in European history (Holsti 1996: ch. 2), and has been declining notably since about 1975. Wallen-steen and Sollenberg (1996: 8–9) report only three interstate wars begin-ning since 1991, two of them in the former Yugoslavia and hence not in what is ordinarily considered to be part of the periphery. SIPRI data (1993) show that territorial conflicts in the Third World actually declined after the Cold War and that the overall level of armed conflict also declined. Similar data are provided by Wallensteen and Sollenberg (1996: 10). Given that there are somewhere in the vicinity of 135 states in the conventionally defined Third World, the low and declining incidence of war is notable.

When we disaggregate the "periphery" into more sensible regions, we find equally compelling evidence that most of these areas have not been and are not likely to be scenes of coming anarchy or chaos in terms of international warfare. There have been minor but violent border disputes but no wars in South America since 1941 – a record that not even the Europeans, the ostensible center of world order, can match. Except for American armed interventions, there have been only two limited wars in Central America and the Caribbean since 1945. There has been peace, if not satisfactory security, in Southeast Asia since the United States withdrew from Vietnam in 1975. There has been no armed combat in East Asia since the Korean armistice more than four decades ago. And Africa, an area where we might expect a high rate of interstate war given the nature of boundaries and other extreme colonial legacies, has been if not a zone of peace, an area remarkably free of armed conflicts between countries.

Most important, not a single war between states in the Third World has threatened the international order as we have defined it above. There has been no Third World incarnation of Hitler or Stalin.[3] Louis XIV, a figure whose pretensions to hegemony could be taken seriously by all Europeans, finds no counterpart in Saddam Hussein, a leader with no followers. Aside from a few Muslim activists who dream of a politically united, transnational spiritual community, Third World governments have been vigorous champions of the Westphalian system, not its challengers. Most have consistently upheld fundamental norms such as territorial integrity, non-intervention, and legal equality. Why? Because it is in their interests as representatives of newly sovereign states to do so. They look upon "no-fly zones," humanitarian interventions, and statements in favor of the national self-determination of "peoples" with deep suspicion precisely because they challenge, weaken, or threaten sovereignty-related norms.

From the perspective of most regions and of the essential elements of international order, then, there is also little empirical foundation for the view of the peripheries as "zones of turmoil," or a "tale of a (violent) world." This kind of thinking just perpetuates the simplistic dichotomies of imperialism and the Cold War. It has led some to argue that the South will now become the new enemy to replace the Soviet Union and that it must be policed, disarmed, and rendered harmless (cf. Krauthamer 1991).

The nature of violence in the peripheries

Defenders of the dichotomy principle and of coming chaos could point to statistics other than those related to the incidence of interstate war. For example, of the approximately forty million deaths by armed conflict since 1945, more than 99 percent have been suffered in the "zone of turmoil." Two-thirds of the new states have used their armed forces *against their own citizens* (Neitschmann 1994: 227), a form of behavior not seen in the "Zone of Peace." Armed violence of one kind or another is ubiquitous in this area, whereas among the OECD countries, roughly, there have been no interstate wars and only a few remaining malignant civil wars, as in Northern Ireland.

The figures do speak for themselves. If we include wars of secession, wars of resistance, civil wars, the breakdown of states, massive humanitarian emergencies, and the like, then there is an empirical foundation of the designation of "zones of turmoil," the "coming anarchy," and the like. But this is not a problem of world order, which is usually characterized as a problem of the relations between states. It is, rather, a problem of the state or more precisely, a problem of the relations between the state and its constituent communities, and between different communities within states.

The figures bear out the generalization. Of the 164 wars between 1945 and 1995 (excluding wars of "national liberation"), 77 percent were domestic (Holsti 1996: ch. 2). More recent data, employing a much looser definition of war or armed conflict (twenty-five battle-related deaths in one year) found, for example, thirty-four ongoing intrastate armed conflicts in 1995, but only one interstate war (Wallensteen and Sollenberg 1996: 8). Everywhere, it seems, people are rebelling, resisting, overthrowing, or massacring. And they are doing these things most of the time in areas designated as the Third World and, more recently, in the post-socialist states. Northern Ireland, Oklahoma City, and Los Angeles are only exceptions that prove the generalization.

Isn't this the sort of evidence to warrant the prediction of "coming chaos" and prove the claim that the Third World has been an arena of chaos for some time? This might indeed be the case. But to get at the sources of the mayhem, we must disabuse ourselves of some of the popular post-Cold War interpretations such as the claim that with the end of that conflict, ancient hatreds and enmities had re-emerged and (new) wars over ethnicity and "identity" had replaced the great contest between freedom and communism.

Wars about the nature of the state, and between the state and its constituent communities, have been going on since the days of colonialism. They are nothing new, and they certainly did not appear suddenly just because CNN finally paid some attention to conflicts which were not an integral part of the Cold War. Let us remind ourselves of just a few major incidents of domestic violence that preceded the onset of the Cold War or began long before the Soviet-American rivalry ended:

- armed resistance and uprisings in Myanmar (Burma) began virtually with the declaration of independence in 1948;
- the partition of India in 1947–8, creating Pakistan, cost several million lives;
- the Eritreans began a secessionist war to tear themselves from the centralizing and oppressive Ethiopian empire in 1961, and finally succeeded thirty years later;
- the partition of Pakistan resulted after central government troops invaded what was to become Bangladesh and killed hundreds of thousands of Bengalis;
- the secessionist Biafra War, starting in 1967, cost several million lives;
- the civil war in the Sudan has been an on-and-off affair since the early 1970s.

The list is just a hint of the total roster of armed violence. It may be trendy to think of these as "ethnic wars" dealing with questions of "identity." But this interpretation is predominantly a projection of contemporary North American social concerns, not an adequate descriptor of what went on in Burma, Eritrea, Nigeria, and the like. It is not even a very good descriptor of what has been going on in places like Tajikistan, where placing the ethnic tag on a war hides what are much more fundamental problems about the state, governance, rule, and communities (Schoeberlein-Engel 1994).

The crises of the state and governance in the peripheries

There are two interrelated problems that have manifested themselves in attempted secessions, state collapse, politicides, and a number of humanitarian emergencies. We can call the first the "crisis of the non-Western state," and the second, the "crisis of governance." Before examining their characteristics, connections, and etiologies, I want to emphasize that these crises are not endemic to or typical of the Third World and the post-socialist states. To use these broad geographic categories to predict vast zones of chaos and anarchy is fundamentally mistaken. We must acknowledge that a great number of former colonies have made a successful transition from pre-colonial polities of an immense variety, to effective modern states. Southeast Asia, with the exceptions of Myanmar and Cambodia, is an area of increasingly strong (meaning legitimacy, not military strength) states that have integrated their multi-community populations reasonably well, provided a range of government services, and directed rates of economic growth that until 1997 were envied in most industrial countries. Human rights problems, corruption, and authoritarian practices persist, but seldom in depth and scope that was seen, for example, in Stalin's Soviet Union, Mussolini's Italy, or today in parts of ex-Yugoslavia. Despite serious structural economic problems in the Caribbean, this region does not seem a candidate for "coming chaos." Despite immense debt problems, the insecure life of indigenous peoples, and the continued, if largely re-defined role for militaries, South and Central America's trajectories are not toward chaos either. If an Israeli-Palestinian peace can be fashioned, the Middle East's prospects are enhanced if not stable and predictable. We are left, then, with three areas where the future is problematic and where serious instabilities remain: West Africa, Central Asia, including Pakistan and Afghanistan, and the Korean peninsula. A fourth major region, China, defies authoritative prognosis. Suddenly, then, our "Third World" has been drastically reduced in size and population. It is no longer possible to throw Malaysia and Liberia, or Trinidad-Tobago and Tajikistan into the same category. Aside from all having been colonies, they have almost nothing else in common. The former have become strong states in terms of legitimacy and economic performance; the latter are weak or collapsing.

The crisis of the state

The modern state is a unique European invention that grew organically through a combination of social-epistemological changes emerging from the Renaissance, the declining political role of the Catholic church, the growth of Protestantism, and the emergence of capitalism and all its technological and scientific accouterments. Bureaucracies, taxation, and armies may be hallmarks of the modern state but they are not unique to it as they were also standard structures of historical empires. The novel and significant aspects of the European state are its fixed territoriality, the concept of citizenship, and the doctrine of sovereignty. All provide a degree of security and legitimacy to political orders that were seldom found in polities elsewhere.

Colonies were never created to become European-type states. They were defined geographically and politically for European purposes, which had nothing to do with the interests of indigenous populations. Yet, in the great process of de-colonization, the political fictions called colonies had to be transformed into European-type states whose defining features in addition to sovereignty and legal equality include (1) a defined and demarcated exclusive territory; (2) a permanent population the members of which are defined as "citizens" and all others as "foreigners"; and (3) access to adequate resources to sustain the population. There are many

other characteristics of the state – including the coercive and tax-extract-
ing capacity of the government – but the three above will suffice to
demonstrate what we mean by the term "the crisis of the state."

Consider the matter of territory. The idea of a permanently bounded
realm is even new to Europeans. The first officially demarcated boundary
lines on the continent were located between France and Spain in the
Treaty of the Llivia (1660). But this treaty arranged only for the cession of
old village jurisdictions. It did not draw lineal boundaries such as those
commonly found in modern frontiers (Sahlins 1998: 36). By the late
1800s, straight lines were drawn with abandon in the new colonies, areas
that previously knew nothing of concepts such as lineal boundaries.
Benedict Anderson (1983) suggests that maps enabled governments in
London, Paris, Brussels, Berlin, St. Petersburg, and elsewhere to create a
classificatory grid which could help identify "our" exclusive spaces from
"theirs." Europeans invented colored spaces called the Ivory Coast,
Guinea, Sierra Leone, Togo, Nigeria, and the Cameroons – places that
did not coincide with any previously known polities. If the imperial
governments had to invent topographical spaces, they also had to invent
nationalities such as "Togolese" or "Nigerian," categories that arbitrarily
and artificially joined Ewes, Yorubas, Ibos, and the like, and separated
other traditional socially coherent groups. These European-defined nationalities were as fictional as the colored spaces in world atlases. The
chaos that seems to recur in some areas of the world derives fundamentally from the gap between European-created fictions and realities on the
ground. Robert Kaplan (1996: 70–1) describes the syndrome which we
might call the people-state disjuncture:

I had come by airplane from Freetown to Lomé, capital of Togo, a country that
may be less fact than fiction. Togo . . . illustrated [West Africa's] geographical
quandary: Population belts in West Africa are horizontal, and human habitation
densities increase as one travels away south from the Sahara and toward the
tropical abundance of the Atlantic littoral. But the borders erected by European
colonialists were vertical, and therefore at cross-purposes with demography and
topography. For example, the Ewe people . . . are divided between Togo and
Ghana. In addition, Togo has been bedeviled by tensions between its southern
peoples and the Voltaic peoples of the north . . . Togo, rather than an organic
outgrowth of geography and ethnicity, was a result of late-nineteenth-century
German greed . . . In 1884, the Germans landed a ship here and staked out a
claim. That was the basis for the national identity of Togo.

Similar problems were created in Central Asia by, first, the Russians,
second by the Persians, and last by Stalin. Boundaries were drawn that
divided peoples, such as the Azeris or Bashkirs, between two or more state
jurisdictions where no lines had existed before. The present-day frontiers

of the former Soviet Central Asian republics thus make little sense from commercial, ethnographic, or geographic points of view. The territorial divisions of Central Asia, as in most of Africa, are fictions created for geostrategic, colonial, and other reasons unrelated to the history, societies, or interests of the local peoples. There will be considerable difficulties trying to create viable states around multi-ethnic and language communities that share little but propinquity. In these circumstances those who try to hold the whole mess together may be tempted to play ethnic cards as a political stratagem.

The act of de-colonization did not alter this disjuncture between communities and the state. The elites who led independence or national liberation movements under the doctrine of national self-determination often had no *nation* to liberate. Rather, they had collections of communities that aside from their dislike of colonialism, had little in common, and certainly no common identity. By accepting colonial borders under the doctrine of *uti possidetis*, the post-colonial regimes continued to split tribes, communities, peoples, and nationalities and fit the remainders into oddly and arbitrarily designed territorial vessels (cf. Ahmed 1996: 9).

The second defining feature of the European state, sanctified in international law, is a permanent population which has a distinct citizenship. Although dual citizenship exists in many jurisdictions, for purposes of travel, work, commerce, and military service – to mention just a few – legal personality is defined in terms of a single state citizenship. One can be an Ongoni, Azeri, Ashkenasi, or African-American, a Christian, Muslim, Jew, or Baptist, a Farsi-, Hebrew-, Arabic-, or English-speaker, but for purposes that take one beyond the state, one is and can only be a Nigerian, Guinean, Iranian (or Turk), or American citizen.

Massive international migration has been a characteristic of the international system for several centuries. Most migrants ultimately substitute the citizenship of their new domicile for their original citizenship. For those who do not migrate but travel, most governments impose time restrictions for visits. One can be a tourist or guest, but not a citizen without undergoing some sort of formal proceeding. In the areas under consideration, however, population movements are incessant and the formalities of citizenship are not involved. Because of porous borders and frontiers, ancient travel and commercial routes, and vast differences of economic opportunities, populations move back and forth with a frequency and volume that mocks frontiers and national census figures. In the Ivory Coast, for example, about half the population is non-Ivorian; about 75 percent of Abidjan's population originates from neighboring countries (Kaplan 1996: 21). In the Gulf states, populations are constituted primarily (actually they are large majorities) of itinerant Indians,

Pakistanis, Palestinians, Bangladeshis, Filipinos, and Koreans. In the mayhem surrounding the collapse of Liberia in 1990 and Sierra Leone in 1992, 280,000 Sierra Leonians fled to neighboring Guinea, while 400,000 Liberians fled to Sierra Leone (Kaplan 1995: 45). We will probably never know how many Hutus escaping from Rwanda will ultimately settle in Zaire; certainly the Zairian authorities will not know. Massive, porous, uncontrolled, and unmonitored zones in Central Asia and Africa, through which millions of people move back and forth, belie the concept of "permanent population" that is the second hallmark of a sovereign state.

These population movements do not necessarily cause chaos, although they might be the results of carnage such as Rwanda. However, they are one more source of the massive explosion of urban populations that results in bush slums, shanty-towns, and more transient communities in which public services are non-existent. In these milieux, diseases are revitalized and the distinction between commerce and criminality breaks down. Politics, drugs, gang warfare, and ethnicity all become entangled in what is by most standards a truly chaotic situation. The political infrastructure of some states, as Goldstone suggests in this volume, cannot possibly provide adequate resources to deal with these communities.

Pakistan is just one example of a polity that cannot meet the third criterion of statehood, reasonable access to resources that can sustain a permanent population. Robert Kaplan, that prescient observer of daily life in the peripheries (as opposed to academic analysts who seldom venture out of the context of their offices and modern hotels), uses Pakistan as the paradigmatic case of a state where inadequate, declining, and squandered resources cannot keep up with population growth and migration. Several indicators that warn of coming difficulties and possible chaos:

- by 1988, illicit drugs accounted for more foreign exchange earnings than all of Pakistan's legal exports;
- Pakistani officials lament that police, magistrates, and tax collectors can no longer perform their jobs, unless paid through graft;
- Karachi's population grew from 400,000 in 1947 to nine million today, with no possibility of providing services much less employment for these numbers;
- drug barons and a variety of criminal organizations fill the void to some extent, but gang warfare that cannot be controlled by the government creates an environment in which security is a scarce commodity;
- massive deforestation and salination of soils reduce Pakistan's food output, in a society that adds 12,000 new mouths to feed daily.

Concluding from such facts, Kaplan (1996: 331) notes:

Benazir Bhutto, rather than a symbol of female empowerment in the male-dominated Moslem world, [was] a symbol of helplessness: the head of a government who can no longer *cope*, because overpopulation and depleted resources have reached the point of saturation, thus destabilizing the state institutions.

The combination of population growth, environmental destruction, porous borders, and uncontrolled population movements is only part of the general crisis of the state, but it is the part which reveals best the extent to which some Third World and post-socialist states will be the likely scenes of future violence. Unlike the Malaysias, Trinidads, and Fijis of the world, their trajectories are downward. They are "phantom states" (Gros 1996), states that exist on paper, have a UN ambassador, and a government. But civic functions (including security) are provided by local agents, including gangs, warlords, and ethnic barons. Others become "collapsed states" (Zartman 1995). Collapsed states often explode into chronic warfare. Somalia is the paradigmatic example, but Sierra Leone, Liberia, Tajikistan, and possibly Zaire can be added to the roster. Russia, Albania, and Pakistan remain candidates for failure. While all of these cases have their international ramifications, with the possible exception of Russia, none poses a major security threat to the region or to world order in general. Indeed, the collapse of Liberia, Sierra Leone, and Tajikistan has barely been noted in Western media. Apparently it takes a major catastrophe of Rwandan proportions to make the headlines, even though those headlines were insufficient to bring a coordinated Western or African response. The argument that the "coming chaos" in the Third World will challenge the security of the OECD world is not credible. These problems are not a threat to major international institutions such as sovereignty, diplomacy, or international law.

The crisis of governance

If the crisis of the state is confined to a few locales and does not warrant any generalizations about all of the Third World or the "periphery," the crisis of governance is more ubiquitous. One can sympathize with the magnitude of the problems faced by many post-colonial and post-socialist states and their governments. Yet many governments inherited colonial polities that were socially coherent, richly endowed with resources, and bound together with infrastructure. Many legacies of colonialism – borders being one of the main ones – made an easy transition to statehood almost impossible, but there were other legacies that provided the foundations for successful state-building projects. The fortunes of Singapore, Malaysia, Lesotho, Tunisia, and dozens of others illustrate the point.

But in some areas, the concept of governance as a *service* or social responsibility never outlived colonialism. Post-colonial governments became the avenues to personal enrichment, clientelism, nepotism, and massive corruption. The term "kleptocracy" best describes polities such as Mobutu's Zaire, the Duvaliers' Haiti, Somoza's Nicaragua, the Marcoses' Philippines, and Ne Win's Burma, to mention just a few of many. Kleptocracies have taken many organizational forms, but they share this one feature in common: the "right to rule" (legitimacy) – the basis of all prolonged governance – is *purchased* rather than earned. The purchased include family members, cronies, the military, and clients of numerous characteristics. Loyalty is based on favors granted rather than services performed.

Polities based on purchased loyalties are inherently unstable because by their very nature they must grant privileged access to the few whose loyalty matters and exclude others. Frequently the exclusions are deliberate and based on ascriptive characteristics. This is "playing the ethnic card," a stratagem of rulers who exclude some in order to shore up their rule among others. The forms of exclusion can range from informal non-violent discriminations, such as Idi Amin's expulsion of Asians from Uganda in 1972, through formal exclusion such as *apartheid*, to violent politicides directed at certain populations.

The details differ from case to case, but the many examples in the Third World and in some post-socialist states share one characteristic that allows them to be termed "exclusions." A distinct group or community within society is systematically excluded from access to policy-makers and political office, or is denied certain or all government services. Hardin (1995: 57) makes the distinction between *positional goods* (public office), *distributional goods* (services), and *the interactions between these two*. In many new weak states and kleptocracies, those who hold positional goods resist sharing them with others who make claims to them, and in order to maintain those goods, they must concentrate distributional goods on those who are loyal to them, thereby excluding outsiders. The history of the Hutus and Tutsis in Rwanda and Burundi demonstrates the consequences that can derive from the monopolization of office and services in a society. A particularly volatile and dangerous situation arises when a minority systematically excludes a majority (Ahmed 1996: 25, 70). Even in states in which rulers represent significant majorities, popular validation of officials through elections may serve only as a census, further justifying exclusions of minorities. The principle of majority rule, in such societies, translates to *permanent* rule by one group over others.

We have, then, a fundamental disjuncture between the concept of the *citizen*, which is intrinsic to the idea of the state and which precludes discriminatory treatment based on ascriptive criteria, and the form of *governance* that in some Third World and post-socialist states has been based on discrimination. Until this contradiction is resolved, we will continue to see one of two different responses: (1) apathy and indifference toward the government, with effective rule taking place at the local level, if at all; or (2) resistance, rebellion, and internal war.

We move beyond kleptocracies and corruption when we enter the realm of politicides. Contrary to much of the post-Cold War literature which characterizes "ethnic wars" as reflecting primordial inter-communal hatreds, most of the massive killings in this century have been organized *by states against their own citizens* (Rummel 1994). The threat to the average peasant or city-dweller in many areas of the world is not the ethnically different neighbor next door (although that is sometimes the case, as in Bosnia or Rwanda), but the state, that European vessel whose main historical function was to provide security for the citizen. This is not a question of the killings that result from state collapse, or of occasional communal conflicts such as in India following the assassination of Indira Gandhi. At question here is the deliberate killing of large numbers of people who are defined as a social and political threat to political incumbents. They may or may not represent an ethnic group.

Politicides are not an invention of the supposedly violent ex-colonial areas. They do not take place within a particular social, cultural, or economic context. Genghis Khan slew millions, often on whim. Emperor Shaka, a regional ruler of nineteenth-century Southern Africa, killed both friends and foes indiscriminately. The Ottomans massacred millions of Armenians during World War I as a matter of deliberate policy. Hitler selected Jews and Gypsies for special treatment, while Stalin killed, transported, or imprisoned perceived "enemies of the state" and "counter-revolutionaries" of many nationalities, languages, and ethnicities. He deliberately starved to death about eleven million Ukrainians in the early 1930s. Since 1945, we have seen politicides in China (post-revolution, the Great Leap Forward, and the Great Proletarian Cultural Revolution), Indonesia (the massacres of 1965–6), Pol Pot's holocaust (focused primarily but not exclusively on the urban middle class), Macias Nguema's killings in Equatorial Guinea, Idi Amin's 300,000 (estimate) victims in Uganda, the work of the death squads in El Salvador during the 1970s, and the most recent genocide of Tutsis and their collaborators in Rwanda in 1994. Of the politicides since 1945, only Rwanda and Bosnia are clear examples of "ethnic war."

We cannot provide a theory of politicides because so many contain idiosyncratic sources and personalities. It is difficult to imagine a Holocaust had Hitler not lived. In contrast, the genocide in Rwanda was a broadly based and broadly organized enterprise. The killings under the Great Proletarian Cultural Revolution were committed by thousands, perhaps millions, of spontaneous groups, with no legal sanction. Idi Amin's murders were as whimsical as those of Genghis Khan or Emperor Shaka, while in Indonesia in 1965–6 an attempted coup d'etat unleashed massive killings unofficially sanctioned by the military, but perpetrated by thousands of citizens who took the occasion to settle private scores. There seems to be no particular trajectory or set of political, economic, or social conditions that can predict politicides. The problems of weak states and kleptocracies that give rise to armed resistance, secession, and civil wars are easier to understand and predict.

The new mediaevalism

Since the American and French revolutions, Western publics, philosophers, and politicians have thought of the state and political legitimacy in terms of an implicit contract in which citizens agree to tax extractions in exchange for government services. Popular sovereignty is the doctrine which vests governors with the "right to rule" over a fixed population, on the basis of consent. In this conception of governance, the state is a massive service agency. If it does not provide the services which are paid for by citizens, the people have a presumptive right to change both the type of government and its personnel.

In some areas of the world, conceptions of government and the state are different. We have already mentioned the problems of kleptocracies, where the state apparatus is used as a medium for personal enrichment and dynastic ambitions. In the case of very weak and collapsing states, we are now seeing a new phenomenon: the state as a private enterprise. Governance is founded not upon traditional authority, consent, and the provision of services – however imaginary or inadequate – but on a ruler's ability to manipulate access to resources, to create business connections with foreign corporations, and to organize mercenary forces to maintain power. The state in terms of a realm of *public* authority has in fact collapsed, to be replaced by networks of private business arrangements and personal loyalties. This type of rule is in direct conflict with the welfare of the state's population.

Recent examples include Liberia and Sierra Leone. Both states collapsed into civil war and the destruction of all central authority – Liberia in 1990, and Sierra Leone in 1992. Both countries had been typified by the existence of rule based on local strongmen. Both faced severe economic crisis as the result of the end of the Cold War, when the influx of foreign aid and other payments drastically declined. Both saw the emergence of private armies that protected and advanced the economic interests of strongmen. There were differences in the two countries, but the overall structure of power and authority in each has a distinctly mediaeval character: rule for personal interest; authority that is fragmented and localized; private armies and mercenaries. Only the sources of funding are modern. In mediaeval Europe, status and wealth derived from patrimony and serfdom. In contemporary neo-mediaeval states, there is no claim of a right to rule based on some principle such as heredity, military leadership, or popular sovereignty. Local warlords simply convert the territories they control into economic enterprises, based on access to resources, transborder smuggling of consumer products, and gun-running. The money they earn through selling resource assets such as minerals, rubber, and timber to foreign firms is not used to deliver services to the population, but rather to hire soldiers and foreign mercenaries such as Gurkha Security Guards, Ltd, and the South African-based Executive Outcomes, to protect their assets. From 1990 to 1993, Charles Taylor, the Liberian warlord who rules something called "Taylorville" – partly Liberian, but slopping over into neighboring countries – earned about $450 million annually from commercial operations in mining, logging, and agricultural exports. Aside from purchasing mercenaries, he also used the funds to distribute economic opportunities as patronage to build political alliances (Reno 1996: 10). There is no role, here, for citizens, and no implicit contract which exchanges tax extractions for public services. To the extent that there is something remotely called a "state," it is essentially a private enterprise that doles out some largesse for reasons of public relations. The state-as-enterprise is closely connected with foreign organizations, both commercial and humanitarian. Foreign firms are eager to purchase access to resources at bargain prices, and NGOs can be manipulated to obtain "aid" and other services which the personal ruler has no interest in providing. The state has become a giant firm, accountable to no one except local clients and foreign share-holders.

The new mediaevalism is demonstrated most dramatically in the nature of armed conflict in these states. War has become de-institutionalized in the sense of central control, rules, regulations, etiquette, and armaments. Armies are rag-tag groups frequently made up of teenagers paid in drugs, or not paid at all. In the absence of authority and discipline, but quite in keeping with the interests of warlords, "soldiers" discover opportunities for private enterprises of their own. They can extort food from farmers, set up roadblocks – a ubiquitous feature of the African landscape – from which they take "tolls" from passersby, including commercial vehicles, and engage in looting when no one is looking. This is the "Kalashnikov Lifestyle," that elevates kids and young men to the top of the local economic pyramid and provides a permanent incentive to engage in war (Reno 1996: 10).

From Montreal, New York, Paris, or Vancouver, this may all look like chaos. It is chaotic if our basis of judgment is how a modern state *should* function. But in some parts of Africa and Central Asia, there is a kind of pre-state politics, where war, insecurity, and predation are normal, and where law, regularized economic activity, and government services are scarce commodities. State frontiers, permanent populations, and rule based on consent are relatively meaningless in these contexts. They are part of our mental maps, but those maps do not apply in these regions.

The conditions of the new mediaevalism reflect fundamental weaknesses of social organization and state capacity. Such weakness cannot serve as a foundation for challenges to world order. The contemporary world order, defined in terms of the fundamental norms and institutions of international relations, is strong, well articulated, and developing toward universality. That order cannot be challenged by rag-tag groups of African teenagers, by minuscule mercenary armies, or by bankrupted national treasuries. Rogue states pose problems of a different type and magnitude, as Paul's chapter indicates, but there is little evidence that they have become role models for the vast majority of countries in South America, Asia, the Middle East, or Africa. Chaos may come to particular societies as a result of the incompatibilities between peoples and states, population growth and available resources, or as a consequence of inept rule, but the images of transnational or civilizational mega-wars, of "coming anarchy" throughout the Third World and post-socialist societies, reflect old imperial mental habits. They do not belong in the domain of evidence-based analysis.

Given the unique sources and character of violence in some areas of the world, significant policy and ethical problems nevertheless arise. Krauthamer's prescriptions are not likely to find much favor because they are based on limited or faulty assumptions and evidence and because there is no domestic constituency in Europe or North America to support the type of policing operations implied in the idea of the South as a threat. A more likely response, given international reactions to Rwanda, Zaire, Liberia, and Sierra Leone, is to pass on conflict-management responsibilities to NGOs, smaller countries, or even to private security enterprises. Another possibility is to create *cordons sanitaires* around the areas of violence so that migrations, disease, and other consequences can be contained within the affected areas. There is not likely to be much enthusiasm for such policies, but at least the implications of neo-imperialism and paternalism implied in foreign military interventions would be avoided.

No one can predict the incidence of politicides, state collapse, or the continuation of existing kleptocracies, although there are certainly many early warning signals for the latter two syndromes. My bet, however, is that for most states in the Third World and for some in the former socialist countries, state strength, legitimacy, and coherence are on trajectories of improvement. The most difficult years, those following the collapse of the Soviet Union, are probably behind us. They were characterized by considerable turmoil and, in the case of Yugoslavia, by two particularly brutal wars. There was not, however, a kind of chaos or anarchy commonly predicted in the early 1990s, and there is even less ground today for thinking that such predictions will come true. It is now time to put in the closet our imperial-era mental constructs and to begin looking at the Third World not as a zone of chaos or of the exotic, but as an area as complex and multi-faceted as the rest of the world, and one in which local problems, driven by local dynamics, prevail.

World order conceived as the set of essential rules and norms that govern most international relationships is not threatened by the types of domestic disorders described above. The vast majority of states in what was called the "peripheries" have strongly supported Westphalian norms, and with a few possible exceptions such as Iran, there are no serious challengers to those norms existing today. But if we conceive of order as the absence of serious conflict and a high range of predictability in bilateral and multilateral relationships, then there are causes for concern. Humanitarian emergencies, state collapse, and secessionist movements are almost common phenomena in our era and are not likely to disappear in the foreseeable future. Many of the chapters in this volume are concerned with these issues, but successful palliatives are rare. Power balancing does not seem to be a particularly relevant strategy in an era when most threats are domestic rather than international. American leadership and commitments of armed strength are not readily available for conflicts in which direct American stakes are not involved. As indicated in the Rwanda, Liberia, Sierra Leone, and other recent episodes of domestic turmoil, American policy responses have been characterized more by benign neglect than compelling action. The analyses of other countries in this volume do not point toward significant involvements either. Japan took part in its first peacekeeping operation in Cambodia, but judging by the strident debates that enterprise generated in the country, there is not much prospect of Japanese leadership in future operations of this sort. India and China appear to be preoccupied with problems in their immediate neighborhoods, and their suspicion of peacekeeping operations as essentially post-colonial ventures suggests that they will continue to be followers at best.

Some countries face profound structural problems that generate internal conflict and violence. Imperial or Cold War-type analyses, or facile generalizations such as "ancient ethnic hatreds" do not help serious diagnostic efforts. Nor do they help in fashioning prescriptions. Sometimes facile solutions only compound the problems, as many learned in Somalia, but there are several strategies and steps that may at least help prevent the worst types of conflicts. The list below is only suggestive.

- early warning systems, which already exist, but which are not adequately utilized by members of the United Nations in a preventive sense;
- diplomatic pressures on governments that exclude significant communities from the political process or political and economic resources;
- the manipulation of trade and aid policies as leverage against states that practice systematic abuses of human rights;
- the promise of non-recognition of armed secessionist movements, unless those movements are essentially based on self-defense against predatory governments;
- heavier emphasis on political development (including civil society) foreign aid;
- less use of plebiscites and referenda in communally divided societies, and more emphasis on development of civil liberties, independent judiciaries, free press, and the like.

These and other palliatives are likely to succeed only if there are proper diagnoses of the sources of conflict and violence in weak states. To date, the diagnoses have been fundamentally conditioned by imperial and Cold War conceptual and perceptual habits. Many of these are flawed and inadequate and may thus help to exacerbate problems. Western policy failures such as Angola, Somalia, Nicaragua, and Rwanda had their roots in faulty analyses, and those can often be attributed to outmoded mental constructs and concepts. Much of the post-Cold War literature on world order suffers from similar limitations. The analysis above suggests that there are few if any threats to world order that emanate from the areas formerly known as the Third World. That vast area is comprised of many different varieties of states. Some have made a reasonably successful transition from colonialism (non-states) to strong statehood and economic growth. A few others are the likely scenes of internal violence, not usually occasioned by "ancient ethnic hatreds," but rather by identifiable government practices. Some also face extreme population pressures which outstrip governments' capacities to provide services and resources. But a large majority are slowly moving in an upward trajectory of increasing democratization and reasonable economic growth, hopeful signs that they will not continue to be sources of instability. Whatever the prospects, however, the world order of the first part of the twenty-first century is not likely to diverge significantly from its Westphalian roots. The fundamental norms of the international system remain intact, and indeed are likely to grow in strength as formerly weak states begin to see the benefits of substantive as well as theoretical sovereignty.

NOTES

1 Some of the ideas developed here were expressed in Holsti (1997).
2 The United Nations refused to classify conflicts of national liberation as wars. They were deemed legitimate acts of emancipation against oppression and had nothing to do with "threats to peace, breaches of the peace, or acts of aggression" as defined in chapter 7 of the UN Charter.
3 Pol Pot bears resemblance in terms of domestic politics, but not foreign policy.

REFERENCES

Acharya, Amitav 1998, "Beyond Anarchy: Third World Instability and International Order After the Cold War," in International Theory and War in the Third World, Stephanie Neuman (ed.), New York: St. Martin's Press, pp. 159–211.
Ahmed, Ishtiaq 1996, State, Nation, and Ethnicity in Contemporary South Asia, London: Frances Pinter.
Anderson, Benedict 1983, Imagined Communities, London: Verso.
Armstrong, David 1993, Revolution and World Order, Oxford: Clarendon Press.
Bull, Hedley 1977, The Anarchical Society, London: Macmillan.
Escobar, Arturo 1995, Encountering Development, Princeton: Princeton University Press.
Fukuyama, Francis 1989, "The End of History?" The National Interest 16: 3–18.
Goldgeier, James and McFaul, Michael 1992, "A Tale of Two Worlds: Core and Periphery in the Post-Cold War Era," International Organization 46: 467–92.
Gros, Jean-Germain 1996, "Towards a Taxonomy of Failed States in the New World Order: Decaying Somalia, Liberia, Rwanda, and Haiti," Third World Quarterly 17: 455–71.
Hardin, Russell 1995, One for All: The Logic of Group Conflict, Princeton: Princeton University Press.
Hoffmann, Stanley 1991, "Watch out for a New World Disorder," International Herald Tribune, February 26, 6.

Holsti, Kalevi J. 1967, *International Politics: A Framework for Analysis*, Englewood Cliffs, NJ: Prentice-Hall.

1994, "The Post-Cold War Settlement in Comparative Perspective," in *Discord and Collaboration in a New Europe*, Douglas T. Stuart and Stephen F. Szabo (eds.), Washington, DC: The Foreign Policy Institute, School of Advanced International Studies, Johns Hopkins University, pp. 37–70.

1996, *The State, War, and the State of War*, Cambridge: Cambridge University Press.

1997, "Legacies of Imperialism and Conflict in the World's Periphery," in *Korea in the 21st Century*, Eun Ho Lee (ed.), Chongju, Korea: Chongju University Press, pp. 15–50.

Hurd, Ian 1997, "After Anarchy: Legitimacy, Authority, and Sovereignty in International Politics," paper delivered at the Annual Meeting of the International Studies Association, Toronto, Canada, March 18–21.

Jackson, Robert H. 1990, *Quasi-States: Sovereignty, International Relations and the Third World*, Cambridge: Cambridge University Press.

Jackson, Robert H. and Zacher, Mark 1997, "The Territorial Covenant: International Society and the Stabilization of Boundaries," Vancouver, Canada: Institute of International Relations, University of British Columbia, Working Paper No. 15.

Kaplan, Robert D. 1994, "The Coming Anarchy," *The Atlantic Monthly* 273: 44–76.

1996, *The Ends of the Earth: A Journey at the Dawn of the 21st Century*, New York: Random House.

Krauthamer, Charles 1990/1, "The Unipolar Moment," *Foreign Affairs* 70: 23–33.

Neitschmann, Bernard 1994, "The Fourth World: Nations versus States," in *Reordering the World: Geopolitical Perspectives on the 21st Century*, George J. Demko and William B. Woods (eds.), Boulder, CO: Westview, pp. 225–42.

Reno, William 1996, "Humanitarian Emergencies and Warlord Politics in Liberia and Sierra Leone," paper delivered at the United Nations University/World Institute for Development Economics Research conference on The Political Economy of Humanitarian Emergencies, Helsinki, Finland, October 6–8.

Rummel, Rudolph J. 1994, *Death by Government*, New Brunswick, NJ: Transaction Books.

Sahlins, Peter 1998, "State Formation and National Identity in the Catalan Borderlands During the Eighteenth and Nineteenth Centuries," in *Border Identities*, Thomas M. Wilson and Hastings Donnan (eds.), Cambridge: Cambridge University Press, pp. 31–61.

Schoeberlein-Engel, John 1994, "Conflict in Tajikistan and Central Asia: The Myth of Ethnic Animosity," *Harvard Middle Eastern and Islamic Review* 1: 1–55.

Singer, Max and Wildavsky, Aaron 1993, *The Real World Order: Zones of Peace/Zones of Turmoil*, Chatham, NJ: Chatham House Publishers.

SIPRI Yearbook 1993: World Armaments and Disarmament, Oxford: Oxford University Press.

Wallensteen, Peter and Sollenberg, Margareta 1996, "The End of International War? Armed Conflict 1989–95," *Journal of Peace Research* 33 (2): 353–70.

Wan, Marilyn A. 1992, "Naturalized Seeing/Colonial Vision: Interrogating the Display of Races in Late Nineteenth Century France," MA Thesis, Department of Fine Arts, University of British Columbia.

Zartman, William (ed.) 1995, *Collapsed States*, Boulder, CO: Lynne Rienner.

15   Political religion in the twenty-first century

Peter van der Veer

Introduction

The fall of the Berlin Wall marked the end of the Cold War tripartite division of the world. On the ruins of the Berlin Wall old ideas of civilization with strategic consequences have reemerged. According to Samuel Huntington (1993: 22), "the great divisions among humankind and the dominating source of conflict will be cultural . . . The fault lines between civilizations will be the battle lines of the future." Huntington took the title of his essay, "The Clash of Civilizations?" from an observation made in an article about Muslim politics by the leading Middle East-expert in the US, Bernard Lewis.[1] It is obvious that for both Huntington and Lewis the essential civilizational border is that between Christianity and Islam, although Huntington takes pains to also delineate fault lines between Orthodox Christianity and Western Christianity as well as to pay some attention to the "Confucian" civilization of China, to Japanese civilization, Hindu civilization and a few others. Islamic civilization is the old enemy of the West from the Crusades onwards and the seemingly unending Israel-Palestine hostilities, the rise of so-called Islamic fundamentalism, as well as the threat by openly anti-Western governments in Iran, Iraq, and Libya made it the appropriate successor of the evil empire of Communism.

The success of Huntington's article and his subsequent book (1996), which develops his argument at greater length, can be explained by the timeliness of a rethinking of America's geopolitical role after the collapse of the Soviet empire by an important theorist of International Relations. It is fascinating to see that the collapse of the Soviet Union has not resulted in a triumphalist mood in the USA, but rather in a gloomy, declinist vision which predicts that in the early decades of the next century the "age of Western dominance" will be over and power will have to be shared increasingly with core states in other civilizations.[2] Regardless of this immediate American context, however, Huntington raises important questions about the role of civilizations and religions in the international order of the twenty-first century which are worth reflecting upon.

Our reflections have to start with the question: what is a civilization? A famous definition has been given by the nineteenth-century anthropologist E. B. Tylor: "culture or civilization, taken in its wide ethnographic sense, is that complex whole which includes knowledge, belief, art, morals, law, custom, and any other capabilities and habits acquired by man as a member of society." In this definition one can find a universalist aspect and a particularist one. The universalist aspect stresses that every human being acquires something called civilization, while the particularist aspect distinguishes different civilizations belonging to different societies. This definition attempts to be neutral, but the concept of "civilization" is in its long history developed to distinguish the civilized from the uncivilized. In the words of Norbert Elias, "this concept expresses the self-consciousness of the West. One could even say: the national consciousness. It sums up everything in which Western society of the last two or three centuries believes itself superior to earlier societies or 'more primitive' contemporary ones. By this term Western society seeks to describe what constitutes its special character and what it is proud of: the level of *its* manners, the development of *its* manners, the development of *its* scientific knowledge or view of the world, and much more" (Elias 1994: 3).

Elias connects the emergence of the concept of "civilization" to the rise of national consciousness in Europe and argues that there are great differences between the English and French use of the word, on the one hand, and the German use of it, on the other. The connection between the rise of the nation-state and the emergence of the concept of civilization is premised on the demise of what Benedict Anderson (1991: 36) has called "the great transcontinental sodalities of Christendom, the Islamic Ummah, and the rest." It is ironic that the term "civilization" as Huntington uses it has only emerged when the social and political significance of civilizations had declined in the process of the making of national states. This makes it immediately clear that the relation between civilization and nation-state is a complex one that Huntington, deliberately but wrongly, ignores.

Huntington does away with the application of the term "civilization" as a universalist Western standard to judge societies, and emphasizes the lack of universal standards and the existence of essential differences between civilizations that have their own normative standards. In his view there cannot be a universal civilization, since the central elements of any civilization, language and religion, do not show any sign of developing into one universal language or one universal religion (Huntington 1996: 57). Huntington also rejects the traditional view of modernization theory that modernization means Westernization (78). He thus chooses the particularistic option in his use of the term "civilization" and ends up with a set of irreducibly different, but modern civilizations which together make up the world order. While Huntington is obviously right in noticing the fatality of linguistic diversity which prevents the emergence of a universal language, he ignores the importance of the nation-state in creating national languages. Civilizational languages like Latin and Sanskrit have been replaced by national languages. Perhaps Arabic can still be seen as an example of a civilizational language, but even there one can discern important national differences in the spoken language. Moreover, Arabic is the language of the Koran, but not by the same token of Muslim civilization, since most Muslims do not command Arabic.

Huntington sees religion as a central defining characteristic of civilizations (47). He correctly notices the failure of secularization in many societies, but he pays no attention to the function of religion in the creation of national cultures. He argues that modernization, in many cases, did not bring the death of religion, but its resurgence (97). The term "resurgence," like the term "revival," however, is problematic, since it suggests the return of something that was on its way out. Especially when the revival is said to be largely caused by the "psychological, emotional, and social traumas of modernization" (100), I feel that we bring the old modernization theory back in through the backdoor. By further arguing that the revival of non-Christian religion is directly related to anti-Westernism Huntington connects his theory of civilizational difference with the widely felt fear of Islamic fundamentalism (100–1).

My main objection to Huntington's argument is that by emphasizing civilizations at the expense of nation-states he gives no interpretation of why and how the role of nation-states in international politics will change, and that he ignores the connection between religion and nationalism. It is the analysis of this connection which leads to a better understanding of so-called fundamentalism and the resurgence of religion. In the next section of this chapter I will examine the role of religion in the development of national cultures. In the third section I will look at the possible decline of nation-states as the result of globalization and at the role of transnational religion in this. Finally, I will come back to Huntington's theory of the clash of civilizations in my conclusion.

Religion and the nation-state

The emergence of the European nation-state is commonly seen to depend on three connected processes of centralization: "the emergence of supra-local identities and cultures (the 'nation'); the rise of powerful and authoritative institutions within the public domain (the 'state'), and the development of particular ways of organizing production and consump-tion (the 'economy')" (Grillo 1980: 1). According to Ernest Gellner's influential theory of nationalism, national culture has by definition to be secular, since economic and cognitive growth are only possible when the absolutist claims of the earlier agrarian (namely, preindustrial) age are replaced by open scientific inquiry (Gellner 1983: 77, 142). For Gellner the historical process is clear both in Europe and in the rest of the world: a society can only develop into a modern nation-state when it becomes secular. In a later book he qualifies his point of view by arguing that Islam defies the secularization thesis (Gellner 1992: 18). I would suggest, how-ever, that Christianity itself defies the thesis in the history of Western Europe and the United States, the empirical core of secularization theory.

Let us take Britain and Holland as two prime examples of the results of the Protestant reformation and of modern nation-states, as they emerged in nineteenth-century Europe. It should be evident that the social signifi-cance of religion increased during the industrial and political transfor-mation these societies went through in the nineteenth century (Wolffe 1994; van Rooden 1996). It is precisely the mobilization of large groups of the population for the political goals of democracy which makes religion such a useful resource. The evangelical movement in the nineteenth century has played a crucial role in the transformation of populations into a modern public, necessary for the modern nation. As I have argued elsewhere, religion has been central to the development of modern institu-tions, such as democracy, in many Western societies (van der Veer 1997).

The secularization of British and Dutch societies did not take place in the ninteenth century as a result of the industrial revolution or the rise of the modern nation-state, but, for a host of specific historical reasons, only in the twentieth century and then in periods so different from each other that it defies universal explanation by a secularization thesis. Britain secularized gradually from the early decades of the twentieth century despite a brief religious resurgence during the Second World War, while Holland only secularized in the 1960s. It should be observed in passing that the USA, a major modern nation-state, offers a different picture altogether, in which secularization is very uneven and religion continues to have a strong public presence even today. The continuing strength of American Christianity appears to be largely the effect of the aggressive recruitment patterns of religious organizations which have not (as yet) been as successful in Western Europe.

In a recent book Jose Casanova (1994) has tried to save the seculariz-ation thesis in a modified form, despite its failure to explain the historical developments outlined above. He points out that there are three elements in the secularization thesis which have been taken to be essential to the development of modernity. First of all, there is the increasing separation of religion from politics, economy, science. Secondly, there is the privatization of religion within its own sphere. Thirdly, there is the declining social significance of religious belief, commitment, and institutions. Casanova argues that only the first and the third element are crucial to modernity, while the element of privatization is not. In a number of case studies of Western secular societies he shows that public and political manifestations of religion do occur without threatening the basic requirements of modern society, including democratic government. He argues, convincingly, that in some cases the work of modernization is done by religious forces rather than by secular ones.

A major element in Casanova's theory, then, is to distinguish, as it were, between "good" and "bad" religions. Good religions are those that further the construction of civil society and bad religions are those that try to undermine it. Though this is not so easy as it seems. Casanova's case material is all about Western Christianity and it might well be possible (and even likely) that different religious traditions have different views of what "civil society" entails, what public debate amounts to, and certainly what role religious arguments should play in public debate (cf. Asad forthcoming). Casanova seems to disregard the possibility that people who argue from non-Christian religious standpoints might have very different views about authority, free debate, and civil society than those who argue from an Enlightenment tradition of secularism. He also seems to disallow the possibility that state-society relations are very different in different parts of the world and that the public sphere is accordingly also different.

It is precisely at this point that one should recognize that theories of secularization, modified or not, only deal with Christianity in the West, that is Western Europe and the United States of America. Secularization theory then is a particular argument about the changing place of Christianity in modern Western society and not about religion as such. It is hardly applicable to the history of Islam, Hinduism, Buddhism, and most other religions. In the latter cases the empirical question about the social significance of religion in terms of church attendance and membership cannot even be raised, since there are no churches. The organization of religion, the place of religion in society, the patterns of recruitment, and indeed the religious traditions are so different that not only secularization theory itself, but also the empirical and theoretical problems which are derived from it in the context of Western Christianity become hard to address. The question, therefore, is not whether Muslim or Hindu or Buddhist societies secularize, but what the role of religion actually is, how it is organized, what it supports, and what it opposes. Since most societies in the world have adopted the nation form, it is important to see how religion shapes the national cultures involved and vice versa. It should be clear that as much as in the European and American case, religion and politics belong together in non-Western societies. In the latter case religious politics is often condemned as "fundamentalism."

The fact that non-Christian religions tend to have a public role is not what disturbs Western observers, since they are more or less aware of that role in their own societies. It is the unfamiliar nature of non-Christian religious arguments in the public sphere, especially about gender-related issues and human rights, the violence involved in some of the disputes, and the threat they seem to pose to secularists and the secular state which are disturbing. The general term used for "bad" religious politics is "fundamentalism."

The term "fundamentalism" was first used in the United States in 1920 to designate a broad Protestant movement in defense of biblical literalism. Especially after the Iranian revolution of 1979, however, it has gained wide currency among journalists and politicians to designate a wide variety of religious movements in the world. To say that this broad application of the word "fundamentalism" is a journalistic invention does not weaken or depoliticize it. It is a crucial term not only in the media coverage of world politics, but also in the creation of world politics itself. A powerful language or discourse is not something one can choose to accept or reject; it can be critiqued and deconstructed, but that will not make it go away.

The greatest enemies of "the open society," for whom the language of utter rejection and condemnation is used, are located not in the West, but in the Rest. If they are found in the West they are from the Rest. Mostly, they are "fanatic Muslims" which threaten the status quo in the Middle East, where Western industrial societies have vital interests in the production of oil. Not all Muslim fundamentalists are enemies, though. Saudi Arabia, Kuwait, and Pakistan, but also the militant groups in Afghanistan fighting Soviet imperialism are often exempted from the strong, condemning tone used for Sudan and Iran as well as for the militant groups fighting the state in Egypt, Algeria, and Palestine. A crucial characteristic of "fundamentalism" is therefore that it is anti-Western. Another is that it is against the secular state. These two characteristics are often conflated in the notion that these are movements which see the secular state as an alien, Western phenomenon. The "fanatic muslim" serves as a template to talk about other fundamentalists, such as the Sikh Khalistanis and Hindu nationalists in India.

Since the term "fundamentalism" is in common usage to describe religio-political movements, a clear definition should be given, so that the term can be used in social theory. A recent endeavor to give such a definition and develop a theory of the phenomenon has been made by Martin Riesebrodt (1994), a Chicago-based sociologist who compares the emergence of modern fundamentalism in the United States and Iran. Riesebrodt argues that fundamentalism is a social phenomenon that occurs during rapid social change, is marked by a profound experience of crisis, and tries to overcome that crisis by a revitalization of religion and a search for authenticity. This revitalization is characterized by what he calls a mythical regress to the revealed and realized order – and authenticity is realized in rational fundamentalism by a literalist reading of sacred texts and in "charismatic" fundamentalism by the experience of a gift of grace. Further, he argues that fundamentalism implies a rejection of the world, but that can take the form of either fleeing the world or mastering the world by forming a political party or religious movement, or secret society. Riesebrodt's central thesis is that fundamentalism refers to "an urban movement directed primarily against the dissolution of personalistic, patriarchal notions of order and social relations and their replacement by depersonalized principles" (9). He asks for attention to the ideology of these movements as well as to the movement's carriers, defined as social units formed in a particular "sociomoral milieu," that is by the coincidence of several structural dimensions.

Riesebrodt's definition and theoretical approach is subtle and fairly typical of the sociological approach to fundamentalism. It is very similar to the guiding ideas behind Chicago's huge, multi-volume Fundamentalism project, under the directorship of Martin Marty and Scott Appleby. This project covers Christian, Jewish, Muslim, Buddhist, and Confucian fundamentalism in a great variety of societies, ranging from the USA to China, and Italy to the Andes. The underlying idea is that fundamentalism is a global phenomenon in so far as it is a response to global processes of social transformation. One could say that it provides sociological support to the journalistic, and geopolitical notion of fundamentalism.

Riesebrodt's theoretical framework, like that of Marty and Appleby, is in fact not very different from modernization theory, focusing on processes like urbanization, industrialization, and secularization. Their opinion seems to be that fundamentalism or politicized religion is a successful defense all over the world against modernity and shows the failure of secularization. Huntington, by and large, accepts this understanding of the "resurgence of religion." As I have argued above, this approach fails to explain religious and secular developments in the West, and is, even in a modified form (as proposed by Casanova), inappropriate for the analysis of such developments in non-Christian societies.

In my view, the understanding of the "bad" politics of fundamentalism depends crucially on an analysis of processes of state formation as the dominant factor affecting the location of religion in society. This is definitely not to say that the state is the determining factor which can explain everything, but rather that we have to examine the historical process in which the relation between state and society gets defined to understand the shifting place of religious institutions and their hold on their constituencies. These processes are different in different parts of the world and we should not expect a one-dimensional, unilinear story of modernity to emerge. What we need is not only an analysis of the transformation of religion in the modern period, but also an analysis of the rise of secular institutions and the role of secularism as a modern ideology in them.

In a number of contemporary, non-Western societies we have to acknowledge not only that religion is a public affair, but also that there is a more-or-less aggressively interventionist secular state, supported by a secularist elite and a secularist army. I am thinking of Islamic societies, such as Turkey, Egypt, Algeria and Pakistan, but also of India, whose population is in majority Hindu. Our analysis of Islamicist and Hindu movements in these societies has to take the role of the secular state into account without adopting the uncritical, normative stance that the secular state is by definition progressive, since it brings secular modernity. The so-called fundamentalist movements can be understood, to an important extent, as responses to secularist interventionism in both the public and the private sphere (van der Veer 1994). This kind of state that was put in place in most cases by colonial powers is directed at the material and moral transformation of entire populations.

The politico-religious movements do not so much defend a traditional society against those interventions, but creatively try to interpret religious tradition so as to come up with alternative models of societal transformation. It is essential to see that these movements are not conservative or reactionary, but aim at a far-going transformation of society. In these societies a struggle between secularist movements and religious movements takes place over the control of the state apparatuses. This is a violent struggle in which often a secularist army is pitched against terrorist groups. It is a violence that tends to upset us more than usual, because these are civil wars in which actors are religiously motivated. Since most of these societies have experienced "the West" in the form of colonial power and because the postcolonial secular state is so much the institutional heir of the colonial state, anti-secularist movements are at the same time often radically anti-Western. Nevertheless, the struggle in which fundamentalist groups engage is by and large internal to specific nation-states despite sporadic terrorist attacks against airliners or office buildings in the West.

An uncritical support of secularists in non-Western societies by Western powers can only support the idea of an unholy alliance between secularists and "the West" and will do much to destabilize the relations between the state and Muslim immigrants in Western societies, especially in Europe. It would be good to take a step back and examine what the struggle between secularists and fundamentalists in these societies is really about and to what extent there are viable alternatives to the Western construction of the public sphere and civil society which these movements try to develop. One of the questions to be asked is what we understand democracy to be, since there can be no doubt that these movements are deeply involved in the democratic revolution in their societies, in which more and more people become involved in the political process. The extent to which the Iranian Revolution of 1979 has furthered democratic participation of the population comes as a surprise only to those who believe that democracy is alien to Islam.

If we look at Muslim politics (or, for that matter, in South Asia at Hindu or Sikh politics) it is striking to what extent religious politics is framed by nationalism. In itself, this is not different from the Western, Christian cases. An important difference, however, does lie in the fact that in the period of the formation of modern nationalism in British India and the Middle East the state was controlled not by compatriots, but by Western, Christian colonizers. In these societies the colonial state adopted often a neutral, secular stance in order not to provoke resistance on religious grounds. The crucial religious and cultural difference between colonizers and colonized, however, profoundly influenced the interpretation of religion and secularism as the basis of anti-colonial independence struggles.

More than in Europe and the USA, secularism became a major ideology, carried by elite groups, rather than a result of the gradual decline of the power of religious organizations or of the radical separation of church and state. Secularism (often combined with socialism), carried forward by leaders such as Nehru and Nasser, continued to be an elitist ideology in societies which were characterized by strong religious commitments. Since both the independence struggle and the postcolonial building of nations depended on mass politics the mobilization of religion could never be avoided. What we see therefore in many societies in Asia and the Middle East is a religious nationalism which confronts a secular nationalism. To speak of a religious resurgence in the last few decades is therefore a misnomer, since religious politics have never been removed from either independence movements or postcolonial national politics.

To acknowledge the direct linkage between nationalism and religion immediately problematizes Huntington's civilizational essentialism.

There are a great number of nation-states in the world which have conflicting interests. The great geopolitical conflicts in this century, the First and Second World Wars, have been largely between co-religionists, belonging to different nation-states. The violent conflicts in the Muslim world are also between co-religionists: Iraq against Iran, Iraq against Kuwait, Pakistan against Bangladesh. Moreover, these conflicts were based upon national interest, not upon religious difference. If the connection between nationalism, the nation-state, and religion is as strong as I have argued here, the question arises to what extent it would be affected by a supposed decline of the nation-state due to contemporary processes of globalization. I want to address that question in the next section.

Religion and globalization

Nation-states operate in a global context or, as Balibar (1990) puts it, in a world system of nation-states. Despite all the arguments in liberal economic theory about Free Trade, anti-Protectionism and the like, modern economies are national economies within a capitalist world system. Similarly, nation-states interact in transnational bodies of world politics, such as the United Nations. In that sense, nation-states have always been globalized, or, perhaps more precisely, have existed in dialectical relation with global processes. This conventional wisdom has, over the last decade, been challenged by a growing literature on globalization and transnational processes. In this literature attention is given to the speed with which production and consumption is globalized, and with which transnational migration is on the increase. According to Roger Rouse (1995), there has been a shift from *multinational corporations* which integrate more-or-less self-contained production and marketing facilities in a number of different national sites to *transnational corporations* that take a single production process and redistribute it across sites in different areas of the world. The latter is only possible thanks to a huge improvement of communication technologies which has taken place over the last decade. Similarly migrants increasingly do not move from one nation-state to another, but maintain more and more complex networks of linkages between sites. They live, so to say, in many places more or less simultaneously. According to a number of theorists of globalization and transnationalism, these phenomena indicate a crisis of "the national" and force nation-states to adapt to "the transnational" (Appadurai 1996; Hannerz 1996). One way of interpreting Huntington's move to the civilizational level is precisely to relate it to the perceived crisis of the nation-state.

It is hard to deny that we witness in our times a significant increase in the speed and frequency with which people, goods and information move across the boundaries of states. The question is to what extent and in what direction that fact transforms or replaces people's identification with their national culture. If 95 percent of the population increase will be in the poorest regions of the world, one does not have to be a prophet of doom like the journalist Robert Kaplan (1996) to predict that migration to the rich regions of the world has only just begun. Migration, however, may reinforce nationalism rather than weaken it.

According to Eric Hobsbawm (1987), mass emigration played an important role in the emergence of the later phase of European nationalism. The half-century before 1914 witnessed the greatest international migration in history. This migration produced nationalism in two ways. It created xenophobia among the people already well established, both the middle and working classes, in the countries of immigration. This led to forms of nationalism that emphasized the "defense of the nation" against the threatening immigrant. We can see something similar happening today in Western Europe and the USA. The imposition, through xenophobia, of a negative identity certainly also enhanced nationalist sentiment among migrants. The element of romanticization that is present in every nationalism is even stronger among nostalgic migrants, who often form a very rosy picture of the country they have left. Benedict Anderson (1992) refers to an aphorism of Lord Acton that "exile is the nursery of nationality" to emphasize the political importance of migrants in the formation of what he calls "long-distance nationalism." The example Hobsbawm gives is that of Thomas Masaryk signing an agreement in Pittsburgh to form a state uniting Czechs and Slovaks, since Slovak nationalism was more alive in Pennsylvania than in Slovakia. The transformation Anderson sees from the exile nationalism of the late nineteenth, early twentieth century to the transnationalism of today is that migrants do not return to their countries of origin to participate in nationalist struggles, but support them from abroad. The transnational networks established thanks to the new possibilities of communication are put to the use of nationalist causes.

What role does religion play in the dialectic between national and transnational? World religions, by their very nature, of course transcend national boundaries. It is true of Christianity, Islam, Buddhism, and to a lesser extent, Hinduism that they have a message for mankind. They have, traditionally, been organized in a globalizing fashion to further worldwide expansion or, to put it in religious terms, missionization. Nevertheless, as I have argued in the previous section, religion has been used in a great many cases to build national cultures. The tension between the national and the transnational is therefore not at all novel for religions.

What can be argued, however, is that the transnational element in religion gets new possibilities thanks to the growth of transnational migration. In fact, we do see the flourishing of large transnational religious movements, such as Pentecostalism in Christianity, the Tablighi Jama – at in Islam, and the Vishwa Hindu Parishad in Hinduism. Interestingly, it is the Muslim movement which is, contrary to what Westerners would expect, avowedly apolitical and not aligned to nationalist politics. Worldly affairs do not matter directly for it. Its view is that the world will improve when every Muslim simply tries to be a good Muslim by fulfilling one's duties. However, as I have argued elsewhere (van der Veer 1994), this stance does have political consequences. For migrants, its message is a perfect defense against assimilation. In that sense the movement may come up strongly against the policies of some states. Despite the ubiquitous discourse on the universal community of Islam, the "umma," there is a clear tendency of localization, of becoming involved in the politics of the nation-state in which one lives (Eickelman and Piscatori 1996: 149– 50).

The Vishwa Hindu Parishad, on the contrary, has explicit political aims and is deeply involved in Hindu nationalism. It is directly allied to the Hindu nationalist party, the Bharatiya Janata Party (Indian People's Party). It is highly successful among Hindu migrants in the USA, the Caribbean, Britain, and South Africa or, better, wherever one finds Hindu communities in the diaspora. The Pentecostalist movements are often deeply involved in the politics of national culture in the societies in which they are active. There is no evidence that processes of globalization and transnationalism impair the contribution of religion to the various nationalisms in the world.

Conclusion

In Huntington's view, future conflicts in the world will be between civilizations. The Gulf War which took place just before the publication of Huntington's *Foreign Affairs* article could be taken as an example of such a civilizational war between the Muslim civilization and the Western (Christian) civilization. On close examination, however, it immediately shows the pitfalls of a civilizational interpretation of world order. In fact, the Gulf War completely divided both the Arab world and the Muslim world. Islamic arguments were used to support Iraq and they were used to support Kuwait and Saudi Arabia. For many Muslims it was a sorry sight to see the secularist Saddam Hussein trying to use Islam for his purposes. Only when there was a massive build-up of US troops in Saudi Arabia did popular sentiment in the Muslim world revert to its standard anti-

Americanism, which has as much to do with America's role in Israel as with anything else, and make Hussein into an unlikely Muslim hero standing up against American hegemony (Esposito 1992: 194–5). Governments, however, such as those of Morocco, Turkey, and Egypt, continued to support the Western alliance. It is not that Islamic issues did not play a role in the Gulf War, but that neither the causes of the war nor its unfolding can be explained by them.

If the civilizational approach is so weak in explaining conflicts of the recent past, why did Huntington's theory receive so much attention? It is perhaps illuminating to examine the use that has been made of civilizational ideas, such as those of Huntington, in Europe. Huntington writes about the West in Atlantic terms, joining the US and Western Europe, but it is in Europe and especially in the Mediterranean region where the civilizational borders between Islam and Christianity are drawn.

When the Wall fell the discussion about the future of Germany was held between "Wessies" and "Ossies," forgetting – as usual – that Berlin, the new capital of unified Germany, is the third largest Turkish city in the world after Ankara and Istanbul. What indeed is the place of Turkey and that of Turkish citizens who reside in Western Europe? Is the border between Muslim Turkey and Christian Greece the significant one for a unified Europe and is this border internally reproduced as a boundary between secular Christian citizens and religiously minded Muslim residents? An affirmative answer to this question seems to be the implicit message of a recent summit of European Christian-Democrats under the leadership of the German Chancellor, Helmut Kohl. These Christian politicians want to deny Turkey membership of Europe since it does not belong to the Christian civilization.

We have here the long-standing competition and enmity between Christian Europe and the Ottoman Empire, of which the Bosnian War, the Bulgarian troubles, and the tense relation between Greece and Turkey are the historical offshoots. It is fair, however, to remind oneself of the fact that there has not been an Islamic military threat to Europe since the defeat of the Ottomans at the gates of Vienna in 1683. On the contrary, European powers have colonized large parts of the Ottoman Empire in the nineteenth century. The struggle has been won by the Western powers and it has led to the dismantling of the Ottoman Empire and the formation of a modern, secular nation-state Turkey. Nevertheless, the old question of the colonial period emerges again, but now in the metropoles of the former colonizing nations. Are people of other race, other religion capable of reaching the endpoint of civilizational evolution, European modernity? To what extent can Muslims become modern; to what extent can they be equal to modern Christians? What we have here is a tension between the universal principles of the Enlightenment and their rootedness in Christian civilization. The Christian-Democrats want to put the struggle between secularist and fundamentalist Muslims in Turkey outside Europe without engaging the fact that that struggle also takes place within its own global cities.

The relation of Turkey to the Western world is a question that can also be raised in Atlantic terms. Turkey is part of NATO, and in 1995 NATO's Secretary-General Willy Claes declared that Islamic fundamentalism was the enemy that had succeeded communism and that NATO was entering strategic alliances with cooperative, secular governments in North Africa and the Middle East to stem the tide of this new danger to democracy. In such a view, different from the current Christian-Democratic one, there is a clear acknowledgment of the fact that secularists in Turkey (backed up by the army) have to be supported in their choice for secular values. But NATO chose to act exactly as Islamicists argue that the West does, by propping up so-called secular governments (often with a reputation for corruption) against which large groups in the population revolt. A narrow definition of secular versus religious politics, which ignores a large part of Western Europe's political history, prevents Europe from making a sharp analysis of what is going on in the Mediterranean area. Every support of corrupt secularism only fuels the Islamicist struggle. One often forgets that when one speaks about Europe and the Mediterranean area one is dealing with a postcolonial situation. The dirty war in Algeria today was preceded by a dirty war with France in the fifties. Nobody can be surprised about Algerian bombs exploding in the Parisian metro, just as nobody can be surprised about Irish bombs exploding in the London subway. These wars do not respect the borders of nation-states or the civilizational borders between Europe and the Rest, since these borders have never been respected before in the colonial period.

Western Europe is also an interesting case for examining the effects of transnational migration and globalization. In marked contrast to the US, Western European nation-states do not define themselves in terms of immigration. On the other hand they have started upon a long process of European unification to facilitate the flow of goods, persons, and money across their borders. While the internal borders of Western Europe become less important, Europe's external borders gain an importance, especially with regions from which Europe fears large-scale immigration.

The end of the colonial era has brought large groups from the former empires into the metropole. By and large, they went to their "own" metropoles, reminding those who were already there that their countries had indeed been metropoles of larger entities. These were citizens settling in the metropolitan part of the former empires. Besides that, Western Europe attracted labor migrants from the Mediterranean area. As long as these were Southern Europeans, Spanish, or Italians, there was little objection in the host societies, but Turkish and Maghrebian immigrant laborers became much more easily the subject of political debate. In the 1960s postcolonial and labor migration became politicized and in the 1970s Europe witnessed a whole range of measures restricting immigration and access to citizenship.

Migration from Islamic countries is one of the most charged political issues in Western Europe. Despite all the political rhetoric in, especially, France and Germany, the presence of large groups of Muslims, as of large groups of Jews in an earlier period, is a fact that will continue to disrupt any civilizational illusions one might have about the Christian West and the non-Christian Rest. The struggle is really for the acceptance of the stranger without desiring to obliterate him either by assimilation or by multiculturalism. There are differences in the world and, as Montaigne observed, "each calls that Barbarism what is not his own practice." To live with each other's barbarism, without violence, in one and the same multicultural society is the challenge of the twenty-first century.

Although the issue of multiculturalism is not straightforwardly examined in Huntington's book, it does seem to motivate his entire project. As he puts it at the end of his book in the following, revealing passage: "Some Americans have promoted multiculturalism at home; some have promoted universalism abroad; and some have done both. Multiculturalism at home threatens the United States and the West, universalism abroad threatens the West and the World. Both deny the uniqueness of Western culture. The global monoculturalists want to make the world like America. The domestic multiculturalists want to make America like the world. A multicultural America is impossible because a non-Western America is not American. A multicultural world is unavoidable because global empire is impossible. The preservation of the United States and the West requires the renewal of Western identity. The security of the world requires acceptance of global multiculturality" (Huntington 1996: 318). This ideological message deals with a real issue, faced not only by the United States, but also by a great number of other societies, namely multiculturalism versus cultural assimilation.[3] This issue cannot be solved, however, by projecting multiculturalism out of domestic politics onto the stage of world politics.

NOTES

1 In 1990 Bernard Lewis had given a talk, entitled "Islamic Fundamentalism," as the Jefferson Lecture, the highest honor accorded by the US government to a scholar for achievement in the humanities. A revised version was published under the title "The Roots of Muslim Rage" in the *Atlantic Monthly* 226 (September 3, 1990): 47–54. John Esposito (1992: 173, 174) has this to say about the article: "It reinforces stereotypes of Islamic revivalism and of Muslims and presdisposes the reader to view the relationship of Islam to the West in terms of rage, violence, hatred, and irrationality . . . The title, 'Roots of Muslim Rage,' sets the tone and expectation. Yet would we tolerate similar generalizations in analyzing and explaining Western activities and motives? How often do we see articles that speak of Christian rage or Jewish rage?"

2 The most successful spokesman of this declinist vision in the US is Paul Kennedy (1993).

3 Huntington's theory is therefore successful not only in the US and Western Europe, but, as my student Margaret Sleeboom informs me, also among intellectuals, especially Nakasone's "new nationalists", in Japan.

REFERENCES

Anderson, Benedict 1991, *Imagined Communities*, London: Verso.

1992, *Long-Distance Nationalism*, Amsterdam: The Wertheim Lecture.

Appadurai, Arjun 1996, *Modernity at Large*, Minneapolis: University of Minnesota Press.

Asad, Talal forthcoming, "Religion, Nation-State, Secularism: Some Comments," in *The Religious Morality of the Nation State*, Peter van der Veer and Hartmut Lehmann (eds.), Princeton: Princeton University Press.

Balibar, Etienne 1990 "The Nation Form: History and Ideology," *Review* 13: 329–61.

Casanova, Jose 1994, *Public Religions in the Modern World*, Chicago: University of Chicago Press.

Eickelman, Dale and Piscatori, James 1996, *Muslim Politics*, Princeton: Princeton University Press.

Elias, Norbert 1994, *The Civilizing Process*, Oxford: Blackwell.

Esposito, John 1992, *The Islamic Threat*, New York: Oxford University Press.

Gellner, Ernest 1983, *Nations and Nationalism*, Oxford: Blackwell.

1992, *Postmodernism, Reason and Religion*, London: Routledge.

Grillo, Ralph (ed.) 1980, *"Nation" and "State" in Europe*, London: Academic Press.

Hannerz, Ulf 1996, *Transnational Connections*, London: Routledge.

Hobsbawm, Eric 1987, *The Age of Empire, 1857–1914*, New York: Pantheon Books.

Huntington, Samuel 1993, "The Clash of Civilizations?" *Foreign Affairs* 72: 22–49.

1996, *The Clash of Civilizations and the Remaking of World Order*, New York: Simon and Schuster.

Kaplan, Robert 1996, *The Ends of the Earth*, New York: Vintage.

Kennedy, Paul 1993, *Preparing for the Twenty-First Century*, New York: Random House.

Marty, Martin and Appleby, Scott (eds.) 1991–6, *The Fundamentalism Project* (5 volumes), Chicago: Chicago University Press.

Riesebrodt, Martin 1994, *Pious Passion, The Emergence of Modern Fundamentalism in the United States and Iran*, Berkeley: University of California Press.

Rouse, Roger 1995, "Thinking Through Transnationalism: Notes on the Cultural Politics of Class Relations in the Contemporary United States," *Public Culture*, 7: 353–403.

van der Veer, Peter 1994, *Religious Nationalism*, Berkeley: University of California Press.

1997, "L'Etat moral: religion, nation et Empire dans la Grande-Bretagne victorienne et l'Inde britannique," *Geneses* 16: 77–103.

Van Rooden, Peter 1996, *Religieuze Regimes*, Amsterdam: Bert Bakker.

Wolffe, John 1995, *God and Greater Britain*, London: Routledge.

16 Environmental security in the coming century

Karen T. Litfin

International relations, as both a field of practice and a field of study, has suffered until recently from a profound ecological blindness. "Environment" was the invisible and putatively stable backdrop against which state actors enacted their dramas of conflict and cooperation. To the extent that it was considered at all, nature was seen by and large as a source of state power, whether through geostrategic positioning or natural resource endowments. So long as nature appeared to be perpetually resilient, endlessly abundant, and immutable on a human temporal scale, the study and practice of international relations could proceed despite this blindspot.

The assumptions which upheld this blindspot, however, are no longer tenable. Since environmental issues first catapulted onto the international agenda in the early 1970s, the blinders have been progressively peeled away. For some, particularly those associated with the new environmental security literature, ecological scarcities have already become a source of violent conflict and are likely to become increasingly so in the future, particularly in developing countries. For others, global ecological interdependence is generating new forms of cooperation and international institution-building. Whether environment is seen primarily as a source of conflict or of cooperation, however, there is general agreement that any attempt to comprehend international environmental dynamics must involve a shift away from a state-centric approach.

Ecological degradation – a corollary to industrial-style economic production and consumption, as well as exponential population growth – is increasingly transnational, in both its root causes and its solutions. Neither pollution nor migratory species carry passports. Moreover, since the mid-1980s, a host of global perils, including ozone depletion, climate change, deforestation, and threats to biodiversity, have been thrust onto the international agenda. While many international environmental problems have been addressed through cooperation among states, their causes and solutions typically involve a complex web of nonstate actors:

328

industry, scientists, nongovernmental organizations (NGOs), and indigenous peoples.

This chapter first looks broadly at environment as a new issue area in international relations, then analyzes its relationship to conflict and cooperation in two subsequent sections on environmental security and environmental cooperation. Whether environmental problems are seen as a source of conflict or as an impetus to cooperation, there is a tendency to naturalize the problems and ignore both their deeper social, economic, and political roots and the extent to which they are socially constructed through intersubjective understandings. Since long-term solutions will require a willingness to grapple with these deeper causes, this chapter aims to coax both the environmental conflict and the environmental cooperation literatures in the direction of a more penetrating and reflective analysis. The final section looks at a range of possible scenarios for the future, including both potential threats and innovations for global environmental governance in the twenty-first century.

International relations meets nature

The general indifference of international relations to ecology reflects a wider conviction in the modern era that, with the exception of natural disasters like floods and earthquakes, nature could be taken as a set of relatively permanent systems and attributes. Earth's biological, chemical, and geophysical systems were easily exogenized from both social analysis and practice so long as they were unchanging on a human timescale. A Lockean conception of nature as infinitely abundant and of value merely as a container for human labor was central to the modern notion of both natural resources and human identity in the modern era. Only those industrious individuals who could make property claims by "mixing their labor with nature" were truly human; all others were expendable savages. The appropriation of nature, on ever larger scales and with ever advancing technologies, thus became the hallmark of modernity. But, like other forms of expansion, this unfettered colonization of nature could only continue so long as nature was not pushed beyond its limits. As nature's productive and absorptive limits have become evident, not only international relations, but all fields of social practice and analysis are being compelled to widen their vision.

While the ecological shift is only in its infancy, there are important signs that it has taken root. Most tellingly, the number of multilateral environmental treaties has skyrocketed – from about fifty in 1969 to 173 in 1994. Including nonbinding and bilateral agreements, the number reaches almost 900 (French 1995). Alongside this proliferation of treaties, and perhaps spurring it on, is a concurrent explosion in the number of environmental NGOs (Willetts 1996). The Commission on Global Governance (1995) finds that the number of transnational NGOs (defined as those operating in at least three countries) grew from 176 in 1909 to 28,900 in 1993, with a large percentage devoted to environmental issues. Although international environmental diplomacy seems to have lost steam since its zenith at the Rio Earth Summit in 1992, the greening of world politics is likely to continue. Major addresses by US Secretaries of State Warren Christopher and Madeleine Albright reveal high-level support for an ecologically orientated US foreign policy. Both have declared that environmental considerations should be incorporated into every foreign policy decision (Christopher 1996; Stilkind 1997).

The ecological move in world politics scrambles conventional understandings of international security. The relationship between coercive power and ecological problems, for instance, raises a host of issues that do not find a comfortable home in traditional international relations discourse. The following section argues that the debates surrounding the concept of environmental security are symptomatic of a deeper ontological and epistemological ferment in the field which is likely to continue and widen in the foreseeable future.

Environmental security as an ambiguous symbol

From national security to environmental security

In this section, I argue that environmental security functions as an ambiguous symbol for a wide array of policy and analytical positions. The ambiguity of the term stems largely from the fact that the two core elements of security discourse, the state and military defense, are rendered problematic by current trends in world politics, particularly in the environmental arena. After examining the relationship between environmental issues and the coercive power of the state, I offer a critique of the argument that ecological problems are likely to lead to violent conflict.

Early on in the Cold War, Arnold Wolfers issued a prescient warning against formulaic calls for national security policy in a classic article entitled "'National Security' as an Ambiguous Symbol." Such calls, he claimed,

may not have any precise meaning at all. Thus, while appearing to offer guidance and a basis for broad consensus they may be permitting everyone to label whatever policy he [sic] favors with an attractive and possibly deceptive name. (Wolfers 1952: 481)

Observing that the symbol was generally invoked in order to suggest the necessity of protection through military power, Wolfers argued that the logic of the security dilemma actually requires that national security policies take the intentions and interests of an adversary into consideration. He also pointed out that, while national security is typically assumed to be rooted in an objective referent, it entails both an objective dimension (the absence of threats to core values) and a subjective dimension (the absence of *fear* that such values will be attacked).

Wolfers' observations are applicable to contemporary discourse on environmental security. Precisely because it functions as an ambiguous symbol, "environmental security" has attracted a remarkable array of proponents, ranging from environmentalists to Western military institutions. For some, like Thomas Homer-Dixon, ecological scarcities are important new sources of violent conflict within and between states. For others, including NATO, the US Pentagon, and weapons labs, environmental security provides not only a new objective in the absence of the Soviet threat, but also an umbrella concept for the greening of military practices. For still others, including the organizers of the 1992 UN Conference on Environment and Development, environmental security is akin to more expansive notions of global or human security, bringing together the quest for development with the quest for sustainability. Finally, some ecologically minded observers promote an alternative biocentric approach as "the ultimate security," according to which species and ecosystems are preserved for their own sake (Myers 1996). One thing unites these diverse perspectives: they all reflect a growing awareness that ecological health must be an essential ingredient in any recipe for international order.

Despite this common reference point, however, the ambiguity of "environmental security" is far greater than Cold War formulations. At least for the superpowers and their allies, such basic questions as what was to be secured, against what threat, and with what methods were relatively straightforward. As the diversity of environmental security proponents attests, contemporary answers to these questions are far from straightforward. Whose interests should be secured: those of the state, the global consuming class, humanity, or the biosphere? What is the threat: political instability, overpopulation, overconsumption, uneven development, or nature itself? How should we, whoever "we" may be, address the "threat": through self-defense, cooperation, or technological fixes?

Coercive power, environment, and the military

From a broader perspective, one should note that the environmental security debates are rooted in two key trends in world politics: the declining utility of force and the enhanced salience of non-state actors. Traditionally, security and order were about two things: the centrality of the sovereign state and its protection through military means. Given that the axiomatic nature of these core premises has become dubious, the current upheaval in security studies – witness the proliferating definitions of security – comes as no surprise. Thus I argue at the end of this section, although with significant caveats, for a conception of environmental security which decenters both the state and coercive power.

One general trend in international relations, the declining utility of force, is particularly visible through an ecological lens. Discussions of balance-of-power politics, military hegemony, and gunboat diplomacy seem alien to international environmental problem-solving. Military threats are strikingly irrelevant to efforts to persuade China not to fully exploit its high-sulfur coal reserves, for instance, or to convince Brazil and Malaysia not to decimate their forests. The ability of the US to block meaningful reductions in greenhouse gas emissions at the 1997 Kyoto climate change conference was not a function of its ability to wield military power. Despite the handful of instances in which military force has been applied to environmental problems, as in the Canadian-Spanish conflict over turbot fishing, traditional diplomacy and cooperation have been far and away the dominant modes of problem-solving and are likely to remain so.

The relative impotence of coercive power in resolving ecological problems, however, does not dissolve the military/environment link. As Richard Matthew has argued, if there are fewer situations in which force is an appropriate policy tool, then the traditional security community has two options: to expand its mandate or to accept the erosion of its resources (1997: 5–6). The proliferation of military-related "environmental security" projects in the 1990s confirms that the first option has been the response of choice. The environment/security nexus has been institutionalized in the US under the new office of the Deputy Undersecretary of Defense for Environmental Security, which collaborates on projects with the Department of Energy and the Environmental Protection Agency (Memorandum of Understanding 1996). The MEDEA Project, instigated by Vice President Al Gore, brings together environmental scientists and the Central Intelligence Agency through the release of formerly classified satellite data (Kerr 1994). Internationally, NATO has launched a pilot study, "Environment and Security in the International Context," to "assess security risks posed by environmental problems . . . and to devise an action plan to address them – with a strong emphasis on preventive actions" (Dabelko and Simmons 1997: 137).

Yet critics have argued for the decoupling of environment and security, pointing out that the military's claim to environmental leadership is suspect at best and dangerous at worst (Deudney 1990). The toxic legacy of the Cold War alone, which will likely be inflicted upon citizens and ecosystems well into the next century, is sufficient to cast a shadow of doubt upon the military as supplier of environmental security. Traditionally, military institutions have been more foe than friend to the environment, with the US and the Soviet defense establishments earning the dubious honor of being considered the world's worst polluters (Käkönen 1994; Feshbach and Friendly 1992). There is some evidence, however, that at least some agencies are cleaning up their act. The Pentagon's Environmental Security office has overseen a 50 percent reduction in the US military's toxic waste production, developed cooperative international military-to-military partnerships for nuclear and hazardous waste clean-up, and involved itself in promoting compliance with international environmental treaties (Department of Defense 1995). While these developments are consistent with the contemporary ecological trend in international relations, they do not authenticate the military as a guardian of environmental security.

Military agencies specialize in responding to threats which involve a clear enemy – generally a foreign aggressor. Critics of the environment/security linkage point out that environmental perils do not fit well into this traditional threat-defense mechanism, and that casting them in this light may lead to serious misconceptions and misguided policy (Deudney 1990; Wæver 1995). Their point is well taken. Despite the fact that industrialized countries are the world's primary environmental offenders, there is a disturbing tendency in the environmental security literature to focus disproportionate attention on developing countries, a tendency which unreflectively reinforces the sort of "chaos-in-the peripheries" historical bias which Kal Holsti argues in this volume pervades Western discourse on international order. Statements, for instance, that population growth in developing countries represents a "national security threat" to the US because of its contribution to illegal immigration are unlikely to promote international order because they encourage an "us-versus-them" mentality which does not address the underlying economic and environmental roots of the problem.

Environment and violent conflict

Although it makes an important contribution to an ecological approach to international order, the most prominent strand in the environmental security literature, that associated with the study of ecological degradation as a source of violent conflict, falls prey to this error by focusing on developing countries as the primary source of environmentally induced international instability. The preliminary work of Thomas Homer-Dixon and his Environmental Conflict and Security Project hypothesized four social effects of environmental degradation which would lead to three types of "acute conflict" (Homer-Dixon 1991). The primary sources of international instability in the model were considered to be developing countries, which are more vulnerable to environmentally caused violence. The four social effects were economic decline, reduced agricultural production, population displacement, and disruption of legitimized social relations. The three types of acute conflict were simple scarcity conflicts, group identity conflicts, and relative deprivation conflicts. The main problem with the model, however, is that it exogenized the social, political, and economic causes of environmental damage, and thereby naturalized a spurious phenomenon labeled "environmentally induced violence."

The project's research conclusions, presented in *International Security* three years after the model was developed, recognize this problem and, to some extent, attempt to address it by concluding that "environmental scarcity," which is itself a combination of environmental change, population growth, and unequal resource distribution, leads to violent conflict. The empirical findings, however, only support a more nuanced conclusion than this, since virtually every example – from the Senegal and Jordan River valleys to the Ganges-Brahmaputra flood plain – highlights the pernicious impact of inequalities in wealth and access to natural resources. Nor do the findings reflect an awareness of the ability of Third World states to conclude agreements in this area, e.g., the various agreements India has made with Pakistan, Nepal, and Bangladesh to share river waters.

The findings do support two important conclusions: that diffuse and persistent subnational violence is a more likely outcome than acute international violence, and that environmental degradation can contribute to the delegitimation of the state. This body of work also confirms a key insight of an ecological approach to international relations: strengthening the environmental component of conflict resolution efforts is essential to efforts to promote international order. While Homer-Dixon's work is problematic for its lack of insight into the root causes of both violent conflict and environmental degradation, it usefully decenters the state and points in the direction of a conception of environmental security which is decoupled from traditional national security discourse.

Towards environmental security in the twenty-first century

While it may be tempting to throw out the term environmental security, there are important practical and epistemological reasons for not doing so. First, since the trends which have so fundamentally challenged the field of security studies are unlikely to subside, alternative formulations of security will continue to demand a hearing. The two principal trends which have thrown the field of security studies into tumult – the declining utility of force and the growing salience of nonstate actors on the world scene – are likely to persist and must be incorporated into any notion of environmental security. Second, climate-change-induced sea-level rise, land degradation and desertification, the largest wave of species extinctions since the dinosaurs, and multifarious pollutants will become sources of insecurity for much of the world in the twenty-first century. Thus it makes sense to speak of environmental security, or at least environmental *insecurity*. Third, limiting security language to military threats cedes too much ground to the security traditionalists.

Ole Wæver argues convincingly that one of the pitfalls of security language, whether of the traditional or alternative schools, is the assumption that "security" signifies some reality with a concrete external referent. Rather than being a sign for something more real, security is most aptly understood as a speech act: "the utterance *itself* is the act" (1995: 55). While his critique could provide the basis for a more reflective conception of security as a socially constructed set of concerns, Wæver opposes an expanded notion of security, including the "securitization of the environment," on the grounds that "[s]ecurity is articulated only from a specific place, in an institutional voice, by elites" (57). In other words, only those concerned with classic state-centric threat-defense dynamics are entitled to perform security speech acts.

But this reading not only ignores the fact that security speech acts are performed on a daily basis by an increasingly diffuse group of scholars and practitioners, it also abdicates too much terrain to the security traditionalists. The state is not the sole subject of security, nor is coercive power the sole means of seeking it. To assume otherwise entails neglecting significant sources of perceived insecurity in the world. If Cold War hawks could seize upon the ambiguous symbol of national security, there is no reason that contemporary actors and analysts cannot employ the ambiguous symbol of environmental security. But to do so reflectively, without falling prey to the sorts of ideological excess which characterized Cold War security discourse, they should be conscious of how they construct their speech acts.

As Wæver's critique implies, an objectivist epistemology has characterized security language. This is a particularly relevant concern with respect to the language of environmental security, which may call upon the authority of science to demonstrate the existence of "objective" threats (Krause and Williams 1996: 233). While scientific information is clearly of great importance in putting environmental issues on the international agenda, it by no means provides an objective factual basis upon which rational policy can be formulated. Knowledge and information are framed and interpreted in light of specific interests and contending discourses, so that information begets counterinformation (Litfin 1994). Even in the context of real material dangers, the invocation of environmental security threats is fundamentally about socially constructed risks (Beck 1992; Lash, Szerszynski and Wynne 1996).

Arnold Wolfers observed over forty years ago that the subjective dimension of security, the absence of fear that core values will be endangered, is at least as important to security language as the existence of material threats (1952: 482). Likewise, "environmental scarcities" are not objective phenomena, but are socially constructed and culturally dependent. As Richard Matthew notes, an individual requires four to six liters of water per day to survive. On this basis, potable water is abundant for most of the world. Yet social scientists routinely define scarcity as less than 2,740 liters per person per day, based upon consumption rates in advanced industrialized countries (Matthew 1997: 4). Likewise, invocations of environmental security tend to naturalize what are essentially social, political, and economic problems (Lipschutz 1998). If the threat-defense mechanism is mapped onto a naturalized understanding of environmental problems, then the quest for environmental security may deteriorate into a stance against nature as enemy to be controlled and conquered, a tacit stance which may be at the root of the mounting global environmental crisis in the first place (Evernden 1993; Merchant 1990).

An associated pitfall is the tendency to paint environmental dangers in falsely universalizing terms. If security is a speech act, then its proponents need to become self-conscious of the specific interests and cultural biases from which they speak. Calls for environmental security have entirely different policy implications depending upon whether they come from Pacific islanders threatened with sea-level rise as a result of climate change, affluent urban dwellers suffocating from automotive emissions, or subsistence farmers without access to clean drinking water. Thus, if environmental security discourse is monopolized by those with an unreflective bias towards the advanced industrialized world, then it will become an easy target for those in developing countries who are already wary of "environmental imperialism" (Non-Aligned Countries 1990).

A final cautionary note: unreflectively depicting environmental problems as security problems runs the risk of contributing to "a proliferating array of discourses of danger." As Michael Dillon maintains, security is neither a fact of nature nor a noun that names something, but a fact of civilization and a generative principle (1996: 19). Building upon Dillon's position, Simon Dalby argues that if "insecurity is not the problem, but rather the ontological condition of mortal human life, then the solution in terms of security, the assertion of control to ensure life, is ironically potentially a threat to life itself, that which is insecure in the first place" (Dalby 1997: 2). Dalby's point is well taken. The Cold War quest for security, whose toxic and radioactive legacy will perpetuate ecological and medical insecurity for decades to come, should offer a sobering lesson. More generally, who can doubt that the primary dynamic driving global environmental degradation is the unrestrained pursuit of material security? Barring a major shift either in consumption practices or in the use of sustainable technologies, this trend will inevitably increase in the coming century. The quest for security, depending upon how it is approached, can perpetuate environmental insecurity.

The greatest challenge in developing a useful ecological approach to security for the coming century will be finding the willingness to recognize and act upon the *root causes* of environmental insecurity. The consumption habits of the affluent, for instance, are only possible because their true ecological costs are externalized onto both future generations and far-flung "shadow ecologies" which serve as sources and sinks for the global economy (MacNeill, Winsemius and Yakushiji 1991). Likewise, population growth in the Third World is fueled not only by deeply rooted gender inequality, but also by the "primary producers' squeeze," itself a consequence of global economic dynamics (United Nations Population Fund 1994). Given the complexity of the material sources of environmental insecurity, to say nothing of the subjective psychological dynamics involved, the agenda for the twenty-first century will be exceedingly full.

In drawing out elements of a "human security" program with an emphasis on environmental concerns, Michael Renner of the Worldwatch Institute outlines an extensive agenda. His list includes the strengthening of civil society, the building of local-global links, a renewed commitment to environmental diplomacy, greater inclusion of NGOs in environmental governance, the shrinking of military budgets, increasing the transparency and accountability of corporate decision-making, and the reduction of deep social and economic inequities which breed environmental insecurity. With respect to the last factor, he suggests a number of positive directions, including a serious commitment to debt relief, land reform in many developing countries, and micro-loan programs for the urban and rural poor (Renner 1997: 128–31). Renner's list gets at many of the root causes of environmental insecurity; it simultaneously suggests that neither a state-centric nor an "us-versus-them" orientation will be helpful.

Environmental interdependence and cooperation

The formulation of an environmental security agenda elucidates the fact that progress will require an immense amount of cooperation, not just among nation-states, but across all social levels. Environmental security therefore brings together realism's preoccupation with tangible physical dangers with idealism's historical emphasis on interdependence and a collective harmony of interests. The dramatic proliferation of environmental treaties since 1972 affirms the observation that international cooperation has been a crucial instrument in the pursuit of environmental security. Although the pace of environmental treaty-making, which reached a peak in 1992 with the Rio Earth Summit, has slowed somewhat, the ecological trend in international relations will inevitably continue as the twin engines of environmental destruction, population and consumption, move into high gear in the coming century.

The evolution of environmental cooperation

Like other forms of international interdependence, the recognition of international environmental interdependence creates a framework for the mutual recognition of common interests and the coordination of policy based upon those common interests. The most tangible expression of the growing awareness of transnational ecological interdependence is the astonishing array of treaties addressing a wide range of environmental problems, including marine pollution (Haas 1989), acid rain (Levy 1993), stratospheric ozone depletion (Litfin 1994), living resources and minerals in Antarctica (Ward 1998), loss of biodiversity (Raustiala and Victor 1996), and the export of toxic waste to developing countries (Miller 1995). This proliferation of treaties is symptomatic not only of the ecological turn in international relations, but also of the fact that environmental protection has become increasingly internationalized (Economy and Schreurs 1997). There is no reason to doubt that this trend will continue and deepen in the coming century.

Two broad observations may be made about environmental cooperation to date. First, while only states can be parties to treaties, and to that extent their formal sovereignty is legitimized and reinforced by the proliferation of environmental treaties, the internationalization of environmental protection is largely driven by nonstate actors: scientists, NGOs, IOs, and industries. State sovereignty is therefore being substantially reconfigured with respect to environmental concerns. The ecological turn in international relations entails the greening of sovereignty and the reconfiguration of patterns of control, authority, and territoriality (Litfin 1997, 1998). Nonstate actors are likely to become increasingly salient in efforts to address international environmental problems in the coming century. Indeed, most proposals for improving the effectiveness of these efforts recommend formally expanding the role of nongovernmental interests in international environmental regimes in all phases of the treaty process, from negotiation to implementation and monitoring (Susskind 1994: 130–31; Stone 1993: 83–8).

The second broad observation that we may make about international environmental treaties to date is that, for the most part, they have been too little and too late. While the planet's life support systems and resource base are undoubtedly in better condition than they would have been in the absence of a quarter-century of international environmental institution-building, the general health of the planet has grown worse, not better, since the first UN environment conference in 1972 (Brown et al. 1998; World Resources Institute 1998). Progress in some areas is better than in others. The ozone regime, for instance, proceeded rapidly from a non-binding convention in 1985, to a regulatory protocol in 1987, to three sets of treaty revisions by 1996. Yet even in what represents the world's greatest achievement in environmental diplomacy, ozone depletion will not peak until early in the next century and the hole over Antarctica is not expected to close for nearly a hundred years, assuming *full compliance* (Litfin 1994: 133). On other pressing environmental issues, such as biodiversity loss and climate change, virtually no progress has been made towards stemming the damage (Raustiala and Victor 1998).

Taken together, these two general observations – that international environmental cooperation to date has precipitated the greening of sovereignty but that it also has accomplished too little too late – spell out some implications for the future. First, if the effectiveness of environmental institutions is to be enhanced, then they will need to move away from band-aid solutions to policies, such as those proposed by Renner in his human security agenda, that get at the root of the problems. Second, if states and societies develop the collective will to address the root causes of global ecological degradation, then the political institutions and practices of the coming century may look quite different from those of today.

Economic and ecological interdependence

The tension between ecological interdependence and economic interdependence is likely to be felt increasingly in the coming years. On the one hand, both concepts stress interconnections and mutual vulnerabilities. Like the biosphere and planetary ecosystems, the global economy is characterized by far-flung causal chains, such that, in John Muir's classic turn of phrase, "everything is hitched to everything else." On the other hand, the global economy confronts Earth's species and life support systems in a generally predatory mode. Global ecological degradation, from tropical deforestation to ozone depletion to toxic waste trade, is a corollary of global economic and industrial practices. The key, then, to a genuine environmental security agenda for the twenty-first century will be harmonizing economic and ecological interdependence. This is the mandate implied in the term *sustainable development*, a mandate which, if taken seriously, would have radical consequences in all spheres of life.

Perhaps because economic practices are the core of the problem, the greening of international political practice appears to be proceeding at a more rapid pace than the greening of the global economy (Esty 1994). In the modern era, nature has been largely excluded from economic calculations because it was assumed to be resilient and abundant as both source and sink. The annual expansion of GNP is still widely viewed as the best indicator of economic progress, and perhaps progress in general, despite the availability of more ecologically inclusive indicators (Daly and Cobb 1989). Growth is the core value informing all of the major international economic institutions: the World Bank, the IMF, the GATT, and its predecessor, the WTO. To the extent that environmental considerations are incorporated into international economic institutions at all, as in NAFTA's environmental side agreement or the World Bank's Global Environmental Facility, their impact is relatively small. Rather than being acknowledged as the fundamental challenge it actually represents, the language of sustainability has been grafted onto the liberal international economic order, without any real transformation of economic practices. While the early discourse of environmentalism stressed that there were "limits to growth," the discourse of sustainable development problematically insinuates that growth can be sustained indefinitely (Torgerson 1995). Even worse, affluence is sometimes recommended as the recipe for sustainability (Brenton 1994); according to this reasoning, environmental values are a luxury that only the prosperous can afford.

Consider, for instance, the widely read *Our Common Future*, which first popularized the notion of sustainable development. The report rightly recognizes poverty and environmental destruction as the two central problems facing humanity at the end of the twentieth century, but then goes on to assert that both can be alleviated only through a five-fold increase in industrial production (World Commission on Environment and Development 1987). The contribution of poverty to ecological damage, primarily through population growth and poor agricultural practices, is highlighted, while the impact of consumption is virtually ignored. The report overlooks the fact that the per capita ecological impact of the advanced industrialized countries prodigiously outstrips that of developing countries (Agarwal and Narain 1991).

The proposed five-fold increase in industrial production will be made possible, in part, by technological changes. Here the report makes a contribution, outlining the sorts of changes in energy and agriculture, for instance, that could facilitate sustainable development. New products and production practices, including clean energy systems and environmentally benign methods of farming, will certainly contribute to sustainable development (Flavin 1996; Rosegrant and Livernash 1996). Likewise, the new field of industrial ecology is finding ways to reduce the traditional tradeoff between ecological health and economic productivity (Ayres 1996; Richards 1997). But it is probably unrealistic to expect that sustainability will be achieved on the basis of technological fixes alone. Not only do some technological fixes, such as genetic engineering, entail major unforeseen social problems (Shiva 1993), but an over-reliance on technology may encourage an ecological blindness by failing to address the likelihood that there are real limits to growth. The marriage of ecological interdependence with traditional liberal notions of interdependence, therefore, cannot be forged either solely or primarily on the basis of technology.

One of the great unacknowledged difficulties in discussions of ecological interdependence is that it, like environmental security, is taken as an objective fact rather than a socially constructed phenomenon. Just as "security" is a speech act enunciated from a certain place and with a particular voice, so too is "interdependence" a speech act. While ecological interconnectedness has a biological basis, the language of interdependence too often masks important social inequalities and differences, generating such platitudinous phrases as "our common future." Yet the future in central Africa is likely to look quite different from the future in Western Europe (Lohman 1990). If interdependence language applied to economics generates a false sense of mutuality, as the dependency theorists have rightly argued, then that same language applied to ecological issues in an unequal world will do the same. Environmental degradation is not a natural phenomenon, but is rather driven by social, political, and economic dynamics.

The perception of ecological interdependence, it should be noted, can nonetheless generate certain opportunities for developing countries. As Marian Miller (1995) argues, developing countries seem to fare best in regime negotiations when the perception of interdependence is greatest, as it is for common property resources. Because the industrialized countries perceived interdependence to be high with respect to ozone depletion, developing countries were able to exact significant concessions – most importantly the technology transfer fund – in exchange for their willingness to cooperate. Since perceived interdependence was not as high for the toxic-waste trade issue, developing countries did not have as much leverage in those negotiations. Claims about ecological interdependence constitute speech acts which, broadly speaking, are oriented towards a preference for cooperation and collective action. A generalized increase in the perception of interdependence may have important implications for the creation of innovative North-South partnerships in the coming century, so long as environmental change is gradual and not catastrophic.

The climate change negotiations offer a potential arena for such a partnership, yet key states have so far failed to seize the opportunity. While industrialized countries, with less than 20 percent of the world's population, emit 70 percent of all energy-related greenhouse gases, developing countries are expected to surpass them within a generation (IPCC 1995). Rather than pushing for meaningful reductions in greenhouse gas emissions, three of the largest per capita emitters (the US, Canada, and Australia) called for either stabilization or minuscule reductions of emissions early in the next century. In the end, largely because of European pressure, the Kyoto conference agreed that industrialized countries would reduce overall emissions by at least 5 percent below 1990 levels in the commitment period of 2008 to 2012 (Conference of the Parties, Article 3). The ink was barely dry on the treaty when prominent members of the US Senate announced that they would block ratification unless developing countries were also required to limit their emissions. Even with US backing, however, the Kyoto Protocol would do little to achieve the 60 percent reduction in greenhouse gas emissions that scientists believe is required to stabilize the world's climate (IPCC 1990). Such an accomplishment will require not only major economic and technological changes, but also a strong North-South partnership.

Global environmental governance in the twenty-first century

This section explores two broad scenarios for global environmental governance. In the first, environmental change continues at a gradual pace, whereas in the second, environmental change occurs rapidly, precipitating a sense of crisis. In general, the prospects are much brighter under the first scenario; a wider range of creative policy options will present themselves, existing institutions can continue to evolve, and violent conflict and coercive responses will be less likely. In either scenario, it should be noted, the ecological turn in world politics that began in the latter part of this century will continue into the next. The primary question is whether that turn will be socially and politically benign or harsh. Preventive efforts and policies that address the root causes of environmental problems are therefore preferred on the basis that they will tend to avert the more catastrophic scenarios.

Gradual environmental change

Assuming that environmental change proceeds gradually, we can anticipate several interrelated trends: a progressive strengthening of existing international environmental institutions, the increasing transnationalization of global environmental governance, and greater linkage of environmental concerns with human rights and development issues. The broad assortment of international instruments developed since 1972 provides a basis for further institutionalization. As the history of international regime-building evinces, environmental agreements and institutions are open to revision on the basis of new information. New species in danger of extinction can be added to the control list of the Convention on the International Trade in Endangered Species (Mofson 1997); toothless conventions can be superseded by binding regulatory protocols, as they were for acid rain and ozone depletion (Litfin 1994; Gehring 1994); and minke whales can be exempted from the whaling moratorium when they are no longer in danger of extinction (Mitchell, 1998). If countries are dissatisfied with the pace of reform, they may opt for unilateral action, which in turn fuels the revision process (Levy 1993). Or if a significant group of affected countries objects to the weakness of a treaty's provisions, it might negotiate an alternative treaty, as developing countries did in the case of toxic-waste trade (Miller 1995). Thus at least some of the groundwork for future international environmental cooperation has been established.

Two important caveats, however, are in order. First, existing institutions for what are likely to be the some of most challenging issues in the coming century are quite weak. The biodiversity convention adopted at Rio in 1992, for instance, includes no binding measures to address the problem, while the Kyoto Protocol represents at best a symbolic first step towards addressing climate change. While each of these issues is likely to have severe repercussions in the coming century, they have proven especially difficult to address in international fora because they involve entrenched economic interests and complex equity issues. Second, international environmental agreements have historically accomplished too little, too late. International law is a notoriously slow and laborious process. Consider, for instance, the much-vaunted international ozone regime. It was not until 1996, twenty-two years after scientists first linked chlorofluorocarbons to stratospheric ozone depletion, that an international ban on the chemicals finally took effect. Innovative environmental responses which do not rely solely upon international legal mechanisms should therefore be pursued, such as full-cost pricing, which would internalize environmental costs into the price of products, or an international labeling system designed to make producers more accountable for the ecological impact of their goods (Wapner 1998).

Frustrated with the slow pace and mediocre effectiveness of international law, nonstate actors are increasingly assuming responsibility for moving the world towards sustainability. NGOs negotiated their own "treaties" at Rio; development NGOs more and more tie their work to the pursuit of sustainability; municipal governments are making efforts to incorporate sustainability into local practices; and a greening of business practices has taken hold in pockets of the world (Ekins 1992; Hawken 1993). To a great extent, the emerging global civil society, comprising decentralized transnational networks of knowledge and action, has its roots in environmental concerns (Lipschutz 1996). These networks, which find their concrete expression in such phenomena as the internet-based Econet, are increasingly linked via information technologies, a trend we can expect to increase in the coming century. Similarly, the links between the local and global which are being increasingly forged on the basis of information technology will become a central component of global environmental governance (Borja and Castells 1997). Thus while international law will evolve to take into account future environmental developments, global environmental governance will not necessarily be centered in the state. Assuming that the pace of environmental change does not accelerate much beyond current rates, cooperation will most likely increase across all levels of social organization.

One important mechanism for slowing the pace of environmental change may be the adoption of "no-regrets" policies which would make sense even if the global environment were not threatened, e.g., increased reliance on clean and efficient energy sources (Wilbanks 1994). While no-regrets policies are typically linked to the climate change issue, they could also be developed for other issues. Tropical deforestation, for instance, is not only ecologically devastating, but usually economically unsound in the long run; sustainable harvesting and ecotourism can offer viable alternatives that make sense for economic, and not just ecological, reasons. Some no-regrets policies offer multiple environmental benefits:

stemming the tide of tropical deforestation contributes to both conservation of biodiversity and stabilization of climate; decreasing coal use would have a positive impact not only on the global climate system, but also on human health and acid precipitation.

If we are honest with ourselves, we must recognize that the primary obstacle to these sorts of sorely needed policies is the habit-driven nature of political and economic practices. Indeed, the history of international environmental action suggests that policies are most likely to change when there is a sense of crisis, whether it be species on the verge of extinction, dramatic oil spills, the Chernobyl disaster, or the ozone hole over Antarctica. For the most part, international environmental responses have limped from crisis to crisis, patching up problems with band-aid solutions – a disturbing pattern that bodes ill for the future. If states cannot find the political will to adopt policies which are proactive and directed to the root causes of global environmental degradation, then it is quite possible that the cascade of environmental problems which has emerged in recent decades will swell into a tidal wave in the coming century.

Catastrophic environmental change

In light of the fact that effective solutions to virtually all international environmental problems require cooperation, enhanced cooperation at all levels of social organization is the most likely scenario for the coming century. It is possible, however, that crises could develop as a result of environmental change which might ignite violent conflict or coercive responses. Homer-Dixon's general argument to this effect may not hold much water historically, but then again, the past may not be a good guide to the future on these questions. While environmental cooperation is built upon the premise of interdependence and a commonality of interests, a crisis situation could provoke an us-versus-them response in which certain states or classes attempt to shore up their interests against those of others. States rendered insecure by environmental crisis might respond in a variety of potentially unnerving ways (Del Rosso 1995). Indeed, some analysts predict that only highly centralized and authoritarian forms of governance will be able to contend with the social disorder that would accompany large-scale ecological collapse (Ophuls 1977).

Since climate influences virtually every aspect of global ecology, climate instability is probably the single most likely source of catastrophic environmental change in the coming century. The impact on international social and political order could be tremendous. Scientists predict that global warming will increase the spread of infectious diseases and agricultural pests (Pirages 1995), aggravate the loss of biodiversity (Peters

and Lovejoy 1992), greatly intensify weather extremes, including floods
and droughts (Vogel 1995), and lead to a global decline of food supply
from land and water (Bright 1997). One consequence of global warming,
rising sea levels, will impact hundreds of millions of people living on small
islands and low-lying coastal regions. The specter of millions of environmental refugees, particularly from the world's poorest countries which
are least equipped to adapt, could become a reality. Likewise, existing
ethnic and class conflicts could be exacerbated by the negative social
impact of catastrophic environmental change.

In international terms, the most obvious us-versus-them scenario
would pit the North against the South. In one futuristic French novel,
Camp of the Saints, dangerously overloaded boatloads of starving people
virtually invade Western Europe (Raspail 1982). A strong anti-immigra-
tion sentiment has already taken root in many Western countries, and
could grow more virulent in a world populated by millions of environmental refugees. Put bluntly, if a world of ten billion people living an
affluent lifestyle is not sustainable, then the affluent will have two choices:
either to cut their consumption, or to defend their consumption against
incursions from others. Given the absence of a trend in the first direction,
there is a real danger that environmental security in the twenty-first
century could take on the more noxious us-versus-them connotations
associated with national security discourse during the Cold War. Rather
than the integrity of ecosystems or well-being of humanity becoming the
objects to be secured, consumption could become the object of security.
"Environmental security" could become the speech act uttered by the
haves against the have-nots.

Pay now or pay later

Future generations will bear a large chunk of the environmental costs of
contemporary practices, from climate change caused by the fossil-fuel-
based global economy to a scarcity of resources due to deforestation and
desertification. A general perception persists that the costs of a serious
worldwide movement in the direction of sustainability are simply too
great to be borne by the present generation. The world spends roughly
$800 billion annually on military preparedness, suggesting that conven-
tional understandings of national security continue to dominate. A fraction of the world's "national security" expenditures would go a long way
towards promoting sustainability through investment in clean technologies, family planning, land reform, and debt relief. At this point, however,
the political will to reorient policy in the direction of a comprehensive
understanding of environmental security is largely absent.

We should note that, because the attention of citizens and leaders alike is limited, efforts to address seemingly unrelated economic and traditional security problems will have an important effect on environmental global governance. The tremendous outpouring of environmental concern in the late 1980s and early 1990s was not a response to greater ecological degradation during that period, but was instead largely a function of the opening window of attention that accompanied the end of the Cold War. People preoccupied with violent conflict in the Balkans and the Middle East, financial crises in East Asia, and a nuclear arms race in South Asia are unlikely to focus their attention on a creeping ecological catastrophe, particularly given the Lockean assumptions embedded in the political economy of modernity.

Nonetheless, given the severity of environmental problems facing the world, the ecological trend in international relations that began in the final decades of the twentieth century is likely to accelerate in the coming century. Whether this development will follow the current trend towards ever more extensive modes of cooperation, or whether it will devolve into more conflictual scenarios depends largely upon the pace of environmental change and the degree to which the present generation is willing to make a serious commitment to sustainability. Some solutions will be relatively easy no-regrets policies. Others, like the greening of the global economy and the amelioration of social inequities which drive environmental degradation, will be more deeply challenging. Under the most optimistic scenario, the ecological shift in international relations could be part of a more general cultural shift which includes the greening of business, education, psychology, and religion, and the emergence of a new form of planetary identity based upon establishing harmonious intra- and inter-species relationships (Deudney 1998; Pinkerton 1997). If the root causes of environmental degradation are not addressed, then the degradation will only increase. The cost of sustainability may be great, but other options will be more costly. The costs can be postponed, but in the meantime, the interest accumulates.

REFERENCES

Agarwal, Anil and Narain, Sunita 1991, *Global Warming in an Unequal World*, New Delhi: Center for Science and Environment.
Ayres, Robert U. 1996, *Industrial Ecology*, Cheltenham: Edward Elgar.
Beck, Ulrich 1992, *Risk Society: Towards a New Modernity*, London: Sage.
Borja, Jordi and Castells, Manuel 1997, *The Local and the Global: Management of Cities in the Information Age*, London: Earthscan.
Brenton, Tony 1994, *The Greening of Machiavelli*, London: Royal Institute of International Affairs.

Bright, Chris 1997, "Tracking the Ecology of Climate Change," in Lester R. Brown et al., pp. 78–94.

Brown, Lester R. et al. 1998, *State of the World 1998*, New York: W. W. Norton.

Christopher, Warren 1996, "American Diplomacy and the Global Environmental Challenges of the 21st Century," Speech at Stanford University, 9 April.

Commission on Global Governance 1995, *Our Global Neighborhood*, New York: Oxford University Press.

Conference of the Parties 1997, *Kyoto Protocol to the United Nations Framework Convention on Climate Change*, (Document FCCC/CP/1997/L.7/Add.1.) New York: United Nations.

Dabelko, Geoffrey D. and Simmons, P. J. 1997, "Environment and Security: Core Ideas and U.S. Government Initiatives," *SAIS Review* 17: 127–46.

Dalby, Simon 1997, "Lacunae and Lapses: The Silences in Environmental Security Discourse," paper delivered to the Annual Meeting of the International Studies Association, Toronto, March 18–22.

Daly, Herman E. and Cobb, John B. 1989, *For the Common Good*, Boston: Beacon Press.

Del Rosso, Stephen J. 1995, "The Insecure State," *Daedalus* 124: 175–207.

Department of Defense 1995, "Report of a Joint U.S.-Russia Ecological/Environmental Seminar" Washington, DC, May 15–19.

Deudney, Daniel 1990, "The Case Against Linking Environmental Degradation and National Security," *Millennium* 19: 461–76.

   1998, "Earth Orders: Intergenerational Sovereign Publics, Republican Earth Constitutions, and Planetary Identities," in Litfin (ed.), pp. 299–325.

Dillon, Michael 1996, *Politics of Security: Towards a Political Philosophy of Continental Thought*, London: Routledge.

Economy, Elizabeth and Schreurs, Miranda (eds.) 1997, *The Internationalization of Environmental Protection*, Cambridge: Cambridge University Press.

Ekins, Paul 1992, *A New World Order*, London: Routledge.

Esty, David 1994, *Greening the GATT*, Washington, DC: Institute for International Economics.

Feshbach, Marray and Friendly, Alfred, Jr. 1992, *Ecocide in the USSR*, New York: Basic Books.

Flavin, Christopher 1996, "Power Shock: The Next Energy Revolution," *World Watch* 9: 10–21.

French, Hilary 1995, "Environmental Treaties Grow in Number," in *Vital Signs 1995*, Lester Brown, Nicholas Lenssen and Hal Kane (eds.), New York: W. W. Norton, pp. 90–1.

Gehring, Thomas 1994, *Dynamic International Regimes: Institutions for International Environmental Governance*, Frankfurt: Peter Lang.

Haas, Peter 1989, "Do Regimes Matter? Epistemic Communities and Mediterranean Pollution Control," *International Organization* 43: 377–404.

Hawken, Paul 1993, *The Ecology of Commerce*, New York: Harper Business.

Homer-Dixon, Thomas 1991, "On the Threshold: Environmental Changes as Causes of Acute Conflict," *International Security* 16: 76–116.

   1994, "Environmental Scarcities and Violent Conflict: Evidence from the Cases," *International Security* 19: 5–40.

Intergovernmental Panel on Climate Change (IPCC) 1990, *IPCC First Assessment Report*, Geneva: World Meteorological Organization and United Nations Environment Programme.

Käkönen, Jyrki (ed.) 1994, *Green Security or Militarized Environment?* Brookfield: Dartmouth Publishing.

Kerr, Richard 1994, "The Defense Department Declassifies the Earth – Slowly," *Science* 263: 625–6.

Krause, Keith and Williams, Michael C. 1996, "Broadening the Agenda of Security Studies: Politics and Methods," *Mershon International Studies Review* 40: 229–54.

Lash, Scott, Szerszynski, Bronislaw and Wynne, Brian 1996, *Risk, Environment and Modernity*, London: Sage.

Levy, Marc A. 1993, "European Acid Rain: The Power of Tote-Board Diplomacy," in *Institutions for the Earth: Sources of Effective International Environmental Protection*, Peter Haas, Robert Keohane and Marc Levy (eds.), Cambridge, MA: MIT Press, pp. 75–132.

Lipschutz, Ronnie D. 1998, "The Nature of Sovereignty and the Sovereignty of Nature: Problematizing the Boundaries Between Self, Society, State and System," in Litfin (ed.), pp. 109–38.

Lipschutz, Ronnie D. and Mayer, Judith 1996, *Global Civil Society and Global Environmental Governance*, Albany: State University of New York Press.

Litfin, Karen T. 1994, *Ozone Discourses: Science and Politics in Global Environmental Cooperation*, New York: Columbia University Press.

1997, "Sovereignty in World Eco-politics," *Mershon International Studies Review* 41: 167–204.

(ed.) 1998. *Sovereignty Moves: The Greening of Authority, Control, and Territoriality*, Cambridge, MA: MIT Press.

Lohman, Larry 1990, "Whose Common Future?" *The Ecologist* 20: 82–4.

MacNeill, Jim, Winsemius, Pieter and Yakushiji, Taizo 1991, *Beyond Interdependence: The Meshing of the World's Economy and the Earth's Ecology*, New York: Oxford University Press.

Matthew, Richard 1997, "Rethinking Environmental Security," paper delivered to the Annual Meeting of the International Studies Association, Toronto, March 18–22.

Memorandum of Understanding 1996, Memorandum of Understanding Among the Environmental Protection Agency, the Department of Energy, and Department of Defense Concerning Cooperation in Environmental Security, July 3.

Merchant, Carolyn 1990, *The Death of Nature: Women, Ecology and the Scientific Revolution*, New York: Harper Collins.

Miller, Marian 1995, *The Third World in Global Environmental Politics*. Boulder: Lynne Rienner.

Mitchell, Ronald 1998, "Forms of Discourse, Norms of Sovereignty: Interests, Science and Morality in the Regulation of Whaling," in Litfin (ed.), pp. 141–71.

Mofson, Phyllis 1997, "Zimbabwe and CITES: Illustrating the Reciprocal Relationship Between the State and the International Regime," in Economy and

350   Karen T. Litfin

Schreurs (eds.), pp. 162–87.

Myers, Norman 1996, *Ultimate Security: The Environmental Basis of Political Stability*. New York: W. W. Norton.

Non-Aligned Countries 1990, Ninth Conference of Heads of States of Government of Non-Aligned Countries, "Statement on the Environment" *International Environmental Affairs* 2: 82.

Ophuls, William 1977, *Ecology and the Politics of Scarcity*, San Francisco: W. H. Freeman and Co.

Peters, Robert L. and Lovejoy, Thomas E. 1992, *Global Warming and Biological Diversity*, New Haven: Yale University Press.

Pinkerton, James 1997, "Enviromanticism: The Poetry of Nature as Political Force," *Foreign Affairs* 76: 2–7.

Pirages, Dennis 1995, "Microsecurity: Disease Organisms and Human Well-being," *Washington Quarterly* 18: 5–12.

Raspail, Jean 1982, *Camp of the Saints*, Norman Shapiro (trans.), Alexandria, VA: Institute for Western Values.

Raustiala, Kal and Victor, David G. 1996, "Biodiversity Since Rio: The Future of the Convention on Biological Diversity," *Environment* 38: 17–20, 37–45.

(eds.) 1998, *Implementation and Effectiveness of International Environmental Commitments*, Cambridge, MA: The MIT Press.

Renner, Michael 1997, "Transforming Security," in Lester R. Brown et al., pp. 115–31.

Richards, Deanna J. (ed.) 1997, *The Industrial Green Game: Implications for Environmental Design and Management*, Washington, DC: National Academy Press.

Rosegrant, Mark W. and Livernash, Robert 1996, "Growing More Food, Doing Less Damage" *Environment* 38: 6–11, 28–32.

Shiva, Vandana 1993, "Women's Indigenous Knowledge and Biodiversity Conservation," in *Ecofeminism*, Maria Mies and Vandana Shiva (eds.), London: Zed Books, pp. 164–73.

Stilkind 1997, "Albright Says Cooperation Can Save Global Environment," US Information Agency Press Release, Washington, DC, April 22.

Stone, Christopher 1993, *The Gnat Is Older Than Man: Global Environment and Human Agenda*, Princeton: Princeton University Press.

Susskind, Lawrence E. 1994, *Environmental Diplomacy*, New York: Oxford University Press.

Torgerson, Douglas 1995, "The Uncertain Quest for Sustainability: Public Discourse and the Politics of Environmentalism," in *Greening Environmental Policy*, Frank Fischer and Michael Black (eds.), New York: St. Martin's Press, pp. 3–20.

United Nations Population Fund 1994, "The ICPD Programme of Action," *Populi* October: 6–11.

Vogel, Shawna 1995, "Has Global Warming Begun?" *Earth* (December): 24–35.

Wæver, Ole 1995, "Securitization and Desecuritization," in Lipschutz (ed.), pp. 46–86.

Wapner, Paul 1998, "Reorienting State Sovereignty: Rights and Responsibilities in the Environmental Age," in Litfin (ed.), pp. 275–97.

Ward, Veronica 1998, "Sovereignty and Ecosystem Management: Clash of Concepts and Boundaries?" in Litfin (ed.), pp. 79 108.

Wilbanks, Thomas J. 1994, "Improving Energy Efficiency: Making a 'No-Regrets' Option Work," *Environment* 36: 16–20, 36–44.

Willetts, Peter 1996, *The Conscience of the World: The Influence of Nongovernmental Organizations in the UN System*, Washington, DC: Brookings Institution.

Wolfers, Arnold 1952, "'National Security' as an Ambiguous Symbol," *Political Science Quarterly* 67: 481–502.

World Commission of Environment and Development 1987, *Our Common Future*, New York: Oxford University Press.

World Resources Institute 1998, *World Resources 1997/1998*, New York: Basic Books.

17 Demography, domestic conflict, and the international order

Jack A. Goldstone

In the 1990s, the world seems to have finally turned the corner on population growth. A combination of increased education for women, national and international support for policies of population planning, and the spread of economic development and accompanying movement along the demographic transition frontier has led to falling population growth rates around the world. Whether among the behemoths – China and India – or among the smaller but rapidly growing nations – such as Saudi Arabia, Kenya, and Malawi – population growth rates have dropped dramatically in the last decade (see Table 17.1).

Yet while population growth rates have dropped around the world, they remain high in some areas. In particular, many nations in the Middle East, southeast Asia, and Central and Northern Africa are still growing at nearly 3 percent per year, a growth rate that leads to a doubling of population in approximately twenty-five years. Moreover, although in most countries the *rate* of population growth has slowed, the absolute number of people being added to the world's population has not; the large number of women of childbearing age in the developing world, who represent the momentum of past population growth, ensures that even while growth rates fall as a percentage of the existing population, the number of new births each year continues to rise. For example, although China's growth rate has fallen to 1.2 percent per year, China will still grow by thirteen to fifteen million people per year for the next fifteen years. The world as a whole will add roughly ninety million people per year, or another 900 million (e.g., another India) in the next decade (Population Reference Bureau 1996).

Rapid population growth itself is no cause for alarm, as it can accompany economic growth and development. But when population growth occurs in countries that have either slow or highly uneven economic growth, in countries whose governments lack the capacity and legitimacy to draw resources needed for development and public services with the consent of the population, and in countries whose elites are deeply

352

Table 17.1. *Countries that have significantly reduced population growth in recent years*

	Pop. growth rates				Pop. growth rates	
	1980–90	1990–4			1980–90	1990–4
Saudi Arabia	5.2	3.2	Costa Rica		2.8	2.1
Kenya	3.4	2.7	Egypt		2.5	2.0
Zimbabwe	3.3	2.5	India		2.1	1.8
Malawi	3.3	2.8	Brazil		2.0	1.7
Algeria	2.9	2.3	Thailand		1.8	1.0
Mongolia	2.8	1.9	China		1.5	1.2

Source: World Bank (1996), *World Development Report 1996* (Oxford University Press), pp. 194–5.

divided by ethnic and/or regional rivalries, then population growth *is* a cause for concern. In such cases, growth can exacerbate pressures on governments and conflicts among elites, increase both the grievances and the mobilization capacity of the population, and heighten the likelihood that conflicts over policy and control of the government will erupt into violent regional and nationwide struggles.

With the end of the Cold War, violent domestic struggles – with their consequences of civil wars, refugee flows, and demands for military and humanitarian intervention – are increasingly the major threat to a stable and peaceful international order (Baldwin 1995). As Susanne Rudolph (1997: 4) has remarked,

Even as political developments in advanced industrial democracies make it vir-tually impossible to engage in interstate wars that create domestic casualties, the fatality counts in civil conflicts [have risen] to figures approximating or over-whelming figures for inter-state wars.

Population and political institutions

To understand the impact of population growth on domestic conflict, one must go well beyond simple aggregate numbers. To determine whether population growth will produce a more unstable and dangerous world in the next two decades, we need to identify the precise institutional path-ways through which it creates political crises.

The obvious fears of the last twenty years – that we will run out of food, of water, of energy, of land, etc. – have been proven false, at least on a global scale. Julian Simon and his followers are correct that over the long haul, the human race has survived repeated crises to become richer and more numerous than ever (Simon 1981; Simon and Kahn 1984). However, *over the short run and for specific regions*, all of these shortages have occurred and will occur, with severe consequences. To ignore this fact and say that "population is not a problem" is like saying that since the human race has triumphed over numerous diseases to fill the earth, we need no longer concern ourselves with medical research or clinical treatment of diseases. In fact, we devote enormous resources to medical research and treatment not merely to save the human race (although large parts of it would surely perish without it), but to mitigate suffering and improve the quality of our lives. It is for these same reasons, rather than only to avert apocalypse, that the effects of population growth demand our attention.

Given that many of the crises we now see stemming from population growth and accompanying environmental degradation are short-term and local in their effects, economists and political scientists sometimes argue that the real problem is not population growth; the problem lies in the political and social institutions that fail to distribute the available resources. This is fair enough; in theory one could view a situation in which population growth is overwhelming the immediately available supply of housing as one in which better policy should have previously allocated more resources for building houses. But *in practice*, if a locality faces a housing shortage, certain questions must be answered – can the supply of housing be quickly increased? Is anticipated population growth going to overwhelm existing supplies for new construction? Most important for politics, will there be inflation, riots against housing authorities, fights over existing housing, migration to new areas?

Although economists have little to say about the distribution of goods and resources, seeing that as a political issue, it is precisely on distributional issues that population growth has its largest impact. Every human society has its cleavages. They may be based on economic status, race and ethnicity, regions, religion, education, or some combination of these; but societies also develop social, political, and economic institutions designed to manage the conflicts that such cleavages can produce. Systems of patronage, justice, and governance may be fair or unfair, they may mitigate or sustain inequalities, but if they are working at all, they discourage violence by producing stable expectations regarding different groups' shares of land, power, and income. As long as those expectations are met, societies tend to remain politically stable. It is when large numbers of people, both elites and popular groups, find their expectations are *not* met that demands arise for dramatic change. It is an unfortunate consequence of population growth that its distributional effects tend to undermine expectations in distressing ways.

In particular, population growth, whether in the context of economic stagnation or rapid development, often distributes resources away from those who labor – such as peasants and traditional workers – to those who employ labor, raising the resentment and fears of the working poor. Moreover, if different elite groups have different degrees of influence over the growing population, and differential access to the fruits of their labors, intra-elite competition and conflicts may increase. And finally, population growth often distributes resources away from the government, as demands for development and social services increase faster than government revenues, weakening the legitimacy of government and its ability to manage conflicts just at the time that social conflicts are growing more intense.

To illustrate how these effects arise, let us examine a hypothetical developing society. For simplicity's sake, let us say that this society has only two sectors: a labor-intensive sector comprising local crafts, migrant or hacienda labor, and agricultural production for local consumption; and a human and financial capital-intensive sector of professions, government, industrial production, and processing and wholesaling of agriculture for export. In developing countries, it is usually a minority of the population that is ensconced in the capital-intensive sector, and a majority that remain in the labor-intensive sector. If the flow of individuals into both sectors matches the growth of job- and income-creating opportunities in these sectors, then conflict is unlikely. But in practice, that rarely happens. Generally, the fastest rate of population growth occurs in the labor-intensive sector, where the job and income opportunities are most limited by resource constraints: especially the amount of land available for peasant farming, but also the incomes of local families who provide the market for traditional foods and crafts. As a result, underemployment and income stresses build in the labor-intensive sector, creating pressures for migration and redistribution of income.[1]

Moreover, the growth of such pressures is highly nonlinear. To continue with our example, let us suppose that one-fifth of the population has jobs in the capital-intensive sector, three-fifths of the population has jobs or a livelihood in the labor-intensive sector, and one-fifth of the population is un- or under-employed. What happens if the population grows by 20 percent? If the labor-intensive sector has reached a point of saturation – whether through population growth or deterioration of land and other resources – that sector can no longer provide expected jobs and incomes. What then happens to that additional population? Assuming that the capital-intensive sector is growing rapidly, it might expand by 50 percent. But since that sector is small, such growth will only absorb *half* the new population, leaving the other half un- or under-employed. This will increase the number of un- and under-employed by fully 50 percent.

Moreover, further population growth leads to ever faster spiraling pressures. If the population grows not by 20 percent, but by 50 percent, then even a doubling of the opportunities in the capital-intensive sector still leaves a 150 percent increase in the un- and under-employed. The result of such arithmetic is clear: even with rapid growth in the capital-intensive sector, the combination of population growth and limited land and other labor-intensive employment resources can lead to wretched distributional problems. Even moderate population growth, if it occurs where resources and opportunities are limited, can lead to underemployment growing much faster than the overall population increases. Given that in many developing countries, populations are projected to double in the next twenty-five to thirty-five years while available land for peasant farming will likely stagnate or decline, the question looms: how will governments provide for and manage the coming tens of millions seeking a livelihood? This question is not merely hypothetical; growing armies of un- and under-employed are major factors fueling unrest in southern Mexico, Algeria, Egypt, and Palestine, and threatening future stability in South Africa and Kenya (Whitmeyer and Hopcroft 1996; Rogerson 1995; Kaplan 1996).

As this question suggests, the immediate effects of population growth are *political*; thus population problems cannot be viewed apart from their institutional context. Unfortunately, far too little attention has been given to the impact of population shifts on political institutions. Well before societies experience widespread absolute deprivation, the institutions that deal with the distribution of goods and power, and the resolution of social conflicts, may be overwhelmed in the face of persistent population pressure and limited resources.

Where such effects occur, institutions, far from being part of the solution to demographic crises, become a major element of the problem. Historical and structural analysis of state failures allows us to trace in some detail the way that population pressures can undermine political institutions (Goldstone 1991). That knowledge can help us intervene in ways to improve and sustain institutions, averting the worst effects of demographic pressures while policies are put in place that will, in the long run, offer hope of alleviating those pressures.

Population growth and political crises in history

That the relationship between population growth and institutional failures leads to revolts, civil wars, and revolutions is hardly new. Europe and classical Asia experienced two major waves of violent political crises since the Renaissance. Between 1580 and 1650 the first such wave rolled across Eurasia, including the English Revolution, the religious civil wars and Fronde in France, rebellions in Catalonia, Portugal, Italy, Sicily, Bohemia, the Ukraine, and the Ottoman Empire, and the collapse of the Ming Empire in China. There followed a century of relative domestic peace, followed by the second wave from 1770 to 1870, this time including the French Revolution, the European Revolutions of 1848, the Pugachev revolt in Russia, and the Taiping rebellion in China. It should come as no great surprise that demographic historians can now document a doubling or tripling of populations in Europe and Asia from 1500 to 1650, followed by a century-long pause, and then a renewed burst of population growth – in Russia and China as well as in Western Europe – from 1730 to 1870 (Goldstone 1991).

After 1870, population growth in the developed world began to slow. However, growth in the developing world just began to take off. Unsurprisingly, we are now in the midst of another worldwide wave of revolts and revolutions beginning right after World War II and continuing to the present day.

As a simple example of the correlation between population pressure and political crises, one can make a list of the twenty-five countries in the world in the low and middle income range with the highest population growth rates of the 1980s (see Figure 17.1). These twenty-five countries represent those nations with population growth at or above 3 percent per year in the decade 1980 to 1991. And although not all of them have been riven by strife and conflict, a remarkable number of the major sites of recent civil wars, revolutions, and violent demonstrations are on this list: Ethiopia, Rwanda, Niger, Congo, the Yemen Republic, Nicaragua, Kenya, Nigeria, Tajikistan (which was one of the most violent of the post-Soviet Union new republics), Iran, and Algeria (which is hovering on the edge of a possible revolution). Other countries on this list – Madagascar, Ghana, Togo, and Côte d'Ivoire – also experienced government crises and national protests, but thankfully in these cases the outcome was movement toward democracy, as elites chose to compromise with each other and institutionalize popular support, rather than create chaos or authoritarian rule.[2] Nonetheless, stability in all of these countries is far from assured, as recent riots in Brazzaville (Congo) have shown.

This correspondence between high rates of population growth and violence is more than just a statistical coincidence. Yet neither is it an iron law. Rather, the answer lies in institutions. Not all institutions are overwhelmed by population pressures. Nor are population pressures the only

Tanzania	Yemen Republic
Ethiopia	Honduras
Madagascar	Cote d'Ivoire
Malawi	Senegal
Rwanda	Jordan
Niger	Congo
Kenya	Tajikistan
Nigeria	Syria
Benin	Namibia
Ghana	Algeria
Togo	Iran
Pakistan	Paraguay
Nicaragua	

(Underlined countries experienced serious domestic political turbulence in the 1980s and 1990s)

Figure 17.1   Countries with population growth rates of 3 percent per year and above, 1980–91

causes of political crises. State corruption, government incompetence, and economic or military setbacks, if sufficiently severe, can all give rise to political crises even in the absence of sustained population growth. However, rapid and sustained population growth is widespread in the developing world, and history shows that such population growth frequently imposed tremendous strains on political and social institutions, leading to their extensive breakdown. Understanding the future of political stability and crises in the developing world therefore seems to require that we grasp the institutional mechanisms by which sustained population growth has produced political crises.

Population pressures and institutional failures: a structural analysis

Figure 17.2 shows the key relationships linking population pressures and political crises. The left-most box lists fundamental factors which, in combination, create difficulties for political regimes: population growth and limited or uneven development. The combination of these factors undermines states through three main routes: (1) bringing a decline in state capacity; (2) producing elite displacement and conflicts; and (3) generating increases in mass mobilization potential.

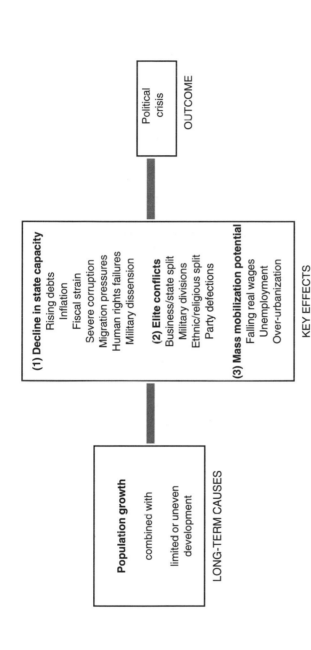

Figure 17.2   Population and political crisis

Decline in state capacity

States need resources. Whether a dictatorship or a democracy, no state can last long if it cannot pay its bureaucrats and its military, if it fails to provide opportunities for its elite supporters, if it cannot assure even minimal standards of work, justice, and security for its middle-class and working populations (Migdal 1988). One of the most striking effects of population growth and resource shortages is the decline of the capacity of the state to carry out the necessary functions of a state, relative to the demands imposed by a growing population. As population rises, the costs of administering justice, providing roads, schools, health care, and education sharply escalate. Subsidies to farmers or city-dwellers, if part of the state budget, can rise precipitously. And frequently, a larger bureaucracy and/or larger military is needed both to absorb a growing number of aspirants to those positions and to carry out the growing tasks of governing. But will a government automatically get the resources it needs to carry out these tasks? All too often the answer is no.

If economic development is slow or uneven, while population grows rapidly, it is likely that for many people per capita income will decline, while for a lucky few wealth will accumulate. This is simply due to the laws of supply and demand. If some resource – land, timber, water, industrial capacity – becomes scarce relative to the number of people who rely on it, then the few people who control that resource will find their wealth sharply rise, while those who depend on that resource will have to pay more and their real incomes will fall. In countries where some key resources are growing scarce as population is rising, elites that control key resources will be enriched and ordinary workers, peasants, and even members of the middle class will find themselves in tighter straits. Where then can the government get the income it needs to cope with sharply rising demands? Either it raises taxes on the majority of the people who are already being hurt by economic trends – which increases resentment and feelings of injustice, or is simply ineffective because they cannot pay much more – or the government tries to take a much larger portion of the new wealth of the elites who are benefiting from scarcity – again a route that is politically dangerous or impossible because of the influence of those enriched elites.

Since both of these approaches often fail, the government simply becomes weaker, increasingly unable to maintain justice, order, and welfare or to keep elites in line. What are the early warning signs of this condition? The government may take on a rising load of debt or print money, creating inflation. The government may show fiscal strain through a measurable decline in income and defaults on obligations.

Severe corruption may replace regular pay as the main sustenance of state servants. Migration – either internal by the jobless seeking work or external by economic refugees leaving for greener pastures – may burden cities or neighboring countries, creating more problems of disorder. Human rights failures may indicate the breakdown of law and order. And an underpaid military, chafing at the rising impotence and failures of the state, may stand aside and not support the troubled regime, or even talk of taking matters into its own hands through a coup.

In short, the combination of rising population and limited or uneven development in developing countries may lead to a recognizable "syndrome" of state capacity decline. This may include rising debt, inflation, fiscal strain, severe corruption, mass migrations, human rights failures, and military dissension, in varying combinations. Even strong states – such as China – are not immune from such pressures. China's agricultural sector, despite its astounding progress in the last fifteen years, is in the process of being overwhelmed by a combination of rapid population increase (an expected 200–250 million in the next fifteen years) and a need to create greater efficiency by substituting capital for family labor (Smil 1993). With agriculture unable to provide a reserve to absorb the growing labor force, the only place for the population to turn is to the cities. The result has been a headlong rush of migrants – perhaps 100 million – to the cities, resulting in a building boom and rapid inflation. As economic wealth has mushroomed in the cities, mainly in the new private and foreign-investment sectors, agriculture and state-owned enterprises have, by comparison, grown slowly. As a result, the income of the central government – dependent on the latter two sectors – declined from 34 percent of GNP in 1970 to 19 percent in 1990 (Hornik 1994). Efforts to increase tax collection have not yet fully reversed this slide, although they have raised massive protests against tax collectors (Perry 1995). Faced with this decline, the government has sped up the printing of money, let credit balloon, and taken on a vast increase in state debts, which have grown from just US$17 billion in 1985 to US$118 billion in 1995 (World Bank 1997). Due to these measures, as Richard Hornik (1994: 29) wrote in *Foreign Affairs*, "China's fiscal and monetary policies remain a shambles," with a state deficit approaching 25 percent of government revenues. Raising government revenues remains the critical goal of China's new leadership under Jiang Zemin, and the stability of the regime depends on its success.

Not surprisingly, as China's private sector offers rapid and concentrated wealth, and the resources of the state have declined, corruption has become a way of life. Internal migration has overwhelmed the old system of residence registration and party control, and the panicked party leadership has turned to various repressive and human-rights violating policies to try to preserve its privileges and some kind of order. Yet the military, reeling from the public distrust and disapproval of its actions in suppressing the Tiananmen Square protests, has tried to professionalize and distance itself from party/society conflicts. Many provincial governments are now openly defying decrees from Beijing, and the rising impotence of the central government combined with the rapid growth of private industry reminds many of the waning days of the Chinese Empire in 1900–10 (Miles 1996; Goldstone 1995).

If a country with a government as powerful as that of China can undergo massive state capacity decline, it is hardly surprising that weaker states, facing even faster population growth and resource degradation, are wallowing in debts, corruption, human rights failures, mass migrations, and dangerously independent militaries. From Somalia to Rwanda to Haiti, the burdens on states have shattered regimes, leading to civil wars, coups, and humanitarian problems that have humbled the ability of the developed world to provide solutions.

What is more, if several weak states facing population pressures are clustered in an area, spillover affects can spread political crisis. In East Africa, the collapse of the Zairian regime, a weak state whose collapse had long been expected, was triggered by the refugee flows and attendant conflicts over land coming from the chaos in Rwanda. The conflicts in Sudan and Ethiopia also link refugee problems and civil wars across states. A similar pattern of spreading crisis and disorder has obtained in the past in Uganda and Rwanda, in Pakistan and Afghanistan, and in Liberia and Sierra Leone (Weiner 1992/3).

Elite displacement and conflicts

The decline of state capacity would not be fatal in a society that had the capacity for renewal. A society basically wealthy in resources and with loyal elites united in their support for the government could effect reforms to help put the government on a sound fiscal basis. But state capacity decline can trigger devastating civil wars and humanitarian disasters in countries that are *not* so united. Where deep fissures divide society's elite groups, and the conflicts between those elites and their supporters is exacerbated by population pressures and resource scarcities that enrich certain groups and hurt others, the ability of a strong government to keep order, provide an outlet for elite ambitions, and offer a framework for compromise and distribution of society's wealth is absolutely vital. Where government weakens, elites will go into business for themselves, resolve their conflicts by force, and, all too often, turn on the government or tear their societies apart.

Where ethnic or regional divisions exist, population growth and re-source shortages can intensify them. These factors can also create splits between the state and the business community, within the military, and within ruling parties. These phenomena can be grouped under the concept of "elite displacement." When a population grows, the number of people who aspire to elite positions – positions of leadership, wealth, and influence – is also going to grow. In a healthy society that is rich in resources and is building its institutions and its economy, there is usually room to accommodate a growing elite. But if a country does not have a sufficiently fast-growing economy, various factions or groups may contest for a stagnant or declining pool of resources to support elite positions. In many developing countries, there simply are not enough positions in the government, and the military, or enough wealth in the ordinary channels of society, to satisfy growing numbers of elite families and their offspring, who themselves aspire to elite positions. The result is a heightened competition between elites for control of the nation's wealth and its government.

It is such struggles that have convulsed countries like Rwanda and Burundi, where sustained population growth and environmental degradation have undermined traditional Hutu-Tutsi economic roles and created a sharp struggle for the remaining spoils. Rwanda and Burundi were characterized for most of their history by a mix of cattle-raising and farming; Tutsi dominated cattle-raising (and leadership of the societies); the far more numerous Hutus were predominantly farmers. The exchange of cattle for grain helped maintain reciprocal relations among Tutsi and Hutus. But over the course of this century, as population growth led to farming encroachment on range land, cattle-raising diminished, and the Tutsi lost their distinctive livelihood, turning to farming and becoming in many ways (except for an identity system imposed by the Belgian colonial regime) indistinguishable from the Hutus. The efforts of Tutsis to maintain their distinctive position shifted to an effort to control the army and post-colonial government, an effort that was abruptly contravened by the Belgian insistence on a majority-based, Hutu-dominant regime. Tutsis and Hutus have been at war, on and off, ever since. In recent years, with population growing rapidly and per-capita output falling, competition between Tutsi and Hutu elites has intensified with each group seeing political domination as essential to its survival. The result has been a failure of compromise regimes, a military-imposed Tutsi dominance in Burundi, and genocidal warfare in Rwanda (Percival and Homer-Dixon 1995).

If a government loses the confidence of its elites, and the elites are divided and competing for resources, only turmoil can result. If the government weakens, and elites feel that whoever first takes over the vacuum of power will win all the spoils, a situation of apparent peace or harmony, or multi-ethnic or multi-racial government, can rapidly degenerate into an all-out war.

Mass mobilization potential

In addition to bringing state capacity decline and exacerbating conflicts among elites, population growth and resource degradation have yet a third set of destabilizing effects, raising the willingness of people to be recruited to fight in situations of violence.

The two major dimensions determining mass mobilization potential are contentment and control. A population that is relatively content is unlikely to take major risks and follow leaders into revolt. Similarly, even discontented popular groups are unlikely to take the risks of violent action if they are well controlled by the government, either closely monitored or dependent on the state for basic needs.

The keys to keeping a population content are physical security and security of incomes. We have already seen that state decline and elite conflicts can undermine physical security as order breaks down and elites "go into business for themselves," or a state resorts to human rights abuses as normal law and order break down and the state fears it is losing control of society. At the same time, rapid population growth and resource degradation generally lead to falling real wages and various kinds of actual or disguised unemployment for much of the population. China offers a telling example. Despite the most rapid and sustained economic growth in the world for the last decade, eighty million Chinese have persistent worries in finding food and shelter. Two-thirds of China's manufacturing workers still work in state-owned firms, most of which are unprofitable and are laying off millions of workers and cutting wages. The combination of rapid population growth, limited and uneven development, and the degradation of rural resources has produced a situation in which much of the population shares relative poverty, while a small fraction competes for extraordinary wealth.

Whether in the hills of Peru and Colombia, where Sendero Luminoso and the FARC respectively recruit, or in the cities of Iran, Egypt, and Algeria, where Islamic fundamentalists recruit terrorists and popular followings, or in the migrant laborer settlements that are growing in and around the cities of South Africa and mainland China, where independent labor unions have made or are making their mark, various combinations of physical and material insecurity are creating potential foot-soldiers for political violence.

Of course, governments have typically met popular discontent with various kinds of state repression and control. But population growth can defeat those efforts as well. Where population growth interacts with declining resources in the countryside, migration to the cities creates concentrations of population that are increasingly difficult to control. And these migrants are available to be recruited into new kinds of organizations, so that urban growth can greatly increase the number of people mobilized into new opposition movements.

Finally, there is a subtlety to the impact of population growth. When a population grows, it is usually because more children are being born and more of those children are growing up rather than succumbing to the childhood diseases that used to keep population growth low. This means that the population becomes rapidly younger: people do not enter the population nicely distributed across all different age groups, they come in as youngsters, creating a "bulge" of youth in the society. Because youngsters tend to be more swaggering than adults, have less to lose, and more to prove, a large "youth bulge" raises the potential for violence. In fact, major revolutions have generally occurred in societies that had exceptionally large "youth bulges" in the 15–29 year age groups (Goldstone 1991). If a very large youth cohort is coming of age in a situation where normal economic opportunities are contracting and elites are competing to offer opportunities and attract followers, the potential for mobilization into political opposition is high. If in addition the central government starts to collapse, there develops a setting for something like gang warfare to develop on a national scale.

Activating ideologies of opposition

Although the mass killings in Rwanda, the tribal struggles in Somalia, and the ethnic cleansing and battles for territory in Bosnia are redolent of non-ideological, large-scale gang warfare, other struggles that are considered more truly "revolutionary" – in Iran, Nicaragua, Palestine, Peru, the Philippines, Algeria, South Africa – do appear to depend more for their existence on some form of ideological mobilization. It may be based on religious fundamentalism, nationalism, socialism, liberalism, or some combination of these, but giving meaning to civil violence and opposition to the government in terms of pursuing an alternative vision of the social order seems a crucial component of these conflicts.

No doubt such ideological mobilization gives these conflicts a different character from conflicts based mainly on efforts by one group to gain territory or power at the expense of others. Yet even such ideologically colored crises are rooted in material conditions that often stem from the combination of population pressures and weak or uneven economic development. In fact, such material conditions seem to be a necessary foundation for the activation of these ideologies into effective cultures of opposition.

By this I mean that ideologies providing alternative visions of the social order are, in themselves, rather fluid and pervasive. Hardly any societies exist that do not harbor some ideological opponents of the existing regime; more commonly a number of opposition ideologies are in the air, competing for adherents. In the Middle East, this century has seen revolutionary ideologies drawing mainly from Islamic fundamentalism (as in the Wahabi movement in Saudi Arabia) and constitutional liberalism (as in the Constitutional Revolution in Iran) in the first decade of the 1900s; followed by anti-imperialism and nationalism during the era of World Wars I and II; followed by authoritarian state socialism (as Nasserism in Egypt and the Ba'athist regimes in Syria and Iraq); followed by a return to Islamic fundamentalism (as in Iran, Algeria, and Egypt). All of these ideologies were "in the air" throughout the century; all of them provided the ideological basis for revolutionary mobilization at some time in this century (Moaddel 1993).

What distinguished times and places where ideologically inspired revolutionary mobilization became significant from times and places where the existing regime preserved stable rule was *not* the presence or absence of an alternative vision of the social order. What mattered was whether elites and popular groups were motivated to withdraw their assent from the existing order and seek to lead or join opposition movements. Existing ideologies could then be "activated" through the formation of elites and their followers into organized communities of opposition. And this in turn depended on whether the state had the capacity to fulfil its promises and commitments regarding economic development, distribution of goods and power, and conflict resolution; whether elites were satisfied or struggling with the state and other elites to preserve their position; and whether the population found sufficient security and justice in their lives, or felt so lacking in these areas that they were willing to take risks to change the status quo. Where growing populations consistently encountered restricted opportunities and limited state capacity, and where urban migration has created vast new communities to be mobilized against the regime (as throughout the Middle East, much of South Asia, Central America, and sub-Saharan Africa), revolutionary movements have also been consistently recurrent, even though their ideological bases show a bewildering variety of shifts in content over time. Demographic factors can thus play a key role in providing the conditions in which ideologically motivated communities of opposition grow and achieve significance (Foran 1993).

To sum up, the most immediately threatening effects of population growth for a stable and peaceful international order are the effects of that growth on domestic politics. Population growth and resource degradation in developing nations will cause demands for services and opportunities to escalate to levels that many states cannot meet, leading to debt, fiscal distress, inflation, and corruption in the government that ruins its legitimacy and effectiveness. Population growth and scarce resources will also lead to intensified elite conflicts as relative scarcities provide opportunities for a few to get rich while many lag behind. Moreover, population growth and limited resources in developing societies will often mean that the society cannot provide elite rewards to all those who believe they deserve them, leading to struggles for control of the government and economy. Population growth is likely to expand further the number of people willing to take the risk of following leaders into a fight, especially if these people are facing declining employment, rapid urban growth, and a shift toward an ever younger population. Lastly, this combination of material conditions often leads to the "activation" of ideologies of opposition, allowing ideologies which have long been present to become the focus of communities actively mobilizing in opposition to the existing regime.

Preventing and mitigating political crises

There is hardly a major arena of foreign policy that will not be affected by the political consequences of population pressures. In the Middle East and North Africa, burgeoning populations are fueling Islamic radicalism. In Mexico, Central America, the Caribbean, and North Africa, the ill-fit between population growth and economic opportunities is producing huge streams of migrants seeking to enter the developed economies of North America and Western Europe, creating increasing problems in absorbing immigrants, regulating immigration, and dealing with resulting resurgent racial conflicts. In sub-Saharan Africa, population growth, resource decline, and state decay are producing humanitarian crises that place an enormous burden on the will and means of the international community. Affecting all these areas, policies to deal with the sources and consequences of population growth may be the most comprehensive and vital element of international security in the post-Cold War world.

There are two levels of policy that are needed to deal with these problems. The first level is to offer help with the *fundamental long-term causes* of these problems: policies addressed to slowing down population growth, conserving resources, and aiding broad-based (rather than narrow, highly uneven) economic development. The second level is to offer help with the *key political effects* of population growth and resource depletion, namely state capacity decline, elite displacement, and mass mobilization potential. A two-pronged approach involving both levels is vital. Policies addressed to the fundamental long-term causes will take years to have an impact; in the meantime, the short-term political effects of continuing population pressures need to be mitigated or the implementation of longer-term policies will fail. At the same time, policies to mitigate the political impact of population pressures *must* be accompanied by sufficient attention to reducing the long-term population and environmental pressures for conflicts, otherwise the results will be like putting out a forest fire then letting even more dry underbrush accumulate. The long-term result will be an even larger conflagration.

Thankfully, the demographic research of the last thirty years has demonstrated that population growth is relatively easy to address. It is now increasingly clear to the leaders of developing nations that the stability of their own governments and the prosperity of their societies depends on slowing the freight train of population increase (Gulhati and Bates 1994: 56–8). Thailand and Indonesia have led the way in showing what is possible with non-coercive, voluntary family planning made available to the population. Widespread adoption of voluntary contraception in Catholic Latin America and Europe, and even in Hindu and Confucian nations in Asia, points the way to what can be done. Making family planning assistance widely available may save the expenditure of hundreds of billions of dollars on dealing with military conflicts, migration, and humanitarian crises a decade or two later.[3]

With population growth slowed, one fundamental cause of many political crises in the developing world will recede. Yet even with such efforts, population growth and its consequences will be with us for many decades as the demographic momentum developed in the last fifty years plays itself out. Thus policies that mitigate those consequences will also demand attention.

To increase the odds that foreign aid and international policies will contribute to the stabilization of the world order, it will be necessary to pay close attention to the precise pathways by which population and environmental pressures create political crises. That is, policies should be directed in ways that help mitigate state capacity decline, avoid heightening elite conflicts, and reduce mass mobilization potential. For example, current economic aid to governments often addresses state capacity by insisting on a sharp curtailment of government spending (e.g., IMF structural adjustment programs). However, such actions do little to improve political stability, as they do nothing to help the state secure a stable revenue base, while making the state more dependent on foreign assistance than on domestic popular and elite support. It should not be surprising that IMF structural adjustment programs, rather than improving political stability, are strongly associated with an *increased* risk of civil war; moreover, this risk is particularly great in struggling democracies, whom international aid agencies are usually most concerned to help succeed (Hauge 1997).

Where political problems are already well advanced, where state capacity is low and popular mobilization potential is high, different policies are needed. In such cases, the most crucial aid should be addressed to supporting a coalition of moderate elites and thus avoiding the degeneration of elite conflicts into civil wars and revolutions. America's greatest success with such a policy was in the Philippines; by withdrawing support from the Marcos regime and supporting a coalition of moderate elites that had formed around Corazon Aquino, rather than supporting Marcos to the bitter end, an Iranian-style debacle was avoided.

Probably the greatest failure in America's Haiti policy was lack of investment in building a coalition of moderate elites to support the Aristide government. Instead, relations between the Aristide government, which was tending in a populist, anti-elite direction, and Haiti's conservative church and business elites became polarized. As a result, Haiti's wealthy elites felt they would find greater security in a military government than in the Aristide regime, and hence tolerated (and in many cases supported) the military coup. Given Haiti's demographic and institutional conditions – a dense population on scarce and increasingly deforested and eroded land, and a government with weak capacities facing a largely impoverished and underemployed population – it is absolutely vital to any regime's stability that it enjoy a reasonably strong elite, as well as popular support. Indeed, elite factionalization is already threatening Haiti's nascent democracy.

The reduction of mass mobilization potential is a difficult task. Where decades of population growth and resource exploitation have constricted opportunities for productive employment, there is no easy and immediate fix. Yet much can be done by spending current aid allocations differently. One very simple measure is to increase the amount spent on primary education in the developing world as opposed to university education. Currently, typical foreign aid programs will spend about 500 dollars per university student, and one or two dollars per primary student per year in a country receiving educational assistance. Aside from the developmental aspects of these policies, the *political* effects create difficulties. Universities will produce students who expect to have some influential position; in a nation with limited state capacity for administrative positions, this can lead to more aspiring elites jockeying for key roles, and heightened factional conflicts. By contrast, building up primary education leads to the recruitment of large numbers of school teachers. This absorbs labor and broadly increases productivity. If even moderately well paid, that large number of school teachers can be the basis for a widespread, regionally dispersed, conservative middle class.

Conclusion: institutions, international assistance, and the international order

One of the greatest disappointments of the last twenty years is that, while international aid has been successful in reducing the rate of population growth, and – in most areas of the world – in increasing per capita incomes, it has not prevented deadly conflicts. The list of domestic conflicts that have created international problems by giving rise to civil wars, revolutions, the creation of humanitarian crises, and refugee flows continues to grow, including at present those in Angola, Afghanistan, Sudan, Algeria, Cambodia, Burundi, Rwanda, Zaire, Sri Lanka, Bosnia, Sierra Leone, Tajikistan, Liberia, and Ethiopia.

The inability of economic development to avert such conflicts, despite increased per capita incomes, reflects the lack of any simple correspondence between overall income or growth and political stability. What matters for preserving political order is the ability of political institutions to cope with the demands placed upon them by their society. In this respect, development that is capital-intensive, creating state debts and limited opportunities for aspiring elites and the masses newly entering the labor force, can actually be destabilizing, rather than helpful.

As Gurr and Harff (1996) point out, well-intentioned meddling that simply reacts to ongoing problems often increases the risks of violent conflict. What is required instead is an approach to foreign aid and intervention in developing nations that addresses the long-term and structural bases for stability and crisis. A sensitivity to how aid and investment will affect the capacity of states to support themselves from stable revenues, how they will affect the propensities of elites to support or contest the existing government, and how they will absorb rapidly growing labor forces, will be essential if foreign support for developing countries is to ameliorate, and not exacerbate, the potential for domestic political conflicts.

International assistance in the areas of population planning and primary education can reduce some of the long-term demographic causes of domestic political conflicts. International assistance or intervention that reduces the degree of regime conflict with elites, and helps to reinforce moderate coalitions in government, as the US has done in the Philippines, can help nations emerge from short-term crises and move forward on the road to stability. Yet nothing constructive can be done without appreciating the role that strong institutions play in preserving domestic order. If the international community is to help create a new and peaceful international order, resistant to the breakdown of states and resulting dislocations, it will be necessary to address the role that demographic pressures, among other factors, play in regard to the institutions through which states, elites, and populations at large secure their places in their societies.

NOTES

1 In some Asian countries (China, South Korea, Taiwan) land reforms provided for expansion in agriculture; in other areas (e.g., the Punjab in India) the "Green Revolution" accomplished the same end. But in many parts of Africa, Latin America, South Asia, and the Middle East, the expansion of population in the labor-intensive sector has led to land hunger, depressed wages, and/or massive migration to urban centers (see Massey 1996).

2 See Burton, Gunther and Higley (1992) for an analysis of how elite compromise in the face of domestic crisis is key to the development of democratic institutions.

3 Aside from the role of population growth in creating pressures that can cause state crises, population growth causes increases in the *magnitude* of populations at risk, and thus directly increases the number of potential refugees or victims should violent conflict arise.

REFERENCES

Baldwin, David A. 1995, "Security Studies and the End of the Cold War," *World Politics* 48: 117–41.

Burton, Michael, Gunther, Richard and Higley, John 1992, "Introduction: Elite Transformations and Democratic Regimes," in *Elites and Democratic Consolidation in Latin America and Southern Europe*, John Higley and Richard Gunther (eds.), Cambridge: Cambridge University Press, pp. 1–37.

Foran, John 1993, *Fragile Resistance: Social Transformation in Iran from 1500 to the Revolution*, Boulder, CO: Westview Press.

Goldstone, Jack A. 1991, *Revolution and Rebellion in the Early Modern World*, Berkeley: University of California Press.

1995, "China's Coming Collapse," *Foreign Policy* 99: 35–54.

Gulhat, Kaval and Bates, Lisa M. 1994, "Developing Countries and the International Population Debate: Politics and Pragmatism," in *Population and Development*, Robert Cassen et al., New Brunswick, NJ: Transaction Books, pp. 47–77.

Gurr, Ted Robert and Harff, Barbara 1996, *Early Warning of Communal Conflicts and Genocide*, Tokyo: United National University.

Hauge, Wenche 1997, "Development and Conflict," in *Causes of Conflict in the Third World*, Ketil Volden and Dan Smith (eds.), Oslo: International Peace Research Institute, pp. 33–51.

Hornik, Richard 1994, "Bursting China's Bubble," *Foreign Affairs* 73: 28–42.

Kaplan, Robert D. 1996, *The Ends of the Earth: A Journey at the Dawn of the 21st Century*, New York: Random House.

Massey, Douglas 1996, "The Age of Extremes: Concentrated Affluence and Poverty in the Twenty-First Century," *Demography* 33: 395–412.

Migdal, Joel 1988, *Strong Societies and Weak States*, Princeton: Princeton University Press.

Miles, James 1996, *The Legacy of Tiananmen: China in Disarray*, Ann Arbor: University of Michigan Press.

Moaddel, Mansoor 1993, *Class, Politics, and Ideology in the Iranian Revolution*, New York: Columbia University Press.

Percival, Valerie and Homer-Dixon, Thomas 1995, "Environmental Scarcity and Violent Conflict: The Rwandan Case," Occasional Paper, Project on Environment, Population, and Security, The Peace and Conflict Studies Program, University of Toronto, and the American Association for the Advancement of Science, Washington, DC: AAAS.

Perry, Elizabeth 1995, "To Rebel is Justified," paper presented to the Program in Agrarian Studies, Yale University.

Population Reference Bureau 1996, *1996 World Population Data Sheet*, Washington, DC: Population Reference Bureau.

Rogerson, Christian 1995, "The Employment Challenge in a Democratic South Africa," in *The Geography of Change in South Africa*, Anthony Lemon (ed.), New York: John Wiley, pp. 172–3.

Rudolph, Susanne Hoeber 1997, "Introduction," in *Transnational Religion and Fading States*, Rudolph and James Piscatori (eds.), Boulder, CO: Westview Press, pp. 1–24.

Simon, Julian 1981, *The Ultimate Resource*, Princeton: Princeton University Press.

Simon, Julian and Kahn, Herman (eds.) 1984, *The Resourceful Earth*, Oxford: Basil Blackwell.

Smil, Vaclav 1993, *China's Environmental Crisis*, Armonk, NY: M. E. Sharpe.

Weiner, Myron 1992/3, "Security, Stability, and International Migration," *International Security* 17: 91–126.

Whitmeyer, Joseph and Hopcroft, Rosemary L. 1996, "Community, Capitalism, and Rebellion in Chiapas," *Sociological Perspectives* 39: 517–39.

World Bank 1997, *World Development Tables* (CD-ROM), Washington, DC: World Bank.

18 Great equalizers or agents of chaos? Weapons of mass destruction and the emerging international order

T. V. Paul

With the end of the Cold War, the proliferation of weapons of mass destruction (WMD) has arrived at the forefront of issues that challenge the creation of a stable international order. The 1991 Gulf War and the revelations about the Iraqi efforts at producing all the three types of weapons of mass destruction – nuclear, chemical, and biological – generated considerable international attention to the problem. The Indian and Pakistani nuclear tests in May 1998 also brought substantial attention to the subject. Some believe that the Iraqi episode portends the coming chaos caused by the possession of WMD by revisionist states or subnational actors that hold grievances against the regional or international order. The renewed enthusiasm for non-proliferation stems not from any sudden increase in the number of states pursuing the WMD route, since most national actors in question had already begun their quest for weapons of mass destruction during the Cold War period. In fact, the post-Cold War era has witnessed some major successes in non-proliferation, as South Africa, Argentina, Brazil, Ukraine, Kazakhstan, and Belarus have renounced nuclear weapons since 1990. The conclusion of the Chemical Weapons Convention (CWC) in 1993 was another milestone event in WMD disarmament on a global scale.

I argue here that the driving force for non-proliferation comes from the status quo states, especially the United States and its allies, who believe that what will constrain their capacity to manage the international security order in the twenty-first century will be the possession of weapons of mass destruction by smaller actors. As Henry Kissinger characterizes it, weapons of mass destruction, especially nuclear arms, are "great equalizers" (1994: 76) of major-minor power relations, a revolutionary source of change in dominant-subordinate state relations since the dawn of the modern state system. The major powers have been driven by the fear that diffusion would blur the line between major and minor powers, as one of the attributes of major power status has been the ability to intervene in the affairs of minor powers without punishment to their home territory in return. The minor powers aligned with the United States and others threatened by proliferation support these initiatives for fear of being coerced by regional states possessing WMD capabilities in future conflict situations.

The Gulf War powerfully demonstrated to the status quo states that the fears expressed during the early stages of the nuclear age that the spread of nuclear weapons would constitute a fundamental change in the international power structure may be coming true. The character of these weapons, especially nuclear arms, is such that they provide the possessor, who may be weak in other power attributes, a potential capability that could under certain circumstances neutralize a larger state's military and technological advantages.[1] Smaller states armed with WMD could resist interventionary pressures by great powers, especially in times of crises. Diffusion could also depreciate the value of alliances and nuclear umbrellas, especially if the smaller allies of the hegemonic power, fearful of abandonment, are compelled to acquire independent capabilities in order to buttress their deterrent capacities. This chapter looks at the likely consequences of the spread of weapons of mass destruction to international order in the twenty-first century. It traces the efforts by the international community, especially by the major powers, to control the diffusion of such weapons. In the second part, I will explore the reasons why some states acquire WMD, while others do not. The final section will discuss the likely threat and opportunity that WMD diffusion could pose to the creation of a peaceful international order in the twenty-first century. I argue that proliferation has both positive and negative implications for international order and that some of the threat scenarios presented, especially in the Western media and scholarship, are exaggerated.[2]

Why do states acquire weapons of mass destruction?

Explanations for why nations acquire WMD range from security concerns to domestic politics and organizational politics (e.g., Sagan and Waltz 1995; Meyer 1984). The most compelling explanation is, however, based on security variables. Nations acquire WMD in the face of similar efforts by enemies or to balance the nuclear and/or conventional military advantages of their adversaries. It is no accident that a majority of states that have acquired or made serious efforts to obtain such weapons have intense perceived or actual security threats. However, a few states with limited security threats had attempted to maintain nuclear weapons options largely for domestic political reasons. Argentina and Brazil fall in this category of states. It must be noted that these states never crossed the line to actual weapons fabrication. South Africa's choice for nuclear weapons also had its roots in the domestic political order, although exaggerated security threats arising out of the protracted conflicts in southern Africa also influenced the decision by the apartheid regime to build a small nuclear arsenal in the 1980s.

As the nuclear age advanced, it has became obvious to most small/medium states that nuclear acquisition is a costly enterprise and not a path for all countries to pursue. The norm of non-possession took hold in several countries, while the political, military, technological, and normative constraints helped to forestall the choices of several states. The strengthening of the nuclear taboo, or tradition of non-use, also gave some assurance to non-nuclear states (Paul 1995). As the non-proliferation regime became embedded, it became clear that only a few states would break the regime rules or even ignore them altogether. Those nations most likely to acquire nuclear weapons are situated in high-conflict environments, facing a protracted conflict or an enduring rivalry. Cases in point are India, Pakistan, and Israel. To these states, relative gains matter most and they have a high probability of engaging in crisis or war with their regional rivals. Such states are least likely to forgo nuclear weapons, while those states that do not face protracted conflicts or those that have a credible alliance partner are likely to forswear their nuclear options, especially if their nuclear programs are launched for domestic political reasons. Shifts in their security environments and domestic regime changes are key variables in explaining such transformations. The cases of Argentina, Brazil, and South Africa attest to this argument. The strategic choices of states in this respect are heavily dependent on their security interdependence with other states, i.e., the extent to which their security is tied to the security of another state (Paul forthcoming).

The pace of proliferation is determined largely by the nature of the systemic and sub-systemic security environment and conflict processes. During the Cold War era, the high level of systemic rivalry caused all major powers to acquire some form of WMD, the nuclear capability being the most potent one. The acquisition of WMD by some such states with regional rivals, e.g., China, caused countries such as India to search for a countervailing capability. In some cases, the desire on the part of some regional states, such as Iran, Iraq, and North Korea, to withstand intervention by great powers may have provided incentives to acquiring WMD.[3] The main incentive for nuclear acquisition for third-tier states, however, comes from regional security threats and conflictual interactions with their neighboring states. The high intensity and long duration of such conflicts, the lack of economic interdependence, and the dearth of reliable alliance partners, all increase the propensity of regional states to acquire WMD capabilities. However, it is probable that as the revolution in military affairs widens the technological and military gap between major powers and regional states, the temptation on the part of additional states to acquire WMD as a hedge against great power intervention will increase in the twenty-first century.

Curbing proliferation

What explains the intense international efforts to control the spread of weapons of mass destruction? Apart from the fears generated by the horrendous destruction these weapons can cause to human and other living beings and the indiscriminate nature of their effects on the environment, political considerations play a large part in the global efforts at non-proliferation. The logic of the efforts varies for great powers and small powers. A brief discussion of the history of endeavors at containing the spread of WMD is essential to elucidate this point.

International efforts at arresting the spread of nuclear weapons began with the dawn of the nuclear era. The earliest attempt was contained in the Baruch Plan of 1946 when the US representative to the United Nations, Bernard Baruch, proposed an international agency to control nuclear activities, with the national right of possession disbanded. The Soviet Union opposed this plan, fearing that it would disallow Moscow from developing nuclear weapons while at the same time allowing the US to maintain its monopoly for several years. Washington went on to adopt a more benign route to nuclear non-proliferation afterwards. The key step in the development of the regime was the creation of the International Atomic Energy Agency (IAEA), an institution which would administer safeguards against the diversion of nuclear materials for weapons purposes. The proposal for such an institution was contained in the 1957 Atoms for Peace Plan of President Eisenhower, which initiated the distribution of nuclear materials to other countries for peaceful nuclear activities with the expectation that there would be no diversion of such weapons to military purposes. With the arrival of China as a nuclear weapon state in 1964, it became apparent to the US and the USSR that efforts should be made to stop additional countries outside the five-member nuclear club from acquiring nuclear weapons.

The key result of these efforts was the conclusion of the Nuclear Non-Proliferation Treaty (NPT) in 1968. The Treaty prohibited member states from collaborating in the development of nuclear weapons or transferring nuclear weapons to one another, while allowing peaceful nuclear energy activities under international safeguards. It established two types of states: nuclear weapon states (NWS) and non-nuclear weapon states (NNWS). Those states that possessed nuclear weaponry before January 1967 were allowed to keep it, while no state would be legally permitted to enter the nuclear club after that date. The non-nuclear weapon states promised not to develop nuclear weapons in return for assistance with their peaceful nuclear energy programs while the nuclear weapon states agreed not to help other states to become nuclear. Under Article VI of the Treaty, the latter also promised to reduce their weapons progressively in order to achieve general and complete nuclear disarmament. This bifurcation of nuclear "haves" and "have-nots" was deliberate and was the main reason why the Treaty received cooperation from the two superpowers and Britain. Although two second-tier nuclear states, France and China, did not join the Treaty immediately, they also tacitly supported the unequal international arrangement. Indeed, in the 1990s they would join the Treaty, having been assured that their positions in the nuclear hierarchy were secure. In 1995, the NPT was extended in perpetuity, with all five declared nuclear powers and several middle ranking states, especially South Africa, Canada, and Australia, taking the initiative to get it approved by the United Nations.

The NPT was largely an attempt by the satisfied great powers and their allies to forestall the arrival of new nuclear challengers to their power position in the international system. As Martin Wight points out, historically satisfied great powers have been in the forefront of disarmament campaigns if such efforts suited their interests. Thus the British proposal for armaments reduction at the Hague conference in 1907, and the 1946 US Baruch Plan to limit atomic development were motivated largely by the desire to maintain the advantageous positions of these two states. Germany and the Soviet Union, the states these proposals were aimed at respectively, resisted such limitations because they would have hampered their efforts to alter the balance of power in their favor (Wight 1978: 211). Once the Soviets achieved nuclear parity with the United States, their interest in forestalling other states from nuclear acquisition also increased. According to Wight, the NPT was the highest point of US-Soviet common interest in this realm and it marked the successful conclusion of their efforts to give a legal basis to the distinction between nuclear "haves" and "have-nots." "It provided the framework of a technological condominium over international society, by fixing the hierarchy of power" (286). The initial Soviet impetus largely derived from a desire to forestall Germany from becoming a nuclear weapon state.

The NPT was thus a powerful way to refuse acknowledgment of newcomers to the nuclear club. By creating a cut-off date, it was presumed that it would be illegal for a new state to acquire nuclear weapons and that efforts in this regard would not be recognized by the international community as legitimate.[4] Although this sovereignty-sacrificing provision violated the notion of self-help which enshrines the principle that the ultimate responsibility for national defense rests with the sovereign state, it was justified on the assumption that non-great powers do not need nuclear capability to exercise their defense responsibilities.

For great powers, more than anything else, the vulnerability nuclear weaponry causes creates the incentive to arrest proliferation. This sense of vulnerability springs from the realization that adequate defenses do not exist against even a limited nuclear attack and that, unlike conventional weapons, a nuclear-armed small state in possession of appropriate delivery systems can cause physical damage to great powers or their close allies, a revolution of sorts in great-small power relations. As Richard Harknett argues, "while conventional weapons allow for adaptation to costs, nuclear weapons permit little more than the absorption of punishment." This incontestable nature of nuclear weapons "alters the range of options available to states contemplating the use of force" (Harknett 1998: 50). Thus great powers have a rational interest in precluding a situation whereby a small state can threaten unacceptable punishment even if it means the complete destruction of the small state in return. The sheer uncertainty that nuclear weapons cause constrains the great power's capacity to intervene against smaller actors. Great powers are also worried about smaller states acquiring ballistic missile capability, as missiles and WMD can form a deadly combination of capability in the hands of smaller actors and thereby alter power relationships.

The NPT, indeed, was the most comprehensive in a long list of efforts by dominant groups or states to deny new military technology to subordinate groups or states. Around 1,100 BC, the Philistines made efforts to prevent the Israelites from acquiring iron-edged weapons (Burns 1993: 1409). During the mediaeval era, attempts by European nobles to prohibit the use of crossbows in wars against Christians were driven by the desire to maintain their monopoly rights over these weapons which could pierce the armor of the knights and had revolutionary implications (Croft 1996: 24).[5] The resistance to the introduction of firearms in the fifteenth and sixteenth centuries by the knightly class occurred after they realized how commoners could gain them and challenge their dominance. Similarly, the mediaeval ban on siege weapons was motivated by the desire to squeeze mercenaries out of the war business (Johnson 1984: 90). In the Orient, the Chinese Ming dynasty attempted to control and downplay gunpowder as a weapon in order that the nomadic Mongols would not use it to disrupt the unification of the Empire (Elvin 1973: 94; Hall 1996: 41).[6] These efforts, however, pale in significance to the NPT, as their target groups and geographical scope were limited.

Despite the unequal treatment of its adherents, the NPT did receive support from a large number of non-nuclear states, partly as a result of the bargain that was reached to provide nuclear technology to these states for civilian purposes. Several states possess neither the capability nor the intention to pursue nuclear weapons programs. Some such states saw the five-year NPT review conferences as opportunities to remind the nuclear states of Article VI of the Treaty which calls on the NWS to progressively eliminate their nuclear arms.[7] Many non-nuclear states have indeed been more concerned about their neighbors seeking to acquire nuclear weapons (horizontal proliferation) than the superpowers' arms race (vertical proliferation). Consequently, they saw in the NPT a way to increase their security (if their neighboring states also agreed to the Treaty controls) and to receive legal sanction for their non-nuclear policies (Nye 1985). Nuclear states would be unlikely to use such weapons against them as that would be a violation of the spirit (if not the letter) of the NPT. In this sense, the Treaty is unique, as the nuclear and non-nuclear states agreed on an unequal treaty that constrains the sovereignty of the latter for reasons unique to the interests of each other. A normative order in this realm thus fulfills the interests of different types of states in the international system (Paul 1997).

The non-proliferation regime has been buttressed by several other instruments to control the transfer of technology and materials to nuclear aspirants. The London Suppliers Group, consisting of twenty-seven exporting states, has established a set of guidelines to prohibit transfer of dual-use technology to states with nuclear ambitions. Similarly, the Missile Technology Control Regime (MTCR) prohibits the supply of space technology components that can be used for developing missiles.[8] In addition, the nuclear weapon free zones in Latin America (including the Argentine-Brazilian bilateral arrangement), the South Pacific, Southeast Asia, and Africa have further strengthened the regime. Unlike the NPT, the incentive for these zones came from the regional states themselves and was not imposed on them by powerful states. The 1996 Comprehensive Test Ban Treaty (CTBT) further constrains all states from conducting nuclear tests, although it allows laboratory level tests, again to the advantage of the five declared nuclear weapon states.

Nearly five decades of international efforts at curbing the spread of nuclear weapons have created a political and normative climate in which no state can easily declare its nuclear intentions or acquire capabilities openly as in the conventional weapons realm. In this sense, the regime has been fairly successful. This partial success is also due to several factors unrelated to the regime. The unsuitability of nuclear weapons to most military situations, the decline in prestige associated

with nuclear possession, and the slide in civilian nuclear energy programs are some of them. The end of the Cold War and the relaxation
of tensions in several enduring rivalries have indeed reduced the need
for nuclear acquisition by a large number of states. However, acquisition propensities have increased in South Asia, East Asia, and the
Middle East, and the conflict patterns in these regions will largely determine how nuclear proliferation will progress in the twenty-first century. The Indian and Pakistani nuclear tests in May 1998 were a clear
indication of new nuclear states emerging in the developing world with
declared capabilities.

Chemical and biological weapons

Unlike the nuclear weapons sphere, chemical and biological weapons
have been spread to several states, and the international instruments to
control their spread do not discriminate between "haves" and "have-
nots." The spread of chemical weapons and their use in internal and
external wars have been concerns for the international community since
World War I. The use of such weapons, especially poison gas, during
World War I and the preparations during World War II (although not
used by any parties, except Japan against Chinese civilians), and subsequently in the post-war era on several occasions, have contributed to a
general antipathy toward these weapons. Chemical weapons have been
sought by states largely for deterrence purposes, based on the notion of
retaliation in kind, to counter chemical or nuclear weapons of an adversary. Chemical weapons proliferation is presumed to have occurred in the
Middle East on a wide scale. Some states, notably Iraq in recent times,
have pursued the acquisition of chemical weapons for counter-insurgency
purposes and have used them against their own population as well as
adversaries. The Iranian incentive for chemical weapons springs from the
desire to deter any future use by Iraq as happened during the waning days
of the Iran-Iraq War. Several Arab states, notably Syria, Egypt, and
Libya, have viewed chemical weapons as a "poor nation's atomic bomb"
to counter Israeli nuclear capability. For some such dissatisfied states in
the Middle East, chemical and biological weapons could be the "great
equalizers" of the twenty-first century.

In the chemical weapons arena, the major arms control development
has been the 1993 Chemical Weapons Convention which bans the development, production, use, transfer, and stockpiling of such weapons. The
Convention requires the destruction of production facilities by the parties within ten years of its coming into being. It creates a strong verification mechanism, administered by the Organization for the Prohibition of

Chemical Weapons (OPCW).[9] One of the unique characteristics of this Treaty is its stringent verification mechanism. It has a provision for routine verifications involving on-site inspections and verification by challenge, and a procedure for settling violations and bringing them to the UN for final decision if the violation continues. Unlike the nuclear realm, the major powers have all agreed to forgo their chemical weapons under this Convention. Once the Convention is fully ratified by all states, there will not be two categories of haves and have-nots, as in the case of the nuclear regime. The non-discriminatory characteristic of the Convention and the stringent verification regime are two factors that make this Treaty stand apart from other multilateral arms control instruments, including the NPT. The non-discriminatory character arose out of the great power realization that the technology for chemical weapons is all too readily available and that these weapons could indeed become the poor nation's equivalent of nuclear weapons and that a chemical weapons monopoly (unlike the nuclear monopoly) is hard to achieve.

In the biological weapons sphere, the main pillar of international efforts lies in the 1925 Geneva Protocol and the 1972 Biological Weapons Convention (BWC). The Protocol bans the use of asphyxiating poisonous or other gases and bacteriological weapons explicitly by belligerents in war. It was an effort to prevent the recurrence of use of such gases and weapons as in World War I, but it is less than a perfect mechanism of control. Most prominently, it lacks a verification or compliance mechanism, and has no effect on intra-state use of such weaponry. The BWC banned weapons made of microorganisms and toxins and the means of delivery designed to use such weapons. States party to the Convention agree not to develop, produce, or stockpile such weapons. However, the Convention does not prohibit "possession of a production capability," nor are there "provisions for intrusive verification and monitoring of compliance" (Pearson 1993: 120). Up until January 1995, 134 states have become party to the Convention and the membership includes all the five declared nuclear weapon states. The Iraqi developments and the new advancements in biotechnology brought forth the dangers of biological weapons acquisition by determined national governments and sub-national groups. Unlike the nuclear weapons area, there is general agreement on the need for controls, except that national enthusiasm waxes and wanes as the issue gains salience only occasionally in the international agenda. Unlike the chemical weapons sphere, the tradition of non-use, or the taboo, in this area has been strong, partly because of the difficulty in using such weapons effectively to attain military and political objectives without hurting one's own troops.

WMD diffusion and the emerging international order

The further diffusion of nuclear, chemical, and biological weapons and their use are probable in the twenty-first century, despite efforts by the international community, especially the nuclear weapon states, to control such spread. Diffusion in particular will occur in three regions of the world: South Asia, the Middle East, and East Asia. States in these regions that are likely to be targets of external intervention, or are engaged in ongoing regional rivalries and protracted conflicts, or are lacking alliance support, are the most likely candidates for acquisition of some form of WMD. Fears are widely prevalent that, if not managed properly, the diffusion of WMD could become a major source of conflict and instability in the twenty-first century. Conflict could occur between states in the South but it could also assume North-South dimensions. Anytime a country acquires WMD, the most significant effect has been in its immediate neighborhood where other states, fearful that their capacity to deter and defend erodes, undertake counter-measures, leading to the classic problems of security dilemma. In terms of great-small power relations, WMD could be viewed as a challenge to system stability and the direct security interests of great powers and their allies. It has been argued that diffusion could erode great power capacity, monopoly rights, and proclivity for direct interventions.[10] It may also cause strategic disengagements and pressures on allies to search for independent capabilities (Freedman 1994: 48).

All these scenarios need not result in cataclysmic outcomes. The presence of WMD and their delivery systems, especially long-range missiles, in the hands of several states and sub-national actors could affect the nature of warfare as we currently know it. Regional states could develop effective mutual deterrent relationships. The number of interventionary wars could decline, in turn removing one of the main reasons for regional insecurity and major power conflict in the past.[11] Great powers may resort to other forms of statecraft to achieve their objectives vis-à-vis smaller actors. Multilateral and non-discriminatory regimes, similar to the Chemical Weapons Convention, could be created as a result of the difficulties in maintaining the monopoly of a given weapon system. Smaller states armed with WMD could possibly thwart direct great-power interventions. There is some level of agreement that had Iraq possessed deliverable nuclear weapons in 1991, the US would have hesitated over military intervention and that economic sanctions would have been given a chance. Although the Iraqi nuclear weapons could not have posed any threat to the US mainland, Baghdad could have threatened US allies and coalition partners in the Gulf with nuclear attack.[12] Some scholars from the developing world have argued that nuclear proliferation may be essential for changing the international system dominated by an oligopoly of status quo states. To them, the threat of nuclear acquisition could force great powers to modify their behavior vis-à-vis regional powers (Kothari 1977; Mazrui 1980). As Hedley Bull states:

In [the] modern international system, there has been a persistent distinction between great powers and small [powers]. Great powers have not been vulnerable to violent attacks by small powers to the same extent that small powers have been vulnerable to attack by great ones. Once again it is the spread of nuclear weapons to small states and the possibility of a world of many nuclear powers that raises the question whether in international relations, also a situation may come about in which the weakest has strength enough to kill the strongest. (Bull 1977: 50)

Non-proliferation advocates have consistently highlighted other dangers of proliferation. They include: adverse impact on the central strategic relationship; advertent or inadvertent nuclear conflicts due to lack of prudence or experience with nuclear weapons; the possibility of surprise attack and complication in global disarmament efforts (Beaton and Maddox 1962: 202–3). Moreover, nuclear proliferation could upset the traditional balance-of-power system as well as great power capacity to maintain peace and order through alignments and counter-alignments (Barton 1977: 154). However, some of these concerns have proved to be exaggerated, as the record of three decades of proliferation provides a less cataclysmic story. Indeed, the pace of proliferation has been much less than predicted; it hardly affected the central strategic balance, it did not result in any regional nuclear wars, and there is a strong indication that direct military confrontations between regional rivals have been reduced due to the nuclear factor.[13]

What is lacking in these regions are concrete confidence-building measures to produce crisis deterrence and psychological stability. Higher levels of confidence in stable relationships take long periods of diplomatic interactions and it is in the early stages of WMD arms race relationships that instability is most likely to occur. The saber-rattling by India and Pakistan following their nuclear tests in 1998 and renewed conflict in Kashmir brought forth fears of inadvertent nuclear war escalating from conventional flare-ups. Yet the possibility of accidental war between new nuclear states or old nuclear states still persists. The dangers posed by Russia's rapid decline and the spread of weapons materials and technical specialists to several countries are equally problematic. Sanguinity about regional realities or ignoring them, however, will not produce a peaceful international order. The probability of accidental use of weapons, lack of confidence-building mechanisms, and lack of progress in regional peace, all cause genuine concerns even to the utmost proliferation optimists. Deterrence, in the WMD realm, is a costly game; and it does not guarantee the achievement of lasting peace. It is, indeed, the concrete political choices of national leaderships that lead to great rapprochements.

Since the mid-1990s, a growing realization among US analysts that nuclear monopoly cannot be maintained forever has resulted in calls for abolition of such weapons. The abolition group consists of key former generals such as Andrew Goodpaster, Lee Butler, and William F. Burns, and former policy-makers such as Robert McNamara and Paul Nitze.[14] Although most of them are driven by a genuine desire for a peaceful world, for some such advocates the American hegemony and primacy can be multiplied if nuclear abolition takes place since no other actors surpass the United States in conventional military and economic capability. Moreover, the lethality and high accuracy of new conventional weapons would allow performing the tasks assigned to nuclear weapons with less catastrophic effects on the environment or on population centers.

With the rapid advancements in info-tech weaponry, the United States has managed to leapfrog its allies and adversaries in the realm of modern weapons. The new military revolution that the US leads involves technologies of digital communications, global positioning system (GPS) of satellites which facilitates exact guidance and navigation, stealth technology which evades radar, and computer-based data processing ("The Future of Warfare" 1997). If nuclear weapons are removed globally, the US would multiply its power position as none of its allies or adversaries will have the technological edge necessary to develop countervailing systems in the short and medium terms. Under such circumstances, it will not be surprising that in the twenty-first century the United States emerges as the major champion of total nuclear disarmament. As its conventional capability increases in leaps and bounds over all present and potential competitors, it will feel that what constrains its effective use would be WMD and delivery systems in the hands of smaller actors. However, countries with weak conventional capabilities vis-à-vis the US, such as Russia, China, and India, are unlikely to agree to nuclear abolition in the short run. A restructured non-proliferation treaty on the model of the Chemical Weapons Convention would be the outcome if the abolitionist position gets accepted globally. Even without such a universal regime, the current NPT may continue to survive as long as no new great powers emerge with nuclear capability. A key problem though is that from the systemic perspective, the NPT attempts to stop the rise and fall of new great powers. It assumes that the status of the declared nuclear powers is permanent and that no new nuclear states will emerge with systemic aspirations. It neither allows the rise of a new great power nor helps the orderly exit of a declining great power from the nuclear club (Paul 1997).

In the chemical and biological weapons arena, progress has been mixed. While an overwhelming majority of states adhere to the regimes, a handful of states with regional power ambitions or conflict potentials tend to pursue this option, even if they are parties to treaties. The relevant cases are Iran, Iraq, Libya, and North Korea. These states are most insecure and at the same time challengers to the regional and international order based on American hegemony. To these states, chemical and biological weapons could form great sources of equalizers. The developments in info-tech weaponry have substantially added to the US capability to engage in precision-guided attacks against these states, while making frontal conventional wars with it are risky as proved during the Gulf War of 1991. Chemical and biological weapons could serve as effective instruments for dissatisfied regional states and terrorist groups that may support such challengers. In some sense, chemical and biological weapons diffusion is more likely than nuclear arms to pose severe challenges to the emerging international security order. Because the technology requirements are high and the political and military benefits low, only a few states have the capacity or incentive to acquire nuclear weapons and their delivery systems. The monitoring of nuclear activities is relatively easier than the monitoring of the chemical and biological weapons efforts by states or sub-national groups. The latter category of weapons also holds larger value for terrorist groups intending to launch concentrated attacks.

What determines whether global disarmament of WMD, especially in the nuclear arena, will take place? One catalyst could be the threat of further diffusion of such capabilities and their use in a future conflict. Some believe that further proliferation is necessary before a genuine effort will be made to eradicate such weapons. As Johnson states: "Undesirable weapons must reach a kind of 'critical mass' in the armament systems of the nations of the world before any meaningful consensual effort to limit or ban their use can be carried through to success" (1984: 99). Any long-term plans for complete and general nuclear disarmament will still leave behind the capacity for some states to rearm quickly if the situation demanded. Abolitionists have proposed several ways to achieve nuclear disarmament. Others have argued for virtual deterrent capacities, capabilities short of actual weapons that would deter potential states from acquiring nuclear weapons or threatening their use (Schell 1984; Mazaar 1995). The critical challenge for twenty-first-century statesmen will be to develop and apply a foolproof verification regime with the aid of new technologies.

Technological developments and politico-military changes in the international system will be crucial factors in determining how proliferation will proceed. As the advanced states acquire better conventional weapons and intelligence capabilities to monitor arms developments in the developing world, dissatisfied regional states will devise new methods to preserve their autonomy and defensive capabilities. Weapons of mass destruction could acquire new meaning as the ability of regional states to deliver these arms against selected targets of major powers and their regional allies increases simultaneously.[15]

The state of the international political system in the twenty-first century will determine how proliferation will occur, i.e., how the aspirations of rising states and regionally dominant states are met by the power hierärchy in the world system. Other challenges are: first, can the United States provide credible protection to non-nuclear major power states such as Japan and Germany? Second, can effective institutional mechanisms and norms be developed that would forestall the need for national deterrent and defensive capabilities of high conflict variety? Third, will ideological struggles lead to the rise of fundamentalist and millenarian movements determined to change the world around them in their own images? Fourth, will the advanced industrialized states and other major weapons producers place restrictions on their weapons development and thereby reduce the differential in technology of warfare among different states? Finally, will dramatic breakthroughs in capability increase the structural dominance of some actors and the return of new imperial attempts for control and domination of minor powers?

Answers to the above questions are important, as a higher great power propensity to intervene in the affairs of regional states could lead to greater efforts by these states to maintain WMD capability and develop strategies to thwart such attempts. Although guerrilla warfare, terrorist strikes, and political opposition at home and abroad have helped to decrease the tendency to direct intervention, other forms of intervention, interdiction, and surprise military attacks have given more encouragement to dissatisfied regional states to attain capabilities that would prevent such intervention. In the twenty-first century, it is possible that great powers and small powers alike will come up with new strategies to cope with their perceived or actual power losses due to technological and political changes. Great powers may resort to multilateral avenues for intervention, while small powers may develop defensive systems and strategies to ward off such interventions.[16]

Conclusion

To answer the question in the title of this paper, weapons of mass destruction, especially nuclear arms, are at once "great equalizers" and "agents of chaos." The pace of proliferation may be critical in determining benign or chaotic outcomes in regional theaters. Limited diffusion under certain conditions could stabilize regional security environments. What is pivotal for near-term security is the creation of stable deterrent relationships in regions where WMD spread has already taken place, while redoubling efforts to resolve regional conflicts. Controlling the spread of such weapons to regions where the spread has not taken place is equally essential in managing the proliferation problem more effectively.

A significant effort has to be directed towards strengthening the traditions of non-use of nuclear, chemical, and biological weapons and their deliberate depreciation as battlefield weapons. Unambiguous no-first-use pledges are the first steps in that direction. The new policy of the US to keep nuclear weapons as a deterrent against chemical and biological weapons use by smaller states is likely to increase pressure on targeted regional states to seek nuclear weapons. The nuclear weapons states may have to depreciate the current value they give to these weapons as instruments of deterrence, containment, hegemony, alliance cohesion, prestige, power, etc., if they seek a genuine solution to the proliferation problem. In the twenty-first century, universal disarmament of categories of weapons may become essential in order to contain the problem of WMD diffusion more effectively, as the maintenance of monopoly rights becomes untenable with additional states vying for the same weaponry. Denial of technologies and materials can delay but not eliminate the causes of proliferation. The position of the abolitionists may be more valid than ever, as global disarmament efforts may become essential for containing a truly global problem caused by the security dilemma and the opportunities created by technological revolutions.

Finally, the proliferation issue cannot be divorced from the state of international politics of a given epoch. The assumption that minor power behavior has no connection to the security policies and weapons choices of major powers is fallacious. Minor powers that wish to maintain autonomy and regional primacy often develop strategies and acquire weapons with the hope of thwarting major power incursions. Their propensity to arm with WMD arises from their desire to maintain autonomy against potential and actual enemies who possess such weapons. As the revolution in military technology increases the gap between major powers and regional states in the developing world, many dissatisfied states may view possession of WMD as their best hope of equalizing power relationships. Greater international efforts at the peaceful integration of key regional states and rising major powers are essential for genuine disarmament to be achieved. Current system leaders have a key responsibility in this regard.

NOTES

1 Scholars at the early stages of the atomic age had recognized this paradox. To one such scholar, even the strongest state may not be able to protect its cities as nations lower in the power gradient "might get hold of atomic weapons and alter the relationship of great and small states" (Dunn 1946: 5). To Herz, nuclear developments could lead to a situation where military "superiority" loses its meaning as even an inferior power armed with nuclear weapons can saturate its opponent without "first breaking the traditional 'hard shell' of surrounding defense" (Herz 1967: 22).

2 Ethnocentrism is rife in this area. Analysts tend to view nuclear weapons in the hands of their own leaders as safe, while nuclear possession by developing states is often described as irresponsible acts by rogue governments. On this theme, see Van Creveld (1993: 124); Waltz (1981: 11).

3 The tendency to call these states "rogues" has some problems as it is a loaded term. This term also brands such states as outlaws while dismissing any genuine security concerns they may have. Some such states were categorized as normal when they were allied with the US, but when they lost that status they became rogues. Pakistan and Iran were not rogue states when they were allies of the US, although they had begun their quest for weapons of mass destruction during that period itself (Kapur 1996).

4 The Treaty allows a party to withdraw from it by giving three months' notice if its supreme national interests so require. This provision (as North Korea found out) has been characterized as equivalent to the right of the former Soviet republics to secede under the Stalinist Constitution (Kapur 1998).

5 Other attempts by dominant groups or states to prevent weapons from reaching their enemies include the Eleventh Ecumenical Council of 1179 and the Twelfth Ecumenical Council of 1215 that prohibited Christians from supplying ships and shipbuilding materials to the Saracens, the Confirmatio Tractatus Flandriae of 1370 between the English King, Edward III and the Count of Flanders and three other towns preventing the latter from providing by sea arms, artillery, or supplies to any of the enemies of the former, and the agreement between Britain and Spain in 1814 to limit the supply of arms and ammunition by British merchants to rebels in Spain's American colonies (Burns 1993: 1410–11).

6 The observation by a Ming era official, Wang Ming-hao, about the dangers of the spread of gun-making and gunpowder techniques to the barbarians resonates the contemporary discourse about WMD proliferation. He expresses frustration at the difficulty of getting the barbarians to observe Ming policies that were aimed at making sure that "no one should dare lightly to use these matchless weapons, and that the population at large should not be allowed to know how they worked, or spread the knowledge about it privately among themselves." Ming-hao laments the flouting of the embargo on the trade in saltpeter and sulfur and the shortsighted generals in allowing "Miao tribesmen to learn about firearms, in order to remedy a temporary shortage of Han Chinese troops" (Elvin 1973: 94).

7 For the bargain between non-nuclear and nuclear weapon states, see Smith (1987).

8 "MTCR members refrain from selling ballistic and cruise missiles with ranges over 300 kms and payloads greater than 500 KG, or with any range if the seller has reasons to believe that they may be used to carry WMD" (Forsberg, et al., 1995: 75). The regime was established in 1987 by the US and six other advanced industrial states. By 1995, its membership has grown to twenty-two. Its establishment was driven by the fear that ballistic missiles, coupled with WMD warheads, can act as potent sources of deterrent as well as offensive capability in the hands of regional powers. The MTCR guidelines for the transfer of dual use technology and materials have become a powerful source of control by the advanced industrial states on the flow of not only missile but space technology as well (Peruci 1997).

9 This body will be directed by a 41-member executive council, a technical secretariat, an inspectorate, and an advisory board. On the Convention, see Spiers (1994: 131).

10 Radiation and other hazards to troops exposed to destroyed facilities could become a key factor inhibiting great power interventions. There are indications that the destruction of the Iraqi biological facilities unleashed bacteria into the atmosphere causing US soldiers serious health problems, often dubbed Gulf War syndrome.

11 This assumes that technological developments will not lead to a foolproof defense system, or that new info-technology will not produce weapons that can search and destroy WMD facilities of regional states effectively.

12 It must however be noted that the Iraqi capability did not prevent intervention by the US-led coalition, partly because of a belief among coalition leaders that large-scale defensive measures would protect civilians and military personnel in the event of an Iraqi chemical attack. Effective defenses against nuclear attack are non-existent, and therefore deterrent threats carry more credibility.

13 There is some tangential evidence that selective nuclear proliferation may have helped prevent major armed conflicts in South Asia and in the Middle East since the wars of 1971 and 1973. India, Pakistan, Israel, and the Arab states have been more cautious about escalating crisis situations. For a case in point, see Hagerty (1995/6).

14 For a statement of their positions, see *An American Legacy* (1997). These initiatives were preceded by a key report by the Canberra Commission, appointed by the Australian Government, on ways to create a nuclear-weapon-free world.

15 Unless simultaneous changes are achieved in great power behavior vis-à-vis smaller powers, a foolproof non-WMD world may be hard to achieve. Disgruntled regional powers may sign treaties, but may not adhere to them, as proven by the cases of Iraq and North Korea. The bottom line is that disarmament cannot be divorced from the state of international or regional politics.

16 For the military strategies of small states, see Paul (1994).

REFERENCES

An American Legacy: Building a Nuclear Weapon Free World 1997, Report No. 22, Washington, DC: The Henry L. Stimson Center.

Barton, John H. 1977, "The Proscription of Nuclear Weapons: A Third Nuclear Regime?" in *Nuclear Weapons and World Politics*, David C. Gompert et al. (eds.), New York: McGraw Hill, pp. 151–211.

Beaton, Leonard and Maddox, John 1962, *The Spread of Nuclear Weapons*, London: International Institute for Strategic Studies.

Bull, Hedley 1977, *The Anarchical Society: A Study of Order in World Politics*, New York: Columbia University Press.

Burns, Richard D. (ed.) 1993, *Encyclopedia of Arms Control and Disarmament*, Vol. III. New York: Charles Scribner, pp. 1409–19.

Croft, Stuart 1996, *Strategies of Arms Control: A History and Typology*, Manchester: Manchester University Press.

Dunn, Frederick 1946, "The Common Problem," in *The Absolute Weapon*, Bernard Brodie (ed.), New York: Harcourt, Brace, pp. 3–20.

Elvin, Mark M. 1973, *The Pattern of the Chinese Past*, Stanford: Stanford University Press.

Forsberg, Randall et al. 1995, *Non-Proliferation Primer*, Cambridge, MA: The MIT Press.

Freedman, Lawrence 1994, "Great Powers, Vital Interests and Nuclear Weapons," *Survival* 36: 35–52.

"The Future of Warfare," 1997, *The Economist*, March 8: 21–4.

Hagerty, Devin T. 1995/6, "Nuclear Deterrence in South Asia: The 1990 Indo-Pakistani Crisis," *International Security* 20: 79–114.

Hall, John A. 1996, *International Orders*, Cambridge: Polity Press.

Harknett, Richard J. 1998, "State Preferences, Systemic Constraints and the Absolute Weapon," in *The Absolute Weapon Revisited: Nuclear Arms and the Emerging International Order*, T. V. Paul, Richard J. Harknett and James J. Wirtz (eds.), Ann Arbor: The University of Michigan Press, pp. 47–72.

Herz, John H. 1967, *International Politics in the Atomic Age*, New York: Columbia University Press.

Johnson, James T. 1984, *Can Modern War be Just?* London: Yale University Press.

Kapur, Ashok 1996, "Rogue States and the International Nuclear Order," *International Journal* 51: 420–39.

   1998, "New Nuclear States and the International Nuclear Order," in *The Absolute Weapon Revisited*, T. V. Paul, Richard J. Harknett, and James J. Wirtz (eds.), Ann Arbor: The University of Michigan Press, pp. 237–61.

Kissinger, Henry 1994, "How to Achieve the New World Order," *Time* March 14, 73–7.

Kothari, Rajni 1977, "Sources of Conflict in the 1980's," *Adelphi Papers*, No. 134.

Mazarr, Michael J. 1995, "Virtual Nuclear Arsenals," *Survival* 37: 7–26.

Mazrui, Ali. 1980, "Africa's Nuclear Future," *Survival* 22: 76–9.

Meyer, Stephen M. 1984, *The Dynamics of Nuclear Proliferation*, Chicago: University of Chicago Press.

Nye, Joseph S. 1985, "NPT: The Logic of Inequality," *Foreign Policy* 59: 123–31.

Paul, T. V. 1994, *Asymmetric Conflicts: War Initiation by Weaker Powers*, Cambridge: Cambridge University Press.

   1995, "Nuclear Taboo and War Initiation in Regional Conflicts," *Journal of Conflict Resolution* 39: 696–717.

   1997, "Power, Norms and Interests: Explaining Persistence of the Nuclear

Non-Proliferation Regime," paper presented at the American Political Science Convention, Washington, DC, August.

1998, "The NPT and Power Transitions in the International System," in Raju G. C. Thomas (ed.), *The Nuclear Non-Proliferation Regime: Prospects for the 21st Century*, Houndmills: Macmillan, pp. 56–73.

forthcoming, *Power Versus Prudence: Why Nations Forgo Nuclear Weapons*, book manuscript, McGill University.

Pearson, Graham S. 1993, "Biological Weapons: Their Nature and Arms Control," in *Non-Conventional Weapons Proliferation in the Middle East*, Efraim Karsh, Martin S. Navias, and Philip Sabin (eds.), Oxford: Clarendon Press, pp. 99–133.

Peruci, Gamaliel. 1997, "Missile Proliferation and US Policy: Ten Years Under the MTCR," International Studies Association Convention Paper, Toronto, March 18–22.

Sagan, Scott D. and Waltz, Kenneth N. 1995, *The Spread of Nuclear Weapons: A Debate*, New York: W. W. Norton.

Schell, Jonathan, 1984, *The Abolition*, New York: Alfred A. Knopf.

Smith, Roger K. 1987, "Explaining the Non-Proliferation Regime: Anomalies for Contemporary International Relations Theory," *International Organization* 41: 253–81.

Spiers, Edward M. 1994, *Chemical and Biological Weapons: A Study of Proliferation*, New York: St. Martin's.

Van Creveld, Martin 1993, *Nuclear Proliferation and the Future of Conflict*, New York: The Free Press.

Waltz, Kenneth N. 1981, "More May be Better: The Spread of Nuclear Weapons," *Adelphi Papers* No. 171.

Wight, Martin 1978, *Power Politics*, Hedley Bull and Carsten Holbraad (eds.), Leicester: Leicester University Press.

Part IV

Conclusions

The state and the future of world politics

John A. Hall and T. V. Paul

This volume has sought to occasion thought about the shape of international relations in the light both of the end of the Cold War and of the emergence of social forces held by some as signaling entirely novel politics. The purpose of these concluding comments is to summarize what has been learnt, so as then to reflect upon what this means for the future. The discussion is necessarily divided into two sections. It is now nearly a decade since the Cold War ended, and the first task before us is simply that of summarizing the way in which our contributors see the international system within which we live. The second section addresses the longer term. This section begins by offering criticism of the post-positivist claims made by Steve Smith in this volume concerning the relations between epistemology, morality, and order – with a good deal of skepticism then being cast upon the view that the state is about to lose its centrality in the life of humanity. This last argument leads to a prescriptive stance of our own: order in the coming era will depend on how prudently states conduct their relations, irrespective of what power structure emerges in the twenty-first-century international system. More concretely, the intelligence of states needs to be augmented so that they can direct their policies according to the dictates of prudence or enlightened self-interest. To make this assertion is, of course, to insist that the synthetic model outlined in chapter three maintains its importance in contemporary circumstances.

Order at the end of the millennium

It is not at all the case that the editors of this volume stacked the deck of contributions in order to arrive at a particular view of the current international scene. So it is with surprise that we note the emergence of a fairly widely shared view as to the orderly nature of the current global condition. This deserves emphasis before attention is turned to underlining disagreements as to how that order is maintained.

International order at the end of the twentieth century seems to comprise two elements: one at the major power level and the other on the North-South dimension. The great power system is semi-unipolar, with the United States retaining a semi-hegemonic leadership role, while other major powers, especially Russia and China, observe, for the most part, a limited supporter role.[1] The North-South dimension, however, is more complex. The North, despite some conflict, is bound together increasing-ly – by which is meant the addition of new members as well as an ever-greater range of issues – by official and unofficial contacts and a network of institutions designed to prevent catastrophe. In contrast, the South – or, to be precise, the rather different social formations within it – is heavily disadvantaged, in part ignored and in part excluded. Let us consider both these social worlds in turn.

Less than a decade ago it was widely presumed that the pre-eminence of the United States was bound to be lost, with America sure to follow Britain into socio-economic decline (Kennedy 1987). This scenario was always highly implausible: the economic rivals of the United States were geopolitically weak, whilst its geopolitical rival was economically puny – a far cry from the German combination of economic and military power which faced Great Britain in the first half of the twentieth century (Hall, 1990). More generally, it is always important to remember that the United States is practically a continent, and that it is blessed with a political system at once enduring and flexible. Still more important for John Ikenberry is the astonishing and transformative success of the last "new world order" established by the United States during the late 1940s. Over the last several decades, the "core institutions of Western order have sunk their roots ever more deeply into the political and economic structures of the states that participate within the order." Furthermore, American hegemony is held by Ikenberry to be "pen-etrated," that is, sufficiently open to allow lesser-allied states access to the hegemon through a set of liberal rules and institutions. Second-ranking states accordingly benefit from participation without needing to fear coercive enforcement by the dominant power. We argue later that Iken-berry's thesis is a little too rosy, and so want to add an additional, slightly more brutal consideration reinforcing the view of the special position of the United States. That point-in-question is simple: the authors who have analyzed other potential challengers all see such significant military or economic weaknesses within them as to allow the United States to rest on its perch for a good deal longer. Let us consider these semi-great powers in turn.

Jack Snyder properly argues that continual predictions of Russian revanchism have so far come to naught – a point now much reinforced by Russia's increasing lack of military means. Snyder cautions that Russia in the past had experienced temporary collapse of military power, but it was successful each time in reversing the setbacks within a decade or so. What differentiates the current decline is that, unlike the past, attempts at popular mobilization will be weak, unless occasioned by precipitous external threat, which Snyder sees as improbable in the short and medium terms. There are two reasons for this unexpected state of affairs. First, the leading elements of the Russian elite seem able to operate within a new capitalist framework; differently put, the nationalist card is not played because an alternative source of mobility and power is available. Secondly, civil society was devastated both by Tsarism and by communism so completely that it is very hard to organize movements of protest from below.

Both Juan Diez Medrano and Michael Mann stress the extent to which Europe lacks a unified geopolitical purpose and military arm. In this context, the rapprochement of France with NATO, however incomplete, stands as a call for continuity: the French hope is surely that a continued American presence will balance the increase of German power resulting from reunification. European weakness, Medrano suggests, arises from the European Union's lack of operational capacity in the areas of defense and security. Moreover, European states lack a common vision or joint interest to deal with military crisis situations. This situation is unlikely to change in the future even as European states will continue to assert their autonomy vis-à-vis the United States, by further integrating the Western European Union into the institutional structure of the European Union and try to counterbalance the power of the United States within NATO itself.

T. J. Pempel insists that Japan is unlikely to generate any unitary geopolitical drive – with any sign of such ambition being likely to result in the absolute insistence, by many neighboring Asian states, on the continuation of a strong American presence. The tension along three dimensions, between domestic and international forces, regionalism and internationalism, and the different dimensions through which Japan will act in the future, suggests that Japan is likely to play a larger international role in the economic arena, especially through collective frameworks of action. But "the economically dynamic Asian region is moving toward a highly complex interdependence that will serve as a check on any Japanese unilateralism – economically or politically."

China is seen by Steve Chan as a relatively satisfied power, finally prepared to endorse Westphalian norms – which, after all, will increase the autonomy it feels it needs both to guard its domestic politics from foreign influence and to deal with its developmental agenda. Contrary to dominant Western opinions about China, Chan argues that the "post-1949 China has undergone a metamorphosis from being a radical challenger to becoming a status quo proponent of the traditional state-centric order." Chan sees no prospect of any impending system struggle involving China. Perhaps some caution should be expressed about this general view. China has become a defender of Westphalian norms at the precise moment when the United States and its allies are beginning to question at last some of these norms – most obviously, those which give a sovereign state the right to repress its population. There is plenty of room for conflict here. Tying trade to human rights may seem completely legitimate for the Western liberal mindset, but it is viewed in Beijing as an encroachment on Chinese autonomy. China's future may also depend heavily on the ways in which other leading actors respond to its increasing economic and military capabilities – the key question being that of whether such responses do or do not propel an arms race in the region.

India is in a slightly different category. But if there is still no agreement as to whether it is or will soon become one of the great powers, Baldev Nayar makes it quite clear that it lacks both the inclination and the economic and military means to mount a substantive challenge to the ordering of world politics in the short and medium terms, except in the nuclear and missile areas. India is also a strong defender of Westphalian norms relating to sovereignty. Still, its conceptions about international order are as yet unclear. In the long run, India could become a major challenger, especially if it is not fully integrated into the international order. The unwillingness of the five permanent members of the UN Security Council to grant India any meaningful role in international governance makes it a likely candidate for assuming a semi-challenger role in the twenty-first century, especially in the areas of global security regimes. The current system leaders have a responsibility to avoid this by replacing their containment policy with both economic integration and the offer of a meaningful role in institutions of global governance such as the United Nations.

The tone of Nayar's chapter neatly introduces the general finding as to the situation of much of the South. Bluntly, the interests, demands, and desires of the South do not form a major part of the terms of the current international order, as conducted by the Northern states; at this point there is, of course, considerable continuity given that the other side of the benign face of American hegemony shown to Europe and Japan was the harsher and more coercive face shown to the Third World. However, different parts of that world are, as noted, variously disadvantaged. The sheer negligence shown towards Africa is seen in continuous economic decline – which exacerbates ethnic rivalries, which themselves then often

cause major population dislocations. In contrast, the geopolitically critical areas of the South – South Asia, the Middle East, the Persian Gulf,
and East Asia – suffer from more direct interference, most obviously in
terms of weapons transfers and the militarization of regional conflicts. All
in all, the North views international inequality as legitimate. The nuclear
non-proliferation regime, as Paul's chapter points out, is unique in seeking to continue the privileges of the advantaged – although this situation is
one which suits a large number of Southern states. In economic terms, the
North increasingly ignores large portions of the South, despite the economic opening of several of these states to the world market. Mann notes
that the world political economy is not really global: insofar as the
advanced world trades or invests in the South, it does so in those countries whose relative social peace results in large part from their status as
allies. Holsti adds to this an insistence that state structures scarcely exist
in many parts of the South, and are certainly insufficient to challenge the
rules of the international system as a whole. Conflict in these states will
continue, with its effects at present being contained within them or within
their regions.

At this point, of course, there is a measure of disagreement. Jack
Goldstone's demographically based understanding of revolution leads
him to suggest that a few developing states – not surprisingly, usually
those blessed with a history of state-building – may yet have the possibility
of making challenges within and perhaps beyond regions. It is worth
noting in this connection that even an intense regional conflict can begin
to undermine larger patterns of power. Paul adds a crucial consideration
here that turns worry into fear. The proliferation of weapons of mass
destruction *is* one area where small power/major power relations will have
a radical impact, with the potential for conflict to emerge. However, this
diffusion of weapons of mass destruction is largely confined to regions
where protracted conflicts and enduring rivalries persist, such as the
Middle East, South Asia, and East Asia. Large parts of the developing
world where no such rivalries exist, i.e., Latin America, and Africa and
Southeast Asia, have declared their regions nuclear weapons free and are
making efforts to keep the regions away from weapons of mass destruction induction (Paul forthcoming).

If there is a fair measure of agreement that the world polity is relatively
orderly, and unequal, there is a good deal of difference as to the mechanics of that order. To realists, including Mastanduno, the glue that creates
international order is the distribution of power, and, more particularly,
the continuing near-hegemonic position of the United States. In contrast,
Michael Doyle makes a forceful case for the suppression of realism by the
normative solidarities created by a liberal league. Although John Iken-

berry starts by challenging realism on the grounds that the West as a whole is normatively integrated, his ambitious argument then goes a good deal beyond that of Doyle. For one thing, the normative glue of the West is held to comprise more than just liberalism. For another, the polity of the United States is held, as noted, to be open to penetration by pressure groups organized from the outside: this apparently means that American hegemony is replaced with some sort of conjoined rule.

There is doubtless something to these anti-realist points, but many of the scholars in this volume (and more outside) would not feel comfortable proceeding too far with this line of argument. As a background condition, it should be remembered that the United States retains structural power within the core of capitalism, with predominance in the military field – as the result of information technology allowing for precision guided attacks – looking particularly firmly established (Nye 1996: 89; Strange 1987; Paul 1998). There is little sign that the hegemon has abandoned the pleasures of acting unilaterally. Thus access to the American government is not available at every moment nor on all issues (with Michael Mastanduno further making it clear that that is not anyway welcome); further, access of any sort is not easily accepted by the American public. Nor is the liberal league a completely egalitarian affair: as close an ally as Great Britain was told of the bombing of Libya only after the planes had taken off. If this is to say that power still counts, another criticism is of still greater interest since it takes us to the heart of the nature of realism. Europe and Japan may be considered members of a liberal league or of the West more generally, but it is hard to see what evidence would prove this to be the case. The counter-argument to Ikenberry's overstated position is that states allied to the United States still calculate – in this case, that it is in their best interest either to accept American hegemony or to speak the language of a liberal league. Running the world has its psychic benefits but it is not to everyone's taste, not least since the exercise of power can be very costly. The world of the North may be one in which realism leads to cooperation rather than to endless challenge. Most nation-states – the partial exception being the American hegemon itself, keen to retain elements of autonomy in its action – have become, as Michael Mann notes, modest: realizing that the attempt to turn themselves into complete and self-sufficient power containers led to disaster, they have gained more by settling for less.

These generalizations most certainly seem to apply *within* the European Union. In the United States, scholarship on European institutions tends to suffer from spectacular swings, from belief in a new and united Europe to eurosclerosis and now, again, to the belief that Europe is beginning to create a new political form. Research which examines institutions rather than actions makes one doubt the romanticism of this latter view (Milward 1992). European unity was born from and still rests upon the Franco-German condominium. All in all, the increase of international links and meetings that results should not be mistaken for transnationalism. Institutions have helped to conduct trade and allowed a semblance of democratic governance and conflict resolution mechanism to an otherwise unwieldy European state system with a history of violent outbursts to settle disputes. Germany particularly seems to like institutional networks of power, since they provide legitimacy to its power and influence vis-à-vis smaller states.

The lack of clarity in this whole area can be further appreciated by considering liberal institutionalism. Does this approach fit best within the liberal or the realist camp? On the one hand, it is most certainly not realist if that position is held to mean the search to increase power in some purely solipsistic sense. On the other hand, liberal institutionalism is far from many versions of liberalism because its mechanics rest upon the calculations made by states, albeit these take place within a framework of increased information and concern for continuing interaction with other states. Lisa Martin argues that the links between institutions and order are several, although institutions can create "status quo bias" to order at the "expense of neglected distributional effects." Martin inclines toward the liberal position, and she recognizes that some states, especially the powerful, could benefit more from institutions, "but without them all states could end up in worse situations." "The very act of creating an institution binds the hands of the powerful states," and allows weaker states to "develop a response, reducing the ability of the powerful to engage in divide-and conquer tactics." Institutions also provide "predictability and stability" often to the benefit of less powerful and poorer states, especially those undertaking domestic political and economic reforms.

Towards the future

We are much helped when turning towards the future by the claims made by Steve Smith. His fundamental and powerfully sustained skepticism leads us to address three issues. To begin with, we offer a wholly negative critique of his claims relating epistemological practices to political outcomes. We then further disagree as to the salience of the state in the future of world politics, arguing that its role is being hollowed out from below and above far less than he imagines. Finally, we provide prescriptions of our own, in so doing joining with him in stressing the importance of agency – that is, in seeking to establish rules (although, they are not those of Smith himself) which take us beyond what is to what ought to be.

The key moment in Smith's post-positivism – itself uncritically derived from the Frankfurt School (Marcuse 1941; Adorno et al. 1976) – lies in the notion that positivism's concern to investigate facts leads, usually insensibly, to endorsement of the status quo. In the case of international relations theory, the practice of positivism is held by Smith to lead to a preference for order above other values. The charge thus moves from an epistemological point to the assertion of an unthinkingly conservative neglect of the dictates of justice.

Two points here deserve outright refutation. To begin with, the Frankfurter view of positivism is a travesty. Edmund Burke was far more prescient about the power of empirical observation when arguing that the questioning of a mere detail of an old regime could bring it down. It is regimes which fear change that limit empirical investigation, with positivism as social practice being characteristic of societies able to change reasonably peacefully through some sort of messy process of trial and error. It would be possible, secondly, to turn the tables on Smith and to poke fun at the pretentiousness to which his position can lead. Whilst it is no doubt pleasurable to perform as an angel ministering to justice, the lack of credentials for such an awesome role is rather striking. Why exactly should we accept Smith's version of justice? More importantly, how are we to know that this is not just hot air – mere utopianism incapable of anything other than self-congratulation because it is bereft of any sense of the constraints of actually existing power structures?

Argument at this level is apt to become tiresome very quickly, whilst being unlikely to lead to any sort of resolution. Accordingly, it makes sense here to evade some of these issues by calling a truce. For one thing, Smith himself – at least when pushed – admits that beautiful theories mean little without a concrete sense of how they may be practically realized; this view means that he is, in some secret and serious part of his soul, as concerned with establishing the facts about current social structural constraints as are "normal" social scientists. For another, whilst it is certainly possible to be an empiricist and to love the status quo, that is not the position that the editors of this volume entertain. To the contrary, our explicit purpose has been to problematize the nature of order, that is, to ask whether the terms of reference of particular types of order privilege those who create or maintain them. Some empirical comments about the neglect of the South have already been made: they underline the fact that our concern for empirical inquiry does not logically entail support of the precise rules and understandings in place at the end of the millennium. This will become further apparent in a moment when prescriptive points are made as to how international order could be improved through the incorporation of the world order concerns that post-positivists have meritoriously brought back to the center of public attention.

Before offering our prescriptive plea, let us turn secondly to a logically prior issue – namely, that of whether the state should any longer be at the center of our attention. Smith suggests very firmly that the state is losing its salience, to which is added the emotional gloss that those who privilege it somehow help maintain it. Let us ignore the emotional gloss, as we can, given that we have no absolute loyalty to this political form, after replying in kind: how provincial to imagine that all the world is like the advanced North, that is, to ignore the horrors of lawlessness that wrack Liberia and Rwanda! Just a day or two outside the peaceful and settled social world of the advanced Western academy would make Smith realize the continuing relevance of Hobbes. Before saying more about this, however, let us first turn to the substantive charge: is it indeed the case that the power of the state is being lost, as forces both larger and smaller hollow out its capacities? There are very strong reasons for doubting this to be the case, as Michael Mann makes clear, and these can best be marshaled in terms of the macro and micro challenges that face the state.

There is of course a basic and fundamental truth at the heart of the notion of globalization, namely that states must live within a larger surrounding which pushes them to change and rationalize. But there is much more continuity here than is realized: the states of the advanced capitalist world have long had to live inside the larger societies of economic and military competition. The fact that the economic shell is fully global, rather than confined to the advanced world, is of course novel. Still, that novelty is much exaggerated (Hirst and Thompson 1996). Economic competition – in the sense of share of world product that is traded – has only recently regained the level it reached in 1913, whilst military competition is in historical terms abnormally low. Further, a detailed consideration of most of the economic evidence shows that trading interchanges are heavily centered in the North, as are patterns of investment, with the challenge from the South if anything losing some salience over the most recent years (Wade 1996). More important still, the world economy remains open because of an agreement amongst states, meetings between which have precisely the character of a re-iterated game made so much of by liberal institutionalists.

The micro challenge to the modern state is that provided by secessionist nationalism. Hudson Meadwell's chapter recognizes the intractability of an elite of nationalist leaders, but he is very much in line with current research in arguing that secession can be limited by means of accommodationist political arrangements. Secession is caused in largest part by the desire to escape from empire; the desire for exit is bred by the denial of voice (Hall 1993). Despite much sound and fury, it does not seem as if democratic and liberal Spain will disintegrate; equally, developing states with liberal language regimes may well stave off the challenge of secession. Furthermore, nationalism is perhaps not quite the threat it used to be, given key changes in historical circumstances. Nationalism almost automatically led to war when it was allied with geopolitical views that insisted that territorial possession was necessary to secure raw materials and markets. This link has now been broken. What is noticeable about most secessionist nationalisms is that they wish to be modern, to join in large markets rather than to escape from them.

These points about the role of the state can usefully be drawn together. Smith's whole position *is* utopian: it puts forward a (questionable) version of what is desirable, but has no means to realize it – not least since it blithely ignores actually existing power structures. But only a moment's thought is needed to realize that most of the challenges analyzed in this book can only be dealt with through the state – and, more particularly, through the state acting in concert with other states. This is most obviously true in the field of environmental degradation. However, this is not to deny that Smith is right to be suspicious of state power. We accept the point, made by Holsti as well as by Smith, that states in some parts of the developing world can be more of a problem than a solution, that is, that they are so weakly anchored in society as thereby likely to become vicious and predatory. But it does not follow from this that the state should be abandoned. What rather matters is the necessity of creating responsive and intelligent polities within a society of states. To say this is of course to come to our prescriptive position. A useful preface to that stance is Holsti's discovery that international orders in the past failed because they too inflexibly reflected the structure of power within the system. In a sense, this is to say that the future of international order is not, as Smith has it, always to be found "out there": what matters quite as much is political agency – by which is meant the intelligence of the powerful in current conditions as well as in the face of forces of social change.

We believe that our synthetic model has obvious continuing relevance at this point. The creation of a society of states, that is, an international polity based on fundamental normative homogeneity, remains a goal of immense importance. The lack of such homogeneity is most clearly seen in the exclusion of the interests and demands of the developing world. International institutions are at present not much more than a club of the rich and powerful; international order will not be secure, nor any move towards a greater element of justice established, until membership and issue area are extended. But there is a second point that can be derived from Peter van der Veer's argument that discourses in the West, such as that of Samuel Huntington's recent "clash of civilizations" thesis (Huntington 1996), that demonize developing societies are dangerous. For one thing, such discourses treat whole societies as unities, and fail to note that, say, Islam is a site of struggle between harsher and softer voices. For another, to demonize may be to radicalize, that is, to create the conditions in which fears become all too justified. What follows from this is simple. International homogeneity in the long run needs to involve more than state elites. If the international civil society movements mentioned by Smith have as yet little power, that is no reason to discourage their growth.

Still more important is the question of the nature of state power. The key feature of our original synthetic model, that of making the state able to calculate, here retains all its bite. In practical terms this sociological condition of realism can only be fulfilled by turning ever more towards liberalism. Doyle's arguments are of especial relevance here. To begin with, states need to be made responsive by introducing democratic control over foreign policy adventurism. More subtly, Doyle's allegiance to liberalism is not just an emotional reflex, in that it is aware that example and instigation should drive liberal policy towards illiberal regimes for a long time before active intervention is contemplated, not least since intervention is exceptionally hard to carry off successfully. Differently put, liberal regimes need to systematically think how to help replace large, ineffectual, and predatory regimes with ones that are at once leaner, efficient, and bounded. Thought on this topic has scarcely begun. And of course liberalism needs to operate quite as much between states as within them, through both the creation of normative solidarities and the introduction of more – and fairer – international regimes.

Before highlighting the principal policy suggestion that follows from all this, it is as well to confront as openly as possible a tension that is implicit in the argument as a whole. On the one hand, our contributors found a measure of orderliness in the international system as the result of a particular structure of power. On the other hand, we are now arguing that steps should be taken to go beyond that structure. Differently put, if no serious challenge to the North can be mounted by the developing world, why should attention be given to its claims? Are we too not utopian, given that power is not often guided by principle?

Whilst there is a great deal to be said for justice in the abstract, that is, for a set of rules that apply to all humanity rather than a minority, two rather different arguments may convince the powerful of the sense of this general position. For one thing, the challenge from the developing world may not be quite as weak as noted, as Holsti argues. The middle-ranking developing states – that is, large states blessed with oil revenues sitting in the midst of crisis zones – may end up with considerable potential to challenge the structure of world power. For another, the power of the North, and of America in particular, may fade, for all that it is strong at the moment. Demographically the North is losing all the time, whilst industrialization outside the core of capitalism will inevitably lead to a diminution in the share of total world product. Both these forces suggest the wisdom of trying to include now, when power allows for some setting of the terms of debate.

The vital point that needs to be made about policy is one that is exceptionally uncomfortable, both for the North as a whole and for the editors who find themselves recommending disruption to the lives of other people. Bluntly, globalization has not gone nearly far enough. The principal way in which the North could help the South is by opening its own markets, which remain especially closed to the agricultural products in which many developing countries have a comparative advantage. In this sense, the Common Agricultural Policy of the European Union is an obscenity, preventing economic growth in both postcommunist Europe and the Caribbean. But to recommend the introduction of market forces in hitherto protected areas is to expose particular sets of people to enforced change. This is desirable, but it would be madness to hide from the fact that as a policy option it is not likely to have vigorous appeal to many Western leaders.

The intelligent state

We believe that order is both a systemic and a unit level phenomenon. If the distribution of power among major power actors within the system has great importance, unit level processes – notably, the way in which states respond to the opportunities and constraints offered by the system – are critical to the maintenance and transformation of order. Prudence on the part of states is necessary at all times, but perhaps especially today given the challenges posed by globalization, demography, the environment, and by weapons proliferation. Although an international order based in large part on semi-unipolarity is currently in place, this will surely not last forever. If historical experience is any indication, new great powers will arise and some of the existing ones will decline. But strategies for peaceful change are not at the center of any lexicon of great power politics. In fact, as Holsti (1991: 33) points out, peaceful change has all but been forgotten in the post-World War II era, despite the great controversy and debate it engendered in the 1930s. For this very reason, the intelligence of states needs desperately to be improved by democratization and by the extension of international institutions.

We can conclude by placing our argument within general comments about the tendency of social science to embrace polar extremes. One way in which this is particularly true is that of the endless conflict between those who stress human agency as compared to those who insist that our situation is determined. Absolute determination to hang on to either of these extremes is likely to be silly. For the truth of the matter is, at least sometimes, that we have some options within the constraints that face us. Our argument has sought to occupy middle ground. That power has established international order at the end of the Cold War is perhaps remarkable. But the benefits of that order are skewed, with much resentment being shown by the disadvantaged. Hence we have argued that the unthinking terms of a system should be complemented by intelligent action. Such action is needed for two reasons. First, an increase in justice, though hard to manage, would in the end make for a more stable world. Secondly, intelligence is needed to ensure a peaceful transition to a new form of order in the future.

NOTES

1 We call the system semi-unipolar and semi-hegemonic as the United States is the only major power that commands some power elements required for hegemony. However, American power is not such as to claim full hegemony over international society. Militarily the United States *is* preponderant over all other major powers; still, the possession by Russia, China, and India of nuclear arms makes nonsense of claims of unipolarity. In the economic realm, American power is very great – but its share of world product is nonetheless less than it was in the years after 1945.

REFERENCES

Adorno, Theodor W. et al. 1976, *The Positivist Dispute in German Sociology*, London: Heinemann Educational Books.
Hall, John A. 1990, "Will the United States Decline as Did Britain?" in *The Rise and Decline of the Nation State*, Michael Mann (ed.), Oxford: Blackwell, pp. 113–45.
  1993, "Nationalisms: Classified and Explained," *Daedalus* 122: 1–28.
Held, David. 1995, *Democracy and the Global Order*, Stanford: Stanford University Press.
Hirst, Paul and Thompson, Grahame 1996, *Globalization in Question*, Oxford: Polity.
Holsti, K. J. 1991, *Peace and War: Armed Conflicts and International Order 1648–1989*, Cambridge: Cambridge University Press.
Huntington, Samuel S. 1996, *The Clash of Civilizations and the Remaking of World Order*, New York: Simon and Schuster.

Kennedy, Paul 1987, *The Rise and Fall of the Great Powers*, New York: Random House.

Marcuse, Herbert 1941, *Reason and Revolution*, Boston: Beacon Press.

Milward, Alan 1992, *The European Rescue of the Nation-State*, London: Routledge.

Nye, Joseph S. 1990, *Bound to Lead: The Changing Nature of American Power*, New York: Basic Books.

1996, "Home and Abroad," *The National Interest* 45 February: 89–92.

Paul, T. V. 1998, "Power, Influence and Nuclear Weapons: A Reassessment," in *The Absolute Weapon Revisited*, Paul, Richard J. Harknett and James J. Wirtz (eds.), Ann Arbor: University of Michigan Press, pp.19–45.

forthcoming, *Power Versus Prudence: Why Nations Forgo Nuclear Weapons*, book manuscript, McGill University.

Strange, Susan 1987, "The Persistent Myth of Lost Hegemony," *International Organization* 41: 551–74.

Wade, Robert 1996, "Globalization and Its Limits: Reports on the Death of the National Economy are Greatly Exaggerated," in *National Diversity and Global Capitalism*, Suzanne Berger and Ronald Dores (eds.), Ithaca: Cornell University Press, pp.60–88.

Index